Church, Stage, and Studio

Music and Its Contexts
in Seventeenth-Century Germany

Studies in Music, No. 107

George J. Buelow, Series Editor

Professor of Music
Indiana University

Other Titles in This Series

Church, Stage, and Studio

Music and Its Contexts
in Seventeenth-Century Germany

Edited by
Paul Walker

With a Foreword by
Lynn Edwards

U·M·I Research Press

Ann Arbor / London

Produced and distributed by
UMI Research Press
an imprint of
University Microfilms Inc.
Ann Arbor, Michigan 48106

Library of Congress Cataloging in Publication Data

Church, stage, and studio : music and its contexts in seventeenth-century Germany / edited by Paul Walker.
p. cm—(Studies in music ; no. 107)
Includes bibliographies and index.
ISBN 0-8357-1938-3 (alk. paper)
1. Music—Germany—17th century—History and criticism.
I. Walker, Paul, 1953–   . II. Series: Studies in music (Ann Arbor, Mich.) ; no. 107.
ML275.C58   1989
780'.943'09032—dc20   89-4919
                                                                          CIP
                                                                          MN

British Library CIP data is available.

The paper used in this publication meets the minimum requirements of
American National Standard for Information Sciences—Permanence of Paper for Printed
Library Materials, ANSI Z39.48-1984. ∞ ™

Johannes Voorhout, *Domestic Music Scene,* Hamburg, 1674
Johann Adam Reinken (at harpsichord), Dietrich Buxtehude (center, with
music on his lap), and, probably, Johann Theile (left, with gamba).
(Museum für Hamburgische Geschichte)

Contents

Foreword

The anniversaries in 1987 of the births of Samuel Scheidt (1587–1654) and Dietrich Buxtehude (ca. 1637–1707) coincided with a time of renewed interest in many aspects of seventeenth-century German music. The final volume of Scheidt's complete works, completed by Christoph Wolff, appeared in 1984. At the same time that European interest in Buxtehude was waning, a new generation of American scholars published important studies on the composer and his music (Lawrence Archbold on Buxtehude's praeludia, Eva Linfield on the ensemble sonatas, and Sarah Ruhle Kyle on the oratorio *Wacht! Euch zum Streit*). Complementing the resurgence in this country of Buxtehude studies is the anticipated culmination of the publication of the complete works, a project begun in 1925, continued intermittently, and finally abandoned thirty-five years later. The series is now under the editorship of Kerala Snyder, the author of the definitive study of the life and works of Buxtehude (*Dieterich Buxtehude, Organist in Lübeck,* New York, Schirmer, 1987).

To commemorate this important anniversary year, The Westfield Center for Early Keyboard Studies organized an international research conference. The Westfield Center was established by Edward Pepe and myself in 1979 to create a forum for active interchange among scholars, performers, and instrument builders in the field of early music. We have sponsored concerts, publications, and a wide range of educational programs, including a number of scholarly conferences on Buxtehude, the Sweelinck circle, and tuning and temperament. The year 1987, with its focus on two composers whose combined careers spanned the seventeenth century and who represent two distinct regions of Germany, suggested the perfect opportunity for a conference broadened to encompass German music from the entire century. An advisory panel of Kerala Snyder, Christoph Wolff, and Ernest May suggested topics for the conference and recommended scholars working in the field. A call for papers elicited additional contributions. With generous support from the National Endowment for the Humanities, the Massachusetts Council on the Arts and Humanities, and

Lufthansa German Airlines, "From Scheidt to Buxtehude: German Music in the Seventeenth Century" took place June 14–17, 1987.

Several performances complemented the scholarly papers and exchanges. A particular highlight was the complete performance, on three successive evenings, of the large-scale oratorio *Wacht! Euch zum Streit gefasset macht*, preserved anonymously but traced by its editor, Kerala Snyder, to Buxtehude's *Abendmusik* concerts. Performers included the Hannover Boys' Choir, directed by Heinz Hennig, the ensemble *Fiori musicali*, directed by Thomas Albert, and soloists David Cordier, Harry Geraerts, and Richard Wistreich. Organ works of Buxtehude and Scheidt were also performed by Harald Vogel on the 1981 Fisk organ in the Wellesley College Chapel, an instrument ideally suited to this repertory thanks to its quarter-comma meantone temperament and a newly added *Brustpedal* division particularly appropriate for Scheidt's *Tabulatura nova*.

My thanks to Paul Walker, who graciously agreed to edit this anthology; to George Buelow, who recommended UMI Research Press as its publisher; to Edward Pepe for managing the conference; to Kerala Snyder, Christoph Wolff, and Ernest May for serving on the conference's program committee; and to all who prepared papers—both for the conference and for this collection.

In his classic study *Music in the Baroque Era* (1947), Manfred Bukofzer asked if perhaps there was not a new legend in the making "which mistakes the late baroque style for baroque music in general." It is our hope that this volume of essays will serve as a much-needed impetus for further studies—and that, one day, all of seventeenth-century music will receive the attention Bukofzer believed it so richly deserved.

Lynn Edwards
Executive Director
The Westfield Center

Editor's Note

At the conclusion of the Westfield Center's conference of June 1987, a number of the participants felt that the increased interest in seventeenth-century German music demonstrated by this gathering called for still further response. The appropriate next step seemed to be to publish a collection of articles representative of the latest research and written by many of the most prominent scholars currently active in the field. It is in this spirit that we offer the present volume. The book mirrors recent research trends in its emphasis on music's relationship to other important aspects of German culture, such as literature, theater, liturgy, and social structure. Only through familiarity with the contexts within which music functioned can we approach a complete understanding of the music itself.

The musical examples accompanying Cleveland Johnson's article were produced on an Apple Macintosh and Laserwriter using *Professional Composer;* all other examples were produced on a Hewlett-Packard LaserJet using *Theme: The Music Editor*. I wish particularly to thank Mark Lambert of Theme Software and Sal Soghoian of Pixels, both in Charlottesville, Virginia, for their assistance in producing the musical examples. I am also grateful to Eva Linfield for her careful checking of the translation of Werner Breig's article and to Diane Parr Walker for her preparation of the index.

Introduction

1

Dietrich Buxtehude and
Seventeenth-Century Music in Retrospect

Christoph Wolff

From a modern perspective, it is no easy task to define the position of Dietrich Buxtehude in the history of music. To be sure, he readily and rightly escaped the fate of being labelled a *"Kleinmeister,"* largely on account of his extensive and extraordinarily original output of organ music. Nevertheless, in virtually every aspect of his creative activity he continues to be perceived primarily as forerunner or predecessor. The influence of nineteenth-century music historiography, with its emphasis on single heroic figures, has long hindered the historical and aesthetic evaluation of numerous important composers as artists in their own right. Though certain composers—and Buxtehude figures prominently among them—are frequently and correctly characterized as having been part of the "background" for a later master's achievements, they of course made their contributions without being able to anticipate the subsequent evolution of styles and genres.

No less a musicological authority than Philipp Spitta expressly evoked in his Bach biography[1] the image of Buxtehude as forerunner. He placed clear emphasis on Buxtehude the organist, an image that he subsequently reinforced with the first critical edition of Buxtehude's complete organ works.[2] The relationship between the older master and Bach appeared to him so close that he proceeded in his edition to title Buxtehude's multisectional preludes and toccatas as "prelude and fugue" or "toccata and fugue." This unfortunate distortion, though it served his argument, went contrary both to the evidence of the sources and to the structures of the compositions themselves. The serious consequences of this artificial terminology have been with us ever since, and have surely played a role in the prevailing inadequate perception of the interrelationship of two very different organ repertoires and their premises.

Spitta developed little if any interest in the vocal output of Dietrich

Buxtehude, and therefore he chose not to complement his edition of the organ works with the publication of Buxtehude's vocal music. Furthermore, his knowledge of the vocal repertoire was necessarily quite limited, since the majority of Buxtehude's surviving vocal works were discovered only in the late 1880s in the Düben Collection at Uppsala.[3] Spitta's prejudices against the quality of Buxtehude's vocal music prevailed even after André Pirro's extensive Buxtehude monograph, where much space was devoted to discussion of the vocal works.[4] Not until 1925, nearly fifty years after Spitta's edition of the *Orgelcompositionen* was there a first attempt at a vocal sequel, this time in conjunction with an ambitious project for a *Gesamtausgabe*. Unfortunately, the project was several times subjected to lengthy interruptions. Today, more than half a century from the start of the complete edition, only nine of a projected fourteen or fifteen vocal volumes have been published.[5] Nevertheless, the available volumes, together with a detailed *catalogue raisonné* of Buxtehude's oeuvre,[6] set the quantitative record straight: not only the vocal works but also Buxtehude's chamber works far outnumber his organ compositions. Yet neither the chamber music nor the vocal works have made any significant impact in twentieth-century musical life. A partial exception is the cantata *Alles was ihr tut* (BuxWV 4), yet although the piece has achieved at least some degree of renown, it is a composition utterly unrepresentative of the overall quality and artistic goals of Buxtehude's vocal works. Its fame has not contributed to any truly increased awareness of the hidden riches of Buxtehude's oeuvre; if anything, its isolated popularity has only served to reemphasize the one-sided preference for the organ music and to reaffirm the persistent image of Buxtehude as forerunner.

Hence, modern-day Buxtehude reception will most likely continue to focus first and foremost on Buxtehude as organist. The subtitle of Kerala Snyder's recent monograph[7] typically refers to the "organist in Lübeck" rather than to the "world-renowned, incomparable musician and composer" (*Weltberühmte Hr. Diederich Buxtehude / Unvergleichlicher MUSICUS und COMPONISTE*), as Buxtehude is addressed on the title page of Johann Caspar Ulich's mourning poem on his death (Lübeck 1707).[8] To which Buxtehude is Ulich referring? Certainly to the organist of St. Mary's, but Buxtehude considered himself to be more than merely that: *"Musicus"* stands for the broadly oriented and talented universal musician, *"Componiste"* for the composer who, in a general sense, is creative, active, and productive in all branches of music. If we wish to understand the notably high esteem accorded to Buxtehude at the time of his death, we need to consider him from the perspective of an early eighteenth-century observer, who would have placed him within the context of seventeenth-century music. And to determine what contributed to the narrowing of Buxtehude's reputation, we must consider later eighteenth-century opinions as well.

Among the most competent, knowledgeable, and reliable observers of the German and European music scene of the early eighteenth century was the lexicographer Johann Gottfried Walther. Through his close personal connections with Buxtehude's friend Andreas Weckmeister, he acquired for his collection many manuscript copies of Buxtehude's keyboard music, specifically autograph tablature copies of the organ chorales.[9] Walther's Buxtehude article in the *Musikalisches Lexikon* (Leipzig, 1732)[10] disappoints, however, in virtually every respect. Besides presenting only meager biographical information, it contains an extremely abbreviated worklist, and there is scant reference to the scope of Buxtehude's output or to his general reputation. Though we owe to Walther the preservation of the bulk of Buxtehude's organ chorales,[11] his famous dictionary contributed little to the documentation of Buxtehude's accomplishments.

The first more comprehensive article on Buxtehude appeared in Ernst Ludwig Gerber's *Neues historisch-biographisches Lexikon der Tonkünstler* (Leipzig 1812).[12] The article reveals surprisingly detailed knowledge, despite Gerber's own complaint regarding the general difficulty of obtaining works by Buxtehude; he specifically mentions that not even the otherwise extensive Breitkopf collection in Leipzig contains Buxtehudiana. Nevertheless, Gerber cites twelve published items (among them librettos of the *Abendmusiken),* and mentions in particular the "profound" quality of Buxtehude's keyboard pieces. Although Gerber himself owned only two Buxtehude compositions, and those in somewhat flawed manuscript versions, he states that these suffice for recognition of "the lion by its paws," and that in one piece only the mention of the composer's name in the title prevents him from attributing the work to Johann Sebastian Bach.[13]

For Ernst Ludwig Gerber, Bach provides the obvious and appropriate frame of reference for Buxtehude. We must assume that this reflects a tradition based on the experience of his father, Heinrich Nicolaus Gerber, who had studied during the 1720s with Bach in Leipzig. For Johann Sebastian Bach, Dietrich Buxtehude was anything but an empty name. It seems reasonable, therefore, to attempt to consider Buxtehude from a Bachian perspective, at least as far as that is possible. Interestingly enough, it appears that it was with none other than Bach that the disproportionate emphasis on Buxtehude's organ music originated. As the transmission of the sources indicates, neither Buxtehude's vocal works, nor his chamber music, nor even his harpsichord suites or variations were cultivated in the Bach circle. The organ works, however, especially the large-scale "pedaliter" preludes and toccatas, owe their principal and most reliable, if selective, transmission largely to their importance within the collecting, teaching, and performing activities of Johann Sebastian Bach and his circle.[14] Certain pieces such as the three ostinato compositions (BuxWV 158–60), or the prelude in F♯ minor (BuxWV 146), survived not in North German or Scandinavian tablature sources, but rather in unique copies from the inner Bach circle. It cannot, therefore, be considered a mere coincidence that Spitta saw in Buxtehude the culmination point of organ music before Bach. Bach's contemporaries, as Johann Joachim Quantz testifies, had already taken this position: "The organists and clavier players—among the latter especially Froberger and Pachelbel, and among the former Reinken, Buxtehude, Bruhns and some others—were almost the first to contrive the most tasteful instrumental compositions of their period for their instruments. But particularly the art of organ playing, which had to a great extent been learned from the Netherlanders, was already at this time in a high state of advancement, thanks to the above-mentioned and some other able men. Finally the admirable Johann Sebastian Bach brought it to its greatest perfection in recent times."[15]

To Bach, Dietrich Buxtehude must indeed have appeared as the most impressive representative of an earlier generation, an earlier era, an earlier century. Bach of course encountered other major representatives of the late seventeenth century as well. For instance, he knew Johann Kuhnau from a joint organ examination in Halle in 1716. Later, as Kuhnau's successor in Leipzig, he had to accustom himself to a profoundly traditional office and perspective. Even for the young Bach, connections with the older generation were already manifold. There were distinguished musicians within his own family, especially Johann Christoph Bach of Eisenach. His Ohrdruf brother, Johann Christoph, provided a direct link with Johann Pachelbel. Georg Böhm of Lüneburg and Johann Adam Reinken of Hamburg opened up for him the idiosyncratic North German scene. The influence of all these notables, however, was greatly surpassed by that of Buxtehude, whose artistic impact on the young Bach was far stronger and far more enduring. In addition, the reaction of Bach and his circle to the compositions of the Lübeck master ultimately resulted in the beginning of a Buxtehude reception, one that fundamentally affected later impressions of that composer.

The virtually exclusive emphasis on Buxtehude the organist is not characteristic of the young Bach, but rather of the mature composer, who included Buxtehude's vocal compositions in the category of "the former style of music" that "no longer seems to please our ears."[16] Bach, defending himself in 1706 when reproved for prolonged absence, told the Arnstadt consistory that "he had been to Lübeck [to visit Buxtehude] in order to comprehend one thing and another about his art" (*umb daselbst ein und anderes in seiner Kunst zu begreifen*).[17] This formulation is kept deliberately general and is certainly not limited to keyboard music. What in particular could Bach have learned from Buxtehude's art? In order to determine this, it seems necessary to attempt to understand what Buxtehude's music represented at the very beginning of the eighteenth century. It was music that reflected a broad spectrum of compositional choices and stylistic possibilities, since Buxtehude was no composer of narrow specialization, but rather one who aimed at the ideal type of the universal musician.

The following discussion will examine Buxtehude's music in retrospect and specifically from the vantage point of the young Johann Sebastian Bach, first in more general terms and then on the basis of a close examination of two representative compositions.

It cannot be mere coincidence that Buxtehude attracted the attention of the two men who were later recognized as the most significant composers of the first half of the eighteenth century. Prior to Bach's Lübeck trip, Handel and his companion Johann Mattheson had paid a short visit to Buxtehude in 1703, from which they returned with powerful impressions.[18] For Bach's stated aim to "comprehend one thing and another about his art," a short visit would not have sufficed; he stayed for more than three months. Why and to what end? Certainly not just to get to know and perhaps copy organ compositions so far unknown to him. Certainly not only to attend, and perhaps participate in, the two *extraordinaire Abend-Musiken* (*Castrum doloris* BuxWV 134 and *Templum honoris* BuxWV 135) in December, 1705. Certainly not only to explore the possibilities for employment, if this aspect played a role at all.

For both Handel and Bach, Buxtehude must have represented a kind of "father figure," one who anticipated in many ways the ideal of a later type: the autonomous composer. The bourgeois, commercial, and liberal atmosphere of the Free Imperial City of Lübeck provided Buxtehude with considerable flexibility in developing and realizing his own various projects. He, of course, held the position of organist at St. Mary's Church, an office with specific duties. Nevertheless, his overall activities were characterized by a display of artistic initiative combined with unusual managerial independence. Courtly service would not have permitted such free conduct. Buxtehude was able to develop his career as a virtuoso, he travelled, and he surrounded himself with pupils. He seized opportunities for composing vocal works of both sacred and secular orientation, and as his own impresario, he organized and financed performances of large-scale *Abendmusiken*. For this purpose he created a new oratorio type far beyond the scope of the Carissimi model, and he regularly published the librettos for these works as well. In order to broaden the compass of his activities he printed two chamber music collections, the sonatas op. 1 and sonatas op. 2 of 1694 and 1696, respectively. In other words, Buxtehude conducted his organist office very much in the style of a municipal *Kapellmeister,* thereby providing a clear role model for Telemann in Hamburg and Bach in Leipzig.

Buxtehude exemplified the ideal type of the universal musician in a number of additional ways. First, he balanced theory and practice. Since the generation of Michael Praetorius or even earlier, scholarly theoretical erudition had belonged among the prerequisites for a preeminent musical office, and Buxtehude was no exception. His theoretical background reflected the Italian tradition of Zarlino (supplied most likely through Matthias Weckmann and Reinken),[19] but in comparison with Christoph Bernhard or Johann Theile, Buxtehude placed more emphasis on practice with a strong theoretical foundation. Rather than writing treatises, he demonstrated his contrapuntal sophistication in diverse practical applications such as the *Missa brevis* (BuxWV 114), the *Klag-Lied* of 1675 (BuxWV 76), and the canons (BuxWV 124–24).[20] In this regard, Buxtehude proceeded in a manner comparable to that of Bach in the *Well-Tempered Clavier*, the *Art of Fugue*, and similar works.

Second, Buxtehude involved himself in organology and the technology of musical instruments. As a widely recognized organ expert, he held close ties with Andreas Werckmeister, seventeenth-century Germany's premier musical scientist and speculative theorist. Buxtehude not only became the most prominent advocate of Werckmeister's new systems of temperament,[21] but also explored in his works the immediate compositional implications of a more flexible and expressive harmonic language (through employment of keys with three and more sharps and flats, as well as through a notable preference for "functional" harmony, with frequent use of double dominants and the like).

Third, Buxtehude's compositional orientation included a broad spectrum of styles and genres:

1. Retrospective as well as modern tendencies complemented each other (as in the music of Monteverdi or Schütz);
2. Dutch and Hanseatic traditions (Sweelinck, Scheidemann, Reinken), English elements (viola da gamba writing), French manners (style brisé in keyboard music, Lully-style opera chorus in vocal music), and Italian influence (Frescobaldi, Legrenzi, Carissimi) are discernible, but Buxtehude always aimed at synthesizing them;
3. Practically all new genres of the seventeenth century can be found in his music: concerto, motet, chorale, aria (strophic and free), and recitative in the vocal realm; toccata/prelude, fugue, ciacona/passacaglia, canzona, suite, sonata, dance, and variation in the instrumental realm.

Fourth, around 1678, Buxtehude created the prototype of the large-scale, multisectional German oratorio on the basis of his detailed knowledge of the Hamburg opera convention.[22] Typical is the title of an oratorio presented in 1684: *Himmlische Seelenlust auf Erden über die Menschwerdung und Geburt unsers allerliebsten Heil- und Seligmachers Jesu Christi, in 5 unterschiedlichen Abhandlungen auf der Operen Art mit vielen Arien und Ritornellen. . . .* Keiser's and Telemann's oratorios as well as Handel's English oratorios profited from Buxtehude's ideas. Bach's *Christmas Oratorio* followed the Buxtehude pattern with respect to the presentation of a unified multisectional work over several weeks.

Fifth, Buxtehude redirected two well-established genres of organ music by drawing inspiration from the compositions of his North German predecessors and contemporaries (primarily Scheidemann, Tunder, Weckmann, and Reinken). He established two predominant types: first, the monodic organ chorale for two manuals and pedal with melismatic cantus firmus and structured, polyphonic accompaniment, in both large-scale (chorale fantasia) and small-scale formats; and second, the Praeludium pedaliter as an extended unit of five to seven parts, integrating the aesthetic concept of the *stylus phantasticus* and the formal and compositional devices of the ensemble sonata.

Consideration of Buxtehude and his music in light of the major compositional and stylistic tendencies of the seventeenth century reveals that his works virtually never rely on specific, identifiable models. Yet Buxtehude embodies all the distinguishing features of a powerful integrating figure. He combined as well as redirected various style and form tendencies, with compositional results that are as highly original as they are ambitious. Particularly characteristic in this respect are his oratorios (in their curious mixture of opera and traditional church music), the "pedaliter" organ preludes, and to a certain extent his keyboard suites with their early, perhaps even prototypical movement order (Allemande-Courante-Sarabande-Gigue).[23] There is no seventeenth-century musician who, in comparison with Bach, shows as many clear analogies in virtually all major areas, theoretical and practical.

Two representative examples may serve to illustrate Buxtehude's ability to sum up in his vocal and instrumental music the principal achievements of the seventeenth century. These are the *Templum honoris* (BuxWV 135) and the Praeludium in G minor (BuxWV 149).

Templum honoris (BuxWV 135)

This oratorio was performed on 3 December 1705, one day after its companion piece, *Castrum doloris* (BuxWV 134). It seems reasonable to assume that Johann Sebastian Bach, who stayed in Lübeck for approximately four months until early February 1706, would not have missed the performances of these major and unique *Abendmusiken*. With these two works, respectively, the Free Imperial City of Lübeck mourned the death of Emperor Leopold I and paid homage to his successor, Joseph I. If Bach was indeed present, he was in all probability not merely a member of the audience, but rather a participant in the very large performing ensemble under Buxtehude's direction. After all, Bach had to finance his extended trip, and offering his services as violinist or keyboard player would have been a logical course of action for the young and

Und DU daraus entsprossen bist/
O Tugend - Kind! O Götter - Sohn!
So komm / empfahe hier der Tugend Lohn/
Die Ehren - Krohn:
Die Du/ O JOSEPH/ Du Würdiger Gast/
Durch Rathen und Thaten erworben DIR hast.
Dieweil bey DIR so vieler Völcker Hoffen/
Ist eingetroffen/
Steht DIR mein Tempel offen.

Aria.

Unsterbliche Ehre!
Du theilest zwar den Sterblichen dich mit/
Doch suchst Du nur/ die Tugendhafft vor Andern:
Man sieht Dich nicht/ als solcher Seel nachwandern/
So wie mit Lust/ die Laster-Bahn betritt.
Ritornello, mit 2. Chöre Waldhörnern und Hautbois,
concertirende.

2.
Unsterbliche Ehre!
Wañ JOSEPH nicht geschworn der Tugend-Fahn/
So bald ER nur zu Herrschen war gebohren;
Hätt' IHN das Reich zum Haupte nicht erkohren/
Und Du IHM nicht den Tempel auffgethan. Ritorn.

3.
Unsterbliche Ehre!
Vermehre stets des Käysers Majestät:
Laß Josephs Ruhm mit Josephs Jahren wachsen/
Ausbreite IHN biß an die Sternen-Achsen/
Alsdann Sein Reich und Ruhm niemahls vergeht.
Sinfonia all' unisono à 25. Violin. con Intrada Seconda
mit 2. Chöre Paucken und Trompeten/

& Tutti.
Eja , Euge !
Det, JOSEPHE IMPERATOR
TIBI Famam, Famæ Dator!

Die Klugheit.
Recitat.
ICh/ mit Gottes-Furcht vermählt/
Begleite die Menschen zum Tempel der Ehren/
Nimmermehr der fehlt/
Der nachfolget meinen Lehren/
In was Stand Er sey.
Die Stein=alten Greisen/
Sind nicht allein die Weisen/
Die Weißheit wohnt auch Jungen Herren bey.
JOSEPH/ Deutschlands Salomon/
Kan hievon/
Ein Durchlauchtigs Beyspiel geben.
Glückseelig sind zu nennen/

Die

Figure 1.1a. Page 3 of the Original Libretto of *Templum honoris* (BuxWV 135)

Er beut den Feinden Trutz/
Durch GOTTES des Mächtigen Schutz/
Auff DEN ER Sich verläßt.
Ich geh mit JOSEPH Aus und Ein/
Er soll Glückselig seyn !
Gesegnet aller Wegen/
Mit hümmlisch- und irrdischen Seegen !

Tutti von allen Chören.

Es geh JOSEPH/ dem Hohen Held
Nach Wunsch/ der Hohen in der Welt !

Glückwünschende ARIA.

1.
JOSEPH wachse/ wachse fort/
  Wie an einer Quelle !
Seine Krohn an allem Ohrt/
Scheine Sternen-helle.
Rhodes Sonne/ Stambuls Mond
Müssen voller Ehr-bezeigen
Sich vor Diesem Joseph neigen/
Und wo Heyd und Barbar wohnt.
Ritornello.

2.
Seines Vaters Segen komm
  Starck auff Josephs Scheittel !
Wer dieß wünscht/ist treu und fromm;
  Wers nicht wünscht/ ist Eitel.
Unter Josephs Regiment
Muß man Reiche mit den Städten/
Sehn im Wohlstand einher treten.
Jeder rufft : Glück zu/ Regent !
Ritornello.

3.
Auch DEIN LÜBECK schweigt hier nicht/
  Höchst-gekröhnter Käyser !
Wünscht an Heil'ger Statt aus Pflicht
  DIR viel Sieges-Reißer.
GOTT erhöre unser Flehn/
  Daß/ zu vieler tausend Frommen/
  Stein' und Hirten aus DIR kommen;
Daß wir Josephs Saamen sehn!

I. CHOR. Eja, Euge !
DET, JOSEPHE IMPERATOR,
TIBI PROLEM, PROLIS DATOR!

II. CHOR. Eja, Euge !
DET, JOSEPHE IMPERATOR,
TIBI VITAM, VITÆ DATOR!

Tutti.

Es leb' JOSEPH der Käyser-Held/
Nach Wunsch der Hohen in der Welt !
Worauff zum Schluß:
Una Passagaglia con divers. Instrom. Vivace.

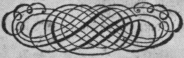

Figure 1.1b. Page 4 of the Original Libretto of *Templum honoris* (BuxWV 135)

ambitious professional musician. The music of *Templum honoris* has not survived, as is the case with virtually all of Buxtehude's oratorios. The printed libretto, however, has come down to us and supplies a number of crucial details that also allow us to infer some of the more important musical features[24] (see fig. 1.1). Thus it is possible to form a general impression of what the young Bach may have experienced.

The libretto indicates that the performances were occasions of grandiose spectacle in the St. Mary's church, which had been specifically decorated and illuminated for the occasion. The musical presentations themselves involved several instrumental and vocal choirs, both large organs and, at least at the end of *Castrum doloris,* the entire congregation as well.[25]

The text of both oratorios represents a curious mixture of sacred and secular elements chosen to suit the politically oriented occasion.[26] The dialog format calls for two soloists as allegorical figures (*Gerücht, Klugheit*) and two choirs. The musical forms include double chorus with *da capo* rounding off, recitative,[27] and strophic aria with instrumental ritornellos. The instrumental requirements of the piece are particularly striking and apparently without precedent or parallel. There are two intradas for two choirs of trumpets and timpani, a ritornello for two concerted choirs of *Waldhörner und Hautbois,* a *Sinfonia all' unisono a 25. Violin,* and at the end a *Passacaglia con divers. Instrom.*[28]

The young Bach had, so far as we know, no opportunity to compose pieces in an oratorio-like format. Elements of Buxtehude-style instrumental splendor seem to be reflected, however, in Bach's two Mühlhausen Town Council Election cantatas, of which one (BWV 71) has been preserved. This piece (published in 1708, well before any vocal work of Handel's or Telemann's was printed) originated one year after Buxtehude's death and only two years after his last two oratorios (BuxWV 134–35). It demonstrates in particular Bach's ambitious and inventive instrumental scoring and may provide, together with the more modestly dimensioned cantatas BWV 150 and BWV 106 from about the same time, the only extant, albeit indirect link to Buxtehude's late vocal music. The oratorio *Wacht! Euch sum Streit gefasset macht* attributed to Buxtehude appears to be less suitable for comparative purposes; it has a much more modest instrumental format and, perhaps more importantly, as a work from the early 1680s it belongs to a very different period.

The reason for the virtually complete disappearance of Buxtehude's large-scale *Abendmusiken* cannot be attributed to any lack of artistic worth or compositional quality, but rather to the fact that these oratorios were not conceived as repertory pieces. In this sense they are comparable to the operas of the same time, especially the Hamburg operas which have also not survived. Occasional works were without exception designed to fit specific circumstances. Moreover, the style of these oratorios had to be adjusted to the requirements of the day. The situation was by no means fundamentally different for the vocal works of the young Handel and Bach, and their coincidental, fragmentary transmission can be explained similarly. For Bach, a systematic preservation of his early vocal works would have been utterly unrealistic since these works were no longer even remotely fashionable. Under exceptional conditions a new context could save them, as was the case, for example, with the thorough revision of the very early chorale cantata BWV 4 for a Leipzig performance, or with the transfer of the choral passacaglia *Weinen, Klagen, Sorgen, Zagen* (BWV 12/2) of 1714 into the *B-Minor Mass* of 1748–49. Bach's later self-critical attitude toward his own early vocal oeuvre would in all likelihood not have differed, in principle, from what he must have thought about the slightly older vocal works of Buxtehude and their even more old-fashioned outlook.

Praeludium in G Minor (BuxWV 149)

In later life, Bach appears by the same token to have regarded much of his early instrumental music such as a chorale partita or the ensemble sonata and symphonia as equally passé. There are exceptions, however, most notably involving the genre of pedaliter organ prelude. Again the analogy is quite striking: a substantial number of Buxtehude's preludes and toccatas have survived and so have a goodly number of Bach's compositions from the same category. In fact, the extant Buxtehude repertoire actually outnumbers that of the young Bach, and the explanation for this most likely includes an aesthetic component. Buxtehude's preludes held the rank of *exempla classica* within the Bach circle and throughout virtually the entire eighteenth century. The G-minor prelude, in terms of format and length the greatest of Buxtehude's pedaliter works, may serve as a case in point.

The large-scale structure of the piece comprises five parts of differing lengths: passaggio (mm. 1–20 [see ex.1.1]); fugue (mm. 21–53 [see ex. 1.2]); interlude (mm. 54–76 [see ex. 1.3]); fugue (mm. 77–143 [see ex. 1.4]); and finale (mm. 144–58 [see ex.1.5]).

The overall organization is a model of clarity, and demonstrates how Buxtehude created a novel type which, while it synthesized elements of earlier keyboard traditions, actually went far beyond the scope of the compositions of Tunder, Weckmann, Scheidemann, Froberger, Frescobaldi, or Sweelinck. The work also displays two particularly modern and forward-looking elements.

First, the prelude embodies the sophisticated and deliberate application of a harmonic language that approaches or anticipates functional harmony. That this occurs in conjunction with the minor mode, which before 1700 normally carried strong Dorian implications, is all the more remarkable. The repetitive definition of the G-minor home key happens at the very beginning of the piece. The many surprising harmonic effects, including the prolongation of the dominant of m. 49 in mm. 50–53 through harmonic shifts introducing C- and A-

Examples 1.1a and 1.1b. Praeludium in G Minor, Opening Passaggio

Example 1.2. Praeludium in G Minor, Fugue I

Example 1.3. Praeludium in G Minor, Interlude

Example 1.4. Praeludium in G Minor, Fugue II

Example 1.5. Praeludium in G Minor, Finale

Example 1.5. cont.

Example 1.6. Praeludium in G Minor, mm. 50–54

Example 1.7. Praeludium in G Minor, mm. 125–27

major (ex. 1.6), as well as the Neapolitan cadence in m. 125 (ex. 1.7), always stay within a strong G-minor framework.

Secondly, the work employs a degree of thematic control that results in a multisectional composition of remarkable unity. The *passaggio* figuration introduces in m. 2 a harmonic pattern that is subsequently spelled out in an ostinato subject. The same subject, slightly modified, is treated in both fugal sections. Moreover, the interlude (mm. 67ff.) as well as the finale (mm. 141ff.) return in their bass parts to the melodic and harmonic fundament of the work.

Buxtehude's expansion of the traditional multisectional prelude/toccata of the *stylus phantasticus* genre into an unprecedented large-scale and thematically controlled format suggests a general path that Bach later pursued as well, although in a different fashion. In his later organ works at least, Bach ordinarily separated the fugal and free structures from one another, adhering to the form scheme *Praeludium et Fuga* preferred in Middle and South Germany. As his *Passacaglia* (BWV 582) demonstrates, he invoked this separation even in the ostinato genre, and thereby introduced a clear alternative to Buxtehude's solution. Nevertheless, with respect to the extraordinarily expansive tendencies of prelude and fugue as separate entities, Buxtehude's unprecedented synthesis unquestionably provided the point of departure for Bach.

As BuxWV 149 shows, the seventeenth-century spectrum of compositional forms and types was sufficient for Buxtehude's purposes in designing large-scale structures. What he deemed insufficient was the traditional lack of coherence in genres of composition that originated first and foremost from improvisation. His sense for larger form, corresponding elements, and formal rounding off led to unschematic, highly individual solutions. Bach, on the other hand, accepted and adjusted to the growing tendency toward categorization of instrumental forms (prelude and fugue, sonata, concerto). Nevertheless, the Buxtehudian manner of extreme diversity and individuality was a decisive precedent for Bach.

Handel and Telemann were more open to compromise. Their instrumental concertos and vocal arias, for instance, reveal a much higher degree of standardization and homogenization in terms of musical form and thematic-motivic, rhythmic, and harmonic contents. Bach's compositional solutions, like Buxtehude's, stress the principle of individuality and resist the tendency toward conformity and regularity. All of Handel's oratorios and keyboard suites and all of Telemann's cantatas and concertos actually possess many more elements in common than Bach's Brandenburg Concertos, violin soli, or Passions taken by themselves. Bach, in this sense, preserved the Buxtehudian spirit, just as Buxtehude had in his own right foreshadowed a later ideal.

Notes

1. P. Spitta, *J. S. Bach,* vol. 1 (Leipzig: Breitkopf & Härtel, 1873), pp. 251ff.

2. *Dietrich Buxtehude's Orgelcompositionen,* ed. P. Spitta, 2 vols. (Leipzig: Breitkopf & Härtel, 1876–78).

3. C. Stiehl, "Die Familie Düben and die Buxtehudischen Manuscripte auf der Bibliothek zu Upsala," *Monatschefte zur Musikgeschichte* 21 (1889), pp. 2–9.

4. *Dietrich Buxtehude* (Paris: Fischbacher, 1913).

5. *Dietrich Buxtehudes Werke,* vol. 1–8, ed. W. Gurlitt et al. (Klecken: Urgrino, 1925–58); continued: *Dieterich Buxtehude. The Collected Works,* vol. 9ff, ed. K. Snyder et al. (New York: Broude, 1987–).

6. G. Karstädt, *Thematisch-systematisches Verzeichnis der musikalischen Werke von Dietrich Buxtehude* (Wiesbaden: Breitkopf & Härtel, 2/1985), hereafter cited as Karstädt, BuxWV.

7. K. Snyder, *Dieterich Buxtehude, Organist in Lübeck* (New York: Schirmer, 1987).

8. Reprinted in W. Stahl, *Dietrich Buxtehude* (Kassel: Bärenreiter, 1937), following p. 56.

9. See Walther's letter of 6 August 1729 to H. Bokemeyer (*Johann Gottfried Walther, Briefe,* ed. K. Beckmann and H.-J. Schulze [Leipzig:Deutscher Verlag für Musik, 1987], p. 63).

10. *Musikalisches Lexikon,* reprint, ed. R. Schaal (Kassel: Bärenreiter, 1953), p. 123.

11. Although Buxtehude's tablatures from Walther's collection have not survived, his own copies in staff notation transmit the majority of the Buxtehude chorales known today (cf. Karstädt, BuxWV).

12. Vol. 1 (reprint, ed. O. Wessely, Graz, 1966), pp. 590f.

13. The oldest extant copies of Buxtehude's prelude in F♯ minor (Musikbibliothek Leipzig and Hessische Landesbibliothek Darmstadt, respectively; cf. Karstädt, BuxWV) attribute the work to J. S. Bach.

14. Of particular importance are two early anthologies compiled after 1700 by the Ohrdruf J. C. Bach (the so-called Andreas Bach Book and Möller Manuscript).

15. *The Bach Reader. A Life of Johann Sebastian Bach in Letters and Documents,* ed. H.T. David and A. Mendel (New York: W. W. Norton, rev. 1966), p. 253.

16. Ibid., p. 123. Here Bach does not refer to the sixteenth- and seventeenth-century motet tradition, but to the vocal-instrumental concertato style of the time around 1700.

17. Ibid., p. 51.

18. Cf. J. Mattheson, *Grundlage einer Ehrenpforte* (Hamburg, 1740; reprint, ed. Max Schneider, Kassel, 1969), p. 94.

19. Cf. P. Walker, "From Renaissance 'Fuga' to Baroque Fugue: The Role of the 'Sweelinck Theory Manuscripts.'" *Schütz-Jahrbuch* 7/8 (1985–86), pp. 93–104.

20. Cf. K. J. Snyder, "Dieterich Buxtehude's Studies in Learned Counterpoint," *Journal of the American Musicological Society* 23 (1980), pp. 544–64.

21. Cf. Snyder, *Dieterich Buxtehude*, pp. 352ff.

22. The connection with operas on biblical subjects (e.g., J. Theile's "Der geschaffene, gefallene und auffgerichtete Mensch," [1678] or "Die Geburth Christi," [1681]) appears to be particularly strong.

23. Cf. R. Hill, contribution to Buxtehude Symposium (Lübeck, 1987)

24. Reprint in G. Karstädt, *Die "extraordinairen" Abendmusiken Dietrich Buxtehudes*, Veröffentlichungen der Stadt Lübeck, Neue Reihe, vol. 5 (Lübeck: M. Schmidt-Römhild, 1962).

25. After the concluding aria, according to the libretto, "the act is concluded with the mourning chorale 'Nun laßt uns den Leib begraben' in which all organs, choirs, and the entire Christian congregation and assembly participate" [Worauf dieser Actus, mit dem Gesang und Choral "Nun laßt uns den Leib begraben" von allen Orgeln und Chören, darin die ganze Christliche Gemein und Versammlung mit einstimmet, ganz kläglich beschlossen wird].

26. Cf. the text of Bach's "Staatsmotette" BWV 71, in whose concluding chorus Emperor Joseph I is addressed also.

27. Most likely the first time that Bach could experience recitative style. The earliest surviving sample of Bach's recitative composition can be found in the Hunt Cantata (BWV 208) of 1713.

28. *Castrum doloris* includes also an instrumental "Lamento."

Part One

Organ Music in Seventeenth-Century Germany

2

Organ Music within the Social Structure of North German Cities in the Seventeenth Century

Arnfried Edler

Foundations of the Organist's Position

From ancient times the northern part of Germany had a social structure distinguished from that of the rest of the empire. Since the Middle Ages the federation of the Hanse bound together the port towns around the Baltic Sea. Only in later times were the towns around the North Sea joined to that federation. Therefore, the regions of North Germany maintained close relations with both the Scandinavian and the Baltic countries that today belong to the Soviet Union. The civilization of these commercial towns was so greatly stamped by that mutuality that still today the similarity of church construction in, for instance, Hamburg, Lübeck, Rostock, Danzig (Gdansk), Riga, and Stockholm is readily apparent to the visitor. The same is true for musical culture, which was borne principally by merchants. Therefore, this culture differed early on from the musical culture of the central and southern parts of Germany, the latter stamped less by the Freie Reichsstädte (free Imperial Cities) than by the courts, with their requirement that the arts serve to represent them.

Great areas of the northern coasts of Germany were ruled by foreign powers. Although the duchies of Schleswig and Holstein were a political unity, only Holstein belonged to the Holy Roman Empire of the German Nation. Furthermore, large portions of the two duchies belonged to the Danish king. The western part of Pomerania was annexed by Sweden after the Thirty Years War, and Gdansk belonged to Poland in spite of its German character and population. However, we do not find in this region the splitting up into small principalities that is typical for the other German regions in this epoch; indeed, the lack of a strong central power was the cause of the area's orientation toward the adjoining nations to the north and east. There were relatively few sovereigns of great importance; one might mention the dukes of Mecklenburg and Pomerania as well as the duke of Schleswig-Holstein, whose rule was ended by Denmark at the beginning of the eighteenth century. The Hanseatic towns stood in permanent opposition, rivalry, and tension with those territories of absolute rulers that surrounded them.

The seventeenth century was the epoch during which the Baltic Sea lost its function as the central trade route of Northern Europe. With the beginning of colonization the chief trade routes shifted toward those towns with direct access to the Atlantic Ocean, that is, those situated on the North Sea. This shift caused the decline of the Hanseatic Federation during the seventeenth century, whereas Hamburg experienced a great economic and cultural rise beginning at the end of the sixteenth century. Formally, Hamburg belonged to the duchy of Holstein and became an Imperial town only in 1768. In contrast, Lübeck, the oldest and foremost among the great Hanseatic towns, was confronted with serious economic problems. Hamburg overtook Lübeck not only in population but in economic and political importance.

There was, however, one very important link among all the North German port towns situated on both the Baltic and the North Sea: this was their confession of Lutheran Protestantism. From Braunschweig (Brunswick) the Lutheran reformer Johannes Bugenhagen had introduced the new confession to Hamburg, Lübeck, Pomerania, Denmark, and Schleswig-Holstein by 1530. Sweden and the Baltic countries also adopted Lutheranism. In all these countries or regions the Lutheran conception of music became the starting point for a new musical development. For Luther himself, artificial polyphonic music was extremely important. He preferred artificial polyphony to unison singing. Luther's favorite composer was Josquin Des Prez, and he said that Josquin was the master of the notes, whereas other musicians were forced to do as the notes wished. With this utterance, the command of polyphonic composition is interpreted for the first time in history as an artificial ability and as a gift of God to man. Hence autonomous artificial creation is not only tolerated by the Lutheran Church (as it was in the old medieval church), but it is appreciated and required as the highest of all models of human activity.

In the epoch of Luther, of course, the organ was still not used for accompanying the singing of a Christian congregation. Rather, its function was to execute the liturgical music of the services and the new congregational chorales of the Reformed Church in alternation with the choir, the pastor, and the congregation. By no means did the organ belong to the necessary equipment of a church in the sixteenth and seventeenth centuries. For this reason it is especially remarkable that most of the early Lutheran church regulations already speak to the functions and social status of organists. By comparison, we must realize that the Roman Catholic Church had nothing comparable until the middle of the twentieth century! The sharpest contrast, however, appears in comparison with the depreciation of the organ and organists in the Calvinist confession. The Calvinists considered organ music to be one of the ornamental elements of the medieval service, elements which, like paintings, architecture, and sculptural decoration, divert from the essentials of faith and must be rejected.

The consolidation and rise of the social status of the Lutheran organist took place immediately as the Reformation was introduced, and it advanced continuously during the second half of the sixteenth century. Already by 1540 we read in a Lutheran Church regulation the admonition to congregations to elect their organists with much attention and care, since organists' abilities differ considerably.[1] Even the performance principle is already in force, for this order prescribes explicitly that the salary of an organist should be determined according to his ability. Thus we see that the function of organ playing changes in this time within Lutheranism from a spiritual office (which it had been in the old church) to a profession in the modern sense. This development is a typical consequence of the Reformation as described by the economic historian Max Weber in his famous book *Die protestantische Ethik* (The Ethics of Protestantism) in 1920. The principle of competition on which this modern concept of profession is based resulted in a quick raising of the level of ability. As a result, organists sought occasions to display their abilities. It is not astonishing to find in this time of transition many complaints from pastors in which organists are accused of performing unsuitable solos which interrupt the liturgical course of the services. Even by the beginning of the seventeenth century organists had achieved such mastery of their musical craft that they gradually became serious competitors to the scholarly cantors, the choir masters of the municipal Latin schools who traditionally were the leaders of all church music and who were officially the superiors of organists. Unlike the organist, the cantor was not specialized in practical music but was a teacher in the Latin school, the municipal school where future university students were prepared. The cantor himself was a scholar; he had acquired the degree of a baccalaureus or a magister, occasionally even a doctor. At the Latin school he gave lessons in music theory and other scholarly subjects such as Latin, religion, etc. He usually enjoyed the third rank in the school hierarchy, under the rector and corrector. Obviously he led the school choir in its performances of liturgical chorale or part song in the main churches. The organist was not a scholar. On the contrary, for a long time the citizens considered him representative of instrumental musicians, which means that his social status was near that of *Spielmann,* the medieval folk musician who was accorded little respect by the middle and upper classes and was even considered incompetent in certain legal matters. (A medieval instrumentalist was not allowed to serve as a judge, witness, or juror.) Nevertheless, the Lutheran Church soon succeeded in integrating the organist into the hierarchy of the church by charging him with different duties of administration. In this way instrumental music in general soon gained social esteem. At the end of the sixteenth century, the music of the organist had already gained such great importance that he was able to engage town musicians for making music "from the organ." Formerly only the cantor was allowed to engage such musicians to support performances of the *Kantorei* (the school choir). The importance of this innovation is twofold: First, the organist became a leader of a particular musical ensemble whose placement in the sanctuary accentuated its function as a musical counterpart to the cantor. Second, the organist's performances introduced a new type of music into the church. The music "from the organ" was performed by a small professional ensemble, whereas the cantor's choir consisted of pupils, i.e., dilettantes. The type of music performed by the organist was intended exclusively for listening. The members of the congregation had to listen to this music as attentively as to the sermon of the preacher, even if the music was without words. This manner of reception is the first appearance of the aesthetic listening that became common only in the later age of Viennese classicism and romanticism. The cantor, placed with his choir on the opposite side of the church, performed figural music, i.e., the great works of polyphony, only in high solemn services. The music for the common services was the unison chorale singing, which did not cause any problems of musical perception. There was an additional problem: after 1600 the style of the great polyphonic motets became the "old style," or *stile antico*. By contrast, organists were the main representatives of the modern concerto style with its new invention of the thoroughbass, since this thoroughbass required primarily the participation of a keyboard instrument.

Several events signal the enormous extent to which appreciation of the organist had grown within Luteranism by the beginning of the seventeenth century. One is the convention organized in 1596 by Duke Heinrich Julius of Braunschweig on the occasion of the consecration of the organ of the castle of Gröningen near Halberstadt. More than fifty organists came together from the vast region between Danzig in the north and Thuringia in the south, and the memory of that convention lasted an entire century. Andreas Werckmeister, the great Halberstadt organist and organ theorist of the late seventeenth century, composed a memorial publication. Another important event is the publication of the so-called *Hamburger Melodeyen Gesangbuch* (Hymnal of Hamburg Melodies) in 1604. This hymnal includes the first references to the practice of organ-accompanied congregational singing. It is historically significant that this important publication announcing a far-reaching reformation of church music was not the work of a cantor but a collaborative production of the organists of the four main churches of Hamburg. Living in Hamburg at that time was Hieronymus Praetorius, who must be considered the first important composer among North German organists. Apparently his models were the organists of St. Mark's Cathedral in Venice, whose activities had a dominating influence on musical development of the second half of the sixteenth century. Like those Venetian organist-composers, Hieronymus Praetorius wrote predominantly vocal concertos for several choirs and accompanying instruments. Although there was no official occasion for which an organist might provide such a genre of music, his compositions were so appreciated by the Hamburg citizens that they undertook to print Praetorius's collected compositions under a title borrowed from Orlando di Lasso's *Opus musicum.*

Theological Legitimation and Reception of Organ Music in the Seventeenth Century

We have already seen that there is a great difference between Lutheranism and Calvinism in regard to the recognition of organ playing. In those countries shaped by Calvinism—such as Switzerland, the northern part of the Netherlands, England, and Scotland—organ music was banished from the ecclesiastical services. Consequently it was impossible for the position of organist to become a true musical profession. This rigid attitude did not loosen until the late seventeenth and eighteenth centuries. It is therefore typical for this situation that organ music found its place outside the service. Especially in the Netherlands, capable organists, who could no longer find employment within the church, were employed by the town administrations. Like the town musicians, these organists made their music for nonecclesiastical purposes. The most famous of the Dutch town organists was Jan Pieterszon Sweelinck (1562–1621). His novel conception of an organ music with concert function made a great impression on his contemporaries and successors. He introduced revolutionary new techniques of organ playing by combining elements of the English virginal style with elements of Venetian organ music of the end of the sixteenth century. This institutionalization of the organ recital, the existence of which can also be proven in England, marks a turning point. The organ recital is the first institution in occidental music made exclusively for the purpose of the performance of autonomous instrumental music. The genres of this organ music were not liturgical; rather, they belonged to the courtly and domestic music of the epoch. Adaptations and variations on popular songs, dances, and large virtuous fantasias are combined with the organ idiom of Andrea Gabrieli and Claudio Merulo, and thus begins the rise of an organ music of new quality. Amsterdam was one of the most important harbor towns along the coast of the North Sea and was therefore very rich in amusement and diverse attractions. At this time we read that among these attractions were two favorites: the so-called anatomies (i.e., public autopsies, which were celebrated like feast days) and organ recitals.[2]

Most of Sweelinck's pupils came from the countries around the Baltic Sea: from Scandinavia and from North and Central Germany. Here his teaching had much greater effect than within his own country, where later in the seventeenth century organ music lost its importance. For the Scandinavian and German pupils of Sweelinck, the problem was to adjust the novel concert style of their master's music to the conditions of their native Lutheran sphere of activity. A simple transfer of Sweelinck's forms and manners of playing was impossible. New forms and styles of organ composition had to be found that could mediate between Sweelinck's achievements and the conditions of organ playing in the Lutheran sphere of the epoch.

Even if Calvinism and Lutheranism were strong antagonists at that time, they did not persist in a hermetic mutual seclusion of doctrines homogenous in themselves. On the contrary, the situation is characterized by violent discussions and power struggles between the two camps. Personal constellations played an important part in the sphere of the courts as well as in the civil administrations of the towns. Thus, even within Lutheranism we find strong trends against the open-mindedness and tolerance of artificial elements in the service. The Calvinist concept of music and its function fitted better in the impetuous and fanatic movements that were released by the religious struggles of the seventeenth century. It is not astonishing, therefore, that again and again discussions concerning the legitimacy of organ music flared up. Thus, it was very important that the University of Wittenberg, which formulated the representative doctrines of Lutheranism in two expert opinions of 1623 and 1630, explicitly designated organ playing as a gift of God appropriate to move the minds of men.[3] In 1661 a very interesting controversy flared up which was caused by a polemic pamphlet published by the Rostock professor of Theology Theophil Großgebauer and which indirectly involved the Hamburg organist Heinrich Scheidemann. The debate sheds light on the reception of the organ music of Scheidemann and his contemporaries in about 1650, including among others Jacob Praetorius, Matthias Weckmann, and the young Johann Adam Reinken, who became Scheidemann's substitute in 1658. One important point involved the organists' virtuosity. Großgebauer, who was considerably influenced by Puritan Calvinism, wrote as follows: "There sits the organist. He plays and shows his art: the whole congregation of JESUS CHRIST must sit and listen to the sound of the pipes in order that the art of one man be exhibited. At this the congregation becomes sleepy and lazy: some people sleep, some chat, some look where it is not proper. . . . Some would have liked to pray, but they are so much occupied and distraught by the whistling and roaring that they are not able to do so. . . ."[4]

Apparently Heinrich Scheidemann felt personally attacked by these and other passages of the book, which—according to his witness—was sold in the Hamburg books shops within a few days. On the spot he induced his brother-in-law, Hector Mithobius, pastor in the village of Otterndorf near Hamburg, to write a voluminous reply which, under the title *Psalmodia Christiana*, was not published until 1665, two years after Scheidemann had died. To the above-cited passage Mithobius replied as follows: "The organist sits there not in order to exhibit his art but to praise GOD in an artificial manner and by his lovely harmony to move himself as well as primarily the whole congregation to rest in God, to an ardent devotion, to spiritual thoughts, and to joy in the LORD, and to awaken the spirit and to make the congregation sprightly, gay, and joyful for the service."[5] The virtuous organ music is considered a means to increase the emotional readiness for reception of the word of God. He speaks about those "pieces to which the congregation is accustomed to listen with much devotion. . . . By making music the mouth is not stopped up but rather opened, which especially will take place by lovely roulades and gracious runs. . . . By this the congregation will pray more zealously, then sing the psalms with much more joy, as experience teaches."[6] Mithobius then justifies the expenditure for the great organs and for fine organ playing because the public service by those means is "decorated, and made magnificent and imposing because the organ is virtually the queen and heart of all musical instruments."[7]

This passage is most important because there are few witnesses for the justification of virtuosic and extended organ pieces within the service. One has often wondered whether the extensive chorale fantasias by Scheidemann, Tunder, Reinken, or Buxtehude could find their place in the service at all, since they seemed to be beyond the scope of the liturgy. Now I think it is likely that Mithobius's *Psalmodia Christiana* supplies the justification for just such extensive musical works within the services. This is shown very clearly in the book's appendix, which comprises the sermon delivered on the occasion of the consecration of the Hans-Riege-organ in Otterndorf. Here we learn some negative facts about the circumstances of that reception. Graphically the preacher describes how several members of the congregation leave the church during the organ music in order to pass the time strolling and chatting in the churchyard. On the other hand, those who remain in the church "sit there like stupid and unthinking cattle and do not once consider that they owe thanks to God for this noble ecclesiastical grace; not to mention that they do not pay honor to that noble and very famous art of organ playing and to other kinds of music and to those persons who are appointed for it; on the contrary, they inwardly and outwardly disdain them and do them harm wherever they are able."[8] From these documents we learn the high theological, aesthetical, and social appreciation which indeed never was undisputed, not even during the period of its flowering in the second half of the seventeenth century.

The importance attached by the citizens of the North German towns to the highest quality of organ playing in their representative churches is also revealed through the scholarships they offered to native young talents for the purpose of long-term study with famous foreign organists. Already before 1600, the young Hamburg organist Hieronymus Praetorius was sent to Cologne for several years; later, Scheidemann and Jacob Praetorius, the son of Hieronymus, went to Sweelinck in Amsterdam. Most of the Sweelinck pupils were scholarship holders of their native towns.

The organist charged with the execution of the thoroughbass became the central figure in the performance of seventeenth-century music *in stile moderno*. In this regard, the cantor, who was bound by strict regulations to cultivate the traditional repertory of motets, was no serious competitor. Only the new type of *Kapellmeister* familiar with the style of opera in the second half of the seventeenth century was of possible danger to the organist. Beginning in the eighteenth century, such *Kapellmeister* were appointed to the cantor posts, for instance, Telemann in Hamburg or Bach in Leipzig. This new type of *Kapellmeister/Kantor* was superior to the organist in his musical qualification, but the type was still rare in the seventeenth century.

With few exceptions, seventeenth-century opera in Germany was restricted to the courts and princely residences. The first opera supported by citizens was founded in Hamburg in 1678. One of its founders was the organist Johann Adam Reinken, and there can be no doubt that Buxtehude, who lived in Lübeck and had friendly relations with Reinken, also knew well the operatic style. Generally the organists were more open-minded toward opera than the Latin school cantors. For instance, the Hamburg cantor of the late seventeenth century, Joachim Gerstenbüttel, wanted to save church music from the poison of *die krumme Operen Schlange* (the twisted snake of opera).

Organists were also a moving force in the development of public concerts, the most significant precursor of which, the Collegium Musicum, was first distinctly defined in North German Lutheran territory by the organist of St. Jacob's Church in Hamburg, Matthias Weckmann. Weckmann's activity in the Collegium Musicum during the years 1660–74 is of sociomusical relevance in that one can observe in it a change from musicmaking in the service of the church to privately sponsored public musical activity. Based upon the Hamburg model, Collegia Musica were established in a number of places, mostly under the direction of organists or town musicians. Here professionals as well as amateurs were engaged in learning the newest music, gradually developing a feeling for aesthetic musical judgment.

The close relationship of organists to the new Italian genres of opera and oratorio becomes manifest not only in the cantatas and in the *Abendmusiken* of Dieterich Buxtehude, but also in the arrangements of oratorios by Thomas Strutius in Danzig about 1660 or by Georg Bronner in Hamburg about 1710.[9]

The Practice of Organists

If we wish to inform ourselves concerning the concrete duties of North German organists in the seventeenth century, we must first study the Lutheran church regulations. They give brief instructions or indications for the occasions and manners of organ playing in the course of the different types of Lutheran services. We already have seen that the organ rarely accompanied congregational singing during this period. The first indications for that practice can be found in the *Hamburg Melodeyen Gesangbuch* of 1604, and we know that some organists, such as Paul Siefert in Danzig or Heinrich Scheidemann in Hamburg, occasionally practiced that type of accompaniment.[10] Apparently that practice was still an exceptional one used only in festive services, such as consecrations. We find it very rarely in the regulations; for instance, a Danzig regulation of 1619 indicates that the singing during communion must be executed in this way. The fundamental elements of the seventeenth-century regulations are the same as those instituted by the sixteenth-century reformers, i.e., for the north, primarily Johannes Bugenhagen. In the regulations before 1560, organ music was required mainly at three points in the service: at the Introit, at the Gradual, and during the Communion. We can infer from these indications that the organ participated in alternation with the choral music of the cantor and that it occasionally offered instrumental contributions to the cantor's figural (i.e., polyphonic) music. The choir and the organ executed the verses of the liturgical chant or of the German chorales alternatively, the latter with the participation of the congregation. If no choir was available, the organist could take over its duties. Instead of a vocal motet for the Gradual, for instance, he played an intabulation of the piece. Through this practice, the genre of organ motet or organ ricercar gradually came to be instituted during the second half of the sixteenth century, and a great many of these were no longer transcriptions of vocal music but genuine organ music. "The touching of motets" (*Motettenschlagen*) became a central duty of organists in the seventeenth century. For instance, the regulation of Ratzeburg (1614) assigned organ motets before the sermon and at the end of the service.[11] At Vespers also the organist regularly performed the exit music; furthermore, he was required to play a motet after the Magnificat. In other words, he would follow the unison singing of the Magnificat with a polyphonic elaboration on the organ. Many of the surviving organ elaborations of the Magnificat grew out of that practice.

No church regulation of the seventeenth century explicitly assigns a place for free organ music, that is, pieces in the so-called *stylus phantasticus*. Reports of performances of such organ music are likewise lacking. It was generally considered a disgrace for an organist to execute pieces "from the tablature" instead of improvising upon the tunes of the occasion. We must not think that the *Abendspiele* (evening performances) that Franz Tunder arranged for the merchants of Lübeck were the only activity of this kind. It was perhaps widespread custom for organists to provide for the entertainment of merchants who were preparing for stock exchange operations or had need of respite, which they particularly preferred to take in the market church. For the most part, however, these old traditions were not institutionalized. It is explicitly stated that Tunder's *Abendspiele* had their origin in similar old customs and traditions that were found all over northern Europe.[12] If we look at paintings depicting interiors of churches in the seventeenth century—for instance, those by Emanuel de Witte or Gerrit Berckheyde—we realize that those churches served many more functions than ours today. They were public buildings accessible nearly all day and were situated in the center of the pulsating life of the town. Citizens met together here for business negotiations, children played, dogs and cats ran up and down, and beggars sat along the walls and beside the portals (fig. 2.1). The concomitant phenomenon of organ recitals in such surroundings might have been similar to those described by Constantin Huygens. According to his report, organ concerts in the Netherlands were meeting points for the different classes of people: unmarried persons visited the recital for amorous reasons, married men for commercial ones.[13] In 1585 an examination of a new foreign organist took place in Danzig. A number of noble citizens took much pleasure in listening to him for several hours, but at the same time they played dice and drank wine. We can imagine that in those church rooms full of life there was great variety in the occasions and the manners of performance for the whole spectrum of organ music of the epoch. Again and again organists succumbed to the temptation of letting dances or even amorous pieces slip into the service, as we can see from the numerous prohibitions against so doing.

One of the most-requested capabilities of seventeenth-century organists was naturally thoroughbass playing. It became more and more self-evident that organists accompanied small sacred concertos or sonatas and canzonas for few instruments with the thoroughbass. Tunder's *Abendspiele* must have consisted for the most part of such vocal and instrumental music in concerto style, and this type of music must also have played a large role in the church service. The repertory was on the whole identical with the secular music of the Collegium Musicum and the courts. Often on the title pages of ensemble sonatas we find the instruction "suited for church and table music." There are indications that performances of such music were not closely regulated but could happen as a spontaneous action, as, for instance, in a report of such music being performed in the Hamburg Church of St. Katherine by the violinist Johann Schop and the organist Heinrich Scheidemann as a response to the sermon.[14] Similarly, the description of a consecration service in Otterndorf shows that Scheidemann played only a single organ solo, a prelude at the beginning. All other pieces in which he participated are called "concertos which were to be sung to the organ" (*in die Orgel gesungen*).[15]

Organists who were installed in important posts, such as Reinken and Buxtehude, called themselves "Director organi" on the title pages of their instrumental compositions. This might appear presumptuous, but we must consider that the music "on the organ"—i.e., in the organ loft—was a genre of music that had since been established as an independent one beside the music of the cantor. Furthermore, this "organist music" was appreciated and demanded by

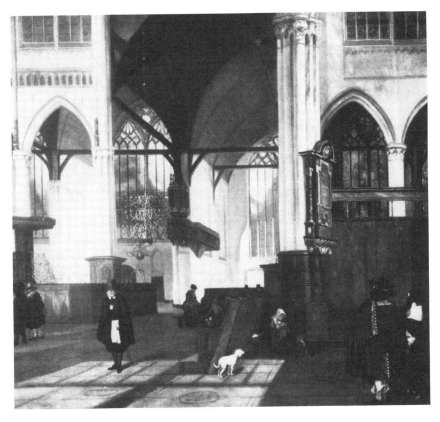

Figure 2.1. Emanuel de Witte, *The Oude Kerk in Amsterdam*, ca. 1656-58
(From Ilse Manke, Emanuel de Witte, 1617-1692, *Amsterdam, 1963)*

the civic society. Thus the title seems not to be improper, even if it was not bestowed officially.

The Chorale Fantasia

The last section of this article will be a consideration of the genre of organ composition that most specifically expresses the idea of organ music in the Lutheran area of North Germany: the chorale fantasia.

The fantasia and its decisive character were developed in England by the Elizabethan lutenists, gambists, and virginalists toward the end of the sixteenth century. The fantasia was decidedly not church music. Rather, it represented for the first time the idea of instrumental music as a work of art in the sense of renaissance art theory. The most concentrated formulation of this idea of the instrumental fantasia was written by Thomas Morley in his *Plaine and Easie Introduction to Practicall Musicke* of 1597. Morley says that in the fantasia "may more art be shown than in any other music because the author is tied to nothing, but he may add, diminish, and alter at his pleasure. . . ."

Jan Pieterszoon Sweelinck transplanted the secular English fantasia for stringed keyboard instruments into the sphere of organ music. Apparently his pupils were fascinated by his large fantasias, which, in contrast to the English ones, are constructed upon a single theme. They could experience in Sweelinck's works the summit of a totally new idea of instrumental form that expanded in wide dimensions and simultaneously exhausted all possibilities of keyboard virtuosity of that epoch. Indeed, it was bound to Sweelinck's individuality. In a sense, he singlehandedly anticipated the structures and presupposed manners of reception characteristic of the autonomous music of 150 years later. Yet Lutheranism offered an opportunity for that premature autonomous music to survive under changed conditions, i.e., through the connection with the Lutheran congregational chorale. The tune of the chorale is treated verse by verse as material for a composition of both subtle contrapuntal technique and immense freedom. The result is a form that had no counterpart in the instrumental music of that epoch; we must consider it an extreme venture into avant-garde composition and virtuosic playing. Here we see a new conception of thematic elaboration that foreshadows procedures characteristic of the sonata of the classic period. We observe the intention of "discussing" the theme, of breaking it up into small motivic particles, of deriving material from it and contrasting motives with each other—all of which is foreign to all other styles of composition of the period. No formal scheme makes possible the foreseeing of any event.

For a prototype of this new genre, let us consider the chorale fantasia *An Wasserflüssen Babylon* by Johann Adam Reinken, who was the pupil and, in 1663, the successor Scheidemann at St. Katherine's Church in Hamburg. This piece, 327 measures in length, is the most extensive of all North German chorale fantasias. It is divided into ten sections, each of which corresponds to one half verse of the chorale. Let us choose the ninth section for an example. It extends to over fifty-five measures from measure 236 to 291 (ex. 2.3). The composer treats the material in two totally different ways: first, with the technique of counterpoint and, second, by broken thematic elaboration. The melodic unity of the half verse is broken up into two constituent motives: a descent within the space of a fourth and a three-note motive shaped by the descending major third and minor second with a repeated note in between (ex. 2.1). The first motive fills the space between the fifth and the upper octave, the second the space between the major third and the sixth of the scale. The contrapuntal first portion of the section (mm. 236–49) realizes this melodic structure by compressing both motives into a continuous eighth-note movement and leading them into a three-part stretto section. Yet the first two strettos end in a citation of the melody that contrasts with the preceding contrapuntal material: it is monody in two different shapes, a syncopated one and a colored one. Within the last one a new motive is developed which in the second part of the section will become an important independent element of contrast (ex. 2.2).

Example 2.1

Example 2.2

The second half of the contrapuntal portion (mm. 250–63) expands the canonic structure based on eighth-note motion by combining it with the melody in augmentation. The listener is involved in the continuous motion; he now hears only tones that belong to the theme, although they are split into two different dimensions of time, i.e., augmentation and diminution.

Whereas the first half (mm. 236–63) shows the tendency toward maximal integration of the material achieved by means of counterpoint, the second (mm. 264–91) involves the process of disintegration. At first the two motives are torn apart into two sharply contrasting shapes. The first motive—the descent within the space of a fourth—is heard without coloration over the violent scalewise ascent of sixteenth notes followed by descending octave leap (see m. 264). The second motive, however, is combined with the figuration motive arising from the colored motive in the first half; it is now changed into an expressive suspen-

Example 2.3. Johann Adam Reincken, *An Wasserflüssen Babylon*, mm. 236–91

Example 2.3, cont.

Example 2.3, cont.

Example 2.3, cont.

sion figure (see m. 265). This procedure of motive-splitting, which renders the motive nearly unrecognizable by comparison with the first subsection, is appropriately repeated on another scale degree. In this way the composer prepares the total isolation of both motives, which is achieved in measures 272 to 285; that is, the first part of this passage is based only on the first, the second part only on the second motive. During the course of musical reflection, both are submitted to such extreme procedures as quick changes of equal and unequal movement, exchanges of upper and lower voices, sequences, and so on.

The entire procedure gives the impression of total fragmentation and disintegration. By no means do I think it unsuitable to suggest an analogy with the characteristic procedures in a classical or romantic sonata or symphony. It would obviously be absurd to assume a direct historical influence. What I think is decisive is that in the sphere of Lutheranism and the early bourgeoisie, one finds for the first time a subjective form of instrumental music that presages the later idea of "absolute" instrumental music.

Notes

1. A. Beutter, "Geschichtliches zur Frage der Organistenbesoldungen," *Monatsschrift für Gottesdienst und kirchliche Kunst* 4 (1899), p. 254.

2. William S. Heckscher, *Rembrandt's Anatomy of Dr. Nicolaus Tulp: An Iconological Study* (New York: New York University Press, 1958), p. 28.

3. Georgius Dedekennus (= Dedekind), *Thesaurus consiliorum et decisionum* [1623], new ed. by Christianus Grübelius (Jena, 1672), vol. 1, p. 559; vol. 3, p. 22.

4. "Da sitzet der Organist/ spielet und zeiget seine Kunst: daß eines Menschen Kunst gezeiget werde/ soll die gantze Gemeine JESU CHRISTI da sitzen/ und hören den Schall der Pfeiffen/ darüber wird die Gemeine schläfrig und faul: Etliche schlaffen/ etliche schwatzen/ etliche sehen, dahin sich's nicht gebühret. . . . Etliche wolten gern beten/ werden aber durch das Sausen und Gethön so eingenommen und verwirret/ daß sie nicht können." Theophil Großgebauer, *Wächterstimme aus dem verwüsteten Zion . . .* (Frankfurt am Main, 1661), pp. 227f.

5. "Der Organist sitzet nicht da seine Kunst zu zeigen/ sondern GOTT künstlich zu loben und durch eine liebliche Harmoniam, so wol sich selbst/ als auch fürnemlich die gantze Gemeine/ zur Ruhe in Gott/ zur brünstigen Andacht/ geistlichen Gedancken/ und Freude in dem HERRN zu bewegen/ und also den Geist zu erwecken/ und die Gemeine munter/ hurtig und freudig zum Gottesdienste zu machen." Hector Mithobius, *Psalmodia christiana . . .* (Jena, 1665), p. 307.

6. "Stücke, denen die Gemeine mit großer Andacht zuzuhören pfleget. . . . Der Mund wird . . . durch das Musiciren nicht gestopffet/ sondern vielmehr eröffnet . . . welches sonderlich also scheinet in lieblichen Coloraturen und anmuthigen Läufflein. Daher betet denn die Gemeine desto eyferiger/ sie singet die Psalmen darauf mit desto grössseren Freuden, wie die Erfahrung lehret." Mithobius, *Psamlodia*, p. 295.

7. "gezieret/ herrlich und ansehnlich gemachet; Weil ja die Orgel gleic˙.sam die Königin und Hertz aller Musicalischen Instrumente ist. . . ." Ibid., p. 293.

8. "sitzen sie da/ wie das tumme unvernünfftige Viehe/ und dencken nicht einmahldaran/ daß sie für diese edle Kirchen Gnad Gott zu dancken schuldig sein: zu geschweigen/ daß die edle und hochberühmte Orgel = Kunst und andere Music/ samt denen Personen/ so dazu bestellet seyn/in gebührenden Ehren halten sollen/ verachten dieselben vielmehr heimlich und öffentlich/ und thun ihnen allen Verdruß an/ wo und wie sie nur können." Ibid., p. 392.

9. Hermann Rauschning, *Geschichte der Musik und Musikpflege in Danzig* (Danzig [now Gdansk, Poland]: Komissionverlag der Danziger Verlags-Gesellschaft, 1931, pp. 261ff; Lieselotte Krüger, *Die Hamburgische Musikorganisationen im XVII. Jahrhundert* (Leipzig/Straßburg/ Zürich: Heitz, 1932), p. 259.

10. Rauschning, Ibid., p. 151; Arnfried Edler, *Der nordelbische Organist. Studien zu Sozialstatus, Funktion und kompositorischer Produktion eines Musikerberufes von der Reformation bis zum 20. Jahrhundert* (Kassel: Bärenreiter, 1982), p. 167.

11. Edler, ibid., pp. 160f.

12. Ibid., pp. 49f.

13. Frits Noske, "Rondom het orgeltractaat van Constantin Huygens," *Tijdschrift van de Vereeniging voor Nederlandse Muziekgeschiedenis* 17 (1955), p. 284.

14. Martin Geck, *Die Vokalmusik Dietrich Buxtehudes und der frühe Pietismus* (Kassel: Bärenreiter, 1965), p. 63.

15. Edler, *Der nordelbische Organist,* p. 166.

3

The Sacred Organ Works of Samuel Scheidt: Their Function, Form, and Significance

Douglas E. Bush

Opinions concerning the organ works of Samuel Scheidt seem to vary greatly. Some scholars have singled out his music as an object for praise (though their actual discussion of his work may be quite brief), while others are considerably less enthusiastic. In his *History of Keyboard Music to 1700,* Willi Apel vascillates between both poles, referring to one piece as "among the most beautiful creations of the period"[1] and calling another "a masterpiece of the first rank,"[2] while he criticizes other works for being "somewhat too long"[3] or admonishes us to be charitable during a fugue "in which a dotted rhythm is hounded to death."[4] In reference to particular echo compositions Apel suggests that Scheidt imitated Sweelinck's style with "about the same success as the apprentice has with the sorcerer's exorcism."[5] Regardless of individual taste, 400 years after Scheidt's birth the composer's work stands as a monument in seventeenth-century music, and his sacred pieces provide a meaningful testament of faith and devotion still capable of stirring one's soul—even in our own "Age of Reason" with its computerized technology.

In considering the sacred organ music of Scheidt, pieces based on Protestant chorales or on other items specifically associated with the liturgical service comprise about two-thirds of the *Tabulatura nova* (1624). Adding to that the one hundred hymns settings of the *Görlitz Tablature* (1650) results in the most extensive body of sacred organ music by any seventeenth-century German composer preserved in printer's ink.

Christhard Mahrenholz, and others, have written much about the form of the sacred works, especially as that relates to the use and placement of the cantus firmus.[6] Likewise, several studies have been made that discuss Scheidt's variation techniques, their different types, and the contrapuntal methods explored within those types. Common in many discussions is the expressed idea that in spite of his publications, Scheidt exerted little or no influence on the musical style of his contemporaries. Indeed, Apel concludes his treatment of Scheidt by saying:

> Scheidt's position and importance in the evolution of German keyboard music, it seems to me, has not always been judged correctly. We know that he had a number of students, but none of them played any role in the field of organ music. There is no trace of an immediate influence of his *Tabulatura nova* on other composers. The development that led from Sweelinck to Bach did not proceed via out-of-the-way Halle, but via Hamburg and Lübeck— not via Scheidt, but via Jacob Praetorius and Heinrich Scheidemann, the teachers of Weckmann and Reincken.[7]

The study of any composer's work with a focus on how that music has influenced other composers, and especially those contemporary to his own time, cannot, or at least should not, be our ultimate objective, for it is very likely that very few composers spend their creative efforts trying to become an influence on others. Rather, it is useful for those of us who enjoy the results of their creativity to study the music in the context of its historical period so that we might better understand those elements that give it its distinctive beauty.

With this in mind, it may be helpful to consider the use of form in Scheidt's chorale-based music as it compares to the work of others. Since an exhaustive treatment is beyond the scope of this study, the comparison will be limited to works based on the chorale *Ich ruf zu dir, Herr Jesu Christ* written by Jan Pieterszoon Sweelinck (1562–1621), Scheidt's illustrious teacher, and Dietrich Buxtehude (1637–1707), perhaps the most famous of all the seventeenth-century German organists. The setting by Sweelinck consists of a number of variations, while those by Scheidt and Buxtehude are contained in a single movement. (One should also bear in mind that Sweelinck's piece was not intended for liturgical use, while the other two most likely were.)

Sweelinck's first variation on the chorale provides a typical treatment one might expect in a set of variations. The cantus firmus appears in the upper voice in an essentially unornamented fashion except for the repeat of the first complete phrase, where it is ornamented and given a distinctive dotted rhythmic pattern. The accompanying contrapuntal voice varies the accompanimental figures used for each phrase segment—often employing a characteristic pattern for each segment (ex.3.1).[8]

Free imitation is used to introduce several phrases of the cantus firmus (including the initial phrase in mm. 21–30), some contrapuntal figures are derived from the cantus firmus (mm. 31–38), and there is some limited use of sequencing motives (mm. 39–42). In its entirety, the variation is forty-five measures in length (ex. 3.2).

Separated from Sweelinck's piece by several decades, Buxtehude's chorale prelude presents a vivid contrast to Sweelinck's variation approach. The prelude

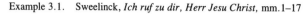

Example 3.1.   Sweelinck, *Ich ruf zu dir, Herr Jesu Christ*, mm. 1–17

begins with two voices, the cantus firmus in the upper voice accompanied by a fantasylike figuration free of any clear reference to the hymn melody. The manual indications, which are reversed when the first hymn phrase is repeated, should be noted (ex. 3.3).[9]

The phrase repetition also introduces additional voices, including pedal, thus providing a textural contrast, while a large part of the cantus firmus is ornamented. The B phrase of the cantus firmus seems to be omitted altogether; in its place a triplet figure is introduced for a brief five measures (ex. 3.4).

In measure 26 the cantus firmus resumes a prominent role (phrase C), further accentuated by another manual change. The next short hymn phrase, D, is repeated in measures 31–33 in a slightly ornamented fashion and the manuals

Example 3.2. Sweelinck, *Ich ruf zu dir*, mm. 21–42

Example 3.3. Buxtehude, *Ich ruf zu dir*, mm. 1–22

Example 3.3, cont.

are changed again. The penultimate phrase of the cantus firmus, E, is highly ornamented and is accompanied with a pedal figure derived from the opening interval of the phrase. The concluding phrase appears in the pedal and is then repeated in an ornamented version in the soprano (again with a change of manuals). Thus in forty-six measures (compared to Sweelinck's forty-five), Buxtehude has given a veritable smorgasbord of ideas. He concludes the piece with a twelve-measure toccatalike coda, at the same time introducing the major tonality with the consistent use of an F♯ (ex.3.5).

Scheidt's setting of this hymn (contained in volume 1 of the *Tabulatura nova*) embodies an altogether different approach. Labeled a "Fantasia," it is not

Example 3.4. Buxtehude, *Ich ruf zu dir,* mm. 26–46

Example 3.4, cont.

concluding c.f. phrase

ornamented c.f. in soprano
- repetition of pedal phrase

Example 3.5. Buxtehude, *Ich ruf zu dir*, mm. 47–58

Example 3.5, cont.

Example 3.6. Scheidt, *Ich ruf zu dir*, mm. 1–40

at all like the *stylus phantasticus* employed by Buxtehude and other North German organists. At the same time, Scheidt's approach to the hymn makes a decisive departure from that of his teacher. A cursory look at the Fantasia shows the use of consistent points of imitation in a manner similar to the motet tradition, beginning with one voice and moving to four-voice texture. The various motives utilized typically present either a hymn phrase or a phrase fragment in foreimitation. After the opening imitative section, Scheidt presents the unadorned cantus firmus in the soprano, while the texture is reduced to two voices to emphasize the appearance of the hymn melody. The cantus firmus is repeated in the tenor voice and the texture is expanded to three voices. The treatment of the initial cantus firmus phrase is concluded with yet one more statement of the melody, now in the bass voice, and the texture grows to four voices. Another imitative section introduces the next hymn phrase, and the foregoing pattern is followed for this and all subsequent phrases of the hymn (ex. 3.6).[10]

The contrapuntal density and the consistency in both style and motivic organization is quite different from that used by Sweelinck in his chorale-based works, although there are similarities to some of Sweelinck's other writings. This is, perhaps, a good example of an instance where Sweelinck's students adapted what they had learned to their own circumstances and musical requirements. Further, in contrast to the music of Sweelinck and the North German organists, whose chorale-based pieces marked "Fantasia" were apparently not intended for the church, Scheidt's Fantasia is no different in style from that used in the first Versus of every hymn setting in the third part of the *Tabulatura nova*.

The matter of style in these imitative works shows a compositional process not unlike the type of imitative writing found in Italian keyboard music of the period. Although no archival evidence exists to prove it, Scheidt almost certainly had some familiarity with the Italian keyboard style, given his direct association with Schütz (for example, the occasion of 15 August 1619 when both Schütz and Michael Praetorius attended the dedication recital Scheidt played on the new organ in the Bayreuth Stadtkirche).[11] As some have pointed out, the very same *Tabulatura nova* makes clear the conscious use of a notational approach new for most German organists, although open score was considered ideal for contrapuntal music, and Frescobaldi extolled its virtues in the prefaces to his keyboard music—also printed in partitur.[12] In any case, it seems probable that Schütz shared with Scheidt his enthusiasm for the fundamentals of music he had learned while in Italy.[13]

When compared to the organ repertories of other German organists who had studied with Sweelinck, or the repertories of their students, Scheidt's sacred organ works reflect a particular fondness for contrapuntal rigor and an awareness of liturgical propriety. Though Sweelinck's "sacred" pieces, as well as those written by his other German students, are masterful and deserving of admiration, Scheidt's music manifests a religious sobriety that perhaps intensified its purpose. As has been commented in reference to J. S. Bach's forty-eight preludes and fugues in the *Well-Tempered Clavier*,[14] Scheidt's preference for conservative contrapuntal writing in his sacred works likewise may well represent the laws and rules of music that he understood and which he had inherited from the great composers of the past. This music might be considered a summary of musical law, a matter of notating that which is musically right. For the devout Lutheran musician, an appellation well-suited to Samuel Scheidt, it would have been very important to use his gift or talent to the best of his abilities in the praise of the God who gave him that talent. In other words, it would be his duty to refine his gift so as to present something to the Creator as near to perfection as his gifts or talents would allow. Again, in reference to music of J. S. Bach, Peter Williams suggests that "reasoning in this way, one reaches a position from which it is easy to comprehend how a composer in the ages of belief would see himself as being at his most devoted and religious precisely when he was writing his most abstract and complicated music. . . . Orthodox . . . Lutheranism would not have cared much for the idea that the duty of the talented few lay in simplifying truth for the quick comprehension by the many, either in music or in theology."[15]

If one entertains that idea, then it seems plausible to consider Scheidt's use of partitur notation instead of the more traditional keyboard tablature as an indication that this music was written for the edification of the "musicus" and was therefore particularly appropriate as an offering in the liturgical service to the glory of God.

In their chronological positions, Scheidt's *Tabulatura nova* and the so-called *Görlitz Tablature* represent the earliest (as well as the largest) published collections of organ music written for the Protestant service. Table 3.1 shows the number of concordant settings of hymns or liturgical items contained in the three volumes of the *Tabulatura nova* both by Sweelinck and other noted contemporaries of Scheidt. (Though not a comprehensive list of composers, it is nevertheless representative.)

Table 3.2 gives the number of concordant settings of the hymns included in the *Görlitz Tablature*. Though some have suggested that the Görlitz settings were used for congregational accompaniment, it seems more probable that they were generally used either to introduce the hymn or were played in alternation with the congregation. However, their intended use also extended into the home, as part of the title suggests: "to be played and sung with Christian churches and congregations—the same also at home—for all feasts and Sundays throughout the entire year."[16]

It is interesting to note the relatively small number of concordant settings among the North German organists, with the possible exception of Buxtehude, compared to the larger number of settings by the Central German organists who worked in the same vicinity as Scheidt. The number of concordances with titles of Pachelbel, Walther, and Bach is consistently higher than with titles of others. A comparison is also provided between the contents of the *Görlitz Tablature* and the hymns Bach listed in the original table of contents for his *Orgelbüchlein*. The greater number of concordances in Central Germany may indicate regional preferences in the hymn repertory that in turn may be the result of the flexibility allowed within the liturgical structure of the Lutheran church. (See table 3.2.)

Christhard Mahrenholz has provided much information concerning the music of the *Tabulatura nova* and its probable usage within the context of the church services of Halle.[17] Table 3.3 provides a basic outline of the Mass and Vespers used at services contained in the *Ordo Cantionum* from the *Laurentiuskirche* in Halle-Neumarkt from the end of the sixteenth century. Even though the order of service as here prescribed does not originate from the churches Scheidt served, it can be assumed that the formats of the various services were very similar. One must keep in mind the structural flexibility of the services as they were observed, with certain items considered optional depending on the feast. Congregational hymns could have been substituted in their place or some parts of the service might have been omitted altogether.[18]

An attempt to reconstruct a service is greatly aided by careful study of the vast musical repertory contained in the published collections of Michael Praetorius and Heinrich Schütz, as well as that of Samuel Scheidt. The music of these composers bears eloquent testimony of the beauty and varied richness of the musical offerings in divine worship in the early decades of the seventeenth century. A study of table 3.3 together with the contents of the *Tabulatura nova*, particularly the works in volume 3, helps clarify the liturgical usage of these pieces. (As can be observed on table 3.1, the Latin hymns are arranged according to the church year. The contents of the *Görlitzer Tabulatur* are likewise organized according to the liturgical calendar. See table 3.1.) For instance, the compositions in *Tabulatura nova III* might suggest the following usage in the mass. The three Kyrie settings may have been used as alternation with either chant or polyphony or they may have been used by themselves without the chant. The Gloria likewise follows alternatim practice with the chant beginning. A motet was generally performed following the epistle, and since there was considerable flexibility in the Lutheran service, any polyphonic piece might have been used. Since the first verset in each of the hymn settings is written in the style of the polyphonic motet, it is possible that these pieces were used in this context. The Credo organ verse may have been used to introduce the German Credo hymn *Wir glauben all an einen Gott,* or it may have been played following the intonation of the minister, or it could have replaced both the intonation and the congregational hymn singing. The "psalmus sub communione" (*Jesus Christus, unser Heiland*) and the various hymn settings contained in the *Tabulatura nova III* all reflect alternatim practice. Again, these could have been used in alternatim with congregational singing, or they may have been used in alternatim with polyphonic choral settings.[19]

Finally, one might wish to ask how widely these pieces were played and how much influence they exerted. A definitive answer is not possible, given the disparity of seventeenth-century sources, not to mention the problem of defining what is meant by the word "influence." However, aside from surviving copies of the printed collection, pieces from both the *Tabulatura nova* and the *Görlitz Tabulatur* that were copied back into the customary keyboard tabulature for easier playing are found in at least ten known manuscripts covering a geographic area from Hungary in the east to Lüneburg and Berlin in the north. Though this may seem like a small number, when compared with the number of concordant sources for works by many other composers it represents a rather respectable quantity.

Even though the specific elements of Scheidt's compositional style may not have been widely copied by his students (we do not know that, however, due to the lack of surviving sources), the imitative processes used by Scheidt remained a hallmark of Central German style and are well-known traits found in the music of Johann Pachelbel, Johann Christoph Bach, Johann Gottfried Walther, and Johann Sebastian Bach—to mention a few. The notion of providing a collection of organ hymns suited for the church year, though not new, carried on to subsequent generations. An assessment of the music by other seventeenth-century luminaries such as Schütz, Schein, or Buxtehude similarly does not indicate that their distinctive musical styles were widely copied by later composers. Each made a particular and very significant contribution to the rich musical life of seventeenth-century Germany. And so it was with Samuel Scheidt. His sacred organ works preserved and transmitted to others the learned contrapuntal style he inherited, and they provided a firm foundation for the work of future German organists.

Table 3.1   Sacred Pieces in Scheidt's *Tabulatura nova*

	J. Praetorius	H. Scheidemann	J. P. Sweelinck	M. Praetorius	M. Schildt
Tabulatura nova III*					
Kyrie dominicale IV. Toni cum Gloria		X			
Credo in unum Deum (Wir glauben all an einen Gott)		X	X	X	
Psalmus sub communione "Jesus Christus, unser Heiland"		X-3			
Hymnus "Veni redemptor gentium" (De adventu Domini)					
Hymnus "A solis ortus cardine" (De nativitate Christi)	X	X		X	
Hymnus "Christe, qui lux es et dies" (Tempore quadragesimali)			X		
Hymnus "Vita sanctorum" (De resurrectione Christi)				X	
Hymnus "Veni creator Spiritus" (De Spiritu Sancto)					
Hymnus "O lux beata Trinitas" (De Sancta Trinitate)		X		X	
Magnificat I–IX†	M-D	I–VIII			I
Modus ludendi pleno Organo pedaliter à 6 Voc.					
Modus pleno Organo pedaliter. Benedicamus à 6 Voc.					
Tabulatura nova I					
Credo (Wir Glauben all an einen Gott)					
Vater unser im Himmelreich	X	X	X		
Warum betrübst du dich mein Herz					
Da Jesus an dem Kreuze stund					
Ich ruf zu dir, Herr Jesu Christ			X		
Tabulatura nova II					
Herzlich lieb hab ich dich, O Herr			X		X
Christ lag in Todesbanden		X			
Christe, qui lux est et dies			X		
Gelobet seist du, Jesu Christ		X			
In te Domine speravi‡					

*Book III is listed first since its contents are exclusively liturgical, whereas books I and II contain a number of secular pieces. It appears that Scheidt intended the final volume to focus on liturgical music.

†The indication I–IX indicates a setting for each of the nine versions of the Magnificat. M-D in the table indicates Deutsches Magnificat (a Magnificat with German text) and I–VIII again indicates the organ settings for various Magnificat chants. The Melchior Schildt setting is for Magnificat Tone I.

‡This text is usually transmitted as "In dich hab' ich gehoffet, Herr" though there is no reference to the hymn tune in this toccata setting.

Table 3.2   Hymn Settings in the Görlitz Tablature

	Sweelinck	J. Praetorius	H. Scheidemann	Tunder	Buxtehude	Pachelbel	J. G. Walther	J. S. Bach*	J. S. Bach
Ach Gott, tu dich erbarmen								X	X
Ach Gott und Herr					X		X	X	X
Ach Gott, vom Himmel sieh darein	X					X	X	X	X
Allein Gott in der Höh sei Ehr	X					X	X	X	X
Allein zu dir, Herr Jesu Christ	X					X	X	X	
Also heilig ist der Tag									
An Wasserflüssen Babylon						X		X	X
Auf meinen lieben Gott				X	X	X		X	X
Aus tiefer Not schrei ich zu dir (2)†			X			X	X	X	
Christ, der du bist der helle Tag								X	X
Christe, der du bist Tag und Licht (2)						X		X	X
Christ ist erstanden								X	X
Christ lag in Todesbanden (2)				X	X	X		X	X
Christum wir sollen loben schon		X					X	X	X
Christ unser Herr zum Jordan kam					X	X		X	X
Christus der ist mein Leben							X	X	X
Christus der uns selig macht							X	X	X
Da Jesus am dem Kreuze stund							X	X	X
Dank sagen wir alle Gott									
Dankt dem Herrn heut und allezeit						X			
Der du bist drei in Einigkeit							X	X	
Der Tag hat sich geneiget									
Der Tag vertreibt die finstre Nacht									
Dies sind die heil' gen zehn Gebot	X					X	X	X	X
Durch Adams Fall ist ganz verderbt	X	X	X		X	X	X	X	X
Ein feste Burg ist unser Gott					X	X	X	X	X

*These correspond to the complete list of titles that were outlined for inclusion in the *Orgelbüchlein*.
†The number indicates two settings of the same hymn.

Table 3.2   Hymn Settings in the Görlitz Tablature, cont.

	Sweelinck	J. Praetorius	H. Scheidemann	Tunder	Buxtehude	Pachelbei	J. G. Walther	J. S. Bach*	J. S. Bach
Ein Kindelein so löbelich (*Der Tag, der ist so freudenreich*)‡					X	X		X	X
Erbarm dich mein, o Herre Gott	X		X			X		X	X
Erhalt uns Herr bei deinem Wort					X	X	X	X	X
Erschienen ist der herrlich Tag							X	X	X
Esaia dem Propheten das geschah									
Es ist das Heil uns kommen her	X		X		X		X	X	X
Es spricht der Unweisen Mund wohl	X				X	X	X	X	
Es war einmal ein reicher Mann									
Es wird schier der letzte Tag herkommen									
Es woll uns Gott genädig sein						X	X	X	
Gelobet seist du, Jesu Christ (2)			X		X	X	X	X	X
Gib Fried, o frommer, treuer Gott							X		
Gib unserm Fürsten und aller Obrigkeit									
Gott der Vater, wohn uns bei						X	X	X	X
Gott hat des Evangelium						X	X		
Gott sei gelobet und gebenedeiet			X				X		
Gott Vater, der du deine Sonn						X	X		
Hats Gott versehn, wer will									
Helft mir Gotts Güte preisen								X	X
Herr Christ, der einig Gotts Sohn	X		X		X	X	X	X	X
Herr Gott, dich loben alle wir		X		X	X	X	X		
Herr Gott, dich loben wir [Te Deum]					X		X	X	X
Herr Jesu Christ, du höchstes Gut (2)								X	X
Herr Jesu Christ, ich weiss gar wohl					X	X	X	X	
Herr Jesu Christ, meins Lebens Licht								X	X
Herr Jesu Christ, wahr Mensch und Gott							X		

‡An alternate text for the same tune.

Table 3.2   Hymn Settings in the Görlitz Tablature, cont.

	Sweelinck	J. Praetorius	H. Scheidemann	Tunder	Buxtehude	Pachelbel	J. G. Walther	J. S. Bach*	J. S. Bach
Herzlich tut mich erfreuen									
Herzlich tut mich verlangen					X	X	X	X	X
Herzlich vertrau du deinem Gott									
Ich dank dir, lieber Herre					X		X		
Ich hab mein Sach Gott heimgestellt						X			X
Ich ruf zu dir, Herr Jesu Christ (2)	X				X	X		X	X
In dich hab ich gehoffet, Herr			X	X		X	X	X	X
In dulci jubilo						X	X	X	X
Jesus Christus, unser Heiland, der den Tod (2)					X	X	X	X	X
Jesus Christus, unser Heiland, der von uns (2)			X	X				X	X
Komm, Heiliger Geist, Herre Gott			X	X	X		X	X	X
Kommt her zu mir, spricht Gottes Sohn					X	X	X	X	
Lobt Gott, ihr Christen allzugleich						X	X	X	X
Mag ich Unglück nicht widerstahn						X	X		
Mensch, willst du leben seliglich			X		X		X		
Mit Fried und Freud ich fahr dahin								X	X
Mitten wir im Leben sind							X	X	
Nun bitten wir den Heiligen Geist			X		X		X	X	
Nun freut euch, lieben Christen gmein (Es ist gewisslich an der Zeit)	X		X		X	X		X	X
Nun höret zu, ihr Christenleut									
Nun komm, der Heiden Heiland (2)	X				X	X	X	X	X
Nun lasst uns Gott dem Herren						X	X		
Nun lob, mein Seel, den Herren					X	X	X	X	
O Christe, Morgensterne									
O grosser Gott von Macht							X		
O Herre Gott, dein göttlich Wort							X	X	X
O Jesulein süss, o Jesulein mild (2)									

Table 3.2   Hymn Settings in the Görlitz Tablature, cont.

	Sweelinck	J. Praetorius	H. Scheidemann	Tunder	Buxtehude	Pachelbel	J. G. Walther	J. S. Bach*	J. S. Bach
O Lamm Gottes, unschuldig						X		X	X
Puer natus in Bethlehem					X		X	X	X
Sie ist mir lieb, die werte Magd									
Singen wir aus Herzensgrund							X		
Surrexit Christus hodie (Erstanden ist der Herre Christ)							X	X	X
Vater unser im Himmelreich	X	X	X		X	X		X	X
Verleih uns Frieden Gnädiglich									
Verzage nicht, o frommer Christ Vom Himmel hoch da komm ich her (2)			X			X	X	X	X
Von Gott will ich nicht lassen					X		X	X	X
Wachet auf, ruft uns die Stimme							X		X
Wär Gott nicht mit uns diese Zeit			X		X		X	X	
Warum betrübst du dich, mein Herz (3)						X		X	
Was Gott tut, das ist wohlgetan							X	X	X
Wenn dich Unglück tut greifen an								X	X
Wenn mein Stündlein vorhanden ist						X		X	
Wenn wir in höchsten Nöten sein						X	X	X	X
Wie schön leuchtet der Morgenstern					X	X		X	X
Wir glauben all an einen Gott	X		X			X	X	X	X
Wo Gott der Herr nicht bei uns hält	X		X			X		X	
Wo Gott zum Haus nicht gibt sein Gunst						X	X	X	
Zion, die werte Gottesstadt									
101 different titles									
Total number of concordant settings	15	4	19	6	33	44	45	80	56

Table 3.3 Scheidt's *Tabulatura nova* and the Order of Service in Halle

	Liturgy	Choir	Organ	Congregation
	MASS			
1.		Introit/Antiphon → Psalm verse Gloria patri Antiphon O →	Introit/Antiphon → Motet →	
2.		Kyrie ant. +	Kyrie ant. +	
3.	Gloria intoned	Et in terra ant. +	Et in terra ant. O	
4.	Salutation R	Salutation R		Salutation R
5.	Collect	Amen		Amen
6.	Epistle			
7.		Alleluia (Sequence)		
8.		(Motet +)	Motet +	
9.		Gradual alt.	Gradual ant.	Gradual alt.
10.	Gospel			
11.	Credo intoned	Patrem + O	German Credo + O	Wir glauben all
12.	Sermon preliminaries	Hymn before sermon		Hymn before Sermon
13.	Sermon	Hymn after Sermon		Hymn after Sermon
14.	Communion lit.	Communion lit. Sanctus +		
15.		J. Chr. u. Heiland + alt.	J. Chr. u. Heiland + alt.	J. Chr. u. Heiland alt.
16.		Communion hymn + alt	Communion hymn + alt	Communion hymn
17.	Concluding lit.	Concluding lit.		Concluding lit.

Table 3.3, cont.

VESPERS

	Liturgy	Choir	Organ	Congregation
1.		Antiphon Psalm Antiphon		
2.		Response R O	Response R O	
3.	Bible lesson			
4.		Latin hymn + alt.	Latin hymn + alt.	(German hymn alt.)
5.	Catechism			
6.			Motet	
7.		Hymn alt.		Hymn alt.
8.	Sermon preliminaries	hymn before sermon		hymn before sermon
9.	Sermon			
10.		Antiphon Magnificat ant. Antiphon	Magnificat ant.	
11.	Versicle R	Versicle R		
12.	Blessing	Benedicamus II +	Benedicamus I +	
13.		Amen		Amen

Legend
alt. = alternatim
R = responsorial
ant. = antiphonal
O = motet may be substituted in place of the
→ = choir or organ
+ = sung in polyphony (when sung in polyphony by the choir the organ would also play a polyphonic setting)

Notes

1. Willi Apel, *The History of Keyboard Music to 1700* (Bloomington: Indiana University Press, 1972), p. 362.

2. Ibid., p. 364.

3. Ibid., p. 358.

4. Ibid., p. 358–59.

5. Ibid., p. 359.

6. See Christhard Mahrenholz, "Die Bearbeitung geistlichen und weltlicher Melodien in Samuel Scheidts Tabulatura nova 1624," *Musicologica et Liturgica* (Kassel: Bärenreiter, 1960), pp. 103–14.

7. Apel, *History of Keyboard Music,* pp. 367–68.

8. Jan Pieterszoon Sweelinck, *Opera Omnia,* ed. Alfons Annegarn, vol. 1, fascicle 2 (Amsterdam: Vereniging voor Nederlandse Muziekgeschiedenis, 1974), p. 33. Other references to this work are from the same edition.

9. Dietrich Buxtehude, *Sämtliche Orgelwerke,* ed. Klaus Beckmann, vol. 2, part 1 (Wiesbaden: Breitkopf & Härtel, 1972), pp. 48–51. Other references to this work are from the same edition.

10. Samuel Scheidt, *Tabulatura nova,* ed. Christhard Mahrenholz, vol. 1 (Leipzig: VEB Deutscher Verlag für Musik, 1979), p. 107.

11. Scheidt makes reference to this in the preface to the *Pars prima concertuum sacrorum* (Hamburg, 1622). These three were also collaborators for the *Concertmusik* in the Magdeburg Dom in 1618. See Hans Joachim Moser, *Heinrich Schütz: His Life and Work,* trans. Carl F. Pfatteicher (St. Louis: Concordia Publishing House, 1959), pp. 101, 108. Further, it is interesting to note that Michael Praetorius's *Syntagma musicum* is expressly based on Italian practice and is dedicated to Hassler, who studied with Andrea Gabrielli.

12. Frescobaldi's keyboard works printed in partitur include his *Il Primo Libro delle Fantasie a Quattro* . . . (1608), *Il Primo Libro di Capricci, Canzon Francese e Recercari* . . . (1626), and the *Fiori Musicali* (1635).

13. These composers, along with their South German and Italian contemporaries, seem to have had particular regard for contrapuntal fluency. Virtually all composers of keyboard music from these regions exhibit their interest in contrapuntal music via their music.

14. See Peter Williams, "J. S. Bach's *Well-Tempered Clavier:* A New Approach," *Early Music* 11 (January 1983), pp. 46–52.

15. Ibid., p. 46.

16. See Christhard Mahrenholz, "Der 3. Band von Samuel Scheidts *Tabulatura nova* 1624 und die Gottesdienstordnung der Stadt Halle," *Die Musikforschung* (1948), pp. 32–39.

17. "Mit der Christlichen Kirchen und Gemeine auf der Orgel/ desgleichen auch zu Hause/ zu spielen und zu singen/ Auf alle fest-und Sonntage/ durch gantze jahr."

18. The flexibility inherent in the Lutheran service is discussed at length in the first chapter of Friedrich Blume, *Protestant Church Music: A History* (New York: W. W. Norton, 1974).

19. The many hymn settings contained in the collections by Michael Praetorius evidence a rich variety of musical practice within the liturgical context.

4

Praetorius, Compenius, and Werckmeister:
A Tale of Two Treatises

Vincent J. Panetta, Jr.

In 1936, Friedrich Blume published a transcription of a manuscript treatise on organ inspection that he had uncovered in the Herzog August Bibliothek, Wolfenbüttel.[1] Apparently a copy of a document written in the early seventeenth century, the treatise bore the following title:

Kurzer Bericht

wass beÿ überliefferung einer Klein und grosverfertigten Orgell zu observiren, wie die fundamentaliter durchgelauffen, mit Fleiss besichtiget, und nach dem Gehör examiniret werden muss. Von Fürstl. Br. Orgeln und Instrumentmachers Esaia Compenio hinterlassen. . . .

Brief Account

of what must be observed upon the delivery of an organ large or small, and how the fundamentals must be examined, thoroughly inspected, and judged by the ear. Left by Esaias Compenius, Organ and Instrument Maker to the Duke of Braunschweig. . . .

Though the *Kurzer Bericht* identified the renowned organbuilder Compenius as its author, Blume offered evidence that the document also bore connections to Michael Praetorius, and suggested that Praetorius had likely shared in its authorship. Blume went no further than this, however, and although his transcription of the treatise has been in print for more than fifty years, the distinct scarcity of that publication has until now kept the *Kurzer Bericht* from receiving the close consideration it deserves.

While Blume did recognize the importance and significance of the *Kurzer Bericht* as a testament of the early seventeenth century, its influence actually extended well beyond its own era. Apparently unknown to Blume was the fact that a copy or version of the *Kurzer Bericht* eventually came into the hands of

Andreas Werckmeister, and that the Praetorius/Compenius treatise served as a primary model for Werckmeister's highly influential *Orgel-Probe* publications of 1681 and 1698.[2] Thus the precepts of the *Kurzer Bericht,* as reflected and amplified in the writings of Werckmeister, served as an important background for much later writing and thinking on the subject of proper organ design and examination. The *Kurzer Bericht* established basic standards that exerted their influence for many generations, both in other treatises and in actual practice. In the process, the document gave rise to a chain of connections that came to involve not only Werckmeister, but also J. S. Bach, Jakob Adlung, and numerous others.

As Blume suggested, the trail of the *Kurzer Bericht* can first be traced in the pages of the *Syntagma Musicum* of Michael Praetorius.[3] Near the end of volume 3 of the *Syntagma,* Praetorius provides a comprehensive list of his compositions and writings, including not only works already in print, but also numerous items apparently planned for future publication. The projected writings include a fourth volume of the *Syntagma,* which would have dealt with composition, a treatise for keyboard players that would have included information on fingering and ornamentation, a manual on the employment of *General-Bass,* and a publication on the subject of temperament for keyboard instruments of all sorts. Of particular interest to this discussion is the second item on page 224.

Orgeln Verdingnis/ Baw und Liefferung/ sowol in Newer verfertigung/ als Alter Orgeln *revision:* allen Christlichen Gemeinen/ Pfarrherrn/ Kirchvätern/ Vorstehern/ Organisten und anderen dessen *Interessenten* zu guter auffacht und nachrichtung gestellet.

Contracting for organs, construction and delivery, covering both new construction and the rebuilding of older organs. Made available in order to provide reliable advice and counsel for all Christian congregations, pastors, church elders, church supervisors, organists, and other interested parties.

This item and the long list that contains it first appeared in 1618, but the ambitious publication plans were brought to an abrupt end by the death of Praetorius in February of 1621. That event left most of the planned treatises in a state now impossible to ascertain, with some perhaps written or at least in preliminary stages, but none published to our knowledge. As further references in the *Syntagma* make clear, however, the Wolfenbüttel *Kurzer Bericht* appears to represent a draft or version of what was intended to be published as the *Orgeln Verdingnis.* Several passages from volume 2 of the *Syntagma* serve to establish and clarify this connection.

The first significant passage appears early in the volume's prefatory material. There, after announcing that volume 2 will include, among other things, certain specifications of new and old organs as well as information on the tuning of keyboard instruments, Praetorius also mentions that there will be a section or chapter on "what should be examined with particular care upon the delivery of an organ" (*was in uberliefferung einer Orgel sonderlich in acht zu nehmen*).[4] This, then, was apparently the original publication plan for an essay on organ inspection, but such a chapter does not in fact appear anywhere in volume 2 or volume 3 of the *Syntagma*.

Part 4 of volume 2 includes a chapter most relevant to this discussion, which appears on pages 158–60. There Praetorius explains in detail why he feels a treatise on organ inspection has become necessary, and outlines his plans for furnishing just such a work. He begins by stating that a guide for those charged with proofing organs should first cover those elements that must be inspected visually, elements that, to use his term, come under the heading of *Augenschein*. Following that, the guide should cover those aspects that must be judged by the ear, or to use the author's term once again, *das Gehör*. Such a handbook, says Praetorius, ought to set out all the relevant criteria regarding bellows, winding systems, chests, the scaling and voicing of pipe work, the discovery of concealed defects, and other pertinent matters.

Praetorius then continues with additional information of interest. He states that while churches often spend considerable sums for new organs or for the rebuilding of existing instruments, all for the glorification of God, the results are in many cases unsatisfactory: keys and sliders stick, chests contain hidden flaws, the wind is too strong in one season and too weak in another (so that extra calcants must be hired), and pipe materials are often too weak, causing the pipes to lean over and fall "like drunken peasants." Faced with all this, says Praetorius, the organist suffers so much anxiety that eventually he would rather set to work threshing in a barn than have to play on such an instrument.

Praetorius then suggests that all of these defects ought rightly to be detected and corrected as the job is being completed, and he notes that instruments that have undergone such careful inspections have been known to function well for fifty, sixty, even eighty years without requiring anything more than minor repairs. Thus, he says, inspectors and church elders need a reference guide to help them through this critical inspection process. Then follows the important passage quoted here.

ein gewiss *Tractetlein* von diesem allen richtig verfasset/ und in druck *publiciret* werde. . . . Derowegen ich . . . *Esaia Compenio,* (welcher mir in vorgesetztem Bericht und Unterricht von alten und newen Orgeln sehr beyräthig gewesen) mit allem fleiss angehalten/ dass er ein solch Tractätlin fassen/ und den Kirchen/Organisten und Orgelmachern zum besten in öffentlichen druck kommen lassen wollte:

Worzu ich ihme dann meines Theils nicht allein beförderlich/ sondern auch nach meinem geringen verstande und vermügen/ beyräthig und behülfflich zu seyn/ dem gemeinem Nutzen zum besten. . . .

Und sol ein solch *Opusculum* und Tractätlin/ weil es sich hier hinten an zu setzen nicht allerdings schickenwollen/ ob Gott wil/ bald folgen.[5]

a certain brief treatise properly covering all these matters will be written and published. . . .
In that regard I have been at pains to urge Esaias Compenius (who was of great help in advising
me on the preceding commentary and instruction regarding old and new organs) to write such
a treatise and to publish it for the benefit of churches, organists, and organbuilders.

Toward which end I, for my part, offered him not only encouragement, but also advice and
assistance, to the best of my humble knowledge and ability, in order to advance the common
good. . . .

And though, to be sure, it has not come to pass that such a modest work or treatise has
been included hereafter, one should ensue before long, God willing.

There are two other significant references that should be noted. At the very
end of the *Syntagma Musicum*, volume 2, Praetorius again mentions his intention to publish a *tractätlein* on organ inspection, and here for the first time he
employs the title word "Verdingnis" in reference to the treatise.

NB.

Was sonsten etwa allhier nicht erinnert worden/ dasselbe wird in dem tractätlin vom Ver-
dingnis/ Bawen/ und Liefferung einer Orgel vielleicht angedeutet werdern.[6]

Whatever has not otherwise been brought up here will perhaps be alluded to in the treatise
on the contracting for, construction, and delivery of an organ.

A final and particularly revealing passage appears at the very end of the
preface to the *Syntagma Musicum*, volume 2. The content of the passage makes
sense only if we assume that this part of the preface was written close to the
date of publication, somewhat after the passage cited above. By this point,
Praetorius was well aware that the state of his health was in decline, and that
he might not be able to complete all of his work in progress.[7] The relevant
passage here reads as follows:

weil Ich etliche Sachen und Tractätlein/ als unter andern vom *General-Bass*, Liefferung der
Orgeln und andere mehre (so in meinem *Operibus* zum theil *promittiret*, und albereit ein guter
Anfang davon gemacht/ auch mit etlichen vornehmen *Musicis*, die sich dessen besser massen
erinnern werden/ in Newigkeit *conferiret*) vielleicht wegen Schwachheit oder andern Zufällen
nicht ganz zum ende möchte bringen können.[8]

perhaps, owing to infirmity or other contingencies, I may not be able to bring to completion
certain items and short treatises, among them those dealing with General-Bass, the delivery
of organs, and others too. Some were promised in the course of my writings, a good beginning
having already been made, and I have conferred anew with certain eminent musicians, who
will surely recall this.

When Praetorius refers here to infirmity or other contingencies, he may have
had more than his own condition in mind: Esaias Compenius, who as we now

know had begun the treatise on organ inspection, had himself died in 1617, perhaps leaving unfinished the work on which a "good beginning" had been made.

To sum up the story thus far, we have learned from the *Syntagma Musicum* that Praetorius felt a treatise on organ examination was important and necessary, and that in compiling just such a tract he had enlisted the help of Esaias Compenius, the highly esteemed organbuilder who had been appointed to the Braunschweig court at the behest of Praetorius. We have also learned that Praetorius himself supplied help in the writing of the document, that it was originally intended to appear as a chapter in the *De Organographia*, and that such inclusion was later deemed impossible (perhaps because the essay remained unfinished). Finally, it seems that Praetorius hoped and planned to publish the treatise as soon as he could, as a separate tract entitled *Orgeln Verdingnis,* but feared on account of his ill health that publication might not ensue.

The *Kurzer Bericht* uncovered in Wolfenbüttel by Friedrich Blume and attributed to Compenius is written in an anonymous scribal hand of the later seventeenth century. Alerted by the attribution, Blume went on to conclude that this manuscript did indeed represent the promised *Orgeln Verdingnis,* citing first of all a reference that appears at the end of the document's title. There, the treatise is identified as the one "promised by Michael Praetorius on page 160 of the preceding treatise" (*von Michael Praetorio in vorgehenden Tractat Fol. 160 versprochen*). It is on page 160 of the *Syntagma,* volume 2, that Praetorius mentions a forthcoming essay on organ examination (see that passage as quoted above). Thus a decisive link is established between the manuscript source and the *Tractätlein* promised by Praetorius. The handwritten *Kurzer Bericht* appears to be a version, perhaps a preliminary version, of the never-published *Orgeln Verdingnis,* and it must at one time have been bound with a copy of the *Syntagma Musicum,* volume 2. In addition, it will be recalled that Praetorius planned his projected treatise to be organized as follows: first, aspects pertaining to *Augenschein,* followed by aspects related to *Gehör.* This is precisely the basis on which the *Kurzer Bericht* is organized, and these two words are used at important points throughout.[9] Though Praetorius is not mentioned on the title page of the *Kurzer Bericht,* evidence to be presented later will show that at least one copy of the treatise circulated in the eighteenth century under his name only.

The remarks of Praetorius cited above serve to underscore the fact that a handbook for organ inspection had become a particular necessity by the early seventeenth century. Malpractice on the part of builders was apparently becoming more and more common, and several possible explanations might be advanced. First, there was a notable boom in organ construction in northern Europe during the late sixteenth and early seventeenth centuries. With the significantly greater number of contracts to be had, it was accordingly easier for unseasoned craftsmen to set up new shops and bid for work. In addition, a considerable number of artisans from the Netherlands were finding their way into northern Germany. In short, many builders without established reputations were appearing on the scene, and the testimony of Praetorius suggests that certain of these purported artisans were less than fully competent and only too willing to fleece the churches. Not only were deficient instruments apparently encountered more and more often at this time, but such problems as did arise were likely to have been more difficult than ever to resolve; the early seventeenth century was an era during which the organ was reaching an unprecedented level of technical complexity, with increasing use of couplers, transmissions, and other sophisticated mechanical features. Finally, because the political scene in northern Europe at that time was one of such diversity, we might also surmise that it would have been easier for an unscrupulous builder to flee an uncomfortable situation, taking his money and leaving behind a malfunctioning instrument.

The *Kurzer Bericht,* the document that resulted as a response to the need perceived by Praetorius, avoids theoretical speculations entirely, presenting instead a wide range of recommendations of a decidedly practical nature. The treatise sets out straightforward criteria for reed and flue pipes, windchests, bellows and wind trunks, tremulants, couplers, and so forth. Certain tests are presented to help examiners identify deficiencies in chests and wind systems, and common tricks used by builders to conceal problems are noted as well. The *Kurzer Bericht* also provides interesting indications regarding contemporary organ aesthetic: that a tremulant's effect was "most lovely" (*lieblichste*) when its speed was regulated to that of the eighth note (*8 schläge uff einen Tact oder Mensur*), that stops of equal length ought not to be drawn together, and that the plenum registration ought not to include Gedackt stops (*dass man keine gedackt Stimme dazu ziehe*).[10]

The *Kurzer Bericht* was apparently never published, and was thus denied, for a time at least, the role that Praetorius had envisioned for it. Nevertheless, it appears to have circulated in manuscript copies, at least one of which found its way to an owner who grasped its importance and guaranteed the perpetuation of many of its precepts over succeeding generations. In his account of the famous organ in the Court Chapel at Gröningen, the *Organum Gruningense redivivum* of 1705, Andreas Werckmeister mentions that manuscripts from the *Nachlass* of Michael Praetorius had come into his possession.[11] That one of these must have been a version of the *Kurzer Bericht* becomes abundantly clear when the Praetorius/Compenius document is compared to Werckmeister's very first published treatise, the *Orgel-Probe* of 1681.

The first paragraphs of the two treatises are strikingly similar.

Praetorius/Compenius
Kurzer Bericht, ca. 1615–20

Beÿ einer ieglichen probation eines Orgelwerckes gebühret einem organico zweÿerleÿ in acht
zu nehmen, dass Ihme mit rechte nicht kan versaget werden, alss
    Zum ersten Besichtigung aller müglichen Dinge
    Zum andern das Gehör und was darzu nöthig ist

For a proper examination of an organ, it is fitting that an organist take two things into
consideration, so that it cannot be denied that everything is correct, namely
    First, an examination of all conceivable aspects,
    Then, the sound and all that pertains to it.

Werckmeister
Orgel-Probe, 1681

Bey probir- und Untersuchung eines Orgelwercks ist von nöthen/ dass man erstlich alle müg-
liche Dinge besichtige/ und dann folgends das Gehör und *Judicium* wohl zu rathe ziehe. . . .

In the proofing and inspection of an organ, it is first necessary to examine all conceivable
aspects, and then the ear and judgment must be brought into play. . . .

This, however, is only the very first of the correspondences to be discovered. Within the long initial chapter of Werckmeister's treatise, many notable
similarities to the *Kurzer Bericht* may be found, both in the specific ideas that
are set forth and in the actual language employed. Excerpts from parallel passages in the two works will more than adequately demonstrate their close relationship (see table 4.1).

The examples given in the table by no means represent all the correspondences that could be cited, but enough have been presented to establish that
these parallel passages cannot be explained as mere coincidence. To be sure,
Werckmeister's 1681 treatise is much longer than the Praetorius/Compenius
document; he covers far more material, he goes into much greater detail, and
he addresses a number of matters that receive no discussion in the *Kurzer
Bericht*. It is nevertheless amply clear that Werckmeister used the Praetorius/
Compenius treatise as a fundamental starting point for his own essay. Existing
opinions as to the "originality" and archetypal character of the *Orgel-Probe*
publications must accordingly be revised.[12]

The material of the 1681 *Orgel-Probe* became the basis, in turn, of two
separate treatises that were published later in Werckmeister's career. The 1681
work is divided into three chapters:

1. *Bey Probirung* (pp. 1–26, on organ inspection);
2. *Von der Stimmung und Temperatur* (pp. 26–40, on the need for and
   application of well-tempered systems);
3. *Etliche Erinnerungen* (pp. 41–52, on the nature of the organ contract).

Table 4.1   Excerpts from Parallel Passages of the *Kurzer Bericht*
and the *Orgel-Probe*

	Praetorius/Compenius *Kurzer Bericht* (ca. 1615–20)	Werckmeister *Orgel-Probe* (1681)
One must determine whether the bellows move properly . . .	ob sie . . . einen feinen satsamen Gang haben	ob sie einen feinen sanfften langsamen Gang haben
whether they are adequately weighted . . .	ob sie auch mit gar schweren Gewichte beleget seyn	[ob sie] mit dem Gewichte recht *aequiriret*
and also that they do not tremble and are easy to pump.	ob sie auch schottern . . . [und] wohl zu treten [sind]	dass sie nicht schüttern . . . und wohl zu treten sind (pp. 1–2)
One must determine whether pipework will not remain long in tune because it is tuned with rims that are bent in or out, or with cuts or ears.	Ob das Pfeiffwerck . . . wegen des Stimmens mit Ecken ein oder auss zerboget, oder mit Einschnitten und Ohren gestimmet sey, dass solches nicht Länger rein bleibet	So muss dasselbe auch nicht wegen des Stimmens mit Ecken / ein- oder aussgebogen / oder mit Ohren oder Einschnitten gestimmet seyn / denn . . . es pflegen solche Pfeiffen felten rein zu seyn (p. 2)
In pipes with chimneys, the lengths of the chimneys must follow precisely the scaling of the pipes.	an den Stimmen so ebene Röhren haben . . . die Röhren fein *ordine* an der Länge nach der *Mensur* den Pfeiffen folgen	Die / so oben Röhren haben müssen fein nach der *Mensur* gerichtet sein (p. 3)
Caps of Gedackt pipes must fit securely . . .	Ob die Gedachte ihre Hüte . . . auff den Pfeiffen zu Grunde stehen	die Hute auff dem Gedackten müssen fein feste umb die Pfeiffen liegen
or problems with tuning will ensue.	daraus folget sonsten leicht Enderung der Reinigkeit	sonsten . . . eine Unreinigkeit verursacht (p. 3)
One must determine whether the feet of the pipes have been drilled through with [bleed] holes . . .	Ob auch das Pfeiffwerck unten in den Füssen mit Löchern zerbrochen sey	ob sie Pfeiffen an Füssen . . . mit Löchern durchboret sind
which is an indication that the chest is defective.	welches auch eine Anzeigung, das die Lade nicht just ist	welches eine Unrichtigkeit des Windladens anzeiget (p. 3)

Table 4.1, cont.

One must determine whether the resonators of reed stops are accurately scaled.	In Schnarrwercken . . . das die *Mensur* der *Corporum* . . . an Länge und Weite richtig [ist]	[In] Schnarrwercke . . . ob die *Corpora* an der Länge und Weite ein jegliches nach seiner Art / gross gnung [ist] (p. 4)
Blocks of reed stops must fit securely into the boots.	Ob auch die Stöcke . . . fein dichte in ihren Löchern stehen und halten	[ob] die Stöcke auch in ihren Löchern . . . feste gnung stehen (p. 5)
One must note whether holes have been drilled through the chest into the wind-channels . . .	Auch ist mit Fleiss darauff acht zu haben, ob auch in Fundament-brete der Laden in die *Cancellen* Löcher gebohret seyn	Es pflegen auch zuweilen die Orgelmacher in die Windladen hin und wieder kleine Löcher zu bohren / welche in die *Cancellen* gehen
for this is an indication that wind is seeping from one channel to another.	welches eine Anzeigung ist . . . dass der Wind auss einer *Cancellen* in die ander sich sticht	darumb der Wind aus einer *Cancell* in die ander sticht (p. 8)
Stop-knobs must draw neither too easily nor too reluctantly.	ob . . . auch die *Registratur* im mittel nicht zu hart oder zu gelinde ziehen lassen	Die *Registraturen* müssen sich wohl ziehen lassen /nicht zu hart / auch nicht zu gelinde (p. 10)
If there are defects in the chest, these can be revealed by playing with no stops drawn.	wen man das *Clavir* stille ohne Pfeiffenwerck begreiffet, so höret man den Wind sausen und brausen	[wenn] alle / oder die meisten *Claves* nieder gedruckt werden / höret man darauff ein sausen / brausen (p. 11)
This trial can be carried out by laying one's arms across the keyboard . . .	mit beiden Armen drauff zu legen	wenn mann mit beyden Armen drauff leget (p. 11)
but during this test one must be sure that the bellows are being pumped and that no ventils have been closed.	Ob auch die Belgen in solcher Probirung getreten werden . . . [und] ob dan nicht etwan eine heimliche Sperventill verhindert wird.	muss man achtung haben / ob die *Ventile* alle offen / und die Bälge getreten werden (p. 12)
Tremulants must beat gently and at an unvarying rate.	sie [sollen] fein sanffte beben, und auch beständig denselben schlag und *Mensur* behalten.	Der Tremulant muss fein sanffte beben / den Schlag oder *Mensur*, nachdem er gerichtet ist / fein beständig behalten (p. 18)

In the second chapter, Werckmeister asserts that the quarter-comma meantone system is outmoded, and he sets forth two circulating unequal temperaments that allow for playing in all keys, without subsemitones and without "wolves." The material of this chapter became the core of the 1691 *Musicalische Temperatur*,[13] in which the tempering schemes of the 1681 volume are presented as Temperaments III and IV. As will be seen shortly, Werckmeister also devoted space in the *Musicalische Temperatur* to a response to certain criticisms that had been lodged against the *Orgel-Probe*.

The 1681 material on organ inspection and contracts found in chapters 1 and 3 was also revised, expanded, and brought forth as a separate publication, namely the *Erweiterte und verbesserte Orgel-Probe* of 1698. Virtually all of the material from the 1681 edition, including the borrowings from Praetorius/Compenius, was kept intact, and was augmented by considerable additional text. Interestingly, however, in preparing this later edition it seems that Werckmeister once again had his version of the *Kurzer Bericht* close at hand, for in several instances material from the Praetorius/Compenius treatise that had *not* been used in the 1681 edition was added at appropriate spots in the 1698 version. In each of the examples in table 4.2, the antecedent portion of the statement is found in *both* versions of the *Orgel-Probe,* but in each instance the second portion, taken from Praetorius/Compenius, was added only in the course of rewriting for the 1698 edition.

Table 4.2   Excerpts from Parallel Passages of the *Kurzer Bericht* and the *Erweiterte und verbesserte Orgel-Probe* of 1698

	Praetorius/Compenius	**Werckmeister**
One must determine whether the pipes stand too closely together . . .	Ob das Pfeiffwerck auch zudichte in einander stehet	Ob das Pfeiffwerck. . . zu dichte in einander stehe (1681, p. 2; 1698, p. 4)
for this will lead to problems in voicing.	den die reine *intonation* sehr dadurch verhindert wird	man es zu keiner reinen *intonation* bringen kan. . . (1698 only, p. 4)
One must determine whether pipework is too thin . . .	ob das Pfeiffwerck auch zu dünne sey	[ob] das Pfeiffwerck nicht zu dünne ausgearbeitet sey (1681, p. 2; 1698, p. 4)
for it will deform and pick up dents when handled	wen man's angreiffet . . . Bäulen und Gruben bleiben . . .	[man] kan [nicht] eine solche Pfeiffe ohne Verletzung und Bäulen . . . angreiffen (1698 only, p. 4)

It is in some respects surprising that Werckmeister felt the need to fall back on another source in compiling the *Orgel-Probe* publications, especially in light of his contemporary reputation as an expert without peer, his own testimony as to his frequent involvement in the examination of organs large and small, and his statement that he had had numerous organs built in his own home.[14] Despite his self-depiction as an autodidact of considerable erudition, Werckmeister apparently decided that to write from that knowledge alone would not be sufficient, and he accordingly made free use of the ideas, method, and language of the *Kurzer Bericht.* Though he surely added much that was drawn from his own experience, he chose to base his work on an existing model, one of unimpeachable authority.

The publication of the first *Orgel-Probe* seems to have aroused considerable ire, especially on the part of organbuilders, who felt that essential secrets of their art had been compromised. The treatise was apparently impugned from many sides, and amid the hailstorm of invective came allegations that the *Orgel-Probe* had indeed been plagiarized from another source or sources. While not all of the charges hurled at Werckmeister by his various detractors can now be traced, the two most prominent accusations of plagiarism appear to have been largely without substance, and did not involve the *Kurzer Bericht.*

In chapters 31 and 32 of the *Musicalische Temperatur,* Werckmeister answers charges that he had relied on the 1677 *Ausführliche Beschreibung des Neuen Orgelwercks auf der Augustus-Burg zu Weissenfels* of Johann Kaspar Trost the Younger,[15] which includes a chapter on the examination of new organs as well as a description of a circulating unequal temperament. While Werckmeister freely admits knowledge of the Trost publication, he denies that he appropriated material from it. Comparison of the two treatises indeed reveals that the *Orgel-Probe* is in no direct way indebted to Trost's organ-proofing recommendations (which are rudimentary at best), and that Werckmeister's 1681 tempering instructions owe little to the somewhat unclear scheme set forth by Trost.[16]

A further charge of plagiarism was evidently leveled at Werckmeister as the result of a cryptic reference in the *Historische Beschreibung der Edelen Sing- und Kling-Kunst* of Wolfgang Kaspar Printz.[17] On page 149 of that work, Printz states that a manuscript treatise by the Züllichau organist Matthaeus Hertel, the *Kurtzer unterricht, was bey überlieferung eines New gebaweten . . . Orgelwerckes ein Organist in acht zu nehmen . . . hat,* had been plagiarized and published "by another under his own name."[18] Many apparently assumed the plagiarist to have been Werckmeister, and Printz felt compelled to offer a lengthy clarification in the *Vorrede* to the 1696 edition of the *Phrynis Mitilenaeus, oder Satyrischer Componist.*[19] There he laments the "gross injury" done to Werckmeister by irresponsible gossips, and he goes on to disclose that the Hertel work was in fact plagiarized (and corrupted to a degree) by one Kaspar Ernst Carutius, in his little-known *Examen organi pneumatici, oder Orgelprobe* of 1683.[20]

Despite these specific accusations, which were and are easily dismissed, Werckmeister nevertheless felt obliged to furnish an elaborate and exceptionally long-winded defense of the 1681 *Orgel-Probe* in the *Vorrede* to the *Musicalische Temperatur*. There he is at pains to assert that organs and their defects can be described only in a very limited number of ways,[21] and that 100 people, if asked, would perforce frame their comments in identical fashion.[22] That, he says, would hardly be grounds for accusations of plagiarism, for "no one can describe something as other than it is."[23]

These arguments, not at all dissimilar to those often advanced in cases of plagiarism even today, sound more like the extenuations of a guilty party than the righteous and indignant proclamations of a truly innocent one (which, we now know, Werckmeister was not). It remains unclear whether any of the critics to whom Werckmeister refers actually knew the *Kurzer Bericht* or realized its relationship to the *Orgel-Probe*. No one, so far as we are aware, had directly accused him of reliance on the Praetorius/Compenius document, but the extent of his belabored apologia perhaps suggests either that his borrowings *had* been noted by someone, or that he was worried that his utilization of the earlier treatise *might* someday be exposed. Clearly, however, he is being entirely disingenuous when he declares:

> Ich kan mit Gott bezeügen/ (dessen Nahme ich nicht missbrauchen will) dass . . . [ich] niemals dergleichen Arbeit gesehen [habe]/ als etwa einen halben Bogen voll/ worinnen ein guter Freund einem *Tyroni* entworffen/ wie ein solch Examen ohngefähr müste beschaffen seyn/ welches doch alles Kinderpossen waren/ jedem *discipul* bekant. . . .[24]

> I am able to swear before God (whose name I do not wish to take in vain) that . . . I have never seen a piece of work that was comparable [to the *Orgel-Probe*], except for one that was no more than a half page in all, in which a good friend roughly outlines for a novice how such an examination must be administered. But this was all child's play, known to every apprentice. . . .

A final predecessor of the 1681 *Orgel-Probe* also deserves brief mention here. One of the most comprehensive treatises ever written on the subject of organ-proofing was completed no later than 1679. Nevertheless, the *Unterricht, wie man ein neu Orgelwerk . . . examinieren . . . und probiren soll* of Werner Fabricius (1633–79) did not appear in print until 1756.[25] The treatise is systematically organized and goes into great detail in its eighty-seven pages. Comparison of its contents with those of the *Orgel-Probe* suggests that Werckmeister was in all likelihood *not* familiar with a manuscript version of the *Unterricht*.

Nor does Fabricius appear to have relied in any way on a copy or version of the *Kurzer Bericht.* Had the Fabricius work actually been published relatively soon after its completion, it might well have obviated the need for Werckmeister to address the same matters himself.

The influence of Werckmeister's *Orgel-Probe* was profound and long-enduring. The 1698 version was reprinted no less than five times, including a translation into Dutch, with the final edition published in the year 1783.[26] This is a remarkable circumstance, and it is difficult to think of a comparable seventeenth-century treatise that was in active demand fully eighty-five years after its initial publication. This speaks not only to the soundness of Werckmeister's advice, but also suggests something about continuity of style in organbuilding: a document employed at the beginning of the eighteenth century to supply criteria for organ design and function was still found useful for the same purpose several generations later. This proposition could be viewed from another perspective as well: the existence and wide dissemination of Werckmeister's treatise surely contributed to a certain consistency in the design, construction, and functioning of instruments.

We also have specific knowledge that Werckmeister's writings found their way into the hands of some of the most influential musicians and organbuilders of his day. The *Lobgedichte* printed at the beginnings of many of Werckmeister's treatises include canons and laudatory poems contributed by such notables as Arp Schnitger, Johann Philipp Bendeler, and Dietrich Buxtehude. These lines, from an acrostic poem by Buxtehude that appears in the prefatory pages of Werckmeister's *Harmonologia Musica,*[27] imply both familiarity with and approval of the *Orgel-Probe:*

> Kömmt es denn auch auf die Proben
> Muss das **Werck** den **Meister** loben.

Interestingly, the play on Werckmeister's name in the second line of this couplet is strikingly similar to lines found in the two *Lobgedichte* that had appeared eleven years earlier in the *Musicalische Temperatur,* perhaps suggesting that Buxtehude owned or had at least examined a copy of that work.

That the *Orgel-Probe* also exerted a significant influence on J. S. Bach has been persuasively argued by Peter Williams. In various writings, Williams has shown that Bach, in preparing certain of his own organ inspection reports, relied heavily on the criteria and even the specific language of Werckmeister's treatise. Williams cites a number of examples in which Bach borrowed key phrases directly from the *Orgel-Probe.*[28] Thus we have Werckmeister paraphrasing Praetorius/Compenius, and Bach in turn paraphrasing Werckmeister, a chain of connections extending back a century and more.[29] For example, Bach, Kuhnau, and Rolle, in their 1716 report on the Liebfrauenkirche organ in Halle,[30] note that they have tested for hidden defects by depressing all the keys of the keyboard with no stops drawn, the same test recommended by Praetorius and Compenius and by Werckmeister in turn.

Bach was not the only organ expert to have been so influenced by Werckmeister, and to his name we can add those of two later Trosts, as well as that of Jakob Adlung. Felix Friedrich has recently called attention to the many correspondences with the 1698 *Orgel-Probe* that are apparent in various documents and disposition plans left by the organbuilders Tobias Gottfried Trost (d. 1718/19) and Heinrich Gottfried Trost (1681?-1759), and we can safely assume that such cases were far from unique.[31] The sections on organ-proofing in Adlung's *Anleitung zu der Musicalischen Gelahrtheit* and *Musica Mechanica Organoedi*[32] are heavily indebted to Werckmeister. Though Adlung often refers directly to Werckmeister and even quotes long passages directly from the 1698 *Orgel-Probe,* at other points he paraphrases substantial sections from Werckmeister without acknowledgment.[33] In many respects, the manner in which Adlung expands upon Werckmeister's text is analogous to the manner in which Werckmeister had previously expanded upon the Praetorius/Compenius essay. In certain cases, language used by Adlung can be traced directly back to the *Kurzer Bericht.*[34]

Another eighteenth-century writer on organs went beyond mere paraphrase of Werckmeister to direct and wholesale borrowing in a published work. The *Grund-Regeln von der Structur und den Requisitis einer untadelhaften Orgel* of Georg Preus II[35] manages to incorporate (though with certain additions and interpolations) nearly the entire text of the *Erweiterte und verbesserte Orgel-Probe,* verbatim. Much of Preus's treatise is in the form of a dialog between *Organist, Vocalist,* and *Calcant,* with Werckmeister's material being delivered by the *Organist.* After discovering Preus's borrowings for myself, I found that they had also been noted by Johann Mattheson, who devotes a lengthy section of the *Grosse General-Bass Schule*[36] to a merciless indictment of the plagiarism. Without ever referring to Preus by name, Mattheson painstakingly documents, complete with page numbers, the borrowings from Werckmeister, and declares, "in all the days of my life I have never seen so blatant a literary robbery."[37] Thus were Werckmeister's advisements disseminated widely in the eighteenth century, and not always under his own name!

Finally, two further manuscript documents cited in the literature, but now impossible to trace, appear to have represented copies or related versions of the Praetorius/Compenius *Kurzer Bericht.* Since their whereabouts are currently unknown, it has not been possible to compare these manuscripts with the Wolfenbüttel document. Nevertheless, certain conclusions can be inferred from the few pieces of information available.

Jakob Adlung, in both the *Musica Mechanica Organoedi* and the *Anleitung zu der musicalischen Gelahrtheit,* mentions his ownership of a manuscript document attributed to Praetorius and bearing the title *Lieferung und Beschlagung oder Probirung einer Orgel.*[38] Adlung asserts that this is indeed the very same essay that Praetorius intended to publish as the *Orgeln Verdingnis.* Additional information concerning the document is conveyed in one of the *Anmerkungen* appended to the text of the *Musica Mechanica* by Johann Lorenz Albrecht, who edited the volume for its posthumous publication. Beyond the difference in titles, Albrecht reports that the document is three pages in length, seven fewer than the ten pages of the Wolfenbüttel manuscript.[39] But though Adlung apparently did not possess the Wolfenbüttel document itself, it will shortly be shown that his exemplar was in all likelihood a related version or even a faithful copy (save the title) of the Wolfenbüttel *Kurzer Bericht.* Albrecht also notes that the manuscript contains "many good things" (*viel Gutes*), and he goes on to state: "Perhaps at some future point I will decide to rescue this useful remnant of earlier times from oblivion, and bring it to publication."[40]

In the 1872 edition of the *Monatshefte für Musikgeschichte* appears an unsigned *Mittheilung.*[41] The short entry refers to a manuscript from the *Nachlass* of the Grafen von Voss, which was at that time in the possession of Emmanuel Mai, a Berlin antiquarian bookdealer. Its title is given as follows:

Michaelis Praetorii, | Weil. Hochfürstl. Braunschweiglüneburgischen | Kapellmeisters in Wolfenbüttel | Kurzer Entwurf, | derjenigen Dinge, | welche | Bey Probirung und Ueber-lieferung | eines neuen | Orgelwercks | in Acht zu nehmen. || Mit einer Vorrede versehen, | und nebst einem | Anhange | von sechs und fünfzig Orgeldispositionen | ans Licht gestellet | von | M. Johann Lorenz Albrecht. | Berlin, || in fol.

This title, and the observation by the author of the *Mittheilung* that the manuscript was *"schön geschrieben,"* suggest that the document in question was a fair copy prepared for publication under the direction of Albrecht, who was apparently following through on his intention to bring the *Lieferung und Beschlagung* manuscript to publication. The manuscript in question, we are told, devoted eight of its pages to the "Praetorius" material, thus making clear that it was a separate copy distinct from the three-page manuscript mentioned by Adlung, and not merely Adlung's exemplar supplied with a new title page. Assuming that he did use as his basis the manuscript from Adlung's estate, Albrecht appears to have provided the document with a *Vorrede,* as well as a new and more ornate title suitable for a printed edition. Nevertheless, no print seems ever to have appeared.

The anonymous author of the *Mittheilung* (quite likely Robert Eitner) did summarize the contents of this *Kurzer Entwurf,* however, providing useful clues as to its relationship with the Wolfenbüttel document. The manuscript, says the

Mittheilung, began by addressing the topics of pipework, reeds, wind chests, and bellows enclosure. Then followed a section covering *Das Gehör:* what must be noted by the *Iudex oder Examinator* when an organ is inspected. Finally, there were sections on *Tremulanten* and *Copulaturen*. A comparison of this summary to the Wolfenbüttel manuscript reveals an exact correspondence of topics and order of presentation. We may tentatively conclude, then, that the *Kurzer Entwurf* prepared for publication by Albrecht was closely related to the Wolfenbüttel *Kurzer Bericht*. If Albrecht did indeed work from an exemplar from the literary estate of Adlung, then Adlung's copy would also have been closely related to the surviving Wolfenbüttel document, despite the differences in length, title, and credited author. Neither Adlung nor Albrecht appears to have realized the relationship of the *Lieferung und Beschlagung* treatise to the *Orgel-Probe* publications of Werckmeister.

One especially important fact emerges from the above details: that an expert as knowledgeable and sophisticated as Albrecht felt that a version of the Praetorius/Compenius treatise was still of sufficient interest and value to merit publication at some point after 1768, fully 150 years after it had been written.

It is now perhaps easier to appreciate just how significant the *Kurzer Bericht* actually was. It was the first attempt since the 1511 treatise of Arnolt Schlick[42] to set standards in an area where they were much needed, and its comments were far more extensive than those of Schlick. The approval of a new organ was a unique and complicated matter, first because an unsatisfactory organ could not simply be returned to the builder like an unsatisfactory violin, and also in that so many different people had to be pleased by the new instrument, including some who had had musical training and others who had not. In this area, the *Kurzer Bericht* established standards and criteria that were found relevant and applicable through the seventeenth and eighteenth centuries, and which have proved useful once again in the *Orgelbewegung* movement of our own era. A direct line of influence can be traced from Praetorius and Compenius to Werckmeister, Bach, Adlung, and beyond.

The author gratefully acknowledges the advice and kind assistance of Christoph Wolff, Harald Vogel, Kerala Snyder, and Evan Bonds.

Notes

1. Praetorius, Michael, and Esaias Compenius, "Orgeln Verdingnis," in *Kieler Beiträge zur Musikwissenschaft*, ed. Friedrich Blume, vol. 4 (Wolfenbüttel and Berlin: Kallmeyer Verlag, 1936), pp. 1–25. The manuscript is still held in the Herzog August Bibliothek (2.3.10 Musica). Blume was led to the document by a previously unheeded mention of it that appears under "Michael Praetorius" in the *Biographisch-Bibliographisches Quellen-Lexicon* of Robert Eitner (vol. 8, p. 47).

2. Andreas Werckmeister, *Orgel-Probe* (Quedlinburg: Theodor Calvisius, 1681). *Erweiterte und verbesserte Orgel-Probe* (Quedlinburg: Theodor Calvisius, 1698; reprint of 1698 edition, ed. and with afterword by Dietz-Rüdiger Moser, Kassel: Bärenreiter, 1970); trans. Gerhard Krapf (Raleigh: Sunbury Press, 1976).

3. Michael Praetorius, *Syntagma musicum*, vol. 2: *De Organographia*, Wolfenbüttel, 1618; second edition, 1619), vol. 3: *Termini musici* (Wolfenbüttel, 1618; second edition, 1619). Facsimile editions of the 1619 prints were published by Bärenreiter in 1958.

4. Praetorius, *Syntagma Musicum*, vol. 2, preface p. 4, 4th leaf.

5. Ibid., p. 160.

6. Ibid., p. 203. See also the related reference on p. 231.

7. Praetorius's final known composition, a five-part setting of psalm 116, was written in anticipation of his own death, as "a farewell to myself." See Walter Blankenburg, "Praetorius," *The New Grove Dictionary of Music and Musicians*, ed. Stanley Sadie (London: Macmillan, 1980), vol. 15, p. 191.

8. Praetorius, *Syntagma Musicum*, vol. 2, preface p.):(11ᵛ.

9. See Praetorius/Compenius, "Orgeln Verdingnis," Blume introduction, p. 7.

10. Praetorius/Compenius, "Orgeln Verdingnis," pp. 23, 21, and 22 respectively.

11. "ich halte dessen Schrifften und Gedächtniss sehr hoch/ mir sind auch seine *Actiones* am besten bekant/ indem mir alle seine *Manuscripta* und *Arcana Musica* ja allerdings seine *Vocationes* und viel Briefe zuhanden kommen." *Organum Gruningense redivivum* (Quedlinburg and Aschersleben: Gottlob Ernst Struntz, 1705), section 54; modern edition, ed. Paul Smets (Mainz: Rheingold-Verlag, 1932).

12. See Dietz Rüdiger-Moser, afterword to the 1698 *Orgel-Probe* facsimile edition, p. iv.

13. Andreas Werckmeister, *Musicalische Temperatur* (Quedlinburg: Theodor Calvisius, 1691); reprint, ed. and with introduction by Rudolf Rasch (Utrecht: The Diapason Press, 1983). Despite Werckmeister's comments in 1681 and 1691, the supplanting of quarter-comma meantone temperament was at best a slow and gradual process; in the *Vorrede* to the *Musicalische Temperatur*, Werckmeister indicates that quarter-comma meantone was still referred to as "the so-called universal temperament" (*die sogenante allgemeine temperatur*). In a recent article, Harald Vogel has presented evidence that in North Germany in particular, many organs were tuned in meantone or modified meantone schemes well into the eighteenth century, and he argues that in the later seventeenth century, application of well-tempering in North Germany can be assumed only for Buxtehude's Marienkirche instruments after 1683. See "Tuning and Temperament in the North German School of the Seventeenth and Eighteenth Centuries," in *Charles Brenton Fisk, Organ Builder*, vol. 1 (Easthampton, Mass.: The Westfield Center for Early Keyboard Studies, 1986), pp. 237–65.

14. See the *Vorreden* of the *Musicalische Temperatur* and the 1698 *Orgel-Probe*.

15. Published in Nürnberg by Wolfgang Moritz Endter and Johann Andreas Endters Erben.

16. *Ausführliche Beschreibung*, pp. 31–39. This chapter of the Trost publication is nevertheless an important early statement of the need for further developments in temperament beyond meantone. In his remarks on organ examination, Trost also mentions a tradition not noted by Werckmeister: that upon successful completion of an instrument, the organbuilder's journeymen and apprentices were by custom rewarded with a quantity of wine equivalent to the amount

that could be held by the largest bass pipe ("Pfleget man/ den alten Gebrauch zu erhalten/ dess Orgelmachers Gesellen und Discipuln so viel gutes Weins/ als die gröste Orgelpfeiffe in sich halten kan/ zu spendiren.") Ibid., pp. 68–69.

17. Wolfgang Kaspar Printz, *Historische Beschreibung der Edelen Sing- und Kling-Kunst* (Dresden: Johann Mieth, 1690; reprint, Graz: Akademische Druck- und Verlagsanstalt, 1964).

18. According to Eitner, the Hertel manuscript was written in 1666, with Anhängen added in 1669 and 1671 that brought the document to a total of thirty-four pages. See Eitner, *Quellen-Lexikon*, vol. 5, p. 150.

19. P·\blished in Dresden and Leipzig by Johann Christoph Mieth and Johann Christoph Zimmermann.

20. Wolfgang Kaspar Printz, *Phrynis Mitilenaeus, oder Satyrischer Componist* (Küstrin: publisher unknown, 1696). No copies of the Carutius treatise are known to be extant. The Carutius plagiarism was also commented upon by Jakob Adlung in a footnote to the text of the *Anleitung zu der musikalischen Gelahrtheit* (Erfurt: J. D. Jungnicol, 1758; reprint Kassel: Bärenreiter, 1953), pp. 342–43, note p; Adlung refers to Carutius as a "mouse-head" (*Mausekopf*).

21. "Die Orgeln und die Beschreibung derer *defecten* können nicht anders beschreiben werden/ als sie an sich selbsten sind. . . ."

22. "Und wenn 100. Leute/ so den Orgel-Bau verstehen/ die Mängel der Orgeln beschreiben solten/so würden sie keine andere Mängel vorstellen können/ als diejenigen/ so bey den Bälgen/ Wind-Laden/ Pfeiff-Wercke und andern dergleichen Dingen sich zu befinden pflegen. . . ."

23. "Niemand kan ein Ding anders beschreiben/ als es an sich selber ist. . . ."

24. Werckmeister, *Musicalische Temperatur, Vorrede.*

25. Werner Fabricius, *Unterricht, wie man ein neu Orgelwerk . . . examinieren . . . und probiren soll* (Frankfurt and Leipzig, n. p.).

26. See Eitner, *Quellen-Lexikon*, vol. 10, p. 228.

27. Andreas Werckmeister, *Harmonologia Musica* (Quedlinburg: Theodor Calvisius, 1702). On the same page, Buxtehude refers to Werckmeister as a "highly esteemed friend" (*hochgeschätzter Freund*). It is also well known that Werckmeister passed along numerous keyboard compositions of Buxtehude to Johann Gottfried Walther. See Johann Mattheson, *Grundlage einer Ehren-Pforte* (Hamburg: author, 1740; reprint, ed. Max Schneider, Berlin: Liepmannsohn, 1910), p. 388. For more on the possible influence of Werckmeister upon the temperament system used in Buxtehude's Marienkirche organs, see Vogel, "Tuning and Temperament in the North German School," and Kerala Snyder, *Dieterich Buxtehude, Organist in Lübeck* (New York: Schirmer Books, 1987), pp. 84–85.

28. Williams's evidence and arguments are presented in the following publications: "J. S. Bach—Orgelsachverständiger unter dem Einfluss Andreas Werckmeisters?" *Bach-Jahrbuch* 72 (1986), pp. 123–25; *The Organ Music of J. S. Bach*, vol. 3: *A Background* (Cambridge: Cambridge University Press, 1984), pp. 139–54.

29. The likelihood that Bach knew and was influenced by other writings of Werckmeister has been discussed by several writers. See, for example, Walter Serauky, "Andreas Werckmeister als Musiktheoretiker," *Festschrift Max Schneider zum 60. Geburtstag* (Halle: E. Schneider, 1935), pp. 118–25.

30. See Williams, *The Organ Music of J. S. Bach*, vol. 3, pp. 144–46.

31. Felix Friedrich, "Werckmeisters Beziehungen zur Orgelbauer und Musikerfamilie Trost," in *Bericht über das Werckmeister-Kolloquium aus Anlass des 340. Geburtstages von Andreas Werckmeister am 30. November 1985. Studien zur Aufführungspraxis und Interpretation von Musik des 18. Jahrhunderts*, no. 30., ed. Eitelfriedrich Thom (Michaelstein: Kultur- und Forschungsstätte Michaelstein, 1986), pp. 93–97.

32. Jakob Adlung, *Musica Mechanica Organoedi*, 2 vols. (Berlin: Friedrich Wilhelm Birnstiel, 1768). Adlung himself states that the treatise was written as early as 1726 (see the *Vorrede* to vol. 2, p. xxiii); reprint, ed. Christhard Mahrenholz (Kassel: Bärenreiter, 1931).

33. See Adlung, *Musica Mechanica*, chapters 13 and 16.

34. For example, the following statement regarding bellows: "Es müssen die Bälge ferner einen feinen gleichen, sanften, langsamen Gang haben . . ." (ibid., vol. 2, p. 38). Many of the most important precepts of the *Orgel-Probe* received further dissemination by way of a summary of the work included in the *Neu eröffnete musikalische Bibliothek* of Lorenz Mizler (Leipzig: author, 1739–54; reprint, Hilversum, Netherlands: Frits Knuf, 1966), vol. 1, part 4, pp. 27–35.

35. Georg Preus II, *Grund-Regeln von der Structur und den Requisitis einer untadelhaften Orgel* (Hamburg: Christian Wilhelm Brandt, 1729).

36. Johann Mattheson, *Grosse General-Bass Schule* (Hamburg: n.p., 1731), pp. 15–28.

37. "Ich gestehe wenigstens, dass ich die Tage meines Lebens keinen solchen groben Schrifft-Raub gesehen habe." Ibid., p. 17. It is unfortunately impossible to assess any possible influence of Werckmeister's *Orgel-Probe* upon the subsequently written but apparently unpublished *Orgel-Probe* of Valentin Bartholomaeus Haussmann (1678–?) mentioned in Mattheson's *Grundlage einer Ehren-Pforte* (pp. 105, 108).

38. Adlung, *Musica Mechanica*, pp. 12, 173–74. Adlung, *Anleitung*, p. 341.

39. Adlung, *Musica Mechanica*, pp. 12–13, fn. 6.

40. "Vielleicht entschliesse ich mich künftig, dies nützliche Ueberbleibsel des Alterthums der vergessenheit zu entreissen, und durch den Druck gemein zu machen."

41. Vol. 4, p. 149.

42. Arnolt Schlick, *Spiegel der Orgelmacher und Organisten* (Mainz: Peter Schöffer d. J., 1511; reprint, transcribed, trans., and ed. Elizabeth Barber, Buren, Netherlands: Frits Knuf, 1980).

5

Towards a Critical Understanding of Buxtehude's Expressive Chorale Preludes

Lawrence Archbold

The expressive chorale preludes of Buxtehude represent the single largest genre of his organ music, if we count by the number of surviving examples. But of course an expressive chorale prelude is considerably smaller than the typical toccata, praeludium, or chorale fantasia. Furthermore, we can be sure that not all of Buxtehude's organ music survives, and we have little way of knowing which genres have suffered the most loss. Indeed, just what constitutes a "genre" in Buxtehude's organ music is questionable. The chorale-based works are today usually divided into several categories: chorale variations, chorale fantasias, chorale ricercares, and chorale preludes.[1] Whether or not organists of the time would have recognized these terms, it seems reasonable to believe that they would have been able to make these kinds of distinctions. The chorale prelude, the most modest of these genres, can almost certainly be taken to be functional music written to introduce the singing of a chorale. It is no secret, even to undergraduate music majors, that there are many types of chorale preludes. One type, however, predominates in Buxtehude's oeuvre: the "expressive" chorale prelude in which the chorale line is decorated—in the manner of a solo vocal line—and heard against a backdrop of accompanimental voices. This type of chorale prelude has been called "monodic"[2] in reference to Scheidemann's works, and indeed there are many similar passages in the cantata repertory. Recently, Christoph Wolff has pointed out provocative similarities between Buxtehude's organ praeludia and his ensemble sonatas, and it is important to remember that the expressive chorale preludes also have their link to the larger world of Buxtehude's music.[3]

Today these chorale preludes are seen by organists and musicologists from different perspectives. Among organists (at least in America), they enjoy a sort of ironic popularity. By virtue of their appearance in several key collections and organ tutors, and their easy availability in reprint, they have found their way into the mainstream organ repertory, if not so much as concert pieces, certainly as functional liturgical music. But the function they provide is rarely that of their original purpose. Serving as preludes, offertories, and in some cases even postludes, and sporting in translation acceptably churchy titles, these works are heard by congregations often ill-prepared to understand them, a fact which is usually of no concern to organists. Music historians, on the other hand, are much better prepared to understand these works, and the canonical status which has been accorded them among the Historically Significant Works is assured. Centrally located on a line of development from Sweelinck and Scheidemann to J. S. Bach, they are everywhere viewed as essential elements in the history of German baroque music. Historians are also more likely to evaluate these pieces within the framework of their original functional intent. And it has been the issues formulated by historians, rather than those of concern to organists, which have shaped our critical view of these pieces. In the nineteenth century, these works posed questions of not only historical development, but also aesthetic quality, particularly regarding the relationship, between the music and the mood of the text of the chorale being set. In our own time—and if Carl Dahlhaus is right, ours is an age of historical rather than aesthetic criticism—the nature of the links between this music and its past and future have been refined, and continue to be fine-tuned.

Critical opinion about Buxtehude's expressive chorale preludes has been mixed. In the early eighteenth century, they evidently interested Johann Gottfried Walther, who copied many of them, and in doing so helped to ensure their preservation. His friend Jacob Adlung, who surely knew some of these works through Walther, claimed that "Buxtehude sets chorales very beautifully."[4] Over 100 years later, the first full-scale critique of Buxtehude's organ music as a whole (by Philipp Spitta, in his Bach biography) was more equivocal.[5] Establishing a pattern copied today, he organized a discussion of Buxtehude's organ music, giving both pride of place and space to the free works. A significantly shorter treatment of the chorale-based works followed, with the larger (though numerically less significant) chorale fantasias leading the way. He characterized the chorale preludes as "full of genius, brilliant, and effective," at the beginning of his discussion, but by its conclusion, he managed to say hardly more than that they are "cleverly written," and to do so in a way that smacks of faint praise. Spitta was troubled by what he saw as a superficiality in these works, related to something that troubled him even more: his inability to find a reflection in the music of the feeling inherent in the chorale itself. Spitta, who without question genuinely admired the free organ works, even went so far as to claim that "Buxtehude entirely lost his characteristics when he ventured on the poetic treatment of the organ chorale." By the word "characteristics" he seemed to have meant those qualities he admired in the big free works, such as the sense of "deep expression directly prophetic of Bach"[6] that he noticed in the Praeludium in F♯ Minor, BuxWV 146. André Pirro, writing early in our century, echoed Spitta's view.[7] For Pirro, Buxtehude was "less powerfully creative" in the chorale prelude than in the free works. Pirro did, however, point to a certain undeniably religious quality in some of these expressive chorale preludes. Finally, in one of the most important recent discussions of this repertory, Willi Apel again conforms to the pattern established by Spitta, namely, an extensive treatment of the free works, followed by a shorter treatment of the chorale-based works, concluding with the chorale preludes.[8] Overall, Apel is kinder to the chorale preludes than was Spitta, and memorably sums them up as works in which "simplicity of presentation and forceful expression are most beautifully combined." He even claims, contradicting Spitta's verdict, that Buxtehude made the expressive chorale prelude "a symbol of the subjective, emotional faith of his time." But in spite of the monumental nature of Apel's book, he finds something nice to say about virtually everything he discusses, and as a result, whatever critical intention he may have had seems compromised. In trying to place these works in Buxtehude's oeuvre, then, it is difficult to avoid the impression that they are in some way the poor cousins of the great free works.

The place of these works in the history of the chorale prelude has received considerable scholarly attention and consensus. Their most important immediate predecessors are surely the chorale-based compositions of Heinrich Scheidemann and Franz Tunder. Scheidemann more or less pioneered this expressive style, but used it chiefly within his chorale variations to set off one variation within the set, rather than as the basis for a single, independently conceived setting. While Scheidemann's chorale settings in this style imitate the sounds of a solo voice and instrumental accompaniment, his solo lines are admittedly only partially vocal in character. The ornamentation is usually florid and more or less continuous, the phrases often exceed in length those possible for the human voice, and the range of the solo line can exceed two octaves. Apel has pointed to Tunder as the composer who created "a new kind of figuration in which a note is stressed expressively by an individual figure only here and there."[9] Yet he readily admits that Scheidemann occasionally did the same thing. As the ornamented line in this expressive style became less systematic in conception (that is to say, more unpredictable—quirky, even—in its ornamentation), it correspondingly took on an increased illusion of the human voice, suggesting improvised vocal ornamentation which is graceful in its spontaneity and cognizant of the need to breathe.

This new kind of expressive keyboard idiom must have seemed the most modern to Buxtehude, at least by his early years in Lübeck; indeed, one of his accomplishments seems to have been the very establishment of the expressive chorale prelude as a genre. This can only be conjectured, though, because so few other expressive chorale preludes written by others of Buxtehude's own generation have come down to us. It is easier to find such pieces by Georg Böhm and Johann Nicolaus Hanff in the next generation (about a half-dozen from each survive), but what of the expressive chorale preludes of Vincent Lübeck or Nicolaus Bruhns? It seems there was, for whatever reason, even less interest in preserving the chorale preludes of the North German organists than in preserving their chorale fantasias or praeludia. Or rather, perhaps there was even less interest in writing them down as actual compositions, for likely most of this "repertory" existed only as improvisation. All this should make us even more grateful for Walther's spark of interest in Buxtehude's chorale preludes and his role in saving so many of them for us.

It seems, then, that Buxtehude selected this unusually effective style of setting a chorale from among the variety of textures to be found in the chorale variation and chorale fantasia and placed it in an effective format and one which, presumably, was very frequently encountered by his listeners. Over twenty of these works survive:

BuxWV	Title
179	*Ach Herr, mich armen Sünder*
180	*Christ, unser Herr, zum Jordan kam*
182	*Der Tag, der ist so freudenreich*
183	*Durch Adams Fall ist ganz verderbt*
184	*Ein feste Burg ist unser Gott*
185	*Erhalt uns, Herr, bei deinem Wort*
186	*Es ist das Heil uns kommen her*
187	*Es spricht der Unweisen Mund wohl*
189	*Gelobet seist du, Jesu Christ*
190	*Gott der Vater wohn uns bei*
191	*Herr Christ, der einig Gottes Sohn*
192	*Herr Christ, der einig Gottes Sohn*
193	*Herr Jesu Christ, ich weiß gar wohl*
197	*In dulci jubilo*
199	*Komm, Heiliger Geist, Herre Gott*
200	*Komm, Heiliger Geist, Herre Gott*
201	*Kommt her zu mir, spricht Gottes Sohn*
202	*Lobt Gott, ihr Christen allzugleich*
206	*Mensch, willt du leben seliglich*
208	*Nun bitten wir den Heiligen Geist*
209	*Nun bitten wir den Heiligen Geist*
211	*Nun komm, der Heiden Heiland*
217	*Puer natus in Bethlehem*

These works range in size from about twenty to sixty measures in length and are remarkable for their similarity. Few obvious qualities set one apart from another in this surprisingly homogenous group of pieces aside from mode, tonality, and meter, inherent characteristics of the chorale.

While we may look in vain to find extant chorale preludes by Buxtehude's contemporaries—such as Bölsche, Heidorn, Ritter, and Werckmeister—one such setting by Andreas Kneller does survive.[10] His composition gives an idea of how the texture of the expressive chorale prelude was handled by a composer manifestly less skillful than Buxtehude, and thus can help illuminate some of the qualities of Buxtehude's chorale preludes that make them more remarkable.

Kneller's chorale prelude on *Nun komm, der Heiden Heiland*[11] (ex. 5.1) invites comparison with that on the same tune by Buxtehude. Kneller's composi-

Example 5.1. Kneller, *Nun komm, der Heiden Heiland*

tion of nineteen measures is almost exactly the same size as Buxtehude's. Clearly, Kneller's plan was to unify this modest, unpretentious work through the repetition of the figure heard at the beginning in the bass part and repeated in that voice in nearly every measure. Yet for all its repetition, the figure creates a sense, not of density or gravity, but of simplicity. While it may not be fair to say that the composition is simple-minded, it is, despite its artifice, undeniably plain. There is no attempt at *Vorimitation;* indeed, the ornamented chorale line and the accompanimental parts literally live in two different worlds. The chorale tune is pleasingly, if simply, graced; the texture thin, on occasion even sparse.

From the very first measure of Buxtehude's chorale prelude on the same tune, BuxWV 211 (ex. 5.2) we notice a significantly richer texture, more elaborate ornamentation of the chorale tune, richer harmony, and a faster harmonic rhythm; indeed, the quarter-note harmonic rhythm is virtually relentless. Later in the work, moments of *Vorimitation* appear, since in this piece the accompanimental voices are flexible enough to encompass everything from simple, quarter-note chords to more elaborate sixteenth-note figurations.

Example 5.2. Buxtehude, *Nun komm, der Heiden Heiland,* (BuxWV 211)

One of the peculiarities of this chorale tune is that its first and last phrases are the same. While Kneller does vary the ornamentation somewhat in his last phrase from that of the first, Buxtehude does so in a much more flamboyant way. Instead of letting the line descend from g' to f' by step as it does in the chorale (ex. 5.3a), he thrusts the line up a seventh from g' to f" (ex. 5.3b). Moreover, this gesture sets the stage for an even more dramatic upward registral shift several measures later, as the tonic arrival (at the last note of the chorale) is extended for a few bars.

Kneller puts the burden of expressivity on the accompanimental voices while the final note of the chorale is prolonged (in its original register); and under an inverted pedal, they have nothing more poignant to offer than subdomi-

Example 5.3a

Example 5.3b

nant harmony. The result is four bars of coda. By making the ornamental line itself bear the expressive burden, Buxtehude creates less a coda or epilogue than a real climax, for this is the first time g″ has been heard, and even a″ follows shortly, supporting the final resting point of the solo line an octave above its normal register (ex. 5.4).

We can notice, then, a richness and a density in Buxtehude's chorale prelude which makes it less immediately accessible than Kneller's: with Buxtehude's piece the listener yearns for a second hearing simply to absorb the abundance of polished detail work, while Kneller's piece seems in comparison "easy listening." Moreover, we also notice a certain nobility of spirit in Buxtehude's music, perhaps a somewhat more formal, certainly a more elevated tone. In all these ways BuxWV 211 is a typical example of Buxtehude's expressive chorale preludes. While these kinds of chorale preludes by Buxtehude are often spoken of as functional music, a comparison such as this reminds us how elaborate they really are, and how much plainer and less interesting merely functional music really is.

Likewise, few expressive chorale preludes survive from North German organists born after the middle of the century, and they are less well known than the praeludia or chorale fantasies of these composers. One of the most interesting of these chorale preludes was written by Daniel Erich, who Gerber tells us was a student of Buxtehude.[12] It provides an opportunity to see what someone from the next generation who knew something of Buxtehude's own chorale preludes did with the genre.

Admittedly, Erich is not a composer of Buxtehude's stature but his *Allein zu dir, Herr Jesu Christ*[13] (ex. 5.5) provides some illuminating points of comparison with Buxtehude's style. The formal layout of Erich's work relies on a rigorous application of *Vorimitation;*[14] while Buxtehude often provides these kinds of passages, he does not enforce a rigid formula. Erich's opening phrase is ornamented in the seemingly casual, irregular fashion typical of Buxtehude: the breath taken in the midst of the chorale phrase certainly could find many parallels in Buxtehude's own writing. The little flourish at the very end of the phrase, though, after the arrival of the finale note of the chorale phrase, is more curious. Unlike anything in Buxtehude's own expressive chorale preludes, it seems unmotivated by the flow that has been established and sounds tacked on. It also comes across as coy. Had Buxtehude felt that some accumulated rhythmic energy needed to be dispelled beyond the tonic arrival, he would likely have provided some less obvious rhythmic motion in the accompanimental parts.

Example 5.4. Buxtehude, *Nun komm, der Heiden Heiland*, (BuxWV 211)

A similar expressive quality reappears in the next chorale phrase, where we find a kind of figuration assiduously avoided by Buxtehude in this sort of context. While Buxtehude himself might have been pleased to have written the opening of the second chorale phrase with its sliding chromaticism melting into a descending scale in the pedal, the figure that appears five measures into the second phrase in the solo, and that is echoed a measure later, again comes across as somewhat heart-on-the-sleeve, and particularly so the second time, when the figure slides into the augmented chord on beat three—the most poignant harmonic event so far. We can admire, as I imagine Buxtehude would have, the way this second phrase expands outward to encompass virtually the whole of the range of the instrument at its peak; but the final little flourish, bigger now than in the first phrase, likewise suffers from the lack of eighth- or sixteenth-note motion during beat one of its bar. Again, the piece seems to have lost that delicate thread of rhythmic and harmonic motion, if only for a split second.

Finally, at the end of *Allein zu dir* (ex. 5.6), there is something almost shameless about the way Erich sentimentalizes one of Buxtehude's most elegant

Example 5.5. Erich, *Allein zu dir, Herr Jesu Christ*

gestures, namely the rising roulade that ascends an octave just after the arrival of the final note of the last chorale phrase. The solo line is cut off before the end of the composition and the final word is left, as it were, to the now-lethargic accompaniment.

These examples uncover something striking about Buxtehude's own expressive chorale preludes: he almost never fails to provide an event—harmonic or rhythmic—on every beat. These events provide a certain tension throughout the works, and in some way (it is hard to say exactly how), they also keep the expressive roulades in focus. Cut loose from a sense of relentless, ongoing motion, the ornamental figures can convey rather surprising emotive messages.

Georg Leyding, another of Buxtehude's students, provides a further point of comparison in his chorale variations on *Von Gott will ich nicht lassen* (ex. 5.7).[15] It is worth noting, perhaps, that the *least* interesting variation in this set is the only one in the expressive style and the only such example of Leyding's to survive. It is the first of six verses, and gets the variation set off to an

Example 5.6.   Erich, *Allein zu dir*

Ninth (Last) Phrase

unpromising start. Leyding seems unable to settle on a figure for the opening *Vorimitation:* first there are dotted notes, then an upbeat triadic figure. This indecision creates an unsettled atmosphere which the appearance of the first phrase in the solo line does little to dispel. The several bars of harmonic stasis, beginning with the last note of the first phrase of the chorale in the solo voice, is also really poor. A characteristic of this chorale tune (not at all uncommon) is that the first two phrases are musically identical; Leyding does not seem to have planned, at least in any clear way, how to handle, let alone take advantage of, this basic fact.

The contrast between Leyding's first variation and Buxtehude's expressive chorale prelude on this tune, BuxWV 220 (ex. 5.8), is almost embarrassing. Admittedly, Buxtehude seems to be working with a slightly different version of the chorale, but that matters little. What does matter is how Buxtehude, realizing that the first two phrases of the chorale are musically identical, chooses to handle that challenge.

Notice how simply—how starkly—the first phrase is handled, in spite of the unpretentiousness of the materials: eighth-note ornamentation, modest enough at that, is held back until the very end of the phrase, so that, in conjunction with the suspension in the pedal at that point, it creates a real sense of climax to the phrase. One notices, too, how Buxtehude artfully increases the rhythmic energy level in the *Vorimitation* to the second phrase, and how the passage avoids the pitfall of harmonic stasis. Furthermore, one observes how the second phrase, with its solo line with its resplendent sixteenth-note elaborations, opens new expressive terrain in the work. And finally, Buxtehude creates a second, even more telling climax, penultimate to the close of this second phrase, by letting the solo line soar up to e″—the highest note of the piece so far—a peak especially well prepared by the florid figurations that precede it.

But this variation set by Leyding amounts to more than just a straw dog, for as the variations proceed, they get more and more interesting, and less and less like Buxtehude. In verse five (ex. 5.9), the expressive chorale style is reconceived to create something no longer monodic or vocal in style, but instrumental, in fact, frankly violinistic. While each phrase of the chorale tune continues to be treated in the solo line, with appropriate gaps between phrases as is customary in the expressive chorale prelude, this variation can no longer be considered "expressive" in the sense that the word has been used for previous examples.

With any subtlety of detail overwhelmed by the driven rhythmic momentum, this variation recalls little of Buxtehude's organ music; it does recall, however, a striking and controversial passage in one of the several versions of the Praeludium in A, BuxWV 151 (ex. 5.10). That passage is curious for two reasons: it does not appear in all the sources and it seems stylistically out of place.[16] Kerala Snyder has recently suggested that this passage is not spurious

Example 5.7. Leyding, *Von Gott will ich nicht lassen* (Verse 1)

Example 5.8. Buxtehude, *Von Gott will ich nicht lassen* (BuxWV 220)

after all, as several scholars, including myself, have argued, but represents Buxtehude's conception of the work from the 1690s.[17] The fifth variation by Leyding cited above gives one pause to ponder whether Buxtehude might also have brought that frankly violinistic kind of style into his (improvised) chorale preludes during the last years of the seventeenth century. After all, we have no reason to believe that Buxtehude's surviving chorale preludes are particularly late works, or that their stylistic homogeneity means that his style of preluding on a chorale tune did not change in the course of his career. Might not this

Example 5.9.   Leyding, *Von Gott will ich nicht lassen* (Verse 5)

variation from Leyding be a not-too-distant echo of Buxtehude's own improvised chorale preludes in a late phase of creative life?

These works by Buxtehude's students point out, then, how delicate a balance of figure, gesture, rhythmic momentum, and harmony Buxtehude was able
to create in his expressive chorale preludes. Moreover, he achieved that balance
over and over again. Perhaps Buxtehude's single-minded vision of the preferred
expressive stance for this genre, overshadowed in his mind each example's
relationship to its chorale text, at least during the phase of his career these works
represent. Elegant, noble, formal without being formulaic, his results are surely
more personal than Scheidemann's, without falling under the shadow of slinki-
ness (as do Erich's) or abandoning altogether the sense of balance (as do
Leyding's).

During which years Buxtehude wrote these works (not to mention the
actual chronology of the chorale preludes) is an issue little discussed by historians, largely because such questions cannot be answered with any real certainty.
Kerala Snyder has pointed out that the actual chorale tunes Buxtehude sets in
this genre are in most cases old, sixteenth-century ones, not newer, seventeenth-
century ones.[18] It would seem, then, that the chorales themselves will not help
very much in building a chronology of these pieces. It does seem reasonable
that Buxtehude would have needed pieces like these—rather a lot of them—at

Example 5.10. Buxtehude, Praeludium in A (BuxWV 151)

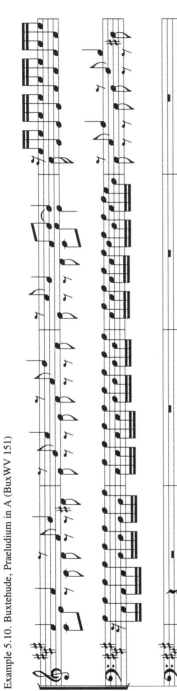

whatever point in his career chorale preludes were required of him in the services for which he played; and that this occasion was early in his career seems probable. It also seems probable that such pieces would have been habitually improvised rather than written down. Moreover, these chorale preludes present far fewer problems of tuning and temperament than do the praeludia. Harald Vogel has recently written that "more than half of the chorale-based settings by Buxtehude use only the five semitones of the pure quarter-comma meantone system."[19] All this might argue for a relatively early origin for many if not most of these works. But it is important to realize that they are accomplished compositions, and perhaps more important, all more or less equally accomplished. In other words, they do not look like student works, in the way that, for instance, the Praembulum in A Minor, BuxWV 158, does.[20] Christoph Wolff has suggested that perhaps these works were written at one time, presumably in Buxtehude's maturity, perhaps on commission.[21] Finally, one wonders about the often-cited report that in 1701 hymnboards were posted in the Marienkirche because many in the congregation could not recognize the chorale on which the organist was preluding. Was this a problem of long standing? Or did Buxtehude for some reason suddenly become more flamboyant? It does seem more than possible, though, that certain of the chorale preludes that do survive could well have confused congregations of the time, as Kerala Snyder has observed.[22] She points to a work such as *Ein feste Burg ist unser Gott*, BuxWV 184, which hides its chorale tune all too well for many of today's listeners—listeners who like Buxtehude's own are familiar with the tune. Yet, we should not be too quick to assume that such troublesome chorale preludes were even in the expressive style. A chorale prelude such as *Von Gott will ich nicht lassen*, BuxWV 221— surely one of Buxtehude's most dazzling chorale settings—would be far more likely to leave a congregation mystified than even *Ein feste Burg*, for it brings together Lutheran chorale and *stylus phantasticus* in such a surprising way that it virtually creates its own genre.

Ultimately, our goal should be the construction of a critical framework that allows for the appreciation of these works as individual compositions rather than as a group or genre. And the best place to begin is by noting the individual chorale preludes that have been singled out. One work stands out as having received the lion's share of critical attention: *Durch Adams Fall ist ganz verderbt*, BuxWV 183. It is mentioned by Pirro, Apel, Shannon, Evans, Marshall, Dirksen, and others,[23] notably for its text painting (falling fifths in the opening pedal line) and its unusually expressive aura. Qualities that distinguish other individual chorale preludes include the gravity of undecorated half-note motion—such as at the opening of *Ach Herr, mich armen Sünder* (BuxWV 179) and *Nun bitten wir den Heiligen Geist* (BuxWV 209)—and particularly poignant harmonic events, as in *Ach Herr*, where the last note of the last phrase of the chorale as presented in the solo line (often an important moment in these works) is unexpectedly supported at first by a seventh chord.[24] But even such a seemingly innocent moment as the curious little codalike gesture in the accompanimental voices in the final two measures of *Gott der Vater wohn uns bei* (BuxWV 190) may hold a special significance. George Buelow has recently pointed out that arias in operas produced at the Hamburg opera during Buxtehude's lifetime often ended with a little instrumental ritornello, although such ritornellos never introduce an aria.[25] And Kerala Snyder's *Dieterich Buxtehude* has certainly made clear Buxtehude's interest in the Hamburg opera. The ending of *Gott der Vater,* more than that of any other of Buxtehude's expressive chorale preludes, has the flavor of a ritornello: it stands relatively independently at a point where Buxtehude's habit is to link seamlessly the end of the final chorale phrase to a carefully calculated spinning-out of the accumulated energy and motivic material of the work.[26] Moreover, *Gott der Vater* does not begin with any of the usual *Vorimitation,* much less a ritornello, but immediately introduces the first phrase of the chorale in the solo voice. It seems not too fanciful, then, to link this piece with the idiosyncratic practices of the Hamburg opera, giving further reason to underline, in an unexpected way, the commonly held notion that these pieces are in many ways like arias.[27]

Perhaps the most revealing way to examine the homogeneity of style in Buxtehude's expressive chorale preludes is to compare two of his settings of the same chorale tune. Of several such pairs that survive, the two settings of *Herr Christ, der Einig Gottes Sohn,* BuxWV 191 and 192, are in some ways the most interesting, because they are not preserved together in the same manuscript (as is the case with the pairs of settings on *Komm, Heiliger Geist, Herre Gott,* BuxWV 199 and 200, and *Nun bitten wir den Heiligen Geist,* BuxWV 208 and 209). Rather, they appear individually in different manuscripts of substantially different content.[28] In addition, one of the settings, BuxWV 191, includes the note A♯ (twice) which, in G major, strains the limits of meantone tuning.[29] This fact may or may not suggest that BuxWV 191 is a more mature composition; however, very few of the expressive chorale preludes are so harmonically daring.

Our most obvious reaction to these two settings is likely to be that they are far more similar than they are different. Overall, BuxWV 192 is the simpler: the ornamentation, while completely typical of Buxtehude's style, is noticeably less florid than in BuxWV 191. The ornamentation is also placed rather differently. In BuxWV 192, flourishes—what Fritz Dietrich some fifty years ago called "apostrophes"[30]—precede the beginnings of some of the chorale phrases in the solo line; such apostrophes in this setting, however, are not found at the ends of the phrases. In BuxWV 191, apostrophes occur both at the beginnings and the ends of the phrases. While the closing apostrophes might seem more daring (they are considerably more unusual in these works than opening apostrophes) both Scheidemann and Reinken used closing apostrophes.[31] One wonders if such closing apostrophes might have had an archaic ring by the time of Buxtehude's maturity. The important point, however, is that the expressive content of these ornaments does not seem to differ much on the basis of where they occur. About all that can be said of these two settings on the basis of their ornamentation is that BuxWV 191 has a certain air of flamboyance that BuxWV 192 lacks. Moreover, the accompanimental voices in these two works are also very similar, in a few spots almost embarrassingly so (for instance, the passage in each case which leads to the appearance of the third chorale phrase in the solo voice). But this should not be taken to mean that BuxWV 191 and 192 are in some way variants of each other, or of some previous, lost version. What is stark in one setting is usually elaborate in the other: while we may enjoy the clever imitation at the beginning of the fourth phrase in BuxWV 191, we can also be jostled by the sudden shift into dotted rhythms during the fifth phrase in BuxWV 192. Again, all this does little to help draw real distinctions between the settings. Indeed, at certain cadential spots at the end of a given chorale phrase, it would actually be possible to switch from one piece to the other without attracting attention.

BuxWV 191, though, is without question distinctive harmonically. It not only has the two A♯s but also one of Buxtehude's most powerful gestures in this genre: the use of a seventh chord to support the concluding note of a chorale phrase (in this instance, the third phrase). This wonderful gesture recalls a similar one, mentioned above, in *Ach Herr, mich armen Sünder*, though in *Ach Herr* this event is saved for the last note of the *last* chorale phrase in the solo line, and thus serves not only as a moment of high expressivity but also as a climactic gesture for the entire piece.

Yet in spite of BuxWV 191's richer harmonic details, the overall tone of these two works—that is to say, their expressive world—is virtually identical. While other expressive chorale preludes are somewhat starker than BuxWV 191, or even BuxWV 192 (one thinks of, say, *Lobt Gott, ihr Christen allzugleich,* BuxWV 202) this tone, however we may call it, pervades the genre in Buxtehude's hands. Perhaps only a few triple-time pieces, such as *Puer Natus in Bethlehem,* BuxWV 217, achieve a tangibly different aura. In 1933, *The Diapason* published an article by Terence White entitled "Dietrich Buxtehude, Composer of Nobility, Pathos, Romanticism,"[32] and while pathos and romanticism perhaps best characterize the great praeludia, nobility is certainly a dominating trait in the expressive chorale preludes. We may disagree with White in explaining this quality as a racial inheritance, but we can certainly agree with him that Buxtehude did achieve such a quality. That he consistently maintained it in so many expressive chorale preludes deserves our notice and may serve as a key to our understanding of Buxtehude's accomplishment in this genre.

Notes

1. See, for example, Robert L. Marshall, "Chorale settings," *The New Grove Dictionary of Music and Musicians,* ed. Stanley Sadie (London: Macmillan, 1980), vol. 4, pp. 329–36.

2. Werner Breig, *Die Orgelwerke von Heinrich Scheidemann,* Beihefte zum Archiv für Musikwissenschaft, vol. 3 (Weisbaden: Franz Steiner Verlag, 1967). Professor Breig, in his address to the Lübeck Buxtehude Symposium in 1987 ("Die geschichtliche Stellung von Dietrich Buxtehudes monodischem Orgelchoral"), cautions against the use of the term "expressive" in place of "monodic" in the repertory before Buxtehude. I am grateful to Professor Breig for providing me with a copy of his paper.

3. See Christoph Wolff, "Präludium (Toccata) and Sonata: Formbildung und Gattungstradition in der Orgelmusik Buxtehudes und seines Kreises," *Orgel, Orgelmusik und Orgelspiel: Festschrift Michael Schneider zum 75. Geburtstag* (Kassel: Bärenreiter, 1985), pp. 55–64. For comparisons between Buxtehude's cantatas and chorale preludes, see Josef Hedar, *Dietrich Buxtehudes Orgelwerke* (Stockholm: Nordiska Musikförlaget, 1951; Frankfurt: Wilhelmiana Musikverlag, 1951), pp. 304–8.

4. Philipp Spitta, *Johann Sebastian Bach,* trans. Clara Bell and J. A. Fuller-Maitland (reprint ed., New York: Dover Publications, 1951), vol. 1, p. 290.

5. Ibid., pp. 267–90.

6. Ibid., p. 276.

7. André Pirro, "L'Art des Organistes," *Encyclopédie de la Musique et Dictionnaire du Conservatoire* (Paris: Librairie Delagrave, 1925), part 2, vol. 2, p. 1328.

8. Willi Apel, *The History of Keyboard Music to 1700,* trans. and revised by Hans Tischler (Bloomington: Indiana University Press, 1972), pp. 610–22.

9. Ibid., p. 594.

10. Kneller was born in 1649 in Lübeck, worked in Hannover and then from 1685 in Hamburg until his death in 1724.

11. This work was attributed to Anton Kniller by Straube (Karl Straube, ed., *Choralvorspiele alter Meister* [New York: C. F. Peters Corporation, n.d.], p. 88); the attribution was corrected to Andreas Kneller by Apel (*History of Keyboard Music,* p. 625, n. 78). The piece has recently been published by Beckmann (Klaus Beckmann, ed., *Andreas Kneller: Sämtliche Orgelwerke* [Wiesbaden: Breitkopf & Härtel, 1987], p. 21).

12. As reported in Hugh J. McLean, "Daniel Erich," *New Grove,* vol. 6, p. 228. Erich was born ca. 1660, was an organist in Güstrow, and died ca. 1730.

13. Straube, ed., *Choralvorspiele alter Meister,* pp. 61–63.

14. In his use of *Vorimitation,* Erich recalls Hanff's chorale preludes, as Apel points out (*History of Keyboard Music,* p. 640).

15. Klaus Beckmann, ed., *Georg D. Leyding: Sämtliche Orgelwerke* (Wiesbaden: Breitkopf & Härtel, 1984), pp. 22–29. Leyding was born in 1664 in Bücken and made his career as an organist in Brunswick, where he died in 1710.

16. See Lawrence Archbold, *Style and Structure in the Praeludia of Dietrich Buxtehude* (Ann Arbor: UMI Research Press, 1985), pp. 261–62.

17. Kerala J. Snyder, *Dieterich Buxtehude: Organist in Lübeck* (New York: Schirmer Books, 1987), pp. 341, 345–47.

18. Ibid., p. 257.

19. Harald Vogel, "Tuning and Temperament in the North German School of the Seventeenth and Eighteenth Centuries," *Charles Brenton Fisk: Organ Builder*, ed. Fenner Douglass, Owen Jander, and Barbara Owen (Easthampton, Mass.: The Westfield Center for Early Keyboard Studies, 1986), vol. 1, p. 247.

20. Archbold, *Style and Structure*, pp. 243, 247.

21. Comments at "From Scheidt to Buxtehude: German Music in the Seventeenth Century," sponsored by The Westfield Center for Early Keyboard Studies, Wellesley College, June 14–17, 1987.

22. Snyder, *Dieterich Buxtehude*, p. 270.

23. Pirro, "L'Art des Organistes," p. 1328; Apel, *History of Keyboard Music*, p. 622; John R. Shannon, *Organ Literature of the Seventeenth Century: A Study of Its Styles* (Raleigh: Sunbury, 1978), p. 237; Margaret R. Evans, "Dietrich Buxtehude: The Chorale Preludes," *The American Organist* 13 (September 1979), p. 39; Marshall, "Chorale settings," p. 333; Pieter Dirksen, "Die Orgelkoralen van Dietrich Buxtehude," *Het Orgel* 83 (October 1987), p. 386.

24. In m. 42.

25. George Buelow, "Hamburg Opera during Buxtehude's Lifetime: The Works of Johann Wolfgang Franck," this volume, p. 127

26. See mm. 50–51.

27. For example, Crocker's characterization of Buxtehude's chorale preludes as "more modern in their implications than the toccata, being the counterpart of the closed aria forms, rather than the grandiose pathos scenes in recitative characteristic of Cavalli in the 1650s." (Richard L. Crocker, *A History of Musical Style* [New York: McGraw-Hill, 1966], p. 294.)

28. The manuscript locations for these two chorale preludes (two for BuxWV 191: the "Plauener Orgelbuch" [now lost; a photocopy survives in East Berlin Deutsche Staatsbibliothek, Musik-abteilung, Foto Bückebung 129], and Berlin, Deutsche Staatsbibliothek, Musikabteilung Mus. ms. 30245; and two for BuxWV 192: Berlin, Deutsche Staatsbibliothek, Musikabteilung Mus. ms. 22541/1, and the "Frankenbergersches Walther-Autograph") suggest that they were not conceived together as a pair. There are enough differences in the pieces themselves, however, to be certain that they are not variants of the same original work. (Locations of these works in Josef Hedar, ed., *Dietrich Buxtehude: Sämtliche Orgelwerke* [Copenhagen: Wilhelm Hansen, 1952], vol. 4, are BuxWV 191: no. 11b, pp. 28–29; BuxWV 192: no. 11a, pp. 26–27.)

29. See mm. 15 and 26.

30. See Apel, *History of Keyboard Music*, p. 370.

31. As in Scheidemann's *Mensch, willst du leben seliglich*, verse 3, mm. 12–13 (Gustave Fock, ed., *Heinrich Scheidemann: Choralbearbeitungen* [Kassel, Bärenreiter, 1967], p. 103) and in Reinken's *An Wasserflüssen Babylon*, m. 241 (Klaus Beckmann, ed., *Joh. Adam Reincken: Sämtliche Orgelwerke* [Wiesbaden: Breitkopf & Härtel, 1974], p. 16).

32. Terence White, "Dietrich Buxtehude, Composer of Nobility, Pathos, Romanticism," *The Diapason* 24 (1 April 1933), p. 25.

Part Two

Vocal Music for Obsequies, Opera, and *Abendmusiken*

6

Heinrich Schütz's *Musikalische Exequien:* Reflections on Its History and Textual-Musical Conception

Werner Breig

Premises

No other work by Heinrich Schütz is accompanied by such a wealth of significant and substantial documents as the *Musikalische Exequien*. Not only do these documents touch upon the external chronology of the work's origins, but they also indicate the stimulus behind its commission, as well as the composer's solutions to problems of compositional technique and his text expression. At the same time, this work has for over half a century been covered with a confusing network of contradictory interpretations and hypotheses. This is especially true of the first part of the work, the *Concert in Form einer teutschen Missa,* the text of which is taken from the coffin of Heinrich von Reuß. The important details necessary to understand Schütz's composition—namely the principles according to which the twenty-five-line text is constructed and the composer's role in its distribution—have until very recently been given constantly changing interpretations—occasionally without either clear documentation or sufficient continuity within the discussions of the secondary literature.[1]

It is the goal of this article to present, through renewed examination of the sources, as detailed a picture as possible of the succession of events to which the *Musikalische Exequien* owes its existence. We will thus obtain a clearer understanding both of the degree of autonomy allowed the composer and of his artistic decisions.

Let us first summarize what is already known about the genesis of the *Musikalische Exequien*. The principal sources in this regard are: The *Abdruck / Derer Sprüche Göttlicher Schrifft vnd Christlicher Kirchen Gesänge* ... in which the texts sung at the funeral service are given (hereafter referred to as *Abdruck);*[2] the printed funeral sermon of Superintendent Christoph Richter (hereafter: Richter);[3] the title page of the original print of Schütz's *Musikalische Exequien* (hereafter: Title);[4] and Schütz's preface (*Absonderlich Verzeichnüs . . .*) to the original print (hereafter: Preface). These documents provide a framework of known facts whose succession can be arranged in four phases:

1. The Prehistory. About one year before his death and burial (Richter) Heinrich Posthumus von Reuß had his coffin made and inscribed with a series of biblical sayings and chorale verses "Zu erweck: vnd vbung Gottseliger SterbensGedancken" [for the purpose of awakening and exercising his pious thoughts concerning death] (*Abdruck*). He selected as the sermon text for his interment ceremony verses 25–26 of Psalm 73, "Herr, wenn ich nur dich habe" (Richter, Preface), and he expressed the desire to have the coffin inscriptions, as well as other texts of his selection (including the *Canticum Simeonis*), performed musically for the funeral (*Abdruck,* Title, Preface).

2. The Commissioning of the Composition. Heinrich von Reuß died on 3 December 1635; Heinrich Schütz was asked by the Count's widow and sons to set to music the texts selected by the deceased.

3. Composition and Performance. Schütz composed the *Musikalische Exequien,* which "bey herrlicher vnd hochansehnlicher Leichbestattung" [at the splendid and most notable interment] of Heinrich Posthumus is "vor vnd nach der Leichpredigt gehalten/ vnd . . . in eine stille verdackte Orgel angestellet vnd abgesungen" [held before and after the sermon and . . . placed and sung at a quiet, discreet organ] (Title).

4. Publication. Soon thereafter (the title page speaks of the "recent" burial) the original print of Schütz's *Musikalische Exequien* was published by Wolff Seyffert in Dresden, with a dedication to the widow and sons of the deceased, an obituary poem by Schütz, and an extensive preface.

The reader may perhaps notice the absence of private preperformances during Heinrich von Reuß's lifetime that are mentioned again and again in the Schütz literature.[5] The assumption of such preperformances is, however, based solely on the misinterpretation of a passage from the title page of the *Musikalische Exequien.* When Schütz wrote, "Musicalische Exequien wie solche . . . Jüngsthin den 4 Monatstag Februarii zu Gera / vor vnd nach der Leichpredigt gehalten / vnd ihrer wolseligen Gnaden / bey dero lebzeiten wiederholten begehren nach / in eine stille verdackte Orgel angestellet vnd abgesungen worden, . . ." the time indication "bei dero lebzeiten" [during his lifetime] refers to the immediately following words "wiederholten begehren nach" [repeatedly wished for]. If Schütz had intended them to refer to "angestellet vnd abgesungen worden," additional punctuation would have been necessary: "ihrer wolsehligen

Gnaden bey dero lebzeiten / wiederholten begehren nach / in eine stille. . . ." The punctuation chosen—and without a doubt deliberately chosen—gives the text the unambiguous sense that the obsequies—according to the repeatedly expressed wishes of the deceased (the *Abdruck* states "nach Ihr Wolsel. Gn hiebevorn mehrmals wiederholter anleitung"), were "held . . . placed and sung before and after the sermon." The description of the same event using three verbs has a purpose: "halten" refers to the liturgical function of the music; "anstellen" to the disposition of the performers,[6] for which the thoroughbass instrument, the "quiet, discreet organ," here sets the standard; and the "absingen" to the actual performance. Furthermore, information to the effect that the deceased had already heard his funeral music while he was still alive would not have been appropriate for the official character of the title page. The latter describes the function that the music assumed within the framework of the "state burial" of Heinrich von Reuß; a casual remark about previous private performances would in any case have belonged in the preface, or it could possibly have been woven into the obituary poem.

The notion that Schütz had begun the composition of the *Musikalische Exequien* before December 1635 is as untenable as these theorized preperformances of the music during Heinrich's lifetime.[7] The following will attempt to trace in detail the course of the four phases in the genesis of the work. Though we will adhere as closely as possible to facts supplied by surviving documents, hypothesis will occasionally be employed to fill some the of the gaps in our verifiable knowledge.

The Prehistory

"Prehistory" of the *Musikalische Exequien* will refer here to that phase during which Heinrich Reuß planned his burial, i.e., had his coffin made and inscribed and selected the musical texts to be performed at the funeral service.

Seen from the vantage point of Schütz's *Musikalische Exequien,* the coffin inscriptions are of central interest. It is from these that the first part of the work, the *Concert in Form einer teutschen Missa,* receives its multipartite textual and musical structure. For a long time, the exact arrangement of the texts on the coffin was a matter of conjecture. Hans Joachim Moser attempted to extrapolate from the composition to the coffin—unsuccessfully, as we now know.[8] (Nevertheless, he was on the right track in that he based his interpretation of the strict alternation between Bible verse and chorale strophe in the "Gloria" section on their arrangement on the coffin.)

We owe our current precise knowledge of the placement of texts on the coffin to the *Abdruck / Derer Sprüche Göttlicher Schrifft vnd Christlicher Kirchen Gesänge, . . .* which Rudolf Henning discovered and first evaluated in his article of 1973. The *Abdruck,* which was presumably sent as an invitation to those taking part in the funaral service, not only lists the texts for all of the musical pieces intended for the church service, but it also gives such an exact position of the coffin inscriptions that Henning was able to reconstruct the appearance of the coffin in a perspective drawing.[9] Remarks in the present study are based on table 6.1, which summarizes the arrangement and sources for the twenty-one coffin inscriptions. In order to avoid confusion, the individual texts

Table 6.1   Bible Verses and Chorale Strophes on the
Coffin of Heinrich von Reuß

	[No.]	Text incipit	Source of Biblical Texts OT	NT
coffin lid				
(a) top	I.	*Christus ist mein Leben*		Phil. 1:21
	II.	*Siehe, das ist Gottes Lamm*		John 1:29b
(b) head	III.	*Leben wir, so leben wir dem Herren*		Rom. 14:8
(c) right side	(h) IV.	*Also hat Gott die Welt geliebt*		John 3:16
	V.	*Er sprach zu seinem lieben Sohn*		
	(f) VI.	*Das Blut Jesu Christi, des Sohnes*		I John 1:7b
	VII.	*Durch ihn ist uns vergeben*		
(d) left side	(h) VIII.	*Unser Wandel ist im Himmel*		Phil. 3:20–21a
	IX.	*Es ist allhie ein Jammertal*		
	(f) X.	*Wenn eure Sünde gleich blutrot wäre*	Isa. 1:18b	
	XI.	*Sein Wort, sein Tauf, sein Nachtmahl*		
(e) foot	XII.	*Gehe hin, mein Volk, in eine Kammer*	Isa. 26:60	
middle section	XIII.	*Der Gerechten Seelen sind in Gottes Hand*	Wisd. of Sol. 3:1–3	
coffin base				
(a) right side	(h) XIV.	*Herr, wenn ich nur dich habe*	Ps. 73:25–26	
	XV.	*Er ist das Heil und selig Licht*		
	(f) XVI.	*Unser Leben währet siebenzig Jahr*	Ps. 90:10a	
	XVII.	*Ach wie elend ist unser Zeit*		
(b) left side	(h) XVIII.	*Ich weiß, daß mein Erlöser lebt*	Job 19:25–26	
	XIX.	*Weil du vom Tod erstanden bist*		
	(f) XX.	*Herr, ich lasse dich nicht*	Gen. 32:27b	
	XXI.	*Er sprach zu mir: Halt dich an mich*		

Source of the Chorale Texts. No. V: *Nun freut euch, lieben Christen gmein* (Martin Luther), str. 5; No. VII: *Nun laßt uns Gott dem Herren* (Ludwig Helmbold), str. 6; No. IX: *Ich hab mein Sach Gott heimgestellt* (Johann Leon), str. 3; No. XI: *Nun laßt uns Gott dem Herren* (see no. VII), str. 5; No. XV: *Mit Fried und Freud ich fahr dahin* (Martin Luther), str. 4; No. XVII: *Ach wie elend ist unser Zeit* (Johannes Gigas), str. 1; No. XIX: *Wenn mein Stündlein vorhanden ist* (Nikolaus Herman), str. 4; No. XXI: *Nun freut euch, lieben Christen gmein* (see no. V), lines 1–4 from str. 7, lines 5–7 from str. 8.

Table 6.2   Textual Outline of Part I of the *Musikalische Exequien*

	[No.]	Text incipit	OT	NT	SWV 279
Pro Introitu	1.	*Nacket bin ich von Mutterleibe kommen*	Job 1:21		
	2.	**[Herr Gott, Vater im Himmel]**			
Coffin Inscriptions					"Kyrie" Portion
coffin lid (a) top	3.	*Christus ist mein Leben*		Phil. 1:21	
	4.	*Siehe, das ist Gottes Lamm*		John 1:29b	
	5.	**[Jesus Christus, Gottes Sohn]**			
(b) head	6.	*Leben wir, so leben wir dem Herren*		Rom. 14:8	
	7.	**[Herr Gott, heiliger Geist]**			
(c) right side	(h) 8.	*Also hat Gott die Welt geliebt*		John 3:16	
	9.	**Er sprach zu seinem lieben Sohn**			
	(f) 10.	*Das Blut Jesu Christi, des Sohnes*		I John 1:7b	
	11.	**Durch ihn ist uns vergeben**			
(d) left side	(h) 12.	*Unser Wandel ist im Himmel*		Phil. 3:20–21a	
	13.	**Es ist allhie ein Jammertal**			
	(f) 14.	*Wenn eure Sünde gleich blutrot wäre*	Isa. 1:18b		
	15.	**Sein Wort, sein Tauf, sein Nachtmahl**			
(e) foot	16.	*Gehe hin, mein Volk in eine Kammer*	Isa. 26:60		
middle section	17.	*Der Gerechten Seelen sind in Gottes Hand*	Wisd. of Sol. 3:1–3		"Gloria" Portion
coffin base (a) right side	(h) 18.	*Herr, wenn ich nur dich habe*	Ps. 73:25–26		
	19.	**Er ist das Heil und selig Licht**			
	(f) 20.	*Unser Leben währet siebenzig Jahr*	Ps. 90:10a		
	21.	**Ach wie elend ist unser Zeit**			
(b) left side	(h) 22.	*Ich weiß, daß mein Erlöser lebt*	Job 19:25–26		
	23.	**Weil du vom Tod erstanden bist**			
	(f) 24.	*Herr, ich lasse dich nicht*	Gen. 32:27b		
	25.	**Er sprach zu mir: Halt dich an mich**			

Source of the Chorale Texts: See table 6.1.

are given Roman numerals, while Arabic numbers represent the order of performance for the twenty-five texts (table 6.2).

The coffin inscriptions are bound together by a common theme: they encompass thoughts of mortality, dying, salvation through Christ's death and resurrection, and eternal life. The selection of bibical texts is not original; it corresponds to contemporary conventions. Henning was able to find "almost all the passages from the Posthumus coffin . . . on a dozen coffins of baroque princes."[10] On the other hand, the supplementing of bible verses with chorale strophes appears to be peculiar to Reuß's coffin.

Concerning the arrangement of texts on the coffin, certain hierarchical principles can be discerned. First, one can say in general that the chorale strophes are in each case closely related to the Bible verses that precede them. Furthermore, as Henning has already shown, the three spatial directions are polarized and assigned relative values: "above" is of a higher value than "below," "right" higher than "left," and the head end of the coffin higher than the foot. Thus, texts no. I and II, the most concentrated formulations of the Christian assurance of salvation, were assigned to a prominent position on the top of the coffin above and below the crucifix. The position of texts no. III and XII also appears to have been determined through the relationship of the "head" end to the "foot" end. While the latter ("Gehe hin, mein Volk, in eine Kammer"), at the foot of the coffin lid, expresses the fallen nature of man in death, this thought finds its consoling counterpart in the saying introduced at the head, "Leben wir, so leben wir dem Herren. . . ." and John 3:16 ("Also had Gott die Welt geliebet . . ."), one of the central biblical statements of the Christian faith, has been given an appropriately prominent place near the head.

The hierarchical ordering is most clearly taken into account, however, in the position of relatively higher value assumed by the New Testament sayings, as is evident from the diagram. The separation of Old and New Testament sayings is carried out with such consistency that one can scarcely doubt the presence of an underlying principle. As for the grouping of texts within the two blocks of Old and New Testament, a certain amount of latitude was possible; it would be difficult to prove that the chosen arrangement was the only sensible one. "Encircling a center" would be a better description for the intellectual interrelation of the sayings than "progression in a straight line."

Schütz's Commission of the Composition

If we trust the statement of the *Abdruck,* according to which the "gracious request" for a musical setting of the coffin inscriptions came from the survivors, then Schütz would have received the commission to compose the funeral music in December 1635. Since nowadays we associate a fixed concept with the expression "funeral music for Heinrich Posthumus von Reuß," namely the three-part work published by Schütz under the title *Musikalische Exequien,* the content and form of the request that Schütz received has scarcely been considered. However, a few thoughts on the form of this request might prove helpful to an understanding of the finished work.

The request in its literal sense, that is, the written document in which Heinrich von Reuß's survivors asked Schütz to prepare music for the funeral service, does not survive. We can, however, reconstruct much of its content with the help of the *Abdruck,* which in this context proves again to be a key document for the history of the *Musikalische Exequien.* Namely, for parts I and III of the *Exequien* the text of the *Abdruck* differs from that of Schütz. This indicates that at the time of the *Abdruck's* printing, the performance material of the *Musikalische Exequien* was not yet in Gera. The *Abdruck* must therefore contain the texts for which music had been requested from Schütz and to which, at least in principle, Schütz had apparently already consented.

As it appears in the *Abdruck,* the order of the worship service contained seven texts to be presented musically (the texts of Schütz's *Musikalische Exequien* are printed here in bold type):

1. **Nacket bin ich von Mutterleibe kommen** (*Pro Introitu*) (SWV 279, no. 1)
2. **Coffin inscriptions** (SWV 279, no. 3, 4, 6, 8–25)
3. *Herzlich lieb hab ich dich, o Herr*
4. **Herr, wenn ich nur dich habe** (SWV 280)
5. **Herr, nun lässest du deinen Diener** (*Canticum Simeonis*) (SWV 281)
6. *Mit Fried und Freud ich fahr dahin*
7. *Hört auf mit Weinen und Klagen*

The title and layout of the *Abdruck* place particular emphasis on the coffin inscriptions; they are reproduced in their entirety, whereas for some of the other texts only the beginning is given (nos. 3, 5, and 6). According to the wishes of the deceased, these inscriptions were apparently to form the musical centerpiece of the funeral service, and accordingly they formed the heart of the composition's commissioning. It was for their sake that a new composition was absolutely necessary, since an ad hoc collection of texts was involved. It is possible—given the short period of time—that Schütz was left to decide whether to write new music for the other texts, to use earlier compositions of his own, or to recommend settings by others. This last option is particularly plausible for text no. 7, which was perhaps sung in the widely disseminated setting by Melchior Vulpius.

The *Abdruck* is particularly reflective of the composition's commissioning as it pertains to part I of the *Musikalische Exequien*. It not only informs us about the arrangement of the inscriptions on the various surfaces of the princely coffin, but it also brings these texts into a specific order (that is, Schütz's).

Rudolf Henning thought he could determine through observation of the texts on the coffin "that the sequential order differs from that of Schütz."[11] This is inaccurate. On the coffin, the texts have no sequential order at all ("sequential order" is a linear concept); they are instead arranged in three-dimensional space, so that in their relationship to the composition one can speak neither of identity nor of divergence. Rather, the translation of the spatial ordering into the linear, one-dimensional flow of music demands some sort of guideline or rule to determine the hierarchical order and the direction in which the three dimensions are to be considered. The rule according to which the coffin's texts are reproduced in the *Abdruck* consists of proceeding in order of importance from top to bottom, from head to foot, and from left to right. It was apparently in this order that the texts of the coffin were presented to Schütz for his setting, and it was in this order that he composed them.

Earlier interpretations of the *Concert in Form einer teutschen Missa,* in spite of everything ingenious that they have detected concerning the sequential order composed by Schütz, have overlooked one problem: the relationship of the Old and New Testaments as text sources. The New Testament texts, which on the coffin are logically placed *above* the Old Testament ones, come to stand—as a result of the gathering of texts in the order described above—*before* those of the Old Testament. This forces the composer to proceed from New to Old Testament texts. To sure, the Old Testament Bible verses are to a certain extent placed in a Christian light through the chorale strophes that follow them, yet there is a certain strangeness to this order. Schütz complied with the textual sequence, but it is difficult to imagine that he welcomed it.

Composition and Performance

The manuscript parts from which the music was performed on 4 February 1636 are not extant, so we cannot determine what last-minute changes Schütz might perhaps have introduced into the music before its printing. If we nevertheless treat separately the phases of "composition and performance" on the one hand and "printing" on the other, we do so for two reasons. First, the print exhibits a purely textual layer of relatively independent significance (title, dedication, poetic eulogy, preface, and headings for the movements) which in part requires its own discussion; and second, of the seven texts or textual complexes in the *Abdruck* for which musical performance is expected, we encounter three that are not in the print of the *Musikalische Exequien*. Thus it is perhaps not entirely irrelevant to ask whether the texts in this group were also set to music by Schütz and performed during the funeral service.

These three texts (nos. 3, 6, and 7 in table 6.2) involve chorales, so that congregational singing could also enter in these places. For the first of the chorale texts, *Herzlich lieb hab ich dich, o Herr,* one could surely think—with all necessary caution—of a figural composition by Schütz, namely the six-voice setting that he published in 1648 in the *Geistliche Chormusik* (SWV 387). *Herzlich lieb* is so unrepresentative of the predominating type of polyphonic *Spruchmotette* in this collection that one can scarcely assume Schütz composed the work for this opus. The princely burial of 1636, however, would be a possible occasion for its creation. One could explain its omission from the published version of the *Musikalische Exequien* in that its simple style caused it not to fit with the other pieces. Schütz appears to have viewed the *Geistliche Chormusik,* on the other hand, as a reservoir in which stray compositions could also find a place; one might think of the aria *Also hat Gott die Welt geliebt* or the motet *Der Engel sprach zu den Hirten,* the latter of which represents a German version of a composition by Andrea Gabrieli.

Whereas thoughts concerning the compositions that are called for in the *Abdruck* but not present in the print of the *Exequien* are of a hypothetical nature, we stand on surer ground with nos. 1, 2, 4, and 5 on the list. In the double choir motet on the sermon text, *Herr, wenn ich nur dich habe,* Schütz is in complete agreement with the wishes of the deceased; in his setting of the *Canticum Simeonis* he goes beyond the requirements of his commission by adding to the main text (*Herr, nun lässest du deinen Diener,* sung by the first choir) a second choir with the words "Selig sind die Toten," an addition of frankly theatrical effect which in the preface the composer expressly claims as his invention.

The most difficult task for the composer was undoubtedly the setting of the complex of twenty-one coffin inscriptions. In the following we will attempt to reconstruct the considerations that led from the "raw material" of the texts (see table 6.1) to the basic plan of Schütz's setting. In table 6.2, which reproduces this plan, the individual segments (by now twenty-five in number) are enumerated consecutively with arabic numbers.[12] The texts of the capella sections are in bold type (with textual additions of the composer in square brackets); the slot on the far right, not present in table 6.1, demonstrates the overlaid bipartite division as it is made clear through the two "Intonatio" beginnings and Schütz's statements concerning the analogy to the two-part Lutheran Mass (Kyrie and Gloria).

In planning the work, the most pressing question had to be the way to tie together the large number of individual pieces. Schütz decided to treat the two types of text, Bible verse and chorale strophe, in stylistically different ways. Apparently, the composer's first fundamental decision was to set the Bible verses in the style of the *kleines geistliches Konzert* for few voices and obbligato thoroughbass, with the chorale strophes set for the entire six-voice ensemble using the proper chorale melodies in motet style, i.e., with a basso seguente.[13]

In this way the chorale sections functioned, as it were, like pillars. In order also to being out this function with respect to mode, Schütz decided to let all the chorale sections end on the final of the primary mode (E Aeolian).[14] Only two of the chorale settings allowed transposition to E (nos. 13 and 19); the remainder, on G (nos. 9, 11, 15, 21, and 25) or A (no. 23), are given in each case a coda in the form of a varied repetition of the final line cadencing on E. While in the body of each of these chorale sections Schütz—as he excuses himself in the preface—"aus den Schrancken Noni Toni . . . außschweiffen vnd solchen Kirchen Melodeyen nachgehen müssen" [must digress from the limits of the ninth mode and follow such church melodies], he always returns to the fundamental mode with the codalike constructions described above.

As a rule, a Bible verse is followed in every instance by a chorale strophe. At two points, however, several Bible verses from among the coffin inscriptions stand directly beside each other, namely before the first chorale strophe, *Er sprach zu seinem lieben Sohn* (nos. I–IV in the *Abdruck,* nos. 3, 4, 6, and 8 in the composition) and before the fifth, *Er ist das Heil und selig Licht* (nos. XII–XIV in the *Abdruck,* nos. 16–18 in the composition). Schütz apparently considered the accumulation of Bible verses in the body of the work unobjectionable. In any case he left the given texts untouched and—through musical means (e.g., scoring, harmony, and style of declamation)—fashioned the series of four segments, nos. 16–19, into a large complex that is both varied and coherent.

The opening group of coffin inscriptions was difficult to handle: Here, if Schütz had remained faithful to the original plan for the texts he would have had to set no fewer than four Bible verses in immediate succession before the alternation of verse and strophe could have begun. He chose instead to make an unauthorized textual change: in order also to be able to alternate between few-voiced concerto sections and six-voice capella "pillars" at the very beginning, he added the three parts of the German trinitarian Kyrie. The three Kyrie portions did not fit schematically with the first three coffin inscriptions, since the first Bible verse already contains the name of Christ (which in the Kyrie text is reserved for the second segment). Thus this first manipulation of the given texts occasioned a second: Schütz inserted the verse from Job 1, which in the *Abdruck* was intended for the "Introitus," into the sequence of coffin inscriptions. The first "Kyrie" (no. 2) could easily follow it (no. 1); the two verses on the top side of the coffin lid (nos. 3 and 4) were both attached to the German "Christe eleison" (no. 5), while the words "Leben wir, so leben wir dem Herren . . ." were followed by the third invocation, directed to the Holy Spirit— an association that the text from the letter to the Romans neither invites nor contradicts.

In this way the number of textual segments to be set to music had grown from the original twenty-one coffin inscriptions to twenty-five, but the text as a whole had gained a structure that could serve in its musical setting as the basis for the regular alternation between reduced, soloistic sections and full-voiced, motetlike ones.

Through the bipartite division of the capella portions (A: three-part German Kyrie, B: eight chorale strophes) the whole had taken on a two-part form that was not present in the disposition of the original coffin inscriptions. Schütz made this bipartite form musically clear by allowing the opening segment of each part (nos. 1 and 8) to begin with a monophonic intonation. To lend formal coherence, each of the two parts is enclosed in a frame. In the first part the two outer cries of the Kyrie (no. 2 and 7) cadence on the final E, while the middle one (no. 5) ends on A.[15] The considerably longer second part is also framed, in that in its two outer verse-settings (nos. 8 and 24)—and only here—the entire six-voice ensemble is engaged; at these two places (nos. 8/9 and 24/25) verse and chorale join together to form six-voice blocks.

The Publication

As already stated, the sources offer us no clues for distinguishing between the first performed version of the *Musikalische Exequien* and the version that was published. Therefore, we will assume that the published version is essentially the same as the version heard at the burial service.

The congregation of 4 February 1636 probably followed the music with the aid of the *Abdruck*. The composer's textual additions in parts I and III would in this context certainly not have been felt as something strange but as an enrichment. If our assumption is correct that the Gera listeners were informed about the order of the musical works only through the *Abdruck,* then the first part of the *Musikalische Exequien* would not have been presented to them as a *Concert in Form einer teutschen Missa,* but rather as a setting of the introit text and the coffin inscriptions. Also, Schütz certainly had no interest in bringing the concept of "Deutsche Messe" into play; this would only have diverted attention from that which the deceased apparently considered so important, namely that the inscriptions of the coffin should sound through music.

Furthermore, the way in which, in the preface to the original print, Schütz speaks of the first part as a "Messe" is equivocal. First he leaves no doubt about the source of the texts: they are "Alle die jenigen Sprüche heiliger Schrifft / vnd Gesetzlein Christlicher Kirchen Gesänge / welche Ihre Selige verstorbene Gnaden . . . auf Ihren . . . Sarck / verzeichnen vnd schreiben lassen" [all those verses of the Holy Bible and strophes of Christian hymns that the deceased had drawn and written on his coffin]. The composition of these texts, however, is a "Concert . . . in Form einer Teutschen Missa" (the same is stated in the title of the part-books); and to be more precise Schütz continues, "nach art der Lateinischen Kyrie, Christe Kyrie Eleyson. Gloria in excelsis. Et in terra pax &c." If this formulation suggests terminological reflections concerning the difference between "form" [German: *Form*] and "manner" [German: *Art*] (the "form" of the *Concert* is that of the German Mass, its "manner" that of the Latin), the author undermines such considerations in the following *Ordinantz,* where he writes, "Dieses nach art einer Lateinischen oder Teutschen Missa auffgesetzte Concert. . . ." Between these two formulations, however, stands the heading "Ordinantz des Concerts oder der Teutschen Begräbnis Missa . . . ," in which the concept of the "Missa" is placed alongside that of "Concert." At the end of the *Ordinantz* Schütz proposes its liturgical use "in place of a German *Missa*" and mentions as appropriate places in the church year the feast of the Purification of the Virgin and the sixteenth Sunday after Trinity.

This confusing multiplicity of definitions contrasts conspicuously with the conceptual sharpness with which Schütz generally conceives the prefaces to his other works. The only possible explanation is that the printed edition of the *Musikalische Exequien* served two functions. It was in the first place a document; that is, it preserved in written form the music that was heard in Gera on 4 February 1636, and it demonstrated that the funeral ceremony took place according to the wish of the deceased and the formal request of the survivors (and dedicatees). Second, however, it was Schütz's aim to create for this music an afterlife beyond the original occasion and to reach an outside economic market with its publication. These two functions were easily combined for parts II and III, since their texts were not situation-specific. In part I, the two aims necessarily conflicted. How could a sensible performance opportunity be found for the musical settings of Reuß's coffin inscriptions after the Gera funeral?

Schütz solved this problem, first, by indicating that the piece took the form of the German Mass (i.e., the Lutheran Missa brevis consisting of Kyrie and Gloria) and could be performed as such for use in the church service, and second, by attempting to give the first part of the *Exequien* print a more general character. The explanation for the peculiar shifting conceptions of the various passages of the preface cited above lies in Schütz's need to keep sight of the origin of the text and its compositional occasion while effecting this transformation.

On the basis of the preceding considerations, the frequently discussed problem of the Gloria is easily solved. It involves the following: Whereas the transformation of segments 1 through 7 of part I into a Kyrie by means of capella insertions is textually motivated, complex nos. 8–25 offers no such analogous textual reference to the Gloria of the Mass. Until now, much of the secondary literature has attempted to support Schütz's explicit analogy through the text (i.e., to discover the relationship between the textual constellation of the second major portion and the text of the Gloria).[16] Without going into the (widely varied) results of these interpretations, we should note a fundamental, suspicious fact: whereas the possibility of indicating the first major portion as a troped Kyrie is obvious, the second major portion offers a serious obstacle to all attempts to bring it into clear relationship with the Gloria of the Mass. To be sure, this obstacle can be overcome through interpretational artifice, but only with the resulting cost that an appreciation of its meaning is beyond what even the most attentive listener can experience in the work itself.

Proceeding, however, from the work's history as it can be reconstructed from the sources, one sees clearly that all attempts to trace Gloria-analogies in the texts are exercises in futility. For the textual compilation of part I was not conceived in analogy to the Mass; rather, it arose through a transformation (not without problems, as has been shown) of the coffin inscriptions. To be sure, the composer did expand this succession of texts (which in any case is not in and of itself bipartite) with the insertion of the Kyrie, but he did nothing to tie it in any way with the Gloria text. The Gloria analogy was only later introduced by Schütz into the already-finished work; and it is limited to the analogous nature of its longer, multipartite text, which contains fundamental statements of the Christian faith and which follows a Kyrie. One may find this conclusion disappointing and criticize Schütz's later labeling as misleading, but everything that we know about the genesis of the work indicates that at no stage in the creative process was there any intention of establishing an analogy to the Gloria.

When one attempts to reconstruct the conceptual considerations that guided Schütz throughout his work on the *Concert in Form einer teutschen Missa,* the Gloria portion appears to be less of a problem than the Kyrie portion, i.e., that portion in which the composer moved beyond the given texts. We attempted above to explain the Kyrie insertions based on formal considerations; according to this explanation Schütz would at first have been less concerned with the Kyrie texts than with the possibility of differentiating between solo and capella sections at the beginning of the work. But the Kyrie insertions form at the same time the focal point for his transformation of the coffin inscriptions into the "Deutsche Messe"—a possibility that Schütz must have noticed, if indeed this had not been the impetus for the initial selection of the three introductory capella texts.

The point at which Schütz decided to expand the given texts by means of the three-fold Kyrie could theoretically have occurred between performance and publication, so that the notion of "Deutsche Missa" would have been first introduced afterwards with a view toward a broader market. In this case, however, one would also have to assume the introduction of further alterations; for example, without the two-part structure of Kyrie and Gloria, the two monophonic intonations would make no sense. Since no documents survive concerning the history of the work between the *Abdruck* and the original print of the *Musikalische Exequien,* we know nothing concerning the decisive divergence between the given textual conception of "Introitus and coffin inscriptions" and Schütz's textual-musical conception of a *Concert in Form einer teutschen Messe.*

Conclusions

We have attempted to view the shape of Schütz's *Musikalische Exequien* against
the backdrop of a "simplified" version of the work's genesis as indicated by the
surviving documents, without assuming any further underlying plans on the
part of the composer. In this way it has been demonstrated not only that such
further assumptions are unnecessary for an explanation of the shape of the work,
but that they would contradict certain of its features (e.g., the succession of Old
and New Testament texts, the problem of the Gloria).

If our inquiry has demonstrated that the text of the *Concerto in Form einer
teutschen Missa* is in no way as carefully "composed" or as full of meaning as
has hitherto been assumed, this may at first have a sobering effect. In reality,
however, it is this recognition that finally affords a clear view of the character
upon which the *concerto's* meaning is actually based, namely the musical shap-
ing that Schütz bestowed upon this textual compilation.

Schütz gave the many-colored and relatively loosely ordered nature of the
texts its due. His structural resources are limited to the connection of the whole
to a common mode, the "rhythmicization" of the musical flow through alternation of few-voiced *concerto* sections and full-voiced, motetlike chorale (or
Kyrie) settings, the subdivision into Kyrie and Gloria parts, and the employment
of a musical "frame" within each of these two parts. Otherwise, the variety of
the texts is matched by the similarly great variety of musical means with which
Schütz gives each of the individual sections its own characteristic stamp.

Particularly important in this respect is the special character that the style
of the *kleines geistliches Konzert* attains in part I of the *Musikalische Exequien*
(whose composition, of course, falls within the time period during which Schütz
was preparing the publication of both parts of the *Kleine geistliche Konzerte*
[1636 and 1639]). We know from Schütz's prefaces to this two-part opus that
he entertained serious reservations about this type of composition, and turned
to the genre in a more extensive way only because of the effects of the war. In
this respect, the danger that the small performing forces will be, so to speak,
"overstrained" if one attempts to use them in writing independent works of
larger proportion (as Schütz's concertos of 1636/39 in fact do, since the adjective *klein* refers only to their performing forces) seems to have played a role.
The nature of the task that Schütz faced in setting the coffin inscriptions—with
all of the problems of a multipartite form—seems to have held forth a certain
charm. For here he could realize the particular possibilities of the soloistic
concerto, namely the capacity for both flexible voice leading and differentiation
of textual meaning without needing to stretch the individual pieces to such great
length. The need, dictated by the large number of texts, to compose *concertos*
in miniature format offered at the same time a special opportunity, and Schütz
knew how to use it.

The composer's assessment of the work's success is reflected in his decision to make it available for broader use by assigning it (in its heading and preface) the liturgical function of a Lutheran Missa brevis. Along the same lines, Schütz also accepted the *Musikalische Exequien* into the sequence of his most important works as "Opus 7" in his catalog of 1647. His attempt to detach the work from its original purpose apparently found little resonance among his contemporaries—as we could conclude from the small number of extant copies of the print—just as the argument in the preface that the opening *concerto* could serve in place of a Mass was textually only weakly supported. The composer's wish for an afterlife for the *Musikalische Exequien* could only be granted by the twentieth-century Schütz renaissance, which has in the fullest sense assigned the work—if for aesthetic rather than liturgical reasons—a place of honor within Schütz's "Opera."

Translated by Paul Walker

Notes

1. The most important literature on Schütz's *Musikalische Exequien* is given in the bibliography at the end of this article. A report on the progress of previous research lies outside the intent of this article; agreement and differences with earlier scholarly literature is only noted where it serves to clarify a problem.

2. Only extant copy in the Stolberg Leichenpredigtsammlung, no. 18709; facsimile in Paul Horn, Günter Graulich, and Klaus Hofmann, preface to *Musikalische Exequien*, Stuttgarter Schütz-Ausgabe no. 8 (Neuhausen-Stuttgart: Hänssler, 1973), pp. xlvi–l.

3. Copies in the Stolberg Leichenpredigtsammlung, no. 18709, and in the Universitäts-Bibliothek Göttingen, Stedernsche Sammlung, vol. 215, 1.

4. Title page and foreword are reproduced in all modern editions of the *Musikalische Exequien*.

5. It appears that Othmar Wessely ("Der Fürst und der Tod," *Beiträge 1974/75*, ed. Osterreich-ischen Gesellschaft fur Musik, pp. 60–71) (Wessely, footnote 20) expressed the first reservations about the legend of performances during Reuß's lifetime; the problem is discussed at length in Horn, Graulich, and Hofmann, preface, but in the end the authors were unable to abandon the thesis of the preperformances.

6. In the foreword to the *Musikalische Exequien* Schütz uses the expression in a similar way; further demonstrations can be found within the discussions of performance practice in the prefaces to the *Psalmen Davids*, the *Geistliche Chormusik*, and the *Weihnachtshistorie*.

7. As an aside, an apocryphal contribution to the dating of the *Musikalische Exequien* may be mentioned. In 1962 one could read in the article by Gustav Adolf Trumpff on the *Musikalische Exequien* that "according to a note of Friedrich Ludwig" the *Musikalische Exequien* was composed "between 9 December 1633 and 11 February 1634" (Gustav Trumpff, "Die 'Musikalische Exequien' von Heinrich Schütz," *Neue Zeitschrift für Musik* 123 [1962], pp.120–21). Unfortunately all indications of when and in what context this note arose and on what source it was based are missing. Objectively, it is unlikely. The reputation of Friedrich Ludwig

(1872–1930) seemed to Trumpff (as it has to certain other more recent authors) to demand that any such allusion associated with his name be taken seriously. It is more likely, however, that Ludwig himself, a master of exacting documentary research, would have been extremely surprised that such unverifiable information was believed for so long.

8. Hans Joachim Moser, *Heinrich Schütz—Sein Leben und Werk,* 2nd ed. (Kassel: Bärenreiter, 1954), pp. 141–42. Translated by Carl F. Pfatteicher (St Louis: Concordia, 1959), pp. 157–59.

9. Rudolph Henning, "Zur Textfrage der 'Musikalische Exequien' von Heinrich Schütz," *Sagittarius* 4 (1973), p. 48. Concerning the coffin itself, the remarkable situation exists that it is preserved and its resting place known—the crypt of the Salvatorkirche in Gera—but because of the architectural situation it is not accessible. (For more detail, see Henning, pp. 45f.) As a result of the thorough description in the *Abdruck,* however, it is unlikely that any surprises would be encountered if the original inscriptions could be studied directly on the coffin. The specifications of the *Abdruck* are in any case verified by two photographs of the coffin from the year 1921 (reproduction in Henning, following p. 56, and in Horn, Graulich, and Hofmann, preface, p. xlv).

10. Henning, "Zur Textfrage," p. 53.

11. Ibid., p. 50.

12. Our enumeration of the segments, which is oriented toward the textual units, differs from that of the Stuttgarter Schütz-Ausgabe, which is based on musical criteria (not explained in the foreword and not made entirely clear) and arrives at a total of twenty-seven segments.

13. Only at the beginning of the chorale movement *Er ist das Heil und ewig Licht* is the basso continuo treated independently.

14. We proceed in this respect from the version of the thoroughbass transposed to E. In order to avoid a sharp in the signature, the vocal parts are transposed a fourth higher to A.

15. The close of the second Kyrie on A might be the result of the revision process. In any case Schütz, as he set the succeeding verse, *Leben wir, so leben wir dem Herren,* appears to have proceeded from a preceding cadence on E; the continuo's unthematic bridge passage with which this section begins gives the impression of a later addition.

16. See the interpretations of Rudolf Gerber ("Die 'Musikalische Exequien' von Heinrich Schütz" *Musik und Kirche* 6 [1934], pp. 296–310), Hans Joachim Moser (*Heinrich Schütz*), Gerhard Mittring ("Totendienst und Christuspredigt—Zum Text der Musikalischen Exequien von Heinrich Schütz" in *Musik als Lobgesang—Festschrift für Wilhelm Ehmann* [Darmstadt, 1964]), and Otto Brodde (*Heinrich Schütz—Weg und Werke,* 2nd ed. [Kassel: Bärenreiter, 1972], pp. 137–48).

Literature on the *Musikalische Exequien*

Bolin, Norbert. *"Sterben ist mein Gewinn"—Ein Beitrag zur evangelischen Funeralkomposition der deutschen Sepulkralkultur des Barock 1550–1750.* Dissertation, Cologne, 1984 (typescript).
Brodde, Otto. *Heinrich Schütz—Weg und Werk,* pp. 137–48. 2nd ed. Kassel: Bärenreiter, 1972.
Eggebrecht, Hans Heinrich. "Heinrich Schütz." *Musicological Annual* 8 (Ljubljana, 1972), pp. 17–39. Reprinted in H. H. Eggebrecht, *Sinn und Gehalt—Aufsätze zur musikalischen Analyse,* pp. 106–39. Taschenbücher zur Musikwissenschaft, no. 58. Wilhelmshaven: Heinrichschofen, 1979.
Gerber, Rudolf. "Die 'Musikalische Exequien' von Heinrich Schütz." *Musik und Kirche* 6 (1934), pp. 296–310.

Henning, Rudolf. "Zur Textfrage der 'Musikalische Exequien' von Heinrich Schütz." *Sagittarius* 4 (1973), pp. 44–56.

Horn, Paul, Graulich, Günter, and Hofman, Klaus. Preface to *Musikalische Exequien,* by Heinrich Schütz. Stuttgarter Schütz-Ausgabe, no. 8. Neuhausen-Stuttgart: Hänssler Verlag, 1973.

Krause-Graumnitz, Heinz. "Heinrich Schütz' schöpferische Gestaltung der zyklischen Großform, dargestellt an seinen 'Musikalischen Exequien' des Jahres 1636." In *Heinrich Schütz und seine Zeit—Bericht über die wissenschaftliche Konferenz des Komitees für die Heinrich-Schütz-Festtage der DDR 1972,* pp. 38–49. Edited by Seigfried Köhler. Berlin, 1974. Reprinted in *Heinrich Schütz in seiner Zeit,* pp. 344–57. Edited by Walter Blankenburg. Wege der Forschung, vol. 614. Darmstadt: Wissenschaftliche Buchgesellschaft, 1985.

Mittring, Gerhard. "Totendienst und Christuspredigt—Zum Text der Musikalischen Exequien von Heinrich Schütz." In *Musik als Lobgesang—Festschrift für Wilhelm Ehmann.* Darmstadt, 1964.

Moser, Hans Joachim. *Heinrich Schütz—Sein Leben und Werk,* pp. 138–42, 418–20. 2nd edition. Kassel: Bärenreiter, 1954. Translated by Carl F. Pfatteicher as *Heinrich Schütz. His Life and Works.* St. Louis: Concordia, 1959.

Nowak, Adolf. "Trauermusik und Trauerrede—Zur musikalischen Werkgestalt in der Exequien-Tradition." In *Das musikalische Kunstwerk: Geschichte, Ästhetik, Theorie—Festschrift Carl Dahlhaus zum 60. Geburtstag,* pp. 373–84. Edited by Hermann Danuser, Helga de la Motte-Haber, Silke Leopold, and Norbert Miller. Laaber, West Germany: Laaber-Verlag, 1988.

Rifkin, Joshua. "Heinrich Schütz." *The New Grove Dictionary of Music and Musicians,* ed. Stanley Sadie (London: Macmillan,, 1980), vol. 17, pp. 1–37.

Schöneich, Friedrich. "Zum Aufbau des Gloria-Teils in Schützens Musikalischen Exequien." *Musik und Kirche* 20 (1950), pp. 182–90.

Trumpff, Gustav Adolf. "Die 'Musicalischen Exequien' von Heinrich Schütz." *Neue Zeitschrift für Musik* 123 (1962), pp. 120–23.

Wessely, Othmar. "Der Fürst und der Tod." In *Beiträge 1974/75,* pp. 60–71. Edited by the Osterreich-ischen Gesellschaft für Musik. Reprint edition in *Heinrich Schütz in seiner Zeit,* pp. 329–43. Edited by Walter Blankenburg. Wege der Forschung, vol. 614. Darmstadt: Wissenschaftliche Buchgesellschaft, 1985.

7

Hamburg Opera during Buxtehude's Lifetime: The Works of Johann Wolfgang Franck

George J. Buelow

When Christoph Wolff published his perceptive iconographical interpretation of a painting owned since the 1970s by the Museum für Hamburgische Geschichte,[1] he not only proved the existence of a previously unknown and unique portrait of Dietrich Buxtehude, but he also gave evidence for new speculation concerning Buxtehude's career. The canvas, which was entitled simply *The Music Party* in an American sales catalogue, shows five performing musicians and three other figures in a typical seventeenth-century pose of *Hausmusik*. The central figure at the harpsichord, clothed in an elegant oriental gown, can be identified as Johann Adam Reinken. The figure to Reinken's right, Wolff established, is Buxtehude, shown with a sheet of music paper bearing a canon with a dedication to the *Bruderschaft* of Reinken and Buxtehude. The canon's text is drawn from the opening to Psalm 133: "Behold how good and pleasant it is when brothers dwell in unity."

The painting places the thirty-seven-year-old Buxtehude in the company of his friend Reinken as well as probably Johann Theile, perhaps the composer of the canon, who may be the gambist in the group of performing musicians. This suggests that Buxtehude was at this date in Hamburg with his friends, two of the founding members of the Hamburg opera at the Gänsemarkt. The portrait of Buxtehude shows him rather dreamy-eyed and elegantly dressed, an artist's representation that seems far removed from our usual concept of the Lübeck organist, devout church musician, who apparently wrote little important secular vocal music. Since the painting bears a date of 1674, four years before the opening of the Hamburg opera, it appears that the early development of this most significant German operatic venture may have been another reason to draw Buxtehude to Hamburg from Lübeck. While there is considerable documentation of important musicians who traveled to Lübeck for visits with Buxtehude, previously only one trip to Hamburg by Buxtehude has been documented, to inspect Arp Schnitger's new organ at St. Nicholaus's Church, in May 1687.[2] Therefore, this painting raises the likely possibility that Buxtehude had experienced operatic music over a period of time in Hamburg. This in turn suggests that the music of Hamburg opera may have relevance for the study of Buxtehude's career and his developing musical style.

Opera in Hamburg in the Seventeenth Century

Hamburg became the first city outside of Italy to possess a public opera house on 2 January 1678. The city was especially appropriate for such an artistic venture. Not only was Hamburg called the "Venice of the North," but in the later seventeenth century it became the largest as well as the most cosmopolitan metropolis in northern Europe. Hamburg was the only important city in Germany to remain untouched by the Thirty Years War. Its earlier role as a member of the Hanseatic League and its favorable geographical position on the Elbe river with its access to the North Sea and the Baltic made the city-state a major commercial seaport. Hamburg's more or less liberal political climate attracted a multinational community. Large numbers of political and religious refugees from southern Germany as well as Dutch, English, Spanish, Portuguese, and Jewish emigrants populated the city. To its population of some 70,000 were added numerous transients entering the port of Hamburg, and this international milieu—not unlike Venice's own population—seemed particularly suited to an operatic enterprise. Of the four public opera theaters built in northern Germany in the seventeenth century—at Hanover, Braunschweig, Leipzig, and Hamburg—the latter had the largest theater and served as a model for the other three.

Hamburg's opera was founded and directed for almost thirty years by Gerhard Schott (1641–1702), a lawyer and member of a well-known Hamburg patrician family. In his extensive European travels he may have learned in Venice his skills for organizing and funding a major operatic venture. Schott formed a partnership with another lawyer and later Hamburg mayor, Peter Lütkens, as well as with Johann Reinken, famed organist at St. Catherine's Church. The Venetian architect, Girolamo Sartorio, was summoned to the city to design the theater which was constructed on rented land on the Gänsemarkt, between the present-day opera house and the Binnenalster. The original motivation for an opera as well as some financial backing may have come from Duke Christian Albrecht of Holstein-Gottorp, who lived in exile in the city from 1675 to 1679. He had a known passion for opera, and his court composer, Johann Theile, came with him. Theile was the first Hamburg opera *Kapellmeister* and also the composer of the first opera for that theater.

Opera became a major facet of the cultural and social image of the city.

The season ran from January through December, with closings normally only for Lent, other church holidays, and the summer months. Performances took place on Monday, Wednesday, and Thursday afternoons. And though information regarding repertory for the first decades is sketchy or nonexistent, from 1695 it is known that at least 100 performances were held in any one year, with an average of five new productions each season. As the only accessible public opera in northern Europe where one could experience the most innovative and "modern" musical compositions, Hamburg no doubt attracted not only royalty, aristocrats, politicians, upperclass businessmen and professionals, but also many performing musicians and composers. Even after Hanover (in 1689), Braunschweig (in 1690), and Leipzig (in 1693) opened their commercial opera houses, Hamburg remained the most important center for operatic performance in northern Europe until it faltered and finally closed after sixty years in 1738.[3]

Repertory in the Seventeenth Century

The annual repertory of the Hamburg opera in the seventeenth century is still not established in accurate detail even though we have recourse to the list published by Johann Mattheson in *Der musicalische Patriot* in 1728. Mattheson's information is incomplete and may be inaccurate in some details, since his own relationship with the opera began only in the last decade of the century; nevertheless, much can be extracted from it regarding the nature of opera during Buxtehude's career in Lübeck. During the first decade of performances, when Buxtehude could have been most influenced by Hamburg musical developments, the most important composers were Nicolaus Adam Strungk and Johann Wolfgang Franck. The later 1680s were dominated by Johann Philipp Förtsch and the early 1690s by Johann Georg Conradi. With the exceptions of a performance of Lully's *Acis et Galatée* in 1689 and the Lully-Colasse *Achilles et Polixène* in 1692, all operas were by German composers and sung in German. In 1693 the first Italian works appeared on the Gänsemarkt stage: Cesti's opera, *La schiava fortunata*, in an arrangement by Gianettini and a work by Pallavicino. There were important works by Johann Sigismund Kusser, who at that time became the second director of the theater. The century closed with operas by Steffani and the first of many by Reinhard Keiser, the latter becoming the dominant figure in the opera's musical and financial fortunes in the first decades of the eighteenth century.

Johann Mattheson, an ardent supporter of Hamburg opera, first as a singer and then as a composer, later said of opera: "In my modest opinion a good opera theater is nothing less than an advanced school of many of the fine arts, including together and all at once architecture, perspective, painting, mechanics, the art of dance, *Actio oratoria*, morals, history, poetry, and most especially music."[4] If Buxtehude attended this so-called advanced school, we may find in what has been preserved of the operatic "curricula" in the seventeenth century some of the musical knowledge he himself may have assimilated.

The Operas of Johann Wolfgang Franck

Among the few scores and aria collections still extant from the seventeenth century for Hamburg, valuable clues to the music can be found in works by Franck, Conradi, and Kusser. The earliest known complete manuscript score of an opera written for Hamburg is the *Ariadne* of Johann Georg Conradi (see the year 1691 in Mattheson's repertory list),[5] arias from Kusser's opera *Erindo*[6] remain as well as for his *Ariadne*,[7] although the latter does not seem to have had a performance at Hamburg. Kusser's distinguished talents received praise from Mattheson, but he represents a second generation both as composer and director, and he probably came to Hamburg too late to have had any decisive musical impact upon Buxtehude. Of much greater likelihood is a relationship both personal and musical between Buxtehude and Johann Wolfgang Franck.

From many of his operas composed for Hamburg, aria collections are preserved for *Aeneas* (1680), *Diocletian* (1682), *Vespasian* (1683), and the two-part *Cara Mustapha* (1686), Franck's last opera composed for Hamburg. Although the music in these collections generally shows strong ties to Venetian operatic models, there are many stylistic features contributing to an overall impression of what can only be described as German.

The lyrical pieces in these operas can be classified by type. Some are based on stylized dance rhythms, and these often combine at the same time more-or-less popular or folk like tunes. A second type, more sophisticated in structures, can best be called Lieder. In these the melodic style often suggests the spirit if not also the content of the German chorale. Both of these types frequently employ strophic poems of several verses. A third kind of aria, usually longer and with a tempo and character indication of adagio, engages effective dissonances and dramatic melodic gestures, rhetorical outbursts usually expressing tragic or other kinds of sad affections. These remind one frequently of the Venetian *lamento* tradition, but despite the formulaic concept, the melodic realization lacks what might be described as an Italianate vocal allure. Here as in other types of arias the impression remains that though Franck was familiar with and had absorbed Venetian operatic conventions, ultimately his musical style was in spirit German, not Italian.

Franck's arias, similar to those often found in Venetian operas, often end with instrumental postludes that may repeat the final phrase or phrases of the melodic material. None examined for this study begin either with an instrumental or continuo statement of the opening vocal motive, a style that seems less progressive for opera arias written in the 1680s. Franck seems to be the first

Hamburg composer to accompany arias at times with orchestral instruments, sometimes using short, concerted interjections to highlight a vocal motive or particular expressiveness. This technique has much in common with arias by Venetian composers such as Sartorio, Legrenzi, and Pietro Andrea Ziani. Franck also knew about the Italian fondness for trumpet obbligatos, and these appear in the aria collections.

The melodic writing, when it is not simple Lied or in the style of a folksong can be complex and difficult to sing because of its angularity. Many of the rather long melismatic passages seem more instrumental than vocal in character, a trait that can also be found in Venetian arias from this period. Worthy of a separate study is Franck's harmonic language, the richness of which can be surmised from the numerous figures given in the printed continuo parts. Highly expressive unprepared seconds, sevenths, and ninths are common, as is Franck's frequent recourse to sudden shifts from major to minor for rhetorical impact. While there are few examples in the collections of ostinato basses, when they appear they resemble similar ostinatos found in Venetian opera. However, the slightly later German fondness for ostinatos and pseudo—or freely employed— ostinato motives characteristic of operas by Kusser, Mattheson, Keiser, and early Handel scores, seems uncharacteristic of Franck's works.

Franck combined the form and spirit of the German Lied and the chorale tradition, German folksong elements, as well as wide-ranging style traits of Venetian opera into music not only of solid craftsmanship, but also of originality and vocal beauty. He was clearly a major force in the developing concept of German opera. Like so much music from this period of the seventeenth century, it looks deceptively simple on the page, and only through performance does it suggest its effectiveness and the reasons for its popularity with Hamburg audiences. The following selection of examples can only hint at the musical significance Franck's scores many have had for Buxtehude.

Like the music found in Venetian operas of this period, Franck's scores have many simple songs or Lieder that are often based on popular tunes and popular dance rhythms. The following examples show the opening phrases for three pieces of this type of dance-oriented song. Example 7.1, *Schleppt ihn* from *Vespasian,* typifies the conventional use of the gigue rhythm, pervasive in Venetian as well as German opera. Example 7.2, *Weichet, nur weichet,* from *Diocletian,* has the common rhythmic character of the forlana. Example 7.3, *O blinde Göttin* from *Diocletian,* has another of the cliché rhythmic devices, the sarabande, familiar in so many vocal and instrumental contexts throughout the seventeenth and early eighteenth centuries.

Example 7.4 shows the opening of the aria *Was ist der verliebten Leben?* from *Aeneas,* the earliest extant music of a Hamburg opera by Franck. This Lied-like aria is through-composed, but has elements of structural coherence in its repetitions of melodic motives and a distinctive hemiola cadence (see m. 3).

Example 7.1. Johann Wolfgang Franck, *Schleppt ihn* from *Vespasian*

Schleppt_____ ihn, schleppt   ihn,   wo   der   Ty - ber

Wel - len aus den fris - che U - fern Quel - - - - len aus

Example 7.2. Franck, *Weichet, nur weichet* from *Diocletian*

Wei- chet nur wei- chet ihr rei- zen - de Trie- be   weil ich ohn'

Hoff- nung und Tro- ste jetzt bin   wenn ich muss mis- sen die

Ster- nen der Lie- be   fall ich ohn Füh- rer fall

#6

Example 7.3.   Franck, *O blinde Göttin* from *Diocletian*

Example 7.4.   Franck, *Was ist der verliebten Leben?* from *Aeneas*

Example 7.5.   Franck, *Ist der Glück mir ganz zu wieder* from *Diocletian*

Example 7.5, from the opening part to a strophic Lied from *Diocletian, Ist der Glück mir ganz zu wieder,* typifies another characteristic Lied style in Franck's works, those with apparent relationship to the *Geistliche Lieder* tradition. The opening melodic gesture can also be found as a feature of several of Franck's *Geistliche Lieder* to texts by Elmenhorst.[8] And this Lied appears to be an adaptation or variation on a chorale melody.

A tragic text inspires all Baroque composers to their most intensely expressive musical ideas, and Franck's operas offer many such examples. In triple meter, marked adagio, some of these arias are accompanied by violins and many of them in binary or ternary forms have great length. Example 7.6, *Schickung ach! es ist zu viel,* from *Cara Mustapha* shows some of these features. It is long by Franck's standards (59 measures) and requires repetition for its strophic text, making it a focal point of the act.

Example 7.7 is also in the same genre as the preceding, and presents a fine example of Franck's expressive vocal style, in which he adapts the Italianate dramatic vocal melismas. He creates a tight musical structure through the repetition of these melismas, but also through the frequent repetition in the voice part and the continuo bass line of the opening melodic motive to *Ihr treulose.*

Example 7.8 illustrates one of the less frequent uses in these operas by Franck of the popular Venetian technique of a basso ostinato aria. The ostinato is not employed rigorously, but breaks off to permit the aria to have a contrasting middle section. There is also in this example further illustration of rather awkward vocal writing on long melismas.

Franck's talent for creating a variety of lyrical and dramatic aria forms can

Example 7.6.   Franck, *Schickung ach! es ist zu viel* from *Cara Mustapha*

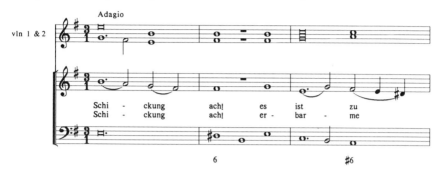

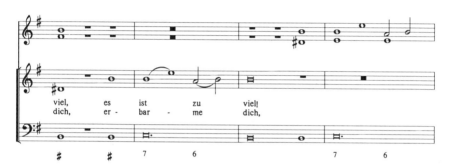

Example 7.7. Franck, *Ihr treulose Himmelsstrahlen*

be seen throughout these aria collections. Not only did he contribute significantly to a major corpus of *Geistliche Lieder,* but he became an important influence in Hamburg, with the performance of many operas during the first decade of the Gänsemarkt theater's history. His music has an inherent German quality, partly the result of employing a melodic style associated with German Lieder, but also with illusions to if not the actual use of chorale tunes. While Franck writes within the parameters of Venetian operatic concepts of the mid-seventeenth century, the result is nevertheless a Hamburg interpretation of Italian or, more exactly, Venetian achievements in those popular musical styles developed for opera. The mold was formed in Venice but the spirit and musical

Example 7.8. Franck, *Eitel ists dem Glücke glauben*

realization changed in its transplantation to the north of Europe. Just exactly what Buxtehude may have thought of these musical developments and how they may have affected his own musical style remains to be considered. It would seem that he must have been impressed by the musicality, popularity, and theatrical excitement he witnessed in Hamburg in the 1680s.

Appendix: Opera in Hamburg in the Seventeenth Century

Year	Composer	Opera
1678	Johann Theile	Der erschaffene, gefallene und wieder aufgerichtete Mensch, Adam und Eva
"		Orontes
	Nikolaus A. Strungk	Der glücklich steigende Sejanus
"		Der unglücklich fallende Sejanus
1679	Johann W. Franck	Die wohl und beständig liebende Michal oder der siegende und fliehende David
"		Die errettete Unschuld oder Andromeda und Perseus
"		Die Macchabaeische Mutter mit ihren sieben Söhnen
"		Don Pedro oder die abgestrafte Eifersucht
1680	Johann W. Franck	Aeneae des Trojanischen Fürsten Ankunft in Italien
	Nikolaus A. Strungk	Die liebreiche durch Tugend und Schönheit erhöhete Esther
"		Doris oder der königliche Sklave
"		Die drei Töchter des Cecrops [or by J. W. Franck, first perf. Ansbach 1679]
"		Alceste [or by J. W. Franck?]
	Johann W. Franck	Jodelet oder Sein selbst Gefangener
1681	Johann Theile	Die Geburt Christi
	Johann W. Franck	Semele
"		Hannibal
"		Charitine oder Göttlich-Geliebte
1682	Johann W. Franck	Diocletianus
"		Attila
1683	Johann W. Franck	Vespianus [or 1681?]
	Nikolaus A. Strungk	Theseus
"		Semiramis Die aller-erste regierende Königin [or by J. W. Franck?]
"		Floretto
1684	Johann Philipp Förtsch	Der hochmütige gestürzte und wieder erhobene Crösus
"		Das unmöglichste Ding
1685	[Theater closed]	
1686	Johann W. Franck	Der glückliche Grossvesier Cara Mustapha, I
"		Der unglückliche Cara Mustapha, II
1687	[Theater closed]	
1688	Johann P. Förtsch	Alexander in Sidon

Year	Composer	Opera
	"	*Die heilige Eugenia*
	"	*Der in Christentum bis in den Tod beständige Märtyrer Polyeuct* [or 1689?]
1689	Johann P. Förtsch	*Der mächtige Monarch der Perser, Xerxes in Abyus*
	"	*Cain und Abel*
	"	*Das betrübte und erfreute Cimbria*
	J. B. Lully	*Acis et Galathé*
1690	Johann P. Förtsch	*Die grossmächtige Thalestris, oder letzte Königin der Amazonen*
	"	*Ancile Romanum das ist des Römischen Reiches Glücks-Schild*
	"	*Bajazeth und Tamerlan*
	"	*Der irrende Ritter Don Quixotte de la Mancia*
1691	Johann Georg Conradi	*Ariadne*
	"	*Diogenes cynicus*
	"	*Numa Pompilius*
1692	Johann G. Conradi	*Carolus Magnus*
	"	*Jerusalem I. Teil: Die Eroberung des Tempels*
	"	*Jerusalem II. Teil: Die Eroberung der Burg Sion*
	[Lully]-Colasse	*Achille et Polixène*
1693	Johann G. Conradi	*Sigismundus*
	"	*Gensericus, der grosse König der afrikanischen Wenden*
	A. Gianettini [Cesti]	*La schiava fortunata* (in Italian)
	Georg Bronner	*Echo und Narcissus*
	Johann G. Conradi	*Pygmalion*
	Carlo Pallavicino	*La Gerusalemme liberata* (in Italian)
	Johann S. Kusser	*Erindo, oder die unsträfliche Liebe*
1694	Georg Bronner	*Venus oder die siegende Liebe*
	Johann S. Kusser	*Der durch Grossmut und Tapferkeit besiegte Porus*
	Reinhard Keiser	*Der königliche Schäfer oder Basilius in Arkadien*
	Johann Philipp Krieger	*Wettstreit der Treue*
	"	*Hercules unter der Amazonen, I & II*
	Johann S. Kusser	*Pyramus und Thisbe, getreue und festgebundene Liebe*
1695	A. Gianettini	*Medea in Atene* (in German)
	Johann S. Kusser	*Scipio Africanus* [or 1694?]
	A. Gianettini	*Die wiedergefundene Hermione*
	Agostino Steffani	*Der hochmüthige Alexander*
	C. Pallavicino	*Armida* [= *Gerusalemme liberata*] (in German)
	J. B. Lully	*Acis und Galathee* (in German)

Year	Composer	Opera
1696	Agostino Steffani	*Der grossmütige Roland*
	Reinhard Keiser	*Mahumet II*
	A. Steffani	*Heinrich der Löwe*
	A. Steffani [?]	*Der siegende Alcides*
1697	Reinhard Keiser	*Der geliebte Adonis*
	A. Steffani	*Der in seiner Freiheit vergnügte Alcibiades*
	Johann S. Kusser	*Jason* [or 1695?]
1698	Reinhard Keiser	*Der bei dem allgemeinen Welt-Frieden von dem grossen Augustus geschlossene Tempel des Janus*
	"	*Irene*
	A. Steffani	*Der vereinigten Mitbuhler oder die siegenden Atalanta*
	Reinhard Keiser	*Der aus Hyperboreen nach Cymbrien überbrachte güldene Apfel* [not 1699]
1699	Johann Mattheson	*Die Plejades oder das Sieben-Gestirne*
	Reinhard Keiser	*Ismene*
	"	*Die wunderbar errettet Iphigenie*
	"	*Die Verbindung des grossen Herkules mit der schönen Hebe*
	"	*Die Wiederkehr der güldenen Zeit*
	A. Steffani	*Il trionfo del fato, oder das mächtige Geschick bei Lavinia und Dido*

Repertory according to J. Mattheson, *Der musicalische Patriot* (Hamburg, 1728), pp. 177–86. Titles according to R. Brockpähler, *Handbuch zur Geschichte der Barockoper in Deutschland* (Emsdetten: Lechte 1964), pp. 200–204.

Notes

1. Christoph Wolff, "Das Hamburger Buxtehude-Bild," in *800 Jahre Musik in Lübeck,* eds. Antjekathrin Graßman and Werner Neugebauer (Lübeck: Der Senat der Hansestadt Lübeck, 1982), p. 64.

2. For further information concerning Hamburg and Buxtehude's relationship to the city and its music see Kerala J. Snyder, *Dieterich Buxtehude, Organist in Lübeck* (New York: Schirmer 1987), pp. 107–20.

3. Hellmuth Christian Wolff's dissertation completed in the 1930s remains the best general study of opera in Hamburg during the Baroque. It was subsequently published as *Die Barockoper in Hamburg,* 2 vols. (Wolfenbüttel: Möseler, 1957).

4. Johann Mattheson, *Die neueste Untersuchung der Singspiele* (Hamburg, 1744), p. 84: "Meines wenigen Erachtens ist ein gutes Operntheater nicht anders, als eine hohe Schule vieler schönen Wissenshaften worinn zusammen und auf einmal Architecture, Perspective, Mahlerey, Mechanik, Tanzkunst, Actio oratoria, Moral, Historie, Poesie, und vornehmlich Musik. . . ."

5. See the author's *"Die schöne und getreue Ariadne,* A Lost Opera by J. G. Conradi Rediscovered," in *Acta musicologica* 44 (1972), pp. 108–21.

6. Published in a modern edition in *Das Erbe deutscher Musik,* zweite Reihe: *Schleswig-Holstein und Hansestädte,* vol. 3 (Braunschweig: Henry Litolff, 1938).

7. *J. S. Coussers Heliconische Musen-Lust, bestehend in einigen Arien aus der Opera: Ariadne* (Stuttgart, 1700).

8. The Elmenhorst Lieder in settings by Franck are reprinted in *M. Heinrich Elmenhorsts . . . geistreiche Lieder, Denkmäler deutscher Tonkunst,* vol 45 (Leipzig: Breitkopf & Härtel, 1911).

8

Lutheran Vespers as a Context for Music

Robin A. Leaver

To speak about the "vesper service," as if there was but one basic liturgical order followed in the orthodox Lutheran churches of northern Germany around the end of the seventeenth century, is perhaps a little misleading. In fact, there were many different types of vesper services; they were held daily, Monday to Friday, throughout the week, on Saturdays, on the eves of major festivals and on saints days, as well as on Sundays, when there could be as many as three different types of vesper services, variously called *Betstunde, Katechismusexamen, Vesperpredigt,* or *Vespergottesdienst.* Each type of vesper service offered a different context for music.[1] This ranged from the simple plainsong psalm-tones and basic hymnody of the daily services to the concerted complexities of choral music with orchestral accompaniment performed at vespers on the major feast days. But before this rich variety of later practice can be explored, the origins of the basic tradition need to be examined.

The Lutheran vespers tradition has its roots in the canonical hours, or daily offices, of pre-Reformation monasticism. Throughout each twenty-four hours, at three-hourly intervals, there were the eight offices of matins, lauds, prime, terce, sext, none, vespers, and compline. They were prayer services primarily based on the chanting of the psalms, together with their antiphons and responsories. Indeed, in the course of every week the whole of the psalter, all 150 psalms, was sung in these services spaced three hours apart. Each service also had its own office hymn which might either be an invariable text, such as *Te lucis ante terminum* at compline, or a *de tempore* hymn which reflected the season or festival of the church year. Of the eight canonical hours, matins and vespers—the principal morning and evening services—assumed priority and importance over the other six. For example, it was incumbent upon secular, parish clergy to say matins and vespers in addition to saying mass each day.

When Luther and his colleagues came to reform the patterns of worship of the churches in Wittenberg and elsewhere, they were critical of the unreformed attitude which regarded these services merely as priestly duty, a duty, moreover, that went largely unfulfilled. For example, in the preface to the Saxon *Kirchenordnung,* first issued in 1539 and signed by such colleagues of Luther as Jonas, Spalatin, and Cruciger, the following is related: "See how they [the papists] laugh at their own canonical hours. One of them said to another, 'I do not have much money or corn, but I do have certain debts and several barns full of unprayed vespers and matins.'"[2] Liturgical reform in Wittenberg began with the abandonment of daily mass, for which Luther substituted revised forms of matins and vespers. However, these services were not considered as priestly duty but rather as communal acts of worship and devotion. They were public services of worship for lay people as well as for clergy, as the title of Luther's small pamphlet dealing with this subject makes clear: *Von ordenung gottis diensts ynn der gemeyne* [Of the order of worship in the congregation], 1523.[3] These weekday services, which each lasted one hour, were introduced in Wittenberg on 23 March 1523. Matins began at 4:00 or 5:00 A.M. and had the following order: Old Testament Lesson (one or two chapters, read consecutively from day to day); Sermon (on the lesson); Collect; Psalmody. Vespers was held at five or six in the evening and had the same structure as matins, except that the lesson was taken from the New Testament, so that there would be, to quote Luther, "reading, interpreting, praising, singing, and praying just as in the morning."[4] Each section had clear musical implications. Concerning the lesson, Luther states that it should be "read, either by pupils or priests, or whoever it may be, in the same manner as the lesson is still read at [unreformed] matins; this should be done by one or two, or by one individual or choir responding to the other, as may seem suitable."[5] In other words, the biblical lessons are to be chanted to the traditional lectionary tones,[6] sung either by various individual voices or groups of singers. The function of the sermon was to explain the meaning of the lesson, so that it would be understood as well as heard. "If this is not done," says Luther, "the congregation is not benefited by the lesson, as has been the case in cloisters and in convents, where they only bawled [the lesson] against the walls."[7] On Sundays at mass and vespers "there should be preaching for the whole congregation, in the morning on the Gospel for the day, in the evening on the Epistle,"[8] and this became the almost invariable practice of later Lutheran Sunday preaching. The collect is connected to the chants of the day: every morning the pastor "shall appoint a fitting responsory or antiphon with a collect, likewise for the evening: this is to be read and chanted publicly after the lesson and exposition."[9] Luther explains the psalmody thus: "Now when the lesson and its interpretation have lasted half an hour or so, the congregation shall unite in giving thanks to God, in praising him, and in praying for the fruits of the Word, etc. For this, the psalms should be used and some good responsories and antiphons."[10] The implication is that there should be half-an-hour of psalm-singing, with the psalms sung to the traditional psalm-tones. What is somewhat revolutionary here is that Luther apparently intended that the whole congregation should sing the traditional psalm-tones, something that only priests, monks, and nuns had done hitherto. There may have been some difficulty in actually getting the Wittenberg congregations to sing these traditional psalm-chants. It needs to be born in mind that this congregational form of daily worship was introduced in the early spring of 1523. Within six months Luther had created the metrical psalm,[11] that is, the biblical psalm rendered into strophic poetry, which is much easier for a congregation to sing, especially a congregation for whom such singing was something of a novelty. But here are the beginnings of the Lutheran tradition of congregational song, the chorale from which developed a rich heritage of choral, organ, and instrumental music.

With these liturgical reforms Luther established the basic elements of the later Lutheran vespers tradition. First, it was essentially a musical order of worship in which traditional plainchant was to continue. Luther states categorically: "Let the chants in the Sunday masses and vespers be retained; they are quite good and are taken from Scripture."[12] Second, the congregation was expected to articulate its prayer and praise in corporate song. Third, with this openness to both traditional chant, on the one hand, and to newly introduced congregational singing on the other, a liturgical environment was created in which organ and choral music could freely develop. Fourth, in contrast to monastic vespers, in which the biblical lections were generally confined to a few verses, substantial portions of Scripture were not only to be read but also expounded and explained in sermons. Indeed, as far as Luther was concerned, if there was no preaching there could be no vespers.[13]

This 1523 pamphlet was written in German and, since it also calls for congregational psalmody, the implication is that these daily services would have been in the vernacular. However, the possibility of employing Latin was not excluded, as is made clear in Luther's *Formula missae et communionis pro Ecclesia Vuittembergensi,* issued later in the same year. In his words on matins and vespers Luther largely repeats what he had said in the earlier German pamphlet, but there is also some new material. For example, he has a particular suggestion regarding the number of psalms sung at these services: "the bishop may reduce the great length [of the services] according to his own judgment so that three psalms may be sung for matins and three for vespers with one or two responsories."[14] This represents a significant reduction in the psalmody. Previously matins had nine psalms and eight responsories, and vespers and compline had eight psalms and one responsory. At first Luther wanted his congregations to sing the traditional psalm-tones, but this was obviously proving to be somewhat difficult, and he was already thinking towards metrical psalmody and strophic hymnody. However, the practice of chanting the psalms was not to be lost to emerging Lutheranism because Luther saw that such psalmody had educational as well as spiritual benefits. Therefore the pupils of the parish schools should take part in the daily matins and vespers. Luther states: "And it is seemly, nay necessary, that the boys should get accustomed to reading and hearing the psalms and lessons from Holy Scripture."[15] The role of the school choir, or *Kantorei* in the liturgy was given particular attention in subsequent months and years in Wittenberg and elsewhere. Luther, in the *Formula missae,* also speaks of retaining the response, *Deo gratias,* at the end of the services, and does so in the general context of congregational hymnody.[16] Earlier in the *Formula missae* he had expressed the desire for as many vernacular hymns as possible for the people to sing in the reformed mass. But as they had yet to be written, he suggested that in the meantime a number of older *Leisen,* such as *Gott sei gelobet und gebenedeiet* and *Nun bitten wir den Heiligen Geist,* could be sung with profit, but the real need was for "German poets to compose evangelical hymns for us."[17] Interestingly in Speratus's German translation of the *Formula missae,* made under Luther's supervision in Wittenberg and issued the following year, 1524, the phrase is expanded to read: "German poets *and musicians* [are needed] to compose evangelical hymns for us."[18]

Over the next months, that is, approximately from mid-1523 to mid-1524, Luther and his colleagues were feverishly at work writing vernacular metrical psalms and hymns for congregational use. However, Luther's first hymnal was not a congregational collection. It was rather a set of part-books for choir use with polyphonic settings of thirty-eight of the hymns that were then being introduced, together with five Latin motets, composed by Johann Walter under Luther's supervision: *Geystliche gesangk Buchleyn,* Wittenberg 1524, the so-called *Chorgesangbuch.* Luther's policy at this stage seems to have been that the hymns would initially be taught in the schools, first from the tenor part-book which contained most of the melodies, then the complete cantus firmus polyphonic settings in three to five voices. When they had been mastered in the school they were sung in the liturgy, as the *Graduallied* in the reformed mass and as the *Hauptlied* in Sunday vespers, in alternation with the congregation, which sang the alternate stanzas in unison supported by the choir. At this stage the congregation used broadsheet copies of the hymns, but within a matter of months a congregational hymnal was issued in Wittenberg containing all the hymns of Walter's *Chorgesangbuch,* together with their associated melodies.[19]

Towards the end of 1525, or early in 1526, Luther issued his *Deudsche Messe vnd ordnung Gottisdiensts,* his German liturgical provisions which were meant to complement rather than replace the *Formula missae.* The pupils from the schools, that is, those who would primarily form the liturgical choir or *Kantorei,* were to play a leading role at matins and vespers. Luther's purpose was partly didactic: "This is what we do to train the boys and pupils in the

Bible."[20] Earlier in the *Deudsche Messe* Luther had reflected on the need for Christian education within the context of worship: "The German service needs a plain and simple, fair and square catechism . . . namely, in these three parts, the Ten Commandments, the Creed, and the Our Father. These three plainly and briefly contain exactly everything that a Christian needs to know. This instruction must be given . . . from the pulpit at stated times."[21] Although the context of vespers is not specifically stated here, once Luther had published his *Small Catechism* in 1529, it became customary to preach on the Catechism at vespers, especially on Sundays.

In the *Deudsche Messe* Luther also outlines the daily services, which remain substantially the same as earlier, except that the New Testament is read in the morning and the Old Testament in the afternoon:

> Likewise at vespers they [the schoolboys] sing a few of the vesper psalms in Latin with an antiphon, as heretofore, followed by a [Latin] hymn if one is available. Again two or three boys in turn then read a chapter from the Latin Old Testament or half of one, depending on length. Another boy reads the same chapter in German. The *Magnificat* follows in Latin with an antiphon or [German] hymn, the Lord's Prayer said silently, and the collects with the *Benedecamus*. This is the daily service throughout the week in cities where there are schools.[22]

What is significant here is that Luther incorporated much more of the monastic office than he did in his daily services issued some three years earlier. In particular, the Latin office hymn, the Lord's Prayer, and especially the vesper canticle (the *Magnificat*)[23] have all returned.

In 1536 Wolfgang Musculus, a pastor in Augsburg, visited Wittenberg to attend a conference of Reformation theologians from many parts of Europe. During his visit he kept a diary which is a valuable eyewitness account of some of the liturgical practices in Wittenberg. On May 14, Cantate Sunday (that is, the Fourth Sunday after Easter) he gives the following description of vespers in Wittenberg. Unfortunately, he does not state whether it was in the Stadtkirche or the Schlosskirche, although the practice is likely to have been the same in both: "The vesper service was held at 1:00 P.M. and throughout followed papistical custom with plainchant, except that the Gospel for the Sunday was sung in the vernacular by a boy in a high place. After Vespers a sermon was given on the second commandment, 'Thou shalt not take the name of the Lord thy God in vain.' Thereafter was sung *Christ ist erstanden.*"[24] There are two matters on which Musculus may have been mistaken. First, the reference to the *Gospel* for the day may be a transcription error, with *Euangelii* being recorded instead of *Epistel*. Two weeks later, on May 28, the Sunday after Ascension, Musculus reported that Luther preached the vesper sermon on the epistle of that day.[25] But Musculus may have been correct for this earlier Sunday, since the practice of preaching on the epistle at Sunday vespers had not yet become thoroughly established (as it certainly did later). Second, in stating that the sermon came after vespers had ended probably means that Musculus was thinking of the traditional vespers at which there was no preaching, and was therefore unaware of the fact that in Wittenberg the sermon was very much part of the vespers service. But once these qualifications have been made, the witness that Musculus gives is very important. In some respects he is a hostile witness in that he was moving in a Zwinglian/Reformed (as opposed to Lutheran) direction; he became professor of theology in Berne, Switzerland, some thirteen years later. It was these Reformed sensitivities which made him record that in his view Wittenberg vespers was virtually unchanged from unreformed monastic use, except for the expanded Bible reading[26] and preaching. This confirms Luther's statements in the *Deudsche Messe,* and elsewhere, that he intended to retain Latin usage where possible, and especially the associated plainchant: the psalm-tones for both the psalms and the *Magnificat*—the traditional chant for those antiphons and responsories which were retained—and Latin plainsong hymnody. In Lutheran vespers, therefore, the monody of the ancient church, and especially the psalm-tones, was preserved as a living tradition which continued well into the eighteenth century.[27] Thus there was a specific liturgical need which led later composers such as Samuel Scheidt, Dietrich Buxtehude, and others, to compose organ music in connection with the basic psalm-tones. It also means that William Porter's recently published essay, in which he suggests that Buxtehude may have used psalm-tone formulas in his free organ works,[28] is not out of the question, since the psalm-tones continued in daily use in northern Germany at this time.[29]

Musculus also gives the information that the subject of the sermon was the second of the Ten Commandments. The implication is that a section of Luther's *Small Catechism* was being taught. For the rest of his life Luther was preoccupied with the Catechism in one way or another. In particular, in addition to preaching many sermons on the various sections of the Catechism (which had now grown to six), he completed a significant collection of catechism hymns:

1. Commandments: *Dies sind die heilgen zehn Gebot*
2. Creed: *Wir glauben all an einen Gott*
3. Lord's Prayer: *Vater unser im Himmelreich*
4. Baptism: *Christ unser Herr zum Jordan kam*
5. Repentance/Confession: *Aus tiefer Not schrei ich zu dir*
6. Lord's Supper: *Jesus Christus, unser Heiland, der von uns*

These hymns, together with the practice of preaching on the Catechism, became a familiar part of Lutheran vesper services. Not only were they sung but they were frequently quoted in catechism sermons. Indeed, some catechism sermons were directly based on the hymns themselves. For example, August Pfeiffer,

Superintendent in Lübeck during Buxtehude's tenure, preached a series of sermons on these catechism hymns of Luther in 1698.[30] Again and again, in the two hundred years or so between the sixteenth and eighteenth centuries, Lutheran composers wrote chorale preludes on the melodies of these catechism hymns. These were clearly for use in vesper services; and the most notable collection of them is that of the large and small catechism preludes in J. S. Bach's *Clavierübung III.*[31] But we need to return to the witness of Musculus in Wittenberg in 1536.

The Augsburg pastor states that following the vesper sermon on May 14, *Christ ist erstanden* was sung. At the Hauptgottesdienst in the morning of the same day Musculus had reported that in between the Epistle and Gospel there was an organ prelude which led into the choir singing the Easter sequence *Victimae paschali laudes* in alternation with the congregation singing the stanzas of the vernacular hymn *Christ ist erstanden.*[32] It is possible that something similar occurred at vespers, although Musculus seems to suggest that only the German *Leise* was sung. Whatever the exact performance practice was, it is likely that the unaccompanied singing of the congregation was preceded by a suitable organ prelude, as had happened in the morning liturgy.

As the Reformation spread throughout Germany, a series of church orders containing outline liturgical forms, usually based on Wittenberg practice, began to appear. For example, when the Reformation was introduced into Albertine Saxony in 1539 a suitable *Agenden-Buch* was published. It contained the following description of vespers:

Church-Order
in Towns and Where There are Schools.
Saturdays and other Feasts.

Vespers shall be held at the usual time after midday; the boys shall sing one, two, or three psalms with the antiphon of the Sunday or feast, and thereafter a Responsory or [Latin] hymn, where a pure one is available. Afterwards let a boy read a lesson from the New Testament. After the lesson the Magnificat is sung with an antiphon of the Sunday or feast, and ending with the collects and *Benedecamus.*[33]

Later it speaks of the weekday vespers, which follows the basic order for Saturdays, but with the additional direction: "And at the end of vespers let a section from the Catechism be taken and expounded in the simplest way to the people. And the portion of the Catechism which has been explained on the Sunday [at Vespers] can be brought before the children for their instruction one or two days in the week, depending on how many or few children attend."[34]

In northern Germany most of the important church orders were drawn up by Johannes Bugenhagen, pastor of the Stadtkirche in Wittenberg, colleague and confessor of Luther, and very much the organizer of the young Lutheran church. He was responsible for the following church orders: Brunswick (1528),

Hamburg (1529), Lübeck (1531), Pomerania (1534), Denmark (1537), Holstein (1542), Brunswick-Wolfenbüttel (1543), and Hildesheim (1544).[35] All of these church orders are very similar in content; in particular those of Hamburg[36] and Lübeck[37] stand quite close to each other in detail.

In general it can be said that the prescriptions for matins and vespers in these church orders closely follow Luther's *Deudsche Messe*. The Lübeck church order of 1531, which remained in force until well into the eighteenth century, deals with daily vespers within the section headed, "On the singing and reading of the pupils in the churches." Like the *Deudsche Messe,* it is a general description rather than a specific liturgy; however, Bugenhagen gives more detail than Luther, and also reduces the service from one hour to half an hour in duration. The service is almost entirely in Latin with only the lesson (read after its equivalent in Latin) and some of the hymnody being in the vernacular:

Antiphon	Sung by two boys
Psalm(s)	One, two, or three psalms, depending on their length, sung antiphonally, "verse by verse," by the pupils, divided into two choirs, to the same tone as the antiphon
Antiphon	
[Responsory	Sung responsorially with the *Gloria patri,* only on eves of feasts and on the feast days themselves]
[Hymn	*De tempore,* only on eves of feasts and the feast days]
Lesson	From the Old Testament (the New Testament being read at matins) chanted by three boys in Latin, then clearly and carefully read in German, "without chant," by a fourth boy
[Litany	Luther's Latin litany, sung antiphonally at Saturday vespers as a penitential preparation for the worship of the next day; the Lutheran form of confession was practiced on Saturday evenings after vespers]
Office Hymn	The hymns of Ambrose and Prudentius are specifically noted
Antiphon	Presumably sung by the two boys, as before
Magnificat	Sung antiphonally by the two choirs, in the same tone as the antiphon, begun by the Cantor singing the first half-verse alone
Antiphon	
Kyrie	Three-fold: Kyrie, Christe, Kyrie eleison

Lord's Prayer
Sermon   Luther had the sermon following the lesson. In later
                          times in Lübeck—as elsewhere—the sermon was re-
                          stored to the earlier position before the Magnificat
Versicles   With responses, both choirs together
Benedecamus   Sung by two boys; presumably the first sang *Benede-*
                          camus Domino, and the second responded *Deo gratias*

On major festivals, following the *Benedecamus* which normally marked the end
of vespers, the *Nunc dimittis,* with the *Gloria patri,* was sung by both choirs
together; then the compline hymn *Jesu redemptor seculi;* appropriate hymns of
the day or season followed.[38] This practice of continuing the musical praise after
the *Benedecamus* on feast days, was later expanded into an opportunity for
more concerted music, and ultimately led to the *Abend Musik* of Buxtehude.

This process of the musical elaboration of vespers was begun under Luther's guidance. His colleague, Johann Walter, Cantor in Torgau from 1526,
produced at least two manuscript collections of polyphonic vesper music, of
which only a few part-books survive.[39] In Wittenberg Georg Rhau, formerly
Thomaskantor in Leipzig, but afterward an important printer and publisher,
issued a number of major collections of mainly Latin polyphonic liturgical
music, written by a variety of contemporary composers such as Resinarius,
Bruck, Senfl, Isaac, Ducis, Dietrich, Walter, and others. The settings ranged
from simple harmonized plainchant to fine examples of polyphony in the
Franco-Flemish style. In 1540 Rhau issued a set of part-books containing music
for vespers, written by a variety of composers: *Vesperarvm precvm officia*
psalmi feriarvm et dominicalivm diervm tocivs anni, cvm antiphonis, hymnis,
et responsoriis (vt vocant) quatuor vocibus ab optimis & celeberrimis Musicis
compositi . . . , Wittenberg 1540.[40] The purpose of this collection was to provide
all the necessary liturgical music for the weekly celebration of vespers. This is
clearly seen when the psalms are examined. There are thirty-five psalms (or
parts of psalms), all of them four-part faburden settings ranging over all eight
psalm-tones, given in seven groups of five, designed for use on each day of the
week:

Sunday	Psalms 109–13
Monday	Psalms 114–16, 119–20
Tuesday	Psalms 121–25
Wednesday	Psalms 126–30
Thursday	Psalms 131–32, 134–36
Friday	Psalms 137–41
Saturday	Psalms 143–47

Also included are numerous settings of the alternate verses of the *Magnificat,* the vespers canticle which was sung every day. These were composed in all the eight tones, and were intended to be sung after the previous verses were intoned monodically. There are also numerous polyphonic settings of *Magnificat* and other antiphons, together with two responsories and four Latin hymns. Rhau later issued more part-books containing polyphonic vesper music: for example, *Novum ac insigne opus musicum,* 1541, containing thirty-six antiphons by Sixt Dietrich; *Sacrum Hymnorum,* 1542, a collection of Latin hymns in settings by various composers, arranged in two parts, the first "Proprium de tempore" and the second "Proprium et commune sanctorum"; *Responsoria . . . de tempora et festis,* 1542, two volumes of responsories composed by Resinarius; and *Novus opus musicam,* 1545, three volumes of settings of Latin hymns and canticles by Dietrich.

Parallel with this developed use of polyphony there was also a concern for an authoritative collection of liturgical monody which would preserve as much of the traditional chant of the church as was consistent with Reformation and biblical doctrines. Up to this point in time each church or group of churches produced their own manuscript versions of preserved and adapted chant. Lucas Lossius—significantly, an educator (the head of the Gymnasium in Lüneberg) with an interest in teaching his pupils the chant they were required at the daily and Sunday services—brought together the basic Lutheran anthology of Latin chant: *Psalmodia, hoc est, cantica sacra veteris ecclesia selecta* [Psalmodia, that is, sacred chant selected from the old church], Nuremberg, 1553. Although it was compiled in northern Germany and published towards the south, in a sense it carried the Wittenberg imprimatur, since Luther's colleague and successor in Wittenberg, Philipp Melanchthon, wrote the preface. It did indeed have wide circulation throughout Germany, being reprinted in 1569, 1579, and 1595.

In the Staatsbibliothek, Berlin, there is a copy of the 1553 edition of Lossius's *Psalmodia* which contains a manuscript description of the liturgical and musical practice of the Laurentiuskirche in Halle.[41] The manuscript is headed "Ordo Cantionem" and probably dates from the end of the sixteenth century. It gives a clear picture of the musical variety of the vespers service. Whereas the earlier Wittenberg practice was for nearly all of the vesper service to be sung to faburdened chant, in Halle greater use was made of unaccompanied monody:

Antiphon	
Psalm	Sung by choir
Antiphon	
Responsory	Sung responsorially by choir, with organ; or replaced by a Motet with organ

Lesson	
Latin Hymn	Choir sings polyphonic setting in alternation with the organ; or a three-way alternation of choir, organ, and congregation which sang the stanza in German translation
Catechism	A section explained by the celebrant or preacher
Motet	For organ; probably a chorale motet
Hymn	That is, the German *de tempore lied,* or hymn of the day or season; sung in unison, the choir alternating stanzas with the congregation
Pulpit Hymn	One or two stanzas, sung by choir and congregation together; during which the preacher enters the pulpit
Sermon	[Prayers of intercession would have immediately followed the sermon]
Antiphon	Sung by choir
Magnificat	*Magnificat* sung by choir in alternation, verse by
Antiphon	verse, with the organ
Versicle	Sung by celebrant
Response	Sung by choir
Blessing	Given by celebrant
Benedecamus	Sung antiphonally by choir in a polyphonic setting
Amen	Sung by choir and congregation together[42]

The Halle manuscript contains a number of features which were to be explored and developed during the following century. First, there is the use of simple Gregorian monody (rather than the four-part faburdens of Rhau and the composers who worked with him), which became the widespread usage throughout the seventeenth century and later. Second, the responsory following the psalmody could be, and often was, replaced by a motet. This indicates that there was a growing flexibility over the musical details of vespers, with alternate music replacing the traditional, especially on feasts and other special occasions. However, the singing of a motet at the beginning of vespers became a widespread and almost standard practice in later times, for example, in Buxtehude's Lübeck and Bach's Leipzig. Third, the *alternatims praxis*, with the organ and choir answering each other in Latin hymnody, became normative during the first half of the seventeenth century—although there was variety in its use. All of the following combinations were possible: 1) unison choir alternating with the organ playing in octaves; 2) unison choir alternating with the organ playing in harmony; and 3) choir in harmony alternating with the organ playing in harmony. Composers wrote specific organ pieces for this purpose. Samuel Scheidt, for example, spent most of his working life in Halle and shared the basic liturgical traditions of the Halle manuscript referred to above. In the third part of his *Tabulatura nova*, Hamburg, 1624 (which was dedicated to leaders in Lübeck, Hamburg, Lüneburg, and Magdeburg), there are settings of six important *de tempore* hymns clearly intended for such *alternatims praxis*.[43] Fourth, the organ "motet" following the catechism instruction developed, over succeeding generations, into the vespers *Hauptmusik,* with an expanded employment of instruments along with the basic choral and organ resources. Here would be performed, for example, the *Psalmen Davids* (1619) of Schütz, the *Musikalische Andachten* (1639–53) of Hammerschmidt, or the cantatas of Buxtehude and Bach. Fifth, the tradition of the choir singing the *Hauptlied* of the day or season in alternation with the congregation, which was begun in Wittenberg with the polyphonic settings of Walter's *Chorgesangbuch* of 1524, continued to be developed, with Hassler, Franck, Praetorius, Schein, and many others composing numerous settings of the chorale melodies for use in this way. Although the concentration on the *Hauptlied* continued, by the end of the seventeenth century the tendency was to let the alternation drop, and the hymn was sung by choir and congregation together. Sixth, the *alternatims praxis* with regard to the *Magnificat* was longer-lived, with composers, such as Scheidt[44] in the earlier seventeenth century, and Buxtehude[45] in the later seventeenth century writing organ pieces on the plainsong tones associated with the *Magnificat*. These were to be played in alternation with the choir, verse by verse.

In general one can say that daily vespers in connection with the schools continued to show a strong Latin content together with the associated plainsong. In those town churches without schools the daily vespers was much simpler and was mostly in German. The order for Saturday vespers was similar to that of the weekdays, and was largely a preparation for the following Sunday. It was therefore the Sunday vespers that developed a particular musical focus, especially on festivals and special days. On these occasions the intoned psalms were replaced by through-composed settings, usually of just one psalm, or replaced by another choral piece on a totally different text but appropriate for the day. Similarly, the *Magnificat* was sung in a concerted setting on the major festivals, or it too was replaced by another piece. If one reads the rubrics Michael Praetorius included before his compositions in his many volumes of music, this "festival flexibility," as it might be called, is clearly detected. For example, in his *Polyhymnia* of 1619, at the head of his setting of *In dich ich hab gehoffet Herr,* he writes: "Since this *Concert* is very long, one can appropriately use it at vespers in place of the Magnificat";[46] and at the beginning of his setting of *Vater unser im Himmelreich:* "Since this is also very long . . . a half-hour work . . . one can use it at vespers in place of the *Magnificat,* or if it is still too long, parts 1 and 2 before, and parts 3 and 4 after, the vesper sermon."[47]

The centenary of the Reformation in 1617 was marked by three days of celebration at the Dresden court, with music composed and directed by the *Hofcapelmeister* Heinrich Schütz. A printed account of the celebrations has survived which includes the following details for the vesper service on the first day, 31 October. Unfortunately most of the music has been lost.

Intoned before the altar: *Deus in adjutorium meum intende.*
Response: *Domine ad adjuvandam &c. Gloria.*
Then follows, for the Introit (the antiphon) *Jubilant hodie omnes gentes,*
    with trumpets, and the hundredth psalm, *Jubilate Deo,* five choirs (possi-
    bly SWV 36, which was later published in the *Psalmen Davids* of 1619),
    sung in-between the repeated antiphon.
"This is the day that the Lord hath made, &c" (Psalm 118.24ff.) as ap-
    pointed for the festival, for one choir.
Item: the Creed (Luther's *Wir glauben all an einen Gott*) sung *figuraliter*
    with the congregation.
After the sermon the *Magnificat,* with six choirs, trumpets and timpani,
    and between each verse stanzas from Luther's German hymn *Erhalt uns
    Herr bey deinem Wort* (sung by the congregation).
Concludes with the congregational hymns *Verleih uns Frieden gnädiglich*
    (Luther), *Gieb unserm Fürsten* (Walter), and the *Benedecamus.*[48]

Another printed source gives us the details of the Christmas/New Year liturgical music of the Marienkirche in Lübeck in 1682–83.[49] As with most of Schütz's music of 1617, Buxtehude's music of 1682–83 is unknown to us. Christmas Day vespers included the following music:

Before the Sermon

Latin hymn, *Corde natus ex parentis* (Prudentius), in an eight-voice setting.
Cantata, *Uns ist ein Kind geboren,* for two sopranos, alto and bass soloists,
    twelve instruments (and chorus?). The five stanzas of the libretto are
    punctuated by instrumental ritornelli which progressively use the melo-
    dies of three Christmas hymns. The Cantata is begun and ended with the
    tutti movement on the biblical words of Isaiah 9.6: "Unto us a child is

born, unto us a son is given," the same words used liturgically as the verse preceding the Collect for Christmas Day at both the Hauptgottesdienst and vespers.

After the Sermon

Magnificat, in a concerted setting: for soprano, alto, tenor bass soloists, four-part choir, and ten instruments. It begins with an opening *Sinfonia,* and is interrupted at various points, similar to Bach's first version of his *Magnificat* (BWV 243a) by various Christmas hymns and canticles, in both Latin and German: *Vom Himmel hoch, Freut euch und jubilirt, Gloria in excelsis deo, Virga jessae floruit,* and *Joseph lieber Joseph mein.* After the *Gloria Patri* there is a final, macaronic addition, beginning, *Psallite unigenito Christo.*

Concerted piece for six soloists, six-part choir, and fifteen instruments: *Dancksagen wir alle.* The form of the libretto is close to that of the traditional collect, and it may well have been a Christmas collect in local use in Lübeck, although I have been unable to locate a source. It therefore links with the collect-verse, Isaiah 9.6, which begins and ends the cantata heard before the sermon, and the item was therefore probably sung after the chanted collects and before the *Benedecamus.*

All the major feasts of the church year, that is, Christmas, Easter, Pentecost, and Trinity, as well as such special days as Advent Sunday, Ascension Day, and others, were celebrated with such musical vespers. But the season of Lent and Passion Week were not neglected, even though in some cities and towns, such as Leipzig, there was generally no concerted music during this time. It must not be forgotten that the great Passions of J. S. Bach were written for the service of vespers on the afternoon of Good Friday.[50] Similarly, I believe, the cycle of seven cantatas by Buxtehude, *Membra Jesu nostri* (BuWV 75), originated as vesper music. The cantatas are based on seven medieval poems, probably written by Arnulf of Louvain (1200–1250), which are addressed successively to the feet, knees, hands, side, breast, heart, and face and of the crucified Christ. They were popular in Lutheran devotion, especially as Paul Gerhardt translated all seven into German, the most famous being the last: *O Haupt voll Blut und Wunden,* the classic passion hymn. Although the seven cantatas were clearly conceived as a unified cycle, with a related key sequence[51] and similar structure, like Bach's *Christmas Oratorio,* they were intended to be performed individually, rather than one after the other on one occasion. Wednesdays during Lent were significant times of devotion in northern Germany[52] when it was customary to read at vespers portions of the conflated version of the passion story, taken from all four Gospels, which had been compiled by Johannes Bugenhagen. This passion history was divided into seven sections and read on these Lenten Wednesdays, and it seems most likely that Buxtehude wrote this cycle of cantatas with these weekly vesper services in mind. Alternatively, it is possible that he intended them for use during Holy Week, at the seven daily vesper services from Palm Sunday to Easter Eve. Either would have been possible, and whatever the specific performance intentions Buxtehude had, these cantatas are obviously devotional vespers passion music.

What had begun as a private, monastic discipline, became in the Lutheran tradition a public, devotional preaching service. This service assumed much of the ancient monody and hymnody of the church, but added to it its own distinctive music and hymnody. By the time of Buxtehude and Bach, the Lutheran vespers tradition had blossomed into a rich musical, liturgical, and spiritual experience, with a wide range of congregational, choral, vocal, organ, and instrumental music.

Notes

1. See R. Freiherrn von Liliencron, *Liturgisch-musikalische Geschichte der evangelischen Gottesdienste von 1523 bis 1700*, (Schleswig: Bergas, 1893), esp. pp. 160–63, and *passim*. See also G. Stiller, *Johann Sebastian Bach and Liturgical Life in Leipzig*, ed. R. A. Leaver (St. Louis: Concordia, 1984), pp. 48–55.

2. "Item, wie sie ihre eigene *Horas Canonicas* verlachten, nicht viel Geld oder Korn hab ich, (sprach einer zum andern) aber gewiss Retardat, und ungebetete Vesper und Metten hab ich etliche Boden voll"; *Agenda, Das ist, Kirchen-Ordnung, Wie sich Pfarrherren und Seelsorger in ihren Aemtern und Diensten verhalten sollen*, . . . (Leipzig, 1712), sig. A3ʳ. The Saxon church order was kept in print and in use until the late eighteenth century, and was therefore followed in Leipzig throughout the Cantorate of J. S. Bach.

3. The document was prepared for the congregation of Leisnig in Saxony but clearly reflects the experiments then taking place in Wittenberg: *D. Martin Luthers Werke. Kritische Gesamtausgabe* (Weimar: Böhlaus, 1883– [= Weimarer Ausgabe, hereafter cited as *WA*]) 12, pp. 35–37; *American Edition of Luther's Works* (Philadelphia and St. Louis: Fortress and Concordia, 1955–86 [hereafter cited as *LW*]) 53, pp. 11–14. See also J. N. Alexander, "Luther's Reform of the Daily Office," *Worship* 57 (1983), pp. 348–60.

4. *LW* 53, p. 13: "und gleych also lesen, aus legen, loben, singen und beten, wie am morgen"; *WA* 12, p. 36.

5. *LW* 53, p. 12: "und daselbs lesen liesse, es seyen schuler odder priester, odder were es sey, gleych wie man itzt noch die Lection ynn der metten liesset. Das sollen thun eyner odder tzween, odder eyner umb den andern, odder eyn Chor umb den andern, wie das am besten gefellet"; *WA* 12, p. 35.

6. See *Liber usualis missae et officii* (Tournai and New York: Desclee, 1961), pp. 120–23; cp. *Handbuch der deutschen evangelischen Kirchenmusik*, ed. K. Ameln, C. Mahrenholz, and W. Thomas, I/1 (Göttingen: Vandenhoeck & Ruprecht, 1932), p. 291, etc.

7. *LW* 53, p. 12: "Und wo dis nicht geschicht, so ist de gemeyne der lection nichts gebessert, wie bis her ynn klostern und stifften geschehen, da sie nur wende haben angeblehet"; *WA* 12, p. 35.

8. *LW* 53, p. 13: "also das man zu beyder tzeytt predige der gantzen gemeyne, des morgens das gewonlich Evangelion, des abents die Epistel"; *WA* 12, p. 36.

9. *LW* 53, p. 14: "eyn feyn Responsorion odder Antiphen mit eyner Collecten ordenen. Des abent auch alsso, nach der Lection und auslegung offentlich zu lesen und zusingen"; *WA* 12, p. 37.

10. *LW* 53, p. 12: "Wenn nu die Lection und auslegung eyn halb stund odder lenger geweret hatt, soll man drauf yn gemeyn got dancken, loben und bitten umb frucht des worts etc. Dazu soll man brauchen der psalmen und ettlicher gutten Responsoria, Antiphon. . . ." *WA* 12, p. 36.

11. See M. Jenny, "Das Psalmlied—eine Erfindung Martin Luthers," *IAH Bulletin* 5 (1977), p. 34 et seq.

12. *LW* 53, p. 13: "Das gesenge ynn den sontags messen und vesper las man bleyben, denn sie sind fast gutt und aus der schrifft getzogen"; *WA* 12, p. 37.

13. "Darumb wo nicht gotts wort predigt wirt, ists besser das man widder singe noch lesse, noch zu samen kome" ("Therefore, when God's Word is not preached, one had better neither sing nor read, or even come together"); *WA* 12, p. 35; *LW* 53, p. 11.

14. *LW* 53, p. 38: "prolixitas mutari potest arbitrio Episcopi, ut tres psalmi pro matutinis, tres pro vesperis cum uno vel duobus responsoriis absolvantur"; *WA* 12, p. 219.

15. *LW* 53, p. 38: "Et pulchrum, imo necessarium est, pueros assuesscere legendis et audiendis Psalmis et lechtionibus scripturarum sanctorum"; *WA* 12, p. 219.

16. *LW* 53, p. 39; *WA* 12, p. 219.

17. *LW* 53, p. 37: "Haec dico, ut, si qui sunt poetae germanici, extimulentur et nobis poemata pietatis cudant"; *WA* 12, p. 218.

18. "Aber es fehlt uns an deutschen Poeten und Musicis. . . ."; *D. Martin Luthers sämmtliche Schriften* (St. Louis: Concordia, 1890–1910), 10, col. 2252.

19. Only an edition of 1526 is known, but since its title page states that this is a revised edition, an earlier issue of 1525, that is, fairly soon after the publication of Walter's *Chorgesangbuch*, seems likely: *Enchyridion geistlicher gesenge vnd psalmen fur die leyen/ mit viel andern/ denn zuuor/ gebessert* (Wittenberg, 1526); see M. Jenny, *Luthers Geistlicher Lieder und Kirch-engesänge. Vollständige Neuedition in Ergänzung zu Band 35 der Weimarer Ausgabe*, Archiv zur Weimarer Ausgabe der Werke Martin Luthers 4 (Cologne and Vienna: Böhlau, 1985), pp. 25–30.

20. *LW* 53, p. 69: "Fur die knaben und schuler ynn der Biblia zu uben gehets also zu"; *WA* 19, p. 80.

21. *LW* 53, pp. 64–65: "Ist auffs erste ym deutschen Gottis dienst eyn grober, schlechter [= schlichter], eynfaltiger guter Catechismus von nöten . . . nemlich die drey stuck, die zehen gebot, der glaube und das vater unser. Inn disen dreyen stucken steht es schlecht und kurze fast alles, was eym Christen zu wissen not ist. Dise unterricht mus nu also geschehen . . . das sie auff der Cantzel . . . fur gepredigt werde"; *WA* 19, p. 76.

22. *LW* 53, p. 69: "Desselbigen gleychen zur vesper singen sie etliche der vesper psalmen, wie sie bis her gesungen sind, auch latinsch mit eyner antiphen, darauff eynen hymnus, so er fur handen ist. Darnach lesen sie abermal eyner umb den andern zween oder drey latinsch aus dem alten testament eyn gantzes odder halbes Capitel, darnachs lang ist. Darnach lieset eyn knabe dasselbige Capital zu deudsch. Darauff das magnificat zu latein mit eyner antiphen odder lied. Darnach eyn vater unser heymlich und die Collecten mit dem Benedicamus. Das ist der Gottis dienst teglich durch die wochen ynn stedten, da man schulen hat"; *WA* 19, p. 80.

23. Luther likewise called for the singing of the *Te deum* and *Benedictus* at matins.

24. W. Herbst (ed.), *Quellen zur Geschichte des evangelischen Gottesdienstes von der Reformation bis zur Gegenwart* (Göttingen: Vandenhoeck & Rupprecht, 1968), p. 72: "Vesperae vero habebantur hora prima pomeridiana per omnia ad morem papisticum in choro, nisi quod lectio Euangelii diei Dominacae vulgariter a puero canebatur ad populum e sublimi et post vesperas contio habebatur de altero praecepto nempe, Non usurpabis nomen Domini Dei tui in vanum etc. postquam canebatur christ ist erstanden"; see also A. Boës. "Die Reformatorischen Gottesdienste in der Wittenberger Pfarrkirche von 1523 an, und die 'Ordnung der gesenge Wittembergischen Kirchen' von 1543/44," *Jahrbuch für Liturgik und Hymnologie* 4 (1959), pp. 22–28.

25. "Ad vesperam concionatus est D. Lutherus tractans Epistolam eius Dominicae"; Herbst, *Quellen*, p. 73.

26. Musculus records that the lesson was read only in German. According to the *Deudsche Messe* it should have been first read in Latin.

27. O. Brodde, "Evangelische Choralkunde (Der gregorianische Choralkunde im evangelischen Gottesdienst)," *Leiturgia. Handbuch des evangelischen Gottesdienstes 4: Die Musik des evangelischen Gottesdienstes*, ed. K. F. Müller and W. Blankenburg (Kassel: Stauda-Verlag, 1961), pp. 343–555.

28. W. Porter, "Psalm-Tone Formulas in Buxtehude's Free Organ Works?," *Charles Brenton Fisk: Organ Builder*, ed. F. Douglass, O. Jander, and B. Owen (Easthampton: Westfield Center for Early Keyboard Studies, 1986), pp. 1, 161–74.

29. It needs to be underlined that the chanting of the psalms continued in those towns and cities where there were Latin schools, or Gymnasia, such as Wittenberg, Torgau, Leipzig, Hamburg, Lüneberg, Lübeck, etc. Elsewhere, vernacular hymnody replaced Latin psalmody. In the various Lutheran court chapels, which maintained musical establishments, especially those with connections with Saxony, the metrical psalms of Cornelius Becker were sung. The model was the Dresden court which used the Becker settings of Heinrich Schütz, 1628/1661, SWV 97–256 (see E. Schmidt, *Der Gottesdienst am Kurfürstlichen Hofe zu Dresden. Ein Beitrag zur liturgischen Traditionsgeschichte von Johann Walter bis Heinrich Schütz* [Berlin: Evangelische Verlagsanstalt, 1961], pp. 74–76). One such chapel was at the court of Weissenfels, which produced its own church order in 1685 and again in 1688 (for the details, see *Johann Philipp Krieger 1649–1725. 21 Ausgewählte Kirchenkompositionen*, ed. M. Seifert and H. J. Moser, Denkmäler deutscher Tonkunst, vol. 53/54 [Wiesbaden and Graz: Breitkopf & Härtel and Akademische Druck- und Verlagsanstalt, 1958], pp. lxi–lxviii.) See also W. Blankenburg, "Der gottesdienstliche Liedgesang," *Leiturgia* 4, pp. 632–35.

30. A. Pfeiffer, *Cithera Lutheri, d.i. Christliche Predigten Uber Die allgemeinen Katechismus-Lieder, . . .* (Lübeck, 1709). Pfeiffer was a favorite author of J. S. Bach, who owned eight of his books. See R. A. Leaver, *Bachs theologische Bibliothek*, Beiträge zur theologischen Bachforschung 1 (Stuttgart: Hännsler, 1983), pp. 37–39.

31. See R. A. Leaver, "Bach's *Clavierübung III*: Some Historical and Theological Considerations," *The Organ Yearbook* 6 (1975) pp. 17–13.

32. Herbst, *Quellen*, p. 71.

33. *Agenda* (Leipzig, 1712), p. 77: "Soll man zu gewöhnlicher Zeit nach Mittage Vesper halten, die Schüler einen, zween oder drey Psalmen und die Antiphon von der Dominica oder Festo, darauff ein *Responsorium* oder *Hymnum*, wo dieselbigen rein vorhanden seyn, singen lassen.

Darnach lass man einen Knaben eine Lection aus dem neuen Testament lesen. Nach der Lection singe man das *Magnificat*, auch mit einer Antiphon von der Dominica oder Festo, und beschlisse mit der Collecten, und *Benedecamus.*"

34. Ibid., p. 81: "und wenn die Vesper aus ist, nehme man ein Stücke aus dem Catechismo für, und lege dasselbige dem Volcke auffs einfaltigste aus, und was man auff den Sonntag aus dem Catechismo für geleget hat, dasselbige soll man die Kinder in der Wochen auff einen Tag oder zween, nachdem der Kinder viel oder wenig, wiederum verhören."

35. The notable north German town for which Bugenhagen did not draw up the church order was Lüneburg (1569). For details of vespers, especially with regard to Bach's time connection with the Michaeliskirche, see G. Fock, *Der junge Bach in Lüneburg. 1700–1702* (Hamburg: Merseburger, 1950), pp. 20 et seq.; and H. Walter, *Musikgeschichte der Stadt Lüneburg. Vom Ende des 16. bis Anfang des 18. Jahrhunderts* (Tutzing: Schneider, 1967), pp. 111–19.

36. E. Sehling, *Die evangelischen Kirchenordnungen des XVI. Jahrhunderts* 5 (Leipzig: Reisland, 1913), pp. (482) 488–540. See also J. Geffken, *Die Hamburgischen Gesangbücher des sechsehnten Jahrhunderts* (Hamburg: Meißner, 1857), pp. 172–74, where the outline of vespers is reprinted from F. E. Ullyseo, *Cantica Sacra* (Hamburg, 1588).

37. Sehling, *Die evangelischen Kirchenordnungen* 5, pp. (327) 324–68.

38. Ibid., pp. 347–48.

39. See C. Gerhardt, *Die Torgauer Waltherhandschriften* (Kassel: Bärenreiter, 1949).

40. See *Georg Rhau Musikdrucke aus den Jahren 1538 bis 1545, 5: Vesperarium precum officia (Wittenberg 1540)*, ed. H. J. Moser (Kassel and St. Louis: Bärenreiter and Concordia, 1960).

41. See C. Mahrenholz, "Der 3. Band von Samuel Scheidts Tabulatura nova 1624 und die Gottesdienstordnung der Stadt Halle," *Musicologica et Liturgica. Gesammelte Aufsätze von Christhard Mahrenholz*, ed. K. F. Müller (Kassel: Bärenreiter, 1960), pp. 114–22; *Handbuch der deutschen evangelische Kirchenmusik*, I/1, 58* et seq.

42. Mahrenholz, *Musicologica et Liturgica*, p. 121; H. J. Moser, *Die evangelische Kirchenmusik in Deutschland* (Berlin: Merseburger, 1953), p. 106. Compare the detailed provisions for figural Vesper music throughout the year in the Michaeliskirche, Hof (north of Bayreuth, found in a manuscript dating from 1592, reproduced in H. Kätzel, *Musikpflege und Musikerziehung im Reformations-jahrhundert dargestellt am Beispiel der Stadt Hof* (Göttingen: Vandenhoeck and Rupprecht, 1957), pp. 109–34. For example, the following is listed as the music for the Eve of Advent Sunday (ibid., p. 109):

Antiphonon:
Hora est iam nos de somno. a 5 vocum. Senffelii.

Psalmus 146:
Laudate Dominum quoniam bonus est psalmus. 8. toni, folio 8 psalmorum figuralium Witebergae excus.

Responsorium:
Ecce dies venient. a 4.

Hymnus:
Veni redemptor gentium. a 5. Ludovici Senffelii [followed by two-voiced versicle: Aperiatur terra]

Magnificat quinti toni. a 5. Orlandi.
Vel loco Benedecamus [Festivale a 4]
Jerusalem plantabis vineam. a 5. Orlandi.

43. *Samuel Scheidt Werke, 7,* ed. C. Mahrenholz (Hamburg: Ugrino, 1954), pp. 18–53; cp. the similar examples of Michael Praetorius, see *Michael Praetorius Sämtliche Orgelwerke,* ed. K. Matthei (Wolfenbüttel and Zurich: Möseler, 1930), nos. 2–6.

44. *Samuel Scheidt Werke, 7,* pp. 54–105. Scheidt offers a composition in each of the eight tones as well as the *Tonus peregrinus.*

45. BuxWV 203 and 204, "Magnificat Primi Toni," and BuxWV 205, "Magnificat Noni Toni," that is, *Tonus peregrinus.* In Bach's day in Leipzig, the *Tonus peregrinus* was the usual, though not exclusive, tone employed for the *Magnificat;* cf. not only his quotation of the melody in *Suscepit Israel* in his concerted setting of the *Magnificat, BWV 243,* but also his four-part setting, BWV 324.

46. "Dieweil dies Concert sehr lang: so könnte man es gar füglich in den Vespern/ anstatt des Magnificats"; *Gesamtausgabe der Muskialischen Werke von Michael Praetorius* 17/2, ed. W. Gurlitt (Wolfenbüttel: Kallmeyer, 1933), p. 293.

47. "Dieweil es auch sehr lang . . . einer halben Stunden Werk ist. So kann man . . . in der Vesper/anstatt des Magnifikats: Oder/ wenn dies auch zu lang währen wollte/ den 1. und 2. Teil vor: den 3. und 4. Teil nach der Vesper-Predigt"; ibid., p. 433.

48. The details of the celebrations were publishd by the Senior Court Preacher in Dresden, Matthias Hoe von Hoenegg, *Chur Sächsischen Evangelischen Jubel Freude, . . .* (Leipzig, 1618); reprinted in Mahrenholz, *Musicologica et liturgica,* pp. 196–204, see esp. 197: "*Intonatio* vor dem Altar: *Deus in adjutorium meum intende. Resp. Domine ad adjuvandem &c. Gloria.* Hier au *pro Introitu, Jubilant hodie omnes gentes,* mit Trommeten/ und der hundert Psalm/*Jubilate Deo,* als ein *Intermedium* zwischen den Trommeten a 5. *Choris.* Diss ist der Tag den der Herr gemacht hat/ &c. auff das Fest gerichtet *per Choros.* Item: Der Glaube *figuraliter* mit der Gemeine. Nach der Predigt. *Magnificat,* mit 6. *Choris* mit Heerpauken und Trommeten/ zwischen jeden Verss/ ein Gesetz/ zum Beschluss/ Verleih uns Frieden gnediglich/ &c. Gib unsern Fürsten/ &c. alles *per Choros. Benedecamus, &c.*" On the vesper services of the Dresden court chapel during Schütz's tenure as Hofcapelmeister, see E. Schmidt, *Der Gottesdienst,* esp. pp. 120–23.

49. *Natalia Sacra Oder Verzeichnüss aller Texte/ Welche in bevorstehenden Heilgen Festen/ als Weinachten/ Neuen Jahr und Heil. drey Könige allhie zu St. Marien sowohl Vor- als Nachmittag . . .* (Lübeck, 1682); reprinted in M. Geck, *Die Vokalmusik Dietrich Buxtehudes und der frühe Pietismus* [Kieler Schriften zur Musikwissenschaft 15] (Kassel: Bärenreiter, 1965), pp. 230–37, esp. pp. 231–33.

50. See R. A. Leaver, *J. S. Bach as Preacher: His Passions and Music in Worship* (St. Louis: Concordia, 1984).

51. C minor, E♭ major, G minor, D minor, A minor, E minor, C minor.

52. See, for example, the "Register über die Psalmen und Kirchen-Gesänge etc." in the court hymnal of Husum, in Schleswig-Holstein, *Ausserlesene Geistliche Lieder* (Schleswig, 1676; reprint, ed. A. Kadelbach, Husum: Husum Druck- und Verlagsgesellschaft, 1986) sig.)( )(ii^v.

9

The Viol Consort in Buxtehude's Vocal Music: Historical Context and Affective Meaning

Eva Linfield

Buxtehude, like many other composers of seventeenth-century Germany, used the consort of viols to highlight special affects in his vocal music. Two traditions concur in the repertory concerning the use of string instruments as accompaniment: 1) the tradition of English consort music for viols, and 2) an Italian tradition of affective string accompaniment that goes back as far as the sixteenth-century Florentine *intermedii*. A particularly strong connection to the Italian tradition presents itself in the affinity between the secular *lamento* of the early Italian opera and the sacred music of *lamento* character in the Lutheran tradition. The German sacred concerto and the *historiae* that have a liturgical affiliation with Passiontide exploit a metaphorically affective use of a string sonority with viols during the seventeenth century. Even the "halo" of a string ensemble (see ex. 9.16) we so closely associate with Christ's voice in Bach's *St. Matthew Passion* and some of his cantatas might be seen as an eighteenth-century culmination of this tradition, by then, however, with a change of instrumentarium from a full or partial consort of viols to that of a "modern" string ensemble.

In the second half of the seventeenth century the consort of viols, consisting of different sizes of viole de gamba, had generally been superseded by the then-modern string ensemble of viole de braccio: two violins, two violas, and violone (an instrument that corresponds to the violoncello). Even in England, the country with a long-standing tradition of viol consort music, musical tastes seemed to be changing as indicated in an account by Roger North, an English gentleman and a major, if rather chatty, music critic of seventeenth-century England: "The old English Fancys . . . fell into a perpetuall grave course of fuge; and if the fuge quickened into a little division, or an air of tripla was prick't, it was extraordinary. For this reason the old English Musick hath passed for dull enterteinement."[1]

In another passage North gives explicit reasons for the change of sonority: "I must observe that the use of chests of violls, which supplyed all instrumentall consorts, kept back the English from falling soon in to the modes of forrein countrys, where the violin and not the treble viol was in use. For the violin is so much more accomodated to the office of an upper part, by a spirit, as well as a pathetick expression, that musick must needs take a new turne."[2]

With the "modes of forrein countrys," North obviously refers to Italy where the violin and the braccio family of string instruments had flourished since the early seventeenth century and where (with rare exceptions, as we shall see later) the consort of viols had become obsolete. Even the bass viola da gamba was rarely heard, as we learn from a letter by Thomas Hill, an Englishman visiting Italy in 1657: "The instrumental music is much better than I had expected. The organ and violin they [the Italians] are master of, but the bass-viol they have not at all in use, and to supply its place they have the bass violin with four strings, and use it as we do the bass-viol."[3]

I offer one example of pictorial evidence for the continuation of viol consort playing and for the existence of different-sized members of the viol family in Germany (see figure 9.1). This painting originated in the mid-seventeenth century and depicts a scene of chamber music at the court of Duke August, the Younger, of Braunschweig-Lüneburg; we see August's children and his third wife, Sophie Elisabeth, who, incidentally, received some compositional advice from Heinrich Schütz.[4]

Against this background of changed tastes noted by Roger North we will look at Buxtehude's vocal works with viole da gamba and investigate his motives for such a scoring. Among the approximately 130 extant vocal works, Buxtehude used the explicit instrumental designation of viole da gamba only five times. Table 9.1 lists those compositions with their respective scoring, along with additional compositions with suggested viol scoring.

The sound of a viol is darker than that of a "modern" string instrument. A full consort of viols creates a warm sonority with introverted character, a somewhat covered sound that could be emulated by an ensemble of violins and violas, but is not inherently characteristic of the braccio-type instruments. It corresponds to the intimacy of strings *con sordino*. In describing the quality of a viola da gamba Mattheson used the endearing adjective "säuselnd" which one might translate as "sweetly singing." He also referred to it as "ein schönes delicates Instrument," (a beautifully delicate instrument).[5] It is precisely this intimate and delicate quality for which Buxtehude strives in the above works specifically designated for viols.

There are only two vocal works in which Buxtehude used the full consort texture: in *Ad cor* and *Laudate, pueri, Dominum*. *Ad cor* is the sixth cantata in

Figure 9.1. Chamber Music at the Court of Duke August the Younger of
Braunschweig-Luneburg, ca. 1645
*(From Meister der Barockmusik, Norddeutsche Musikkultur um Bach und
Händel, Hamburg, 1985)*

Table 9.1   Compositions with Scoring and Suggested Scoring
for Viole da Gamba

Compositions with scoring for viole da gamba

Ad cor, cantata from the cycle *Membra Jesu Nostri*, BuxWV 75
    S,S,B; 5 vg, bc.

Laudate, pueri, Dominum, BuxWV 69
    S,S; 5vg, vlne, bc.

Fürwahr, er trug unsere Krankheit, BuxWV 31
    S,S,A,T,B; 2v, 2vg, vlne or fag, bc.

Herr, ich lasse dich nicht, BuxWV 36
    T,B; 2v, vlne or vg, 3vg, bc.

Auf, Saiten, auf! Laßt euren Schall erklingen! BuxWV 115
    S; 2v, 2vg, bc.

Compositions with suggested scoring for viole da gamba

Herzlich lieb hab ich dich, o Herr, BuxWV 41
    S,S,A,T,B; 2v, 2va, vlne or fag, bc.

Jesu, meiner Freuden Meister, BuxWV 61
    S,A,T,B; 3va, bc.

Nimm von uns Herr, du treuer Gott, BuxWV 78
    S,A,T,B; 2v, 2 violette, fag, bc.

O clemens, o mitis, o coelestis Pater, BuxWV 82
    S; v, 2 violette, vlne, bc.

---

a seven-cantata cycle for Passiontide addressing seven parts of Christ's body, the *Membra Jesu*. The instrumental scoring for all cantatas calls for two violins and basso continuo except for that in *Ad cor* (To the heart). The change to an enriched five-voice texture with the darker and also registrally lower scoring of the viols sets this cantata in relief against its surrounding works and adds a special aura alluding to the most intimate and dearest part of Christ's body, his heart. Structurally the work consists of three solo arias for two sopranos and bass respectively, based on sacred Latin love poetry. A concerted trio with the text *Vulnerasti cor meum, soror mea, sponsa* (Thou hast ravished my heart, my sister, my spouse) from the *Song of Solomon* frames the arias. The sensuality of the biblical love poetry inspired Buxtehude's musical setting with its languishing leaps of a descending minor sixth and the dynamically declamatory rhythmic configuration of the opening line (ex. 9.1a). Also the dissonant anticipation of the word *"cor"* enhances the expression of pathos. Only in the repeat of this trio Buxtehude added the viols (ex. 9.1b). The string sound emphasizes

Example 9.1a. Buxtehude, *Membra Jesu* (BuxWV 75); *Ad cor: Vulnerasti cor meum*

Example 9.1b.   *Vulnerasti cor meum*

the languishing mood and intensifies it with the idiomatic string tremolo that had become a near cliché for pathetic expressivity. An instrumental sonata with sections shifting from duple to slow triple proportions serves as an introduction to the cantata. One of its triple sections and the ritornello that concludes the opening vocal trio explicitly expose a descending tetrachord in the basso continuo (see ex. 9.2). The emblematic association of the descending tetrachord with the *lamento* has been well established and discussed by Ellen Rosand.[6] The immediate association here is not with the lament but with intense love. Since, however, Buxtehude combined a text from the *Song of Solomon* with Latin poetry that refers in its second verse to Christ's Passion, he, in fact, mixed the metaphors of languishing love and lament and found the appropriate musical expression by employing a full consort of viols. Buxtehude's choice of the phrygian mode for the setting of *Ad cor* emphasizes the affect of lament. Christoph Bernhard associates this mode with "wehmütige und traurige Sachen" (pensively melancholic and tenderly sad things);[7] Mattheson calls its affect contemplative, sad, lamenting, but still hopeful of consolation.[8]

The intended affect that accounts for Buxtehude's scoring of the chaconne *Laudate, pueri, Dominum* with a full consort of viols is less obvious. He initially juxtaposed the thick string texture with the unusually high soprano parts. Later on in the piece the sweet vocal lines, at times in imitation, at times in parallel thirds are pitted against the warm string sonority and interwoven with it. This

Example 9.2. Buxtehude, *Vulnerasti cor meum*

Example 9.3.   Buxtehude, *Fürwahr, er trug unsere Krankheit* (BuxWV 31)

particular scoring might have suited Buxtehude's intention to express an affect of mellifluence and innocence suggested by the address to "pueri," (children or young boys).

Führwahr, er trug unsere Krankheit liturgically belongs to the Passiontide. Its text, from Isaiah 53: 4 and 5, refers to Christ as sufferer and redeemer. An introductory *Sinfonia* sets the mood for this passion text with static offbeat tremolo writing, emphasis on appoggiatura motives, and a richly figured basso continuo as the harmonic support for the colorful string ensemble with two viole da gamba as inner parts (ex. 9.3). Only once, at the end of the *Sinfonia* (ex. 9.4), does a melodic line break through the tremolo texture that had been motivically without profile and rise to the flat sixth scale degree while outlining a diminished triad, only to fall back as an ornamental appoggiatura of the fifth scale degree. It is particularly effective to let an inner voice rise out of the texture, in this case the upper viola da gamba. Melodic gesture and harmonic dissonance coincide at this point and amplify the pathos suggested by Buxtehude's choice of text. Here the instrumental genre of the *Sinfonia* stands as a metaphor for the preverbal gestures of the passion text.

The metaphorical use of the viols also comes into play in the accompanied soprano recitative *Aber er ist um unserer Missetat willen verwundet* (He was

Example 9.4. *Fürwahr, er trug unsere Krankheit* (BuxWV 31)

wounded for all our transgressions) in which the three lower strings alone provide a tremolo backdrop (ex. 9.5). The most intense expression, however, occurs as an instrumental interruption of the sentence "der geplaget . . . und gemartert wäre" (who was stricken . . . and afflicted of Him). Twelve measures of tremolo for the three lower strings, with double stops in the upper viola da gamba, represent an emotive power that goes beyond verbal expression.

Since the two compositions *Herr, ich lasse dich nicht* and the wedding cantata *Auf, Saiten, auf!* do not share the affective characteristics discussed above, I am continuing my investigation with a few works that specify "violette" for the inner parts. Although we cannot be certain about the type of instrument Buxtehude used, circumstantial evidence makes it likely that these compositions were also performed with viols. Schütz's *Christmas History* offers a clue: the 1664 print specifies for *Intermedium* I, the angel's annunciation of Christ's birth, the participation of "2. Violetten," whereas the title page in the manuscript version indicates "con due Viole da gamba." Buxtehude's compositions *O clemens, o mitis* and *Nimm von uns Herr,* both prayers, share simple string writing in consort style and some tremolo sections. I am suggesting that the nomenclature of violette, at least in these pieces, also refers to a performance with viole da gamba.

The inconsistencies of scoring indications in the seventeenth century are

Example 9.5.   Buxtehude, *Fürwahr, er trug unsere Krankheit* (BuxWV 31)

well known. A viola could be either a viola da braccio or a viola da gamba. In table 9.1 I listed two works in which the viola designation probably means viola da gamba. *Jesu, meiner Freuden Meister* is a dialogue cantata in the form of a conversation between the soul yearning for solace and Christ.[9] The title page indicates its function as a funeral piece. Buxtehude distinguished the dialoguing characters through scoring: *Die betrübte Seele* (the sad soul) is scored for soprano, alto, and tenor voice with basso continuo, whereas Christ is sung by a bass solo with the accompaniment of the three violas (viols) and basso continuo. These strophic arias in a slow triple proportion are interspersed with instrumental ritornelli exposing the chromatically descending tetrachord in viola I and the basso continuo (ex. 9.6). A performance with viols would stress the affects of lament and emphasize Christ's benevolence.

The chorale cantata *Herzlich lieb hab ich dich, o Herr* resembles *Nimm von uns Herr* in structure and string-ensemble texture. Ex. 9.7 shows a striking instance of text expression heightened by scoring and texture of the string

Example 9.6a. Buxtehude, *Jesu, meiner Freuden Meister* (BuxWV 61)

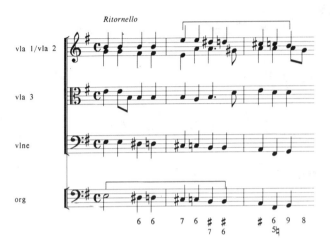

Example 9.6b. *Jesu, meiner Freuden Meister* (BuxWV 61)

Example 9.7. Buxtehude, *Herzlich lieb hab ich dich, o Herr*
(BuxWV 41)

40

45

ensemble. In the last verse Buxtehude isolated the word "ruhn" from the phrase "laß den Leib . . . ohn' einzig Qual und Pein ruhn bis am letzten Tage" (let my body without any suffering or pain rest till the last day). The texture is interrupted, the cantus firmus of the chorale tune does not continue, stasis sets in. An E-major triad with staggered entrances in the vocal parts extends over a twelve-measure pedal on E. The strings participate in this stasis. Only violin I and viola da gamba I are gently rocking in parallel sixths between chord tone and upper neighbor. Buxtehude manipulated his text in order to emphasize the affect of sleep and rest. The low register of the strings and the elimination of cantus I in this passage suggest the darker and introverted sonority of viols to help express the intended affect.[10]

Although the music to most of Buxtehude's *Abendmusiken* is not extant, scoring indications written into the rubrics of their text books reveal some of the composer's musical intentions. *Die Hochzeit des Lamms/Und die Freudenvolle Einholung der Braut zu derselben,* BuxWV 128 (The wedding of the lamb/And the joyful search of the bride) is a dramatic work with texts taken from the Bible, chorale texts, and poetry. The drama emerges without an ongoing narrative but instead in the form of dialogues. The oratorio, as one might call it, is based on the story of the wise and the foolish virgins preparing for the reception of Christ, the bridegroom.[11] One tableau represents an angel appearing to the wise virgins who have fallen asleep. The angel's repeated question "Ach, was wollet ihr nun schlaffen?" (Why do you want to sleep?) receives the virgin's answer: "Ich schlaffe, aber mein Hertz wacht" (I sleep, but my heart is awake [*Song of Solomon*, 5, 2]). This scene is introduced by a *Symphonia* with viole da gamba, and the angel's aria is interspersed with ritornelli, presumably using the same scoring. Here we then have a typical example of viols being used as an emblem of sleep. The following tableau presents the foolish virgins who failed to buy the oil for their lamps in time to light the way and receive their bridegroom. The following poetry acts as a commentary to the foolish virgins' behavior:

> Die Welt erzittert ob den Todt,
> wann einer liegt in der letzten Noht,
> dann will er erst fromm werden . . .
>
> Und wenn er nicht mehr leben mag,
> so hebt er an ein große Klag,
> will sich erst Gott ergeben. . . .
>
> The earth trembles because of death,
> only lying at death's door
> will some return to piety . . .
>
> And when someone does not want to live any longer,
> he starts to wail and to lament,
> and will only then surrender to God. . . .

This aria is sung by a soprano to the accompaniment of "3 viole de gambe" and interspersed with ritornelli played by trombones. The trombones stand for the trembling earth and death as part of the underworld, a metaphorical use of the instruments that goes back to the *intermedii* in sixteenth-century Italy. (We shall return to this later on.) The viols fit into the category with affect of passion and lament.

A dialogue between Christ and the wise and foolish virgins musically recalls Christ's dialogue with the sad soul from *Jesu, meiner Freuden Meister*. Again Christ is accompanied by strings, this time by "5 violi," whereas the virgins are represented by two sopranos and two altos, respectively, with just a basso continuo. This is yet another example of the viol consort highlighting the voice of Christ.

In another *Abendmusik,* a *Natalitia Sacra,* the rubrics inform us again of Buxtehude's setting: a strophic aria in celebration of the newborn child to the accompaniment of two viols, some strophes to the accompaniment of two violins and three viols.[12] A rather sweet and pietistic text alludes to the heavenly Christ child and gives rise to an affect of innocence and tender love which must have prompted Buxtehude's use of the viole da gamba.

From the above investigation, patterns of affective meaning emerge for Buxtehude's vocal works with viol accompaniment. These we can condense into four categories:

1. Affect of lament, used in compositions with passion texts, in prayers, and funeral compositions;
2. Celestial affect, including the affect of tender love, innocence;
3. Affect of sleep;
4. Affect of highlighting a special character, here Christ, with the accompaniment of strings.

The question arises: what is the instrumental tradition in northern Germany that enabled Buxtehude to employ a full or a partial consort of viols in his vocal works? In the early seventeenth century Germany benefited from an influx of English musicians who had left their country originally because of religious conflicts. Also political and marriage ties between England, Denmark, and Germany attributed to the transmission of cultural influences.[13] Of particular importance were those English composers who settled and acquired fame on the continent. Key figures were William Brade (1560–1630) and Thomas Simpson (1582–ca. 1625). They were instrumental in spreading the English tradition of viol consort playing in Germany. Brade was active as Ratsmusikant (1608–10) and director of Ratsmusik (1613–15) in Hamburg. From 1622–25 he functioned as Hofkapellmeister in Gottorf, the court of Schleswig-Holstein. Thomas Simpson started as "violist" at the court of Heidelberg (1608–ca. 1611) and later gained a position at the court of Schleswig-Holstein. During the first quarter of the century, Brade and Simpson had published between them seven collections of instrumental music that appeared in Hamburg, with some of Brade's music simultaneously appearing in Hamburg and Lübeck. These publications contain mostly separate dance numbers for consorts of four, five, and six voices. Brade's prints include a scoring indication on the title page: "auff allerley musicalischen Instrumenten, Insonderheit auff Fiolen. . . ."[14] (on various instruments, particularly on viols). Similar collections of consort music by German composers reached publication during the first decades of the seventeenth century, probably under direct influence and inspiration of their English colleagues. The English had instilled the Germans with a familiarity of the viol-consort sonority and had taught them to play these instruments. As we have seen with Buxtehude's repertory, they lost their common use in the second half of the century but, instead, served a very special function in concerted vocal music, and only in vocal music, to enhance certain affects suggested by the texts to be set.

While the English were responsible for a German tradition of composing for viols, it was the Italians who added a dramatic dimension to this tradition. In the precursors of early Italian opera, the Florentine *intermedii,* consorts of various instrumental groups served as an audio-dramaturgical background.[15] Consorts of viols were rarely used by themselves but most frequently in combination with other groups. Sumptuous consorts of lutes and viols added splendor to the appearance of gods and to celestial scenes in general. Although different-sized viols were still documented, a group of three or four "violoni da gamba" (bass viols) most frequently seemed to represent this family.[16] Two scenes from the *intermedii* for the 1589 wedding celebrations in honor of Ferdinand I and Christine of Lorraine may serve as an illustration of the viols' representational character: 1) a *sinfonia* played in Heaven, scored for a battery of plucked strings and a consort of different-sized viols, 2) a scene in Hell, sung by five devils lamenting their fate, accompanied by four trombones, a lyra viol, and four bass viols.[17] The viols heighten the affect of a celestial scene in the first example, the affect of a *lamento* in the other. (The trombone's association with the underworld continues, of course, beyond Baroque drama, but its tradition probably started with the Florentine *intermedii*).

In his earliest dramatic work, *L'Orfeo,* Monteverdi continues the metaphorical employment of instrumental groups along the tradition of the *intermedii.* Explicit scoring for "Tre bassi da gamba" added to an instrumental *sinfonia* exists in act 3 only. Here the dark sound contributes to Orfeo's rather sad and melancholy mood before entering Hades. Since this scoring is rare, therefore quite special, another occurrence is worth mentioning: the ravishing love song *Con che soavità* from Monteverdi's seventh book of madrigals is scored for soprano and three instrumental choirs. Monteverdi saved the lowest choir of "viole da braccio overo da gamba" as sole accompaniment for the line "che soave armonia" (how sweet would be your concord), sweet words with sexual connotations.

In the context of the viol consort it is interesting to follow the tradition of *lamento* compositions in early Italian opera. One of the most moving and influential laments of the seventeenth century was Monteverdi's *Lamento d'Arianna,* the only surviving composition from his opera *Arianna.* From a contemporary critic we hear: "but best of all was Adriadne . . . who in her musical lament accompanied by 'viole et violini' made many cry for her misfortune."[18] Ellen Rosand documents the conventional feature of a string accompaniment for *lamento* compositions. The string parts were seldom notated or even indicated in the score. This performance reference appeared, however, frequently in the rubrics of the libretti. Opera laments in the second half of the century changed from expressive recitative to aria style. The aria lament clearly stands out from its context for reasons of slow tempo, triple meter, the ostinato structure of a *lamento* bass, and the string accompaniment. In seventeenth-century opera string accompaniments are rarely used and practically confined to laments. This tradition of associating laments with strings extends at least as far back as Psyche's lament, a solo madrigal from the Florentine *intermedii* of 1565. Psyche is accompanied by four viols, four trombones, and a bass lyra before she disappears into inferno with the allegorical figures of Envy, Jealousy, Care, and Scorn. (Notice the parallel to the devils in hell from the 1589 *intermedio*).

The designation of "viole" is a generic description of string instruments. In the *intermedii* and in Monteverdi's early operas performed at the Mantuan

Example 9.8.   Vivaldi, *Juditha Triumphans*

court the reference might have been to either viole da gamba or braccio. Operas performed in public theatres after 1637 would have most likely used modern strings. Although performance records for the Venetian opera houses are sparse, surviving records for the 1657 and 1659 performances of Cavalli's opera *Antioco* at the Teatro S. Cassiano specify four or five viole da braccio, i.e., modern strings.[19]

While evidence points against the use of viols in Venetian opera, there is documentation of their employment in Venetian oratorio productions associated with the orphanage-conservatories. A furniture inventory of 1673 shows the instrumental resources belonging to the Mendicanti: among them the recent acquisition of seven viole da gamba.[20] These instruments by then hardly belonged to the standard orchestra. They were most likely used for special effects in oratorio performances at the *ospedali*. A striking example presents itself as late as 1716, in Vivaldi's oratorio *Juditha Triumphans* which is altogether rich in instrumental scoring with affective meaning. Holofernes has fallen into a drunken sleep when Juditha sings a monologue in recitative style which is accompanied by a five-part ensemble of "voile all'inglese," (English viols) with drawn-out chords (ex. 9.8).[21] The reference to "English viols" shows their outdatedness in Italy and highlights their special effect in Vivaldi's depiction of a sleep scene.

Early opera in Rome had been largely controlled and subsidized by the Barberini family. Although there is no evidence of viols being used in operas, there is plenty of documentation of consort playing and viol instruction at Cardinal Francesco Barberini's household. An inventory from 1634 of Cardinal

Example 9.9.   Cesti, *Il pomo d'oro*

Francesco and Antonio Barberini's court lists: "six viols which make a consort (conserto) in a wooden case painted red with the arms of his Eminence."[22] In 1638 the Landgraf of Hessen assisted at a public festival at Monte Cavallo to which the porter, according to the pay records, had to carry "all viols." The Barberini family seems to have provided a conclave for viol playing at a time when Venice had switched to modern strings with the exception of the rare employment of viols for special effects in performances at the orphanage-conservatories.

Throughout the Baroque period Venetian opera flourished at the Emperial Court in Vienna. One of the most sumptuous spectacles of the seventeenth century was *Il pomo d'oro,* a collaboration between Sbarra and Cesti. It was performed in 1668 in the new Theatre on the Cortina designed by Burnacini. The production was exceptionally elaborate concerning stage design and orchestration and clearly reflected the difference between the means of an Emperial court and "public" opera houses like those in Venice. Nino Pirrotta pointed out that *Il pomo d'oro* is a late example of the influence of *intermedii* in operas.[23] The same affects which were expressed by a metaphorical use of string instruments in Venetian opera and oratorio and also by Buxtehude are emphasized in *Il pomo d'oro:* two laments, one in recitative style, the other an aria, and an aria of sleep are accompanied by three viole da gamba and a graviorgano in chordal style. They are the only examples of such scoring in this opera (ex. 9.9).

Two manuscript scores are extant for the opera *L'Orfeo* by Sartorio, one for a performance in Vienna, probably in 1672, the other for a performance in Venice in 1673.[24] Sinfoniae and ritornelli for a four-voice ensemble in Venice, a five-voice ensemble in Vienna, are notated in two treble, alto, an added tenor for Vienna, and bass clef, presumably indicating an ensemble of viole da braccio. The change of clefs to soprano, alto, alto, tenor in Vienna, and bass in the ritornello preceding Orfeo's lament signifies a change of affect. The composer strives for a darker sound to introduce the lament. While any instrumental designations are absent from the Venetian score, the Viennese score specifies the change of ensemble with the title "Sinfonia di viole." Orfeo's lament itself, although identical in both manuscripts, carries the performance indication in the rubric of the Viennese libretto: "Quest'aria va accompagnata de la sola lira, o viole all'inglese" (an aria accompanied by a lyra or by English viols). Here is an example of a composer probably preferring the accompaniment of a consort of viols to express the affect of lament. An alternative performance with viole da braccio, as seemed to be standard in Venice, does, of course, not change the basic affect. Pay records for the Emperial court indicate that Vienna employed a number of gambists until the early eighteenth century.[25] English influence also contributed to the continued usage of viole da gamba in Vienna, similar to the situation in northern Germany.

A genre that made frequent use of viol consort is the Viennese *sepolcro,* a type of oratorio with the theme of Passion and crucifixion of Christ. Characteristic of *sepolcri* was an ensemble of four or five viols, as we encounter in the *sepolcri* by Draghi and the Emperor, Leopold I himself.[26]

A direct tie exists between the Viennese *sepulcro* or "castrum doloris," as it was often referred to on title pages, and Buxtehude's *Abendmusik* "Castor doloris" which he wrote in honor of Leopold I's death. Unfortunately, neither the music nor any scoring indications in the libretto exist for Buxtehude's work.

Returning to Germany we also find examples of affective viol scoring in operas. Bontempi's *Il paride,* a work similar in scope to Cesti's *Il pomo d'oro,* was written for a performance at the Dresden opera in 1662. One of the *intermedii* consists of an entrée of the graces, a ballet with "Music, con Violen di Gamba," representing a delicate, possibly celestial affect.

In German dramas violin/viol groups are frequently mentioned in librettos with text indication and stage directions to mourning and slumber scenes.[27] Andreas Gryphius indicates "Violen" in his drama *Leo Arminius* in connection with the stage direction "unter während dem Saitenspiel und Gesang entschläft Leo auf dem Stuhle sitzend" (to the continuous sound of string music and song Leo falls asleep while sitting on a chair). In a libretto by Hallmann, Breslau 1667, the rubrics read: "Nachdem sich Urania niederlegt, wird ein liebliches und gleichsam entferntes Stückchen auff etlichen Violen di gamba gespielt werden, bis sie entschlummert" (After Urania lies down a melodious and rather distant sounding little piece will be played on various viols until she falls asleep). Without exact specification adjectival qualifications for string ensembles point to the usage of viols to express certain affects, sometimes with added psychological connotations as, for example, in Rosenmüller's libretto *Der Beständige Orpheus* (The Steadfast Orpheus), 1684. After Orpheus's lament the stage directions read: "Die gelinde Music continirt nach einer stillen Trauermusic" (gentle music continues after a quiet lament), and later the melancholic Orpheus is accompanied by a "getrübtes Saitenspiel" (darkened, overshadowed string sound). The libretto to Keiser's *Nebukadnezar,* written for the Hamburg stage in 1704, also uses adjectives like "lieblich, getrübt, gelinde" (sweet, gentle, darkened) to accompany, for example, Nebukadnezar's dream. We know, however, that there was hardly any use of gambas in the Hamburg opera.

One relevant example, rare because text and music are still extant, is Johann Wolfgang Franck's aria lamento *Schickung, ach! es ist zu viel* from his opera *Cara Mustapha.* (See Buelow article, ex. 7.6.) This aria, from the second part of the opera *Der unglückliche Cara Mustapha,* is in slow triple proportion with the indicated tempo designation "adagio." Its mode is E minor, the old phrygian. Two violins accompany the soprano voice and function as a simple chordal realization of the basso continuo. The composer emphasizes the expression of lament with sigh figures—appoggiaturas and rests—in both vocal and instrumental parts, even in the structural basso continuo. The strings intensify the pathos of the lamento character.

Also the aria for soprano *O, der großen Barmherzigkeit, mein Herz zerbricht in tausend Stücken*, an aria from the third act of *Wacht! Euch zum Streit gefasset macht*, an *Abendmusik* possibly composed by Buxtehude, fits with its string ritornelli into the category of the affective aria lament with introverted string accompaniment, or better, string interjection. The intimate sonority originally associated with viols could, of course, as also demonstrated in the above examples, be emulated by modern strings, just as we have seen it happen in the laments of the Venetian opera.

The strongest tradition of affective string accompaniments originated with the Italian *lamento*. It is this tradition which the Germans, mostly the Lutherans, transformed according to their own liturgical needs and used in compositions connected with Passiontide. The close connection between the operatic, secular lament and the lament as a sacred composition exists already in Monteverdi's output with his *contrafactum Pianto della Madonna sopra il Lamento d'Arianna*, published in 1641 in his collection of sacred works *Selva morale e spirituale*. Matthias Weckmann copied this very lament. His autograph copy together with a large collection of seventeenth-century Italian music is housed in the Ratsbücherei, Lüneburg.[28]

Quite an extensive repertory of concerted vocal music exists in primarily Lutheran areas of northern Germany, the Baltic Sea, and Saxony in which the affects of an Italian *lamento* tradition merge with an English tradition of scoring for viols. The two traditions complement each other in such a way as to amplify the affective content of the compositions. Among the composers in this tradition are Heinrich Schütz who, of course, was the most famous transmitter of the Italian style in seventeenth-century Germany, his pupils Matthias Weckmann and Johann Theile who both moved on to the north, also two composers from the Bach family: Johann Michael and Johann Christoph Bach. The northern German circle is, among others, represented by Franz Tunder (Buxtehude's predecessor in Lübeck), Nicolaus Bruhns (also associated with Lübeck), and Christian Geist (who spent most of his career at the Hofkapelle in Sweden and as organist in Copenhagen, Denmark).

A few pieces may serve as examples. Geist chose an orchestration of three viols only, presumably bass viols (alto, alto, bass clef), for a composition that sets the text of Christ's burial according to the gospel of John: "Es war aber an der Stätte, da er gekreuzigt war." After an introductory *sinfonia* the tenor delivers the biblical text in simple recitative style to the accompaniment of the viols' dark chordal backdrop (ex. 9.10). The texture of the instrumental writing changes to a motet style in the accompaniment of the strophic aria *O*

Example 9.10. Christian Geist, *Es war an der Stätte, da er gekreuzigt war*

Example 9.11.   Weckmann, *Wie liegt die Stadt so wüste*

Traurigkeit, o Herzeleid (O sadness, o sorrow). This aria, in fact, closely resembles an English consort song.

Weckmann has composed a number of sacred concertos with *lamento* character. A highly Italianate and stunningly expressive piece is *Wie liegt die Stadt so wüste* (How desolate lies the city) on a text adapted from the Lamentations of Jeremiah. Weckmann scored the concerto for soprano and bass voice with a five-voice string ensemble of two violins and three bass viols, and organ. The soprano recites the opening question "how desolate lies the city?" in a near monotone above the continuo's *lamento* bass (see ex. 9.11). Jeremiah, represented by the bass voice, follows this arid recitative with his first lamentation

Example 9.12. J. C. Bach, *Ach, daß ich Wassers g'nug hätte*

Example 9.12, cont.

Example 9.13.   Schütz, *Die sieben Worte Jesu Christi am Kreuz*

supported by the full string ensemble. The stark contrast amplifies the *affetuoso* character of the strings. Alexander Silbiger has suggested that "Wie liegt die Stadt so wüste" is the first in a cycle of three concertos with *lamento* character, all scored with an instrumental ensemble of two or three violins and three viole da gamba with organ basso continuo.

My last example of a *lamento* setting is an excerpt from a lament by Johann Christoph Bach, *Ach, daß ich Wassers g'nug hätte,* scored for alto voice, a five-voice string ensemble with violin, three viols, violone, and basso continuo (see ex. 9.12). The striking use of dissonances that rock back and forth between root-position chord and diminished triad over a pedal, the emphatic repeat of the opening motive in the violin, later in the voice, with its falling gesture expressed as a *saltus duriusculus,* the choice of the phrygian-mode notation, and the accompaniment of the string ensemble form a conglomerate of expressive devices that depicts the *lamento* character with unique intensity.

The other genre that ties in with the *lamento* and makes extensive use of affective viol scoring is that of the *historia,* the story of the Passion being its most common exponent. In *Die Sieben Worte Jesu Christi am Kreuz* (Christ's last words on the cross) from ca. 1645, Heinrich Schütz singled out Christ as the only *persona* with an instrumental accompaniment other than just a basso continuo, an accompaniment of two unspecified instruments notated in soprano and alto clef (ex. 9.13). Given the clefs we have to exclude a performance with violins (they are always notated in treble clef). Probably Schütz intended the warmer sound of treble and alto viol to surround Christ with a special aura. It is the Evangelist's part that receives noteworthy treatment in Schütz's "Resurrection History" from 1623. According to Schütz's preface, the Evangelist can be accompanied either by a continuo with organ, lute, or pandora realization or by four viole da gamba without continuo. With his explicit preference for viols Schütz reveals his interest in a more personalized characterization of the Evangelist. As mentioned above, Schütz employed violettae, i.e., viols, in the "Christmas History," 1664. *Intermedia* I, VII, and VIII are scored for soprano, two viols, and basso continuo. In *Intermedium* I the angel announces the birth of Christ to the shepherds. In the latter *Intermedia* the angel appears in Joseph's dreams, first urging him to flee Egypt and eventually telling him that he may safely return to Israel. Schütz added a programmatic subtitle to all three numbers: "Worunter bisweilen des Christkindleins Wiege mit eingeführt wird" (under which the Christ child's cradle is introduced) (ex. 9.14). The rocking cradle is represented by a repeated descending halfstep motive. The emblematic use of viols enhances a celestial affect on the one hand (by association with the angel), and an affect of gentle sleep on the other (by association with dream and cradle).

Johann Theile and Johann Sebastiani used similar instrumental effects to emphasize the words of Christ and those of the Evangelist. Theile specified on

Example 9.14. Schütz, *Christmas History*

Example 9.15.　Keiser, *St. Mark Passion*

the title page of his *St. Matthew Passion* (1673 print) an accompaniment of two viols or violas for the voice of Christ and two violas for the Evangelist. All other characters were to sing in simple recitative style to the accompaniment of a continuo only. Sebastiani used two violins to highlight Christ and three viole da gamba or da braccio in the Evangelist's accompanied recitatives of his *St. Matthew Passion* (1672 print, ms. ca. 1663 or 1664). The alternative performance indication of viole da gamba or da braccio in both Passions suggests a lack of viols in certain places by the last quarter of the seventeenth century.

The tradition of accompanying Christ's voice with a string ensemble continued into the eighteenth century. In his *St. Mark Passion,* ca. 1717, Reinhard Keiser juxtaposed the accompanied recitatives of Christ with simple recitatives for all other personages. The slow chordal writing of an ensemble of two violins and two violas again intimates the special aura around Christ's words (ex. 9.15). Although not specified, it is possible that the inner parts notated in alto and tenor clef might have been performed on viols. Keiser used a viola, not a violoncello, as an obbligato continuo for the chorale *Wenn ich einmal soll scheiden* (Be near me, Lord, when dying). This part exceeds the register of a viola da braccio and was most certainly performed on a viola da gamba. Keiser's *St. Mark Passion* leads us directly to J. S. Bach who himself copied out some of its parts for his own performance of the work. In Bach's *St. Matthew Passion* the seventeenth-century five-voice string ensemble with two darker inner voices of viole da gamba or braccio has been superseded and replaced by the modern quartet with one viola da braccio (ex. 9.16). Although the configuration of the ensemble changed, the *affetuoso* character for the accompaniment of Christ's voice stayed the same.

The previous investigation leads to the following conclusion: the *lamento* of the early Italian opera with its conventional string accompaniment started a tradition whose influence continued into the German sacred concertos and *historiae*. In certain centers of Germany, also in Vienna, this tradition was, until the late seventeenth century, inseparably linked to the sonority of accompanying viols. Pieces with chordal string accompaniment highlighting one very special voice, be it with viole da gamba or braccio, fit Jacob Wilhelm Lustig's description in his *Muzykaale Spraakkonst* (Amsterdam, 1754): "Such pieces, called 'accompagnati,' are eminently suited to arouse and sustain the most powerful and exalted emotions."[29]

Buxtehude's vocal music with the accompaniment of a full or a partial consort of viols is representative of the concurrence of two larger traditions in seventeenth-century Germany: the tradition of English consort music which, apart from its mellow string sonority, did not serve a function of particularly affective meaning, and the tradition of Italian dramatic music in which the string accompaniment stood as a metaphor for certain affects, mainly celestial, sleep and lamenting, and took on the role of "sonorous stage design."

Example 9.16. J. S. Bach, St. *Matthew Passion*

vln 1

vln 2

vla

Jesus

p Mein Va-ter, ist's mög-lich, so ge- he die- ser Kelch von mir, doch nicht wie ich will, son- dern wie du willst.

Bc

Notes

1. *Roger North on Music*, transcribed and ed. by John Wilson (London: Novello, 1959), p. 25. This particular excerpt has been taken from Roger North's autobiography which dates from ca. 1695.

2. Ibid., p. 222. This passage appeared in *An Essay of Musicall Ayre*, ca. 1715–20, in a chapter headed *The Respublica of Consort*.

3. W. Henry Hill, *Antonio Stradivari, His Life and Work (1644–1737)*, (London: W. E. Hill, 1902; reprint New York: Dover, 1963), p. 110.

4. This is a detail of a painting that appeared in the catalogue to the exhibition of "Meister der Barockmusik. Norddeutsche Musikkultur um Bach und Händel" (Hamburg, 1985).

5. Johann Mattheson, *Das neu-eröffnete Orchestre* (Hamburg, 1713), p. 280. The reference here is to the bass viola da gamba.

6. Ellen Rosand, "The Descending Tetrachord: An Emblem of Lament," *Musical Quarterly* 65 (1979), pp. 346–59.

7. J. M. Müller-Blattau, ed., *Die Kompositionslehre Heinrich Schützens in der Fassung seines Schülers Ch. Bernhard*, 2nd ed. (Kassel: Bärenreiter, 1963), p. 95.

8. Mattheson, *Das neu-eröffnete Orchestre*.

9. Søren Sørensen points out that this form of conversation in music was commonly used as a regular feature in funeral ceremonies. See the preface to his edition (Kopenhagen: W. Hansen.)

10. Martin Geck has discussed the last example from *Fürwahr, er trug unsere Krankheit* and the one from *Herzlich lieb hab ich dich, o Herr* in *Die Vokalmusik Dietrich Buxtehudes und der frühe Pietismus*, Kieler Schriften zur Musikwissenschaft no. 15 (Kassel: Bärenreiter, 1963), pp. 176–77. He talks about these sections as showing Buxtehude's interest in musical mysticism.

11. The complete libretto has been reprinted in André Pirro, *Dietrich Buxtehude* (Paris: Librairie Fischbacher Société Anonyme, 1913; reprint Geneva: Minkoff, 1976), pp. 175–84.

12. See Geck, *Vokalmusik*, p. 235.

13. For an impressive list of family connections and other musical contacts and exchanges between England and Germany, see Werner Braun, *Britannia Abundans* (Tutzing: Schneider, 1977), chapter 1.

14. All of Brade's printed collections are housed in the Herzog Albrecht Bibliothek in Wolfenbüttel.

15. See Howard Mayer Brown, *Sixteenth-Century Instrumentation: The Music of the Florentine Intermedii* (N.p.: American Institute of Musicology, 1973).

16. Ibid., p. 50.

17. Ibid., pp. 109 and 122. The instrumental designation "viole" in this case probably refers to the "violoni di gamba" or bass viols. Brown gives a probable disposition of voices and instruments, the bass viols playing parts notated in two tenor, baritone, and bass clefs.

18. Ellen Rosand, "The Descending Tetrachord," p. 350, n. 12.

19. See Lorenzo Bianconi and Thomas Walker, "Production, Consumption and Political Function of Seventeenth-Century Opera," *Early Music History* 4 (1984), p. 209.

20. Eleanor Selfridge-Field, *Venetian Instrumental Music from Gabrieli to Vivaldi* (Oxford: Blackwell, 1975), p. 45. Selfridge-Field mentions an increase of instrumental music and instrumental accompaniment towards the end of the seventeenth century.

21. See facsimile edition of the manuscript score housed in Torino, published by the Accademia Musicale Chigiana, Siena, 1948, p. 142.

22. See Frederick Hammond, "Girolamo Frescobaldi and a Decade of Music in Casa Barberini: 1634–1643," *Analecta Musicologica* 19 (1980), pp. 94–124. The inventory is mentioned in n. 44, p. 109. In 1636, twenty-one sets of viol music were purchased by Mazzocchi. An interest in viol playing seems to have been actively pursued in the Barberini family.

23. Nino Pirrotta, "Early Opera and Aria," *Music and Theatre from Poliziano to Monteverdi* (Cambridge University Press, 1975), p. 271.

24. See Ellen Rosand's introduction to "L'Orfeo," reprint, Milan: Ricordi, 1983.

25. Ludwig Ritter von Köchel, *Die Kaiserliche Hof-Musikkapelle in Wien von 1543–1867* (Vienna: Beck'sche Universitäts-Buchhandlung, 1896; reprint Hildesheim: Olms, 1976). Köchel writes: "Die Viola da gamba . . . war in der Hofkapelle von 1682 (vielleicht auch früher) bis 1740 mit 1,2, bis 4 Gambisten besetzt, von denen Fr. Ant. Schmidbauer excelliert zu haben scheint. Das Violoncell war in der Hofkapelle seit etwa 1680 neben der Viola da gamba in Verwendung." A more recent and also more reliable study is that of Franz Hadomowsky, "Barocktheater am Wiener Kaiserhof. Mit einem Spielplan (1625–1740)," *Jahrbuch der Gesellschaft für Wiener Theaterforschung,* 1951/52. Important, of course, is the fact that Schmelzer, the Hofkapellmeister since 1682, was an excellent gambist and contributed a fair amount of repertory for strings including the viola da gamba. Some of his compositions are rather virtuosic for the viol.

26. On Draghi see Rudolf Schnitzler, *The Sacred Dramatic Music of Antonio Draghi* (Ph.D. diss., University of North Carolina at Chapel Hill, 1971), particularly pp. 200–202.

27. Most of the following information I have taken from Andrew D. McCredie, *Instrumentarium and Instrumentation in the North German Baroque Opera* (diss., Hamburg, 1964).

28. See Alexander Silbiger, ed., *Four Sacred Concertos* by Matthias Weckmann, vol. 46 (Madison: A-R Editions, 1984), p. xxvii, n. 28.

29. Laurence Dreyfus, *Bach's Continuo Group. Players and Practices in his Vocal Works* (Cambridge, Mass.: Harvard University Press, 1987), as quoted on p. 83.

10

Literary Perspectives on the Texts of Buxtehude's *Abendmusiken*

Gloria Flaherty

Reading the libretti of Buxtehude's *Abendmusiken* is like reading an anthology of New High German poetry of the sixteenth and seventeenth centuries. Anyone with some expertise in the German language of today can do so with little or no effort. Except for an occasional archaic word, quaint form, or overwrought expression, the texts are linguistically comprehensible. I stress this because such was not universally the case during the Reformation and Counter-Reformation. At that time, there were multifarious German dialects striving to survive their own relentless evolution from the primordial Indo-European to Proto-German to East, North, and West Germanic, and then on through Old High German to Middle High German and eventually New High German.[1]

Exploration of the means whereby those German dialects could be made mutually comprehensible had been steadily encouraged for political as well as economic reasons. The Chanceries of the Holy Roman Empire of the German Nation had even developed a kind of linguistic common denominator for communicating important matters among each other during the late Middle Ages. Technology, however, was developing at so rapid a pace in the German lands that it made linguistic unification even more realistic. Religion finally saw to the successful implementation of that unification. The movable type invented by Johannes Gensfleisch, who preferred his matronymic, Gutenberg (ca. 1400–ca. 1468), was applied in fantastically farsighted ways by Martin Luther (1483–1546), the outspoken leader of the general movement towards ecclesiastical reform.

Luther helped to liberate the German language from its ageold bondage to Latin. He tried to inculcate a natural grammatical awareness in his countrymen while simultaneously either standardizing certain forms or purging some elements. He rejected the double negation, as, for example, in "Das geht ja kein

Kaiser nix an."[2] He reduced the number of prefixes and suffixes that could be added to any given stem. Finally, he shortened many other words, so that, for example, *Besuchung* became *Besuch,* and *das mittlere Zeitalter* became *das Mittelalter.*[3]

Luther's crafty political sense, much like that of a Chicago ward politician able to turn out the vote, enabled him to get the people to accept not only his message, but also the form in which it was delivered. He advocated hymns and church services in the vernacular. He also instigated a new German translation of the Bible. While that translation might not have united the peoples speaking different German dialects, it did give greater impetus to the development of a unified German language that would be comprehensible in all regions of Middle Europe.

Luther's work on the Bible began during his stay at the Wartburg and lasted throughout his lifetime. As a humanist trained in current philological methods and research techniques, he consulted available scholarly findings and sought sources earlier than the Latin Vulgate, namely those in ancient languages like Hebrew and Greek. His intention was to come to understand such sources well enough to render them into a German language that would be universally comprehensible. His approach involved consulting the devotional publications, mystical tracts, and those translations of the Bible that were available. He also relied heavily on common everyday usage. Conferences with multilingual scholars and theologians as well as with rabbinical experts helped Luther determine which German expressions best suited the meaning of the text at hand. Throughout this process, Luther used the language of the Saxon chancery at Meissen as his model. The common German language that Luther managed to develop spread quickly to all those areas where his reforms had been readily accepted. Because of the technological advances of print culture, that common language had also spread to those areas that remained loyal to the Church of Rome. Despite obvious confessional differences, New High German was very definitely in the ascendancy. By 1622, the Low German literary standard (perhaps best exemplified by the Lübeck Bible), which had been steadily developing from the municipal constitutions and laws of the Hanseatic towns, had already been superseded by New High German.[4]

During Buxtehude's lifetime, there was ever-increasing concern about regulating and refining the German language so that it would be on an equal footing with French and English. Many hoped that a common German language without imported words and forms would have political ramifications—in other words, that it would lead to nationhood with a centralized capital that could influence, if not dictate, style and taste. In addition to the dictionaries of German in German—not of German in Latin or French—there were orthographic reforms, like those indicated in Justus Georg Schottel's (1612–76) *Ausführliche Arbeit von der Teutschen Haupt-Sprache* (1663).[5]

As its syntax became standardized and its vocabulary more and more refined, the German language gained mightily in expressiveness. Its vexatious
prefixes and suffixes, among other features, allowed for the coinage of new
words by mystics, philosophers, and scientists alike. The language began to
shed its rustic aura, slowly gaining the reputation of a sophisticated means for
polite discourse.

This tendency was given support by patriotic societies founded in the
seventeenth century to cultivate things German. Literary scholars refer to them
as *Sprachgesellschaften* because of their ongoing effort to purge foreign influences from the language and thereby from German culture. The *Elbschwanenor-
den,* which was founded by Johann Rist (1607–67) in 1660 and had its effects
as well as members in Lübeck, strongly supported the kind of standardized New
High German that we observe in the libretti of Buxtehude's *Abendmusiken.* Rist
himself provided a brilliant demonstration of that language with his Evangelical
hymn *O Ewigkeit du Donnerwort.*[6] Conrad von Hövelen (fl. 1660), who wrote
under the pseudonym Candorin, published a list of members in the middle of
the seventeenth century.[7] Buxtehude is not among those names, though there
are a remarkably large number of poets talented enough to have entered the
twentieth-century canon of what should be read by members of the Society for
German Renaissance and Baroque Literature.[8] Von Hövelen also wrote a most
interesting treatise defending opera as among the *adiaphora*—that is, middle
things unquestionably acceptable in the secular sphere—and comparing it to
certain kinds of church music.[9]

German rhetoric was also enriched by the results of a weltering assortment
of experiments during Buxtehude's lifetime. Cicero, Quintilian, and Horace
would have been generally known due to the all-pervasiveness of the Latinate
tradition. Rhetoric was part of the school curriculum and would have been
learned deductively through rote memorization of examples and principles.
Once committed to memory, those examples were repeatedly imitated, so that
the pupil had opportunities to practice and adjust. Educated persons had mastered the figures well enough to apply them readily to different situations.
Among the more popular ones during the seventeenth century were oxymoron,
chiasmus, ellipsis, paranomasia, asyndeton, polysyndeton, anaphora, and
epiphora. In the last quarter of the seventeenth century, the treatise on the
sublime attributed to Longinus was rediscovered and translated. It allowed for
rhapsodic usages encouraging transport and the kind of flying high that still is
associated with the trancelike states achieved by some religious enthusiasts.
Sublimity was thereafter often cited as an excuse for rhetorical lapses as well
as infractions against the Franco-Roman neoclassical code of artistic laws.

Understanding of German metrics also underwent great change in the
course of the seventeenth century. The doggerel of earlier popular poetry was
replaced by the alexandrine of French origin. In both cases, accentuation was

related to the number of syllables, often resulting in awkward, if not clumsy German verse. Martin Opitz (1597–1639), whose *Buch von der Deutschen Poeterey* appeared in 1624, gave added impetus to a reform movement when he attempted to discover linguistic laws inductively. He argued that German was inherently very different from the Romance languages. It had dynamic rather than musical accentuation and therefore could not be scanned. Composer-poets, like Johann Hermann Schein (1586–1630), knew Opitz and not only ratified his work with their own but also gave it greater currency by passing it on to their disciples. Schein, like Johann Kuhnau (1660–1722) and others who were to hold the position of *Thomaskantor* in Leipzig, enjoyed very close association with those involved in the literary scene. One of Schein's most successful pupils was Paul Fleming (1609–40), whose poems expressed human feeling and religious fervor deeply enough to become an essential part of the cultural heritage of all German-speaking peoples.[10]

Despite such universal interest and concern, the seventeenth century was not one of the strongest for German poetic achievements. No figures in any way comparable to Shakespeare or Milton emerged. There were many very good, well-trained poets, even some truly excellent ones, but most were poetasters, or just plain awful rhymesters. A later, positivistically oriented philologist and scholar of German literature, Wilhelm Scherer (1841–86) reflected what had become the negative evaluation of such Baroque poetry when he advanced his *Wellentheorie* after reviewing such writings. It prejudicially held that flowering periods came in 600-year intervals, every 300 years producing a wave crest or trough. The glorious period of Middle High German poetry was 1200, Sherer argued, while the age of Goethe conveniently climaxed in 1800. Accordingly, the years 1500, as well as 2100, were considered wave troughs. Scherer pre-dicted that the next great period would be around 2400.[11]

While not one of the greatest periods, the seventeenth century was nonetheless extremely rich in strategies of assimilation, experimentation, and invention. New forms were cultivated, and older forms were given different contents as well as contexts. Opera and other musical theatrical forms abounded as did novels and novellas. And, there were the learned poems and the culturally pretentious (though poetically conservative) *Meistergesänge* in addition to products of oral culture, such as folksongs, incantations, and spells.

Patricians and other burghers counted poetry as one of the basic staples in their social lives. They consumed vast quantities of what were called *Gelegenheitsgedichte*—occasional poems, or greeting-card-type poetry commemorating major passages such as births, weddings, and funerals. These poems were written by *Zeremonienmeister* (masters of ceremonies) as well as by moonlighting lawyers, physicians, businessmen, burgomasters, and ministers. Teachers were frequently involved because they were the ones responsible for giving formal instruction in the techniques of versification in the local schools. Whoever the poet was, he, and an occasional she, could easily avail himself of one of the burgeoning number of how-to books that outlined in great detail the craft of poetry. Books of rhymes and rhetorical figures were as plentiful as manuals of the rules, which were considered indisputable laws due to the regrettably unquestioned acceptance of the Franco-Roman neoclassical code. One such manual purported to teach its purchaser the knack of producing the well-wrought poem in thirty-six hours. In another, it was twelve, and in yet another, only six. The publishing industry had made such great strides in producing handsome profits that the business angle was never overlooked. As a result, how-to books were readily supplied for those people who cultivated poetry-writing among their fashionable diversions. Since there were neither laws of copyright nor notions of plagiarism or originality, borrowing and stealing were rampant. Printers changed texts and publishers produced unauthorized editions, thereby keeping for themselves royalties actually due the poets. Musicians and performers made alterations freely, as did the producers of occasional poems. And then there were those who brazenly filched lines, stanzas, or whole passages for inclusion in their own writings.

Most important among all such literary genres before and after the Reformation were hymns. They represented many different kinds of poetry as well as various sources. Some were contrafacture—love songs, folksongs, or other items were altered to suit the new purpose. Such hymns often circulated on flyers or broadsheets that were printed by entrepreneurs hoping to get rich quickly. They could be bought like other popular tunes. Since at least the fifteenth century, the tradition was to indicate *im ton* or *melodie* as mnemonic devices. Some songs as well as melodies were cited in chronicles as being among the top ten of a particular year. Later on, the most popular hymns were collected in hymnals. Parishioners, especially the very old and the very young, were not at all interested in memorizing words. Their intellectual sluggishness, however, provided the foundation for a lucrative kind of hymnal printing and publishing. The preachers even seem to have conspired with the publishers to sell more and higher-priced books to be read and studied at home. Interestingly enough, the Newberry Library's collection would indicate that seventeenth- and early eighteenth-century German hymnals had similar topical organization, always including a section on *Wachsamkeit* (wakefulness or awareness) and a section on *Kampf und Streit* (fight and struggle).

Due to the Thirty Years War, the Counter-Reformation, and the generally chaotic circumstances of the times, the hymnbooks which became songbooks then became *Erbauungsbücher,* or devotional books. All such books continued to sell very well. Furthermore, as the Enlightenment gathered more momentum in the course of the eighteenth century, hymns and hymnals were subjected to increasingly rational treatment. Consequently, their organization changed radically. The language, the metrics, in sum, the poetic quality improved, yet the religious energy and power of the "original" or earlier versions somehow got lost. Enlightened poets, like the well-known Christian Fürchtegott Gellert (1715–69), persevered in trying to write poetry according to the melodies or metrical schemes of older hymns.[12] However, Frederick the Great (1712–86), who issued an edict in 1740 allowing religious diversity in Prussia, summed up the Enlightenment evaluation of the hymn with his pronouncement of 1780: "A person can believe in my lands whatever he wants as long as he is legitimate. As far as the hymnals are concerned, everyone is free to sing 'Nun ruhen alle Wälder' or whatever other stupid and foolish stuff he wants."[13]

Many were the themes that were treated in this vast and divergent accumulation of printed matter that I have chosen to call seventeenth-century German poetry. The most common had to do with the pastoral life *vis à vis* the one governed by money, commerce, competition, and the capitalistic system. Again and again, *Welt* (world) rhymed with *Geld* (money). The vanity and transitoriness of earthly existence were pervasive in such poems. Elements of Germanic patriotism were everywhere noticeable, as were concerns for the commonweal and for brotherly love.[14]

North European resistance to the Christianization process was also evident in the many references to magic, divining, ritualistic sex, and even cannibalism. In the seventeenth century, the witches of East Prussia and Lithuania were thought to "cure and cause most diseases to such as they love or hate, and this of melancholy among the rest."[15] They were known to use knots, amulets, and philtres, as well as datura, bhang, and other substances that stimulated opium-like reactions of mirth or ecstasy.[16] An eighteenth-century German encyclopedia even reported that although the official religion of Lübeck might have been Lutheran, some church altars openly displayed hex signs while others hid the inscribed incantations that were supposed to ward off the evil spirits that might try to intrude.[17] Apparently organ builders were not the only ones who were superstitious! In northern Europe, not only was there a strong underground belief in witchcraft, but there were also many reports of ecstatic visions, ascensionism, and bilocation. Associated with such practices in the common mind were the Quakers, Shakers, Enthusiasts, and other kinds of convulsives.

Furthermore, in the middle of the seventeenth century, there was generally sustained worry about lycanthropy and cannibalism. In 1649, Paul Einhorn, who opposed the lascivious dances and songs associated with orgiastic rituals, likened contemporary Christianity to a fragile veneer over deeply entrenched pagan beliefs; even during the holiest holiday seasons, he wrote, there were loathsome parties, "with dancing, hopping, singing, and gruesome clamour, in addition to gourmandizing and drinking, whereby they then went from one house to the next in such a dreadful and voluptuous condition and spent the entire night there."[18]

Now it is time to turn to the text of *Wacht! Euch zum Streit gefasset macht*. Whoever might have prepared it managed to call up and apply the exact same skills as the librettist of *Die Hochzeit des Lamms*. Both texts suggest the method of cut and paste so often used by the purveyors of seventeenth-century German occasional poetry. The poetic corpus of Philipp Nicolai (1556–1608), for example, was plundered to the extent that some of his widely known poems were hacked up and appear stanza for stanza, or one stanza here and another one later on. In the *Hochzeit*, the third stanza of his *Wachet auff ruft uns die Stimme* appears four pages after the first two stanzas. On the other hand, number 32 of *Wacht* incorporates the second stanza of *Wie schön leuchtet die Morgenstern*, a text also used by Johann Kuhnau and, subsequently, Johann Sebastian Bach.

Both the *Hochzeit* and *Wacht* texts contain sometimes convoluted examples of contrafacture or the slightly veiled religious application of secular poetry. An example that would have suggested to seventeenth-century Germans the entire poetic heritage of the Judeo-Christian world is the verbally and poetically simple, yet touching *Ich bin dein und du bist mein*. While André Pirro traces it to the biblical Song of Songs, I cannot help but think that the many folksongs, like the one in Middle High German about the heart being a shrine lockable with a key, were intentionally implied:

> Du bist mîn, ih bin dîn:
> des solt dû gewiss sîn.
> du bist beslozzen
> in mînem herzen;
> verloren ist daz sluzzelîn:
> dû muost immer drinne sîn.[19]

There is also widespread inclusion of the hymns that were popular enough to be collected into early eighteenth-century hymnbooks, which meant they appealed to conservative audiences willing to pay hard-earned cash for them. The *Jesu meine Freude, meiner Seelen Weide,* for example, was apparently written by one Johann Franck (1618–77), who is known to historians as an eminent jurist and the burgomaster of Guben. That particular hymn, however, can be traced back to one of Heinrich Albert's Flora arias for an opera published in Magdeburg in 1645.[20] In other words, his eminency the burgomaster produced a contrafacture by changing, among other things, the name Flora to Jesu. Several other pieces of Franck's also became popular hymns.

The *Wacht* text is similarly like a necklace of conservative hymns and poems strung on a very fragile connective thread. In addition to recognizing the second stanza of the Nicolai, I managed to identify some of those pearls that appear at least with their first lines intact, which, unfortunately, is all that literary scholars can rely on, due to the operative indexing principles. The aria, no. 31, *O tausendmal selige, fröhliche Stunden* (O thousandfold blissful, joyful hours) is apparently from the pen of one C. Trincius, according to the *Magdeburgisches Gesangbuch* of 1701. The chorale, no. 45, *Herzlich lieb hab ich dich, o Herr* (Deep in my heart I love you, Lord) is purportedly by one Martin Schalling. The first written record of it I have found dates from 1571, and Mathiam Gastritz, the organist at Ambers, is acknowledged as its composer. It also appears in the Lübeck hymnal of 1607. No. 45 is only the first stanza—albeit divided into three parts—of a poem of three full stanzas, so the element of choice was obviously very important. The chorale, no. 80, *Mit Fried und Freud ich fahr dahin,* appeared in Johann Walters's *Geystliches Gesangk Buchleyn* (Wittenberg, 1524), yet has been attributed to none other than Martin Luther himself. I do not wish to belabor the point, but it strikes me as more than merely interesting that the chorales seem to have been selected from the sixteenth century, when the Lutherans chose to use aggressive, strongly militaristic vocabulary as well as the first-person plural to stimulate unity or at least a sense of community, whereas the arias tend to be from the seventeenth century, when the stress on the individual soul was so strong, as, for instance, in the contributions of Paul Gerhardt (1607–76).

The texts of the Buxtehude *Abendmusiken* employ typically Baroque themes and rhetorical techniques, stressing metaphysical, political, and personal choices. Tripartite schemes are routine. Virtually all the various means of repetition can be found in *Wacht.* The very first aria's *"Wacht! Wacht! Wacht!"* provides a geminatio, iteratio, or epizeuxis by way of introduction. (The current English rhetorical handbooks usually offer the example, "O horror, horror, horror.") While this is continued in the second stanza, it is intensified by the kind of personification that produces allegory. The last provides the final compounding with faith alone as the ultimate weapon, something all Christian soldiers in Luther's army were supposed to believe they were equipped with.

While the extended personification and allegorization suggest an incipient dramatic intent, plot and suspense are, not surprisingly, lacking. (Even German playwrights of the seventeenth century did not have much in their plays that is genuinely dramatic by comparison with Shakespeare or what came afterwards in German drama.) Alternation of individuals and groups counted more than plot in the seventeenth century, and the libretti of the known Buxtehude *Abendmusiken* and the *Wacht* text reflect this. Moreover, there was concern for the visual and for fragrances, as reports of the early North German operatic performances indicate. Those concerning the Hamburg theater, for instance, mentioned the inclusion in scenic design not only of illuminations but also of flower petals and, in one instance, even released starlings.

The reception of all such musical dramatic works in the New High German language was not unanimously positive. The Pietists, along with other charismatic and pentecostal types of Christian believers avidly seeking social acceptance and their own theological legitimacy, were, as to be expected, more conservative about all such public matters, especially those having to do with assuming parts, playing roles, and making believe. They therefore castigated the heathen elements in all public performances, whether operatic treatments of Biblical subjects in Hamburg or generically vague musical pieces performed on Sundays in churches in Lübeck.[21] Their fears did have some basis in reality, since heathenism had still not been completely exterminated in the north.

The *Abendmusiken* in Lübeck and the operas in Hamburg evolved simultaneously during the last quarter of the seventeenth century. Many, many literary affinities indicate continuous, very rich cross-pollination. Johann Theile of Hamburg was, for example, good friends with Buxtehude, whose son-in-law did, indeed, in spite of the many nasty anecdotes, arrive in Lübeck after a stint in Hamburg. Complaints of obstreperous audience behavior on Sundays, the Sabbath, underscored the urgency some folk gave such critical issues.

The penetrating studies of Kerala Snyder and George Buelow have opened up all sorts of new avenues for investigating Buxtehude in light of the early German operatic debates and their concomitant implications for applied criticism. A desired, yet not predictable result would be closer cooperation among those representing all the existing disciplines involved.

Notes

1. John T. Waterman, *A History of the German Language with Special Reference to the Cultural and Social Forces That Shaped the Standard Literary Language* (Seattle and London: University of Washington Press, 1966), pp. 20–22, 42–51. See also Adolf Bach, *Geschichte der deutschen Sprache*, 6th rev. ed. (Heidelberg: Quelle & Meyer, 1956), pp. 73–92.

2. R. Priebsch and W. E. Collinson, *The German Language,* 6th ed. (London: Faber and Faber, 1968), pp. 390–91. Bach, *Geschichte,* pp. 189–95.

3. Waterman, *History,* pp. 128–35.

4. Schottel has been characterized in the twentieth century as "a poet of no mean stature." See Philippe Dollinger, *The German Hansa,* trans. and ed. D. S. Ault and S. H. Steinberg (London: Macmillan, 1970), p. 266. See also Wilson King, *Chronicles of Three Free Cities: Hamburg, Bremen, Lübeck* (New York: E. P. Dutton, 1914), p. 246. Bach, *Geschichte,* p. 179 and Waterman, *History,* p. 118.

5. Curt von Faber du Faur, *German Baroque Literature: A Catalogue of the Collection in the Yale University Library* (New Haven: Yale University Press, 1958), p. 190.

6. Ibid., p. 102.

7. *Candorins Deutscher Zimber Swan Darin des Hochlöbl: Ädelen Swan-Ordens Anfang, Zunämen, Bewandnis, Gebräuche, Satsungen, Ordensgesätse, samt der Hoch-ansähel: Geselschafter Ordens-Namen entworfen* (Lübeck, 1667), is available in the microfilm version of the von Faber du Faur collection at Yale, no. 416, p. 109.

8. Information about that society's activities can be obtained from Professor Barton Browning at the Pennsylvania State University.

9. *Eren- Danz- Singe Schauspiel-Entwurf* (n.p., 1663). Flaherty, *Opera in the Development of German Critical Thought* (Princeton: Princeton University Press, 1978), p. 340.

10. Von Faber du Faur (*German Baroque Literature*, p. 8) wrote, "Schein's musicianship joins in Fleming's lyrics with Opitz' more mature metrics to form the first true artistic lyrics."

11. Wilhelm Scherer, *Geschichte der Deutschen Litteratur* (Berlin: Weidmann, 1883), pp. 18–21.

12. A few composers, among them J. A. Hiller and C. P .E. Bach, claimed to have liked what he produced.

13. I am responsible for this translation, which was made from the German cited by Ernst Moritz von Arndt in *Von dem Wort und dem Kirchenliede nebst geistlichen Liedern* [Bonn: Weber, 1819], ed. Konrad Ameln (Hildesheim and New York: Olms, 1970), p. viii: "Ein jeder kann bei mir glauben, was er will, wenn er ehrlich ist. Was die Gesangbücher angehet, so stehet einem Jeden frei, zu singen: 'Nun ruhen alle Wälder' oder dergleichen dummes und und törichtes Zeug mehr."

14. Flaherty, "Money, Gold, and the Golden Age in Germany," *The Old World: Discovery and Rebirth,* ed. David Daiches and Anthony Thorlby (London: Aldus Books, 1974), pp. 378–80.

15. Robert Burton, *The Anatomy of Melancholy, what it is, with all the kinds, causes, symptomes, prognostickes & severall cures of it,* 3 pts. [Oxford, 1621], ed. Holbrook Jackson (London: J. M. Dent, 1932; reprint, New York: Vintage Books, 1977), pt. 1, p. 205.

16. Ibid., pt. 2, p. 247.

17. Johann Heinrich Zedler, *Grosses Vollständiges Universal-Lexikon aller Wissenschaften und Künste,* 64 vols., 4 suppl. vols. (Halle: Zedler, 1732–54; reprint, Graz: Akademische Druck- und Verlagsanstalt, 1962), S. v. Lübeck, col. 1061.

18. *Historica Lettica, Das ist Beschreibung der Lettischen Nation* (1649) in *Ueber die religiösen Vorstellungen der alten Völker in Liv- und Ehstland: Drei Schriften von Paul Einhorn und eine von Johann Wolfang Böckler, aufs neue wieder abgedruckt mit einer seltenen Nachricht Friedrich Engelken's über den grossen Hunger 1602* (Riga: N. Kymmel, 1857; reprint, Hanover-Döhren: Harro von Hirschheydt, 1968), p. 19.

19. André Pirro, *Dietrich Buxtehude* (Paris: Librairie Fischbacher, 1913; reprint, Geneva, 1976), p. 175. Ludwig Christian Erk, *Deutscher Liederhort, Auswahl der vorzüglicheren deutschen Volkslieder,* rev. ed. Franz M. Böhm, 3 vols. (Leipzig: Breitkopf & Härtel, 1893–94), vol. 2, no. 371, p. 187, mentioned the source: "In einem Liebesbriefe des Wernher v. Tegernsee, 12. Jahrh. Müchner Cod. Tegerns. 1008, Bl. 114b: Daher K. Bartsch, Liederdichter des 12.–14. Jahrh. S. 284 unter namenlosen Liedern." Also mentioned was that the motif was still very popular in Swiss, Austrian, Alsatian, and German folksongs.

20. A. F. W. Fischer, *Kirchenliedlexikon: Hymnologisch-literarische Nachweisungen über ca. 450 der wichtigsten und verbreitetsten Kirchenlieder aller Zeiten in alphabetischer Folge nebst einer Übersicht der Liederdichter,* 2 vols. (Gotha, 1878; reprint, Hildesheim: Olms, 1967), vol. 1, p. 378. See also von Faber du Faur, *German Baroque Literature,* no. 472, p. 128.

21. Gottfried Vockerodt (1665–1727) wrote in *Missbrauch der freyen Künste/ insonderheit Der Music/ nebenst abgenöthigter Erörterung der Frage: Was nach D. Luthers und anderer Evangelischen Theologorum und Politicorum Meinung von Opern und Comödien zu halten*

sey? Gegen Hn. D. Wentzels/ Hn. Joh. Christian Lorbers/ und eines Weissenfelsischen Hof-Musicantens Schmäh-Schrifften gründlich und deutlich vorgestellet (Frankfurt, 1697), pp. 122–30, that such works inculcated heathen topics rather than teaching what their adherents claimed. Martin Heinrich Fuhrmann was yet another who went on record as stating that all dancing, singing, and music excites to lust and lustful acts. See, for example, the following two works: *Das In unsern Opern-Theatris und Comoedien-Bühnen Siechende Christenthum und Siegende Heidenthum/ Auf veranlassung Zweyer wider den Musicalischen Patrioten Sich empörenden Hamburgischen Theatral-Malcontenten, Musandri und Harmonii/ betrachtet* (Berlin, 1728), and, *Die an der Kirchen Gottes gebauete Satans-Capelle/Darin dem Jehova Zebaoth zu Leid und Verdruss/ und dem Baal-Zebub zur Freud und Genuss, (1.) Die Operisten und Comoedianten mancher Orten ihren Zuschauern eine Theologiam Gentilium aus den Griechischen und Lateinischen Fabel-Mätzen, und eine Moral aus des verlohrnen Sohns Catechismo vorbringen; und (2.) Die Menschliche Welsche Wallachen und Amadis-Sirenen aus dem Hohen Lied Ovidii De Arte amandi, liebliche Venus-Lieder dabey singen; und (3.) Die Jubalisten mit Geigen und Pfeiffen nach des alten Adams Lust und Wust darzu klingen; und (4.) Sylvester mit seiner Herodias- Schwester, und Arlequin in einem Frantzösischen Kälber-Tantz herum springen; In einem Wald-Discours Über des Autoris zwey letzte Tractätlein wider die Hamburgischen Operisten* (Berlin, 1729).

11

Buxtehude, the Lübeck *Abendmusiken,* and *Wacht! Euch zum Streit gefasset macht*

Kerala J. Snyder

One of Buxtehude's chief claims to fame in seventeenth-century Lübeck lay in his production of an annual concert series, the *Abendmusiken,* in St. Mary's Church. These concerts took place on the last two Sundays of Trinity and the second, third, and fourth Sundays of Advent each year, immediately following the Sunday vesper service. The *Abendmusiken* did not form part of the liturgy of the church, however, nor was their presentation included in Buxtehude's responsibilities as organist of St. Mary's, the position he held from 1668 until his death in 1707. The financial support for the *Abendmusiken* came almost entirely from individual and corporate donations from the Lübeck business community, as we know from numerous letters of acknowledgment preserved in Buxtehude's hand.[1]

All the music for Buxtehude's known *Abendmusiken* is lost. Three libretti (*Die Hochzeit des Lamms, Castrum doloris, Templum honoris*), the titles of a few other works (*Himmlische Seelenlust auf Erden, Das allerschröcklichste und allererfreulichste,* and the individual titles in the mixed programs for the *Abendmusiken* of 1700), and the topic of one other (the parable of the prodigal son in 1689) are the only sure survivals from Buxtehude's famed concert series. Of more than one hundred preserved vocal works by Buxtehude, not one matches these texts, titles, or theme, although among them several suggest themselves as good candidates for performance in an *Abendmusik* of the type presented in 1700.

Among all the vocal works with sacred texts in German preserved from the latter part of the seventeenth century, only one work is of sufficient length to raise the possibility that it might be a dramatic *Abendmusik* by Buxtehude: an anonymous oratorio in three acts, untitled, with the opening text *Wacht! Euch zum Streit gefasset macht.* It is transmitted in a set of parts copied in the mid-1680s at the Swedish royal court in Stockholm, standing in close proximity to numerous vocal works of Buxtehude copied at the same time and place and preserved in the Düben collection at Uppsala.[2] Its plot concerns the condemnation of an evil soul to hell for the sins of pride, avarice, and wantonness and the parallel reward of heaven to a good soul for devoting herself entirely to Jesus. It is thus closely related thematically to two known *Abendmusiken* of Buxtehude, *Die Hochzeit des Lamms* of 1678, which relates the parable of the wise and foolish virgins in two acts, and *Das allerschröcklichste und allererfreulichste, nemlich Ende der Zeit und Anfang der Ewigkeit,* in five acts, which Buxtehude announced for publication in 1684.

Believing *Wacht! Euch zum Streit* to be the lost *Das allerschröcklichste und allererfreulichste,* Willy Maxton transformed its three acts into five, omitting numerous arias and rearranging each act to end with a chorale setting instead of an aria. He published it under the title *Das Jüngste Gericht* in 1939.[3] In this form it has been performed on numerous occasions—always within the confines of a single performance—and has aroused considerable controversy concerning its authenticity as a work of Buxtehude.[4] In the catalogue of Buxtehude's works, it stands among the doubtful works (BuxWV Anhang 3); and Sara Ruhle, in her recent doctoral dissertation devoted entirely to this work, declined to ascribe its composition to Buxtehude on the basis of the overall simplicity of its musical style. She suggested instead that it "was written by a follower of Buxtehude, a member of his circle familiar with the *Abendmusiken* and with his other sacred dramatic works."[5]

Wacht! Euch zum Streit received its first complete modern performance at Wellesley College in June, 1987, as part of the conference "From Scheidt to Buxtehude," sponsored by The Westfield Center for Early Keyboard Studies. Its three acts were presented in serial form on separate evenings, in the manner of the Lübeck *Abendmusiken,* by the Hannover Boys' Choir and Fiori Musicali. In this form, both the dramatic structure and the music seemed more convincing as possible creations of Buxtehude than they had from Maxton's version. My edition of the complete oratorio will appear as an appendix within the volume devoted to *Abendmusiken* in *Dieterich Buxtehude: The Complete Works.*

While *Wacht! Euch zum Streit* cannot be ascribed with certainty to Buxtehude and remains an anonymous work, confined to appendixes of the *Buxtehude-Werke-Verzeichnis* and *The Complete Works,* the evidence pointed to Buxtehude as the composer of this work is quite compelling. This evidence can be divided into four categories: the physical characteristics of the manuscript, the character of the libretto, the stylistic similarity between the music of *Wacht! Euch zum Streit* and a distinct portion of Buxtehude's vocal music, and documentary information relating to Buxtehude's *Abendmusiken* of 1682.

The Manuscript

The manuscript is a set of parts for two sopranos, alto, tenor, bass, two violins, two violas, and continuo. The parts for each of its three acts are contained in separate wrappers of coarse paper identical to that used in at least two Buxtehude manuscripts in the Düben collection, *Cantate Domino* (BuxWV 12, *S-Uu* vok. mus. i hskr. 67:8) and *Schwinget euch himmelan* (BuxWV 96, vok. mus. i hskr. 70:8). The contents of each wrapper is listed in pencil in a seventeenth-century hand, possibly Düben's. Each part is in folio format, ca. 210 x 330 mm., in gatherings of one to three bifolios, fifty-nine bifolios in all. The Violin I part of act 2 is missing, and this is not a recent loss; it is listed as "Violino 1mo def." on the act 2 wrapper. The Violin II part for the closing aria of act 3 was never copied; despite the note "Verte cito" at the end of the preceding number, one turns the page to find it ruled but devoid of music.

Three different papers were used for the parts of *Wacht! Euch zum Streit.* All of acts 1 and 2 and the vocal parts of act 3 are on paper bearing the watermark "Seven Provinces—DVSVLI." This same paper is found in the following Buxtehude manuscripts in the Düben collection:

> vok. mus. i hskr. 6:13 (*Jesu, meines Lebens Leben,* BuxWV 62), complete set of parts;
> vok. mus. i hskr. 50:11 (*Du Lebensfürst, Herr Jesu Christ,* BuxWV 22), S,A,T,Bc;
> vok. mus. i hskr. 51:8 (*Jesu dulcis memoria,* BuxWV 57), all parts except Violin I;
> vok. mus. i hskr. 83:41–45, fols. 11–14 (earlier pages contain *Pange lingua* [BuxWV 91], dated 1684, and BuxWV 22);
> vok. mus. i hskr. 85:76–88, fols. 1–20 (contains *Schaffe in mir, Gott, ein rein herz* [BuxWV 95], *Lobe den Herren, meine Seele* [BuxWV 71], and *Herr, nun läßt du deinen Diener* [BuxWV 37]);
> inst. mus. i hskr. 13:25 (Sonata in B♭, BuxWV 273), violin and organ parts.

Violin I and Continuo of act 3 are on paper with the watermark "Amsterdam—PBD." This is found in only one Buxtehude manuscript, the tenor part of *Du Lebensfürst, Herr Jesu Christ* (BuxWV 22; vok. mus. i hskr 50:11). Violin II and both viola parts of act 3 are on paper identified by Jan Olof Rudén as "Narr/7—PVL typ 01." Although unique in the Düben collection, he has found nineteen examples of it in the Stockholm archives dated between 1686 and 1689, with eleven examples from 1687.[6] The sharing of two papers with the parts of Buxtehude's *Du Lebensfürst* would seem to indicate that these works were copied at about the same time. The concordant tablature of *Du Lebensfürst* (vok. mus. i hskr. 83:41–45, fols. 6v-10r) follows a work dated 1684 and was probably copied soon afterwards.[7]

The principal scribes of *Wacht! Euch zum Streit* have been identified by Bruno Grusnick as "DBH,b" and "DBH,d," both of whom were active in the copying of works by Buxtehude in the Düben collection.[8] Their hands can be found in the manuscripts of *All solch dein Güt* (BuxWV 3), *Alles was ihr tut* (BuxWV 4), *Eins bitte ich vom Herren* (BuxWV 24), *Erhalt uns, Herr, bei deinem Wort* (BuxWV 27), *Gott hilf mir* (BuxWV 34), *Jesulein, du Tausendschön* (BuxWV 63), *O Gottes Stadt* (BuxWV 87), and *Schwinget euch himmelan* (BuxWV 96), as well as in the works of numerous other composers.[9]

This physical evidence leads to the conclusion that *Wacht! Euch zum Streit* was copied in Stockholm under Düben's supervision, probably between 1684 and 1687, in close conjunction with the copying of many works by Buxtehude. While this by no means rules out other composers represented in the Düben collection as the author of this work, it certainly lends strength to Buxtehude's candidacy.

The Libretto

The libretto of *Wacht! Euch zum Streit*[10] consists mainly of strophic poetry, intermingled with biblical quotations and chorale texts. The first part of act 1 functions as a prologue, introducing as allegorical characters the forces which will be operative in the drama: *Der Geitz* (Avarice), *Die Leichtfertigkeit* (Wantonness), and *Die Hoffarth* (Pride). After the conventional argument as to which of them is the most important, Pride always insisting that its power underlies that of the other two, they agree to stop squabbling and unite their efforts to undermine the German nation. The remainder of act 1 considers the sin of pride, manifest in costly clothing and jewelry. Its closing aria introduces the pious Christian counterpart: Jesus replaces gold, diamonds, and pearls; his drops of blood form a necklace of pearls and coral; his righteousness clothes the soul like silk. It is a theme that will run through the rest of this oratorio.

The dramatic format of acts 2 and 3 is quite different. Two real characters emerge; although they are unnamed in the manuscript, Maxton labelled Soprano I "die gute Seele" and Soprano II "die böse Seele." Act 2 is devoted to avarice: Soprano II relentlessly pursues riches, only to discover that possession produces not satisfaction but only the desire for more and the frustration of having to leave it all behind at death. The quest of the pious Soprano I, on the other hand, results in the discovery of the pearl of wisdom and Jesus as her treasure, which she *can* take with her to heaven.

Act 3 explores wantonness. In the place of the one evil soul in the second act, two appear in the third act: Soprano II represents the soul who eats and drinks too much, and the Alto personifies a whore, whose aria, *Mag dieser nicht werden,* Maxton cut from his edition. Jesus, although he is not named, appears as the Tenor in act 3, offering the pious Soprano I food, drink, and love. His aria, *Schäflein komm nur,* is also missing from Maxton's edition. While Soprano I is intoxicated by the love of Jesus, Soprano II becomes completely drunk. The contrast between these two characters is especially sharply drawn in act 3, and, as is often the case in the visual arts, it is the evil soul that is more colorfully portrayed.

The libretto of *Wacht! Euch zum Streit* shares several features with that of *Die Hochzeit des Lamms,*[11] Buxtehude's *Abendmusik* of 1678, which was performed from four to five o'clock on the second and third Sundays of Advent that year. The purpose of *Die Hochzeit des Lamms* is announced on the title page of its printed libretto: to provide joy and consolation to the pious and to frighten the ungodly. Like *Wacht! Euch zum Streit,* it presents a strong contrast between the pious and the ungodly and the condemnation of the ungodly to the flames of hell. Both oratorios use the chorale *Wie schön leuchtet der Morgenstern* to depict the joyful love between Jesus and the pious. The librettist of *Wacht! Euch zum Streit* may in fact have drawn his images of Jesus as pearl, food, lover, and bridegroom for the arias of Soprano I from this chorale.

The two librettos are made up of the same three textual elements: biblical verses, chorales, and strophic poetry. But whereas the published libretto of *Die Hochzeit des Lamms* draws most of its text from the Bible, with only a few interpolated arias, the reverse is true of *Wacht! Euch zum Streit.* The preponderance of strophic arias in this work has in fact been used as an argument against Buxtehude as its composer. Strophic arias, however, formed the most important element in the operas composed for the new Hamburg opera, which had opened in January, 1678. Buxtehude presumably composed *Die Hochzeit des Lamms* later in the same year, and as far as we know it was his first dramatic *Abendmusik.* By 1684, however, his oratorios had moved stylistically in the direction of opera; *Himmlische Seelenlust,* announced for publication that year, was to be "in opera style, with many arias and ritornelli."[12] In 1688, the Hamburg pastor Hinrich Elmenhorst, a librettist for the opera, wrote that Buxtehude's *Abendmusiken* were in fact operas: "Musicians understand the word *operas* to mean the compositions of poets and composers performed not only in theaters, but also in churches. . . . In this connection I must mention how the world-famous Lübeck musician Diedericus Buxtehude has performed more than one such opera in public churches there in the *Abendmusik* customary at a certain time of year, whose poetry has been published."[13]

The character of Soprano II is certainly more appropriate to the opera stage than to the world of Buxtehude's vocal music as we know it. But the pious Soprano I steps right out of that world. Compare, for example, her aria from act 3 with one from *Nun freut euch, ihr Frommen, mit mir* (BuxWV 80):

Süßer Jesu, Jesu du,
meine Ruh',
banquetieren, jubilieren
kann ich immer fort von dir.
Und so süß ist dein Genuß
daß stets wächset die Begier.

Sweet Jesus, thou Jesus,
My peace,
Banqueting and singing praise
I can do forever with thee,
and so sweet is thy pleasure
that desire grows steadily.

O Jesu, wie süße bist du!
Was bringst du für selige Ruh!
O Jesu, mein Leben,
was soll ich dir geben?
Süßer als Honigseim bist du mir nu.[14]

O Jesus, how sweet you are,
What blessed peace you bring me.
O Jesus, my life,
what shall I give you?
You are sweeter than honey to me.

The first stanza of another of Buxtehude's vocal works, *Was mich auf dieser Welt betrübt* (BuxWV 105) could almost serve as a summary of *Wacht! Euch zum Streit:*

Was mich auf dieser Welt betrübt,
das währet kurze Zeit.
Was aber meine Seele liebt,
das bleibt in Ewigkeit.
Drumb fahr, o Welt,
mit Ehr und Geld
und deiner Wollust hin.
In Kreuz und Spott
kann mir mein Gott
erquicken Mut und Sinn.[15]

What troubles me in this world,
that lasts a short time.
But what my soul loves,
that lasts forever.
So go away, o world,
with your honor and money
and desire.
In cross and derision
my God can for me
refresh courage and spirit.

The worldly values of honor, money, and pleasure that are rejected here are precisely the three qualities portrayed by the allegorical figures in act 1.

The rejection of worldly values manifest in *Wacht! Euch zum Streit* fits very comfortably into the cultural milieu of seventeenth-century Lübeck. Luxury ordinances were of course not peculiar to Lübeck, or even to the seventeenth century, but a mandate of the Lübeck city council, dated 7 November 1680,[16] is reminiscent of the language found in act 1 of *Wacht! Euch zum Streit*. It is entitled *Mandat Wider die Kleider-Hoffart,* to be read from the pulpits of all the Lübeck churches. Citizens of all classes were prohibited from wearing diamonds and other jewels, pearls around the neck and arms, gold and silver ornaments on their clothing. Previous such mandates had been ignored, and God's righteous anger had been provoked, causing war, fire, pestilence, famine, and disease. *Wacht! Euch zum Streit* could be considered an enormous musico-dramatic sermon on this text, summarized at the close of act 1:

Weg mit solchem Koht,	Away with all such filth,
Weg mit solchen Eitelkeiten	away with such vanity,
die der Seelen doch bereiten	which prepare for the soul
einen Ew'gen Todt.	eternal death.
All mein Zieren und mein prangen	All my adornments and my spendor
will in Jesu ich umfangen,	I will embrace in Jesus;
Er soll meiner Ehren schein,	He shall be my honor's glory,
Gold, Demant und Perlen seyn.	gold, diamond, and pearls.

The language of *Wacht! Euch zum Streit* is also well suited to a Lübeck *Abendmusik*. The libretto appears to be the work of a North German literary amateur, perhaps even Buxtehude himself, who enjoyed writing poetry[17] and who may have written and compiled the texts for his *Abendmusiken*. Although the name of the poet is more likely to be found on a seventeenth-century libretto than the name of the composer of its musical setting, Buxtehude's name is the only one listed on the three surviving published librettos of his *Abendmusiken*. The North German origin of the text of *Wacht! Euch zum Streit* is betrayed by one Low-German word, *"Wellenhaven,"* in the aria *Sehet doch, daß Satans Sklaven.*[18] Furthermore, the invocation of *"Das Teutsche Reich"* points to a performance in an imperial free city, such as Lübeck, rather than in a court. The librettos of both *Castrum doloris* and *Templum honoris* call upon *"Teutschland."*[19]

Musical Style

It is chiefly on the basis of its musical style that connoisseurs of Buxtehude's music have hesitated to accept *Wacht! Euch zum Streit* as a work of his; much of it simply does not sound like most of the vocal music of Buxtehude that we know. This common judgment is based primarily on the many strophic arias in the work. Although Buxtehude used many strophic texts in his vocal works, he more often gave them varied musical settings than a purely strophic musical treatment; and when he did use strophic musical form, his settings often contain more subtle nuances—particularly in their rhythm—than can be found in many of the arias of *Wacht! Euch zum Streit*.

Since the composition of vocal music did not lie within Buxtehude's responsibilities as organist of St. Mary's in Lübeck, he probably enjoyed a considerable amount of artistic freedom with respect to the musical style of most of his vocal works. This helps to explain the great stylistic variety within this large corpus of works. For the continued production of the *Abendmusiken,* however, he was dependent on the financial contributions of the business community, so it is quite likely that Buxtehude catered to the taste of the citizens of Lübeck in his composition of these works. One of Buxtehude's preserved vocal works, *Schwinget euch himmelan* (BuxWV 96), was clearly directed toward the businessmen of Lübeck:

Häufe das Käufen mit reichlichem Segen,	Pile rich blessing on business;
Handel und Wandel uns wachse herzu,	let commerce and trade increase;
lasse die Schiffe zum Segen bewegen,	let the ships move profitably,
stärke die Werker mit Leben und Ruh!	strengthen the workers with life and peace.
Betet und ächzet, ächzet und lechzet:	Pray and moan, moan and languish;
Vater, dein segenerfülleter Schoß	Father, from your blessing-filled bosom
mache dein Lübeck erfreuet und groß.	make Lübeck happy and great.

Since the text of this work would have appealed to Buxtehude's financial backers, its music may offer an example of the musical style of his lost *Abendmusiken.* Buxtehude used the same simple, lilting music to set five of the eight strophes of its text (ex. 11.1). Music in a similar style abounds in *Wacht! Euch zum Streit,* as in example 11.2, from the first aria of *Die Leichtfertigkeit* in act 1. This style is also found in the arias of the early Hamburg operas; example 11.3 is drawn from Johann Wolfgang Franck's opera *Vespasian* of 1681.[20]

Buxtehude's sacred vocal works also offer some examples of composition in a simple and direct musical style, nowhere more clearly than in the cantata *Alles was ihr tut* (BuxWV 4). This work, like *Schwinget euch himmelan,* does not rank high on the connoisseur's list of favorite vocal works by Buxtehude, but it appears to have been his most popular vocal work during his lifetime. It is Buxtehude's only vocal work to be disseminated in three independent manuscript sources. Its text, while more general in nature than *Schwinget euch himmelan,* also implies God's blessing of bourgeois business activity. And its music offers a chorale setting, an ensemble aria, and an arioso setting of a biblical text, each of which is markedly similar to analogous movements in *Wacht! Euch zum Streit.*

All of the chorale settings in *Wacht! Euch zum Streit* belong to a category designated by Friedhelm Krummacher as "erweiterte Kantionalsätze,"[21] in which a fairly simple chorale harmonization is enhanced with concertato instrumental interjections; I call this type a concertato chorale harmonization. It is in its chorale settings that *Wacht! Euch zum Streit* approaches the style of Buxtehude's vocal music most closely, as Krummacher has noted. Example 11.4 gives one example from act 2, the second strophe of "Wie schön leuchtet der Morgenstern." Buxtehude employed this same style in the closing chorale of *Alles was ihr tut* (example 11.5).

The ensemble arias of *Wacht! Euch zum Streit* are closely related stylistically to the concertato chorale harmonizations, apart from the obvious fact that in this case no cantus firmus is present. Example 11.6 shows this style in the closing aria to act 2, and Buxtehude used it in the four-voice aria of *Alles was ihr tut* (ex. 11.7).

The passages for bass solo in *Wacht! Euch zum Streit* are arioso settings of biblical texts. In act 1 they are designated as the "Voice of God"; in acts 2 and 3 they function in this way, even though the character is not named.

Example 11.1. Buxtehude, *Schwinget euch himmelan* (BuxWV 96)

Schwin- get euch him- mel- an, Her- zen und Sin- nen, stei- get viel hö- her als

Ad- ler em- por, stei- get viel hö- her als Ad- ler em- por,

Example 11.2. *Nein, Närrin* from *Wacht! Euch zum Streit*

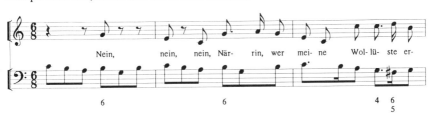

Nein, nein, nein, När- rin, wer mei- ne Wol- lü- ste er-

ken- net, ver- la- - - chet den nich- ti gen Schein.

Example 11.3. Johann Wolfgang Franck, *Schleppt ihn* from *Vespasian*

Example 11.4. "Wie schön leuchtet der Morgenstern" from *Wacht! Euch zum Streit*

Example 11.5. Buxtehude, *Darauf so sprech ich Amen* from *Alles was ihr tut*

Example 11.5, cont.

Example 11.6. *Seine Wunden sind die Minen* from *Wacht! Euch zum Streit*

Example 11.6, cont.

30

Example 11.8 gives one such passage from act 3; its stylistic similarity to the bass solo in *Alles was ihr tut* (ex. 11.9) may be noted.

Schwinget euch himmelan and *Alles was ihr tut* belong to a stylistic category that I have designated as Buxtehude's "music for the ordinary citizen."[22] His concertato chorale harmonizations, German-texted arias in strophic or modified-strophic form, and German-texted concerto-aria cantatas and mixed cantatas also belong to this group. When compared with this smaller group of compositions rather than with the entire corpus of Buxtehude's vocal works, the musical style of *Wacht! Euch zum Streit* provides strong evidence in favor of Buxtehude as its composer.

Buxtehude's *Abendmusiken* of 1682

Although the manuscript, libretto, and musical style of *Wacht! Euch zum Streit* all point to Buxtehude as its composer, the work still appears to be too small

Example 11.7. Buxtehude, *Dir, dir Höchster, dir alleine* from *Alles was ihr tut*

Example 11.7, cont.

Example 11.7, cont.

(both in its length and in its scoring) for an *Abendmusik* by Buxtehude. The
recent performance of *Wacht! Euch zum Streit* at Wellesley demonstrated that
acts 2 and 3 last approximately one hour each, the duration announced for each
act of *Die Hochzeit des Lamms* in 1678. The performance of act 1, however,
requires only thirty-four minutes. We know from Buxtehude's entry in the St.
Mary's account book that the manuscript for his *Abendmusik* of 1679 filled 400
bifolios,[23] whereas the manuscript for the parts of *Wacht! Euch zum Streit* uses
only fifty-nine bifolios. We also know that a setting of "Wie schön leuchtet der
Morgenstern" in *Die Hochzeit des Lamms* called for eleven violins and two
trumpets, and that Buxtehude purchased three shawms and two recorders for the
1679 *Abendmusiken*. The extant parts for *Wacht! Euch zum Streit*, however,
contain only two violin parts and two viola parts, and it is possible that the viola
parts were added in Stockholm. Also, *Wacht! Euch zum Streit* has only three
acts; Buxtehude had already composed two oratorios in the five-act form that

Example 11.8. *Wohlan, alle, die ihr dürstig seid* from *Wacht! Euch zum Streit*

would become standard for the Lübeck *Abendmusiken* by 1684, the year he announced the publication of *Himmlische Seelenlust* and *Das allerer-schröcklichste.*

In 1682, however, Buxtehude presented in his *Abendmusiken* a work of more limited scope than he had wished and intended. In the letter of thanks and solicitation that he wrote to his financial backers the following February, he referred to the *Abendmusiken* of 1682 in the following way:

> Although in the most recent time [I] have not been able to present as complete a work as [I] wished and intended, on account of impediments which have occurred, nevertheless [I] have

Example 11.9. Buxtehude, *Habe deine Lust* from *Alles was ihr tut*

the most respectful confidence in my highly and widely honored gentlemen, that they will have kindly accepted the little that has been presented and will further manifest their good will toward me—already so laudibly shown—for more encouragement of a fuller and larger work in the future, to demonstrate that such [good will] will stimulate me not only for the work desired of my office, but also for particular service to my most highly honored gentlemen, both collectively and individually. . . .[24]

Further information concerning the *Abendmusiken* of 1682 is found in Buxtehude's entry in the St. Mary's account book on 12 January 1683:

Inasmuch as . . . a bass by the name of Jean Carl Quelmaltz had to be brought from Hamburg for the recently presented *Abendmusik,* since the singers in the choir (*Cantorey*) of this school at the present time have been poor, and I could not use them, so I have paid 23 rixdollars in charges spent for the bill at the inn and also to content the aforementioned bass with a gratuity. But because this has caused great damage to my resources, in view of the present bad times and very small reimbursement by the citizenry, my highly honored directors have been so good as to come to my assistance with 10 rixdollars from the church, which is hereby accepted with grateful thanks and entered into the account.[25]

Jean Carl Quelmaltz may have been the same man as the bass named Quellmann who was a member of the *Kantorei* of the Johanneum in Hamburg in 1679 and briefly acted as director of music at the cathedral that year until the appointment of Nicolaus Adam Strungk.[26]

Wacht! Euch zum Streit is a work of more limited scope than we might expect Buxtehude to have composed during the 1680s, and therefore it seems quite possible that it could have been the work Buxtehude presented in his *Abendmusiken* of 1682. If this was the case, then Jean Carl Quelmaltz sang the role of the Voice of God. Even if *Wacht! Euch zum Streit* was not the specific work to which Buxtehude referred in his letter of 1683, that letter offers strong evidence that Buxtehude did not present a large work with opulent scoring in his *Abendmusiken* every year. The shortness of the first act and modesty of scoring in *Wacht! Euch zum Streit* thus lose their strength as arguments against Buxtehude's composition of this work.

Buxtehude's *Abendmusiken* regularly followed Sunday Vespers at St. Mary's, and the Westfield Center's performance of act 1 of *Wacht! Euch zum Streit* was preceded by a reconstruction of such a vesper service. The polyphonic vocal music followed the model presented in *Natalitia sacra,* the text book for the music of the morning and afternoon services at St. Mary's, Lübeck, for the Christmas season of 1682.[27] Three works were drawn from the choir library of St. Mary's: an anonymous motet from Erhard Bodenschatz's *Florilegii Musici Portensis* (1621), a setting of the Magnificat by Hieronymus Praetorius (1622), and a sacred concerto from Andreas Hammerschmidt's *Musikalische Andachten IV* (1646);[28] one vocal work by Buxtehude was also included, *Befiehl dem Engel, daß er komm* (BuxWV 10). Following this vesper service, the first act of *Wacht! Euch zum Streit* struck the listener as genuinely entertaining; its music skillfully juxtaposed the style of the opera house to that of the church. One was reminded of Elmenhorst's comment that the Lübeck *Abendmusiken* were in fact operas. And the closing aria to act 1, which had been excised by Maxton, provided a perfect ending for one evening of a Lübeck *Abendmusik* (ex. 11.10).

The serial performance of *Wacht! Euch zum Streit* at Wellesley lent further strength to the hypothesis that this work was composed for the Lübeck *Abendmusiken* and that Buxtehude was its composer. Acts 2 and 3, when allowed to stand on their own, proved to be dramatically effective, and anticipation for the next installment mounted each day. A definite momentum built toward the third act, in which the depravity of the evil soul reaches its peak, and which as a result proved to be the most entertaining. One could begin to understand why the *Abendmusiken* drew such crowds that, beginning in 1682, the Lübeck police were regularly employed for watch duty during the performances.

Example 11.10. *O der Rasenheit* from *Wacht! Euch zum Streit*

Notes

1. For further information on Buxtehude's *Abendmusiken* and their support by the Lübeck business community, see Snyder, *Dieterich Buxtehude: Organist in Lübeck* (New York: Schirmer Books, 1987), pp. 56–72.

2. *Uu* vok. mus. i hskr. caps. 71. There is no title page, but the wrappers for the parts of each act contain pencil notations in a seventeenth-century hand. The wrapper for the parts of act 1—not included in the microfilm supplied by the Deutsches Musikgeschichtliches Archiv— reads "Actus 1^{mus} / Wacht euch zum Streit / a Soprano 1mo et 2do / Alto / Tenore 1mo et 2do /Basso / doi Violini / doi Violetti / Basso Cont."

3. Dietrich Buxtehude, *Das Jüngste Gericht: Abendmusik in fünf Vorstellungen*, ed. Willy Maxton (Kassel: Bärenreiter, 1939).

4. Summarized in Sara Cathcart Ruhle, *An Anonymous Seventeenth-Century German Oratorio in the Düben Collection (Uppsala University Library vok. mus. i hskr. 71)* (Ph.D. diss., University of North Carolina, 1982), pp. 72–84. See also Friedhelm Krummacher, *Die Choralbearbeitung in der protestantischen Figuralmusik zwischen Praetorius und Bach*, Kieler Schriften zur Musikwissenschaft, 22 (Kassel: Bärenreiter, 1978), pp. 173–74; Georg Karstädt, "Richtiges und Zweifelhaftes in Leben und Werk Dietrich Buxtehudes," *Musik und Kirche* 49 (1979), p. 170; and Snyder, "Buxtehude and *Das Jüngste Gericht*: A New Look at an Old Problem," *Festschrift für Bruno Grusnick zum 80. Geburtstag*, ed. Rolf Saltzwedel and Klaus D. Koch (Neuhausen-Stuttgart: Hänssler, 1981), pp. 128–41.

5. Ruhle, *An Anonymous Seventeenth-Century German Oratorio*, p. 303.

6. Jan Olof Rudén, "Vattenmärken och Musikforskning: Presentation och Tillämpning av en Dateringsmetod på musikalier i handskrift i Uppsala Universitetsbibliioteks Dübensamling" (Licentiatavhandling i musikforskning, Uppsala University, 1968), vol. 1, p. 156.

7. For further details on the manuscripts of *Du Lebensfürst*, see *Dieterich Buxtehude: The Collected Works*, vol. 9, ed. Kerala J. Snyder (New York: The Broude Trust, 1987), pp. 279–81.

8. Bruno Grusnick, "Die Dübensammlung: Ein Versuch ihrer chronologischen Ordnung," *Svensk tidskrift för musikforskning* 48 (1966), pp. 183–84.

9. For a list of compositions in the Düben collection copied by "DBH,b" and "DBH,d," see Ruhle, "An Anonymous Seventeenth-Century German Oratorio," pp. 49–53.

10. No original source for the libretto is known. A transcription from the musical source is found in Ruhle, pp. 325–46.

11. Transcribed in André Pirro, *Dietrich Buxtehude* (Paris: Fischbacher, 1913; reprinted, Geneva: Minkoff, 1976), pp. 175–84.

12. Albert Göhler, *Verzeichnis der in den Frankfurter und Leipziger Messkatalogen der Jahre 1564 bis 1759 angezeigten Musikalien* (Leipzig: Breitkopf & Härtel, 1902; reprint, Hilversum: F. Knuf, 1965), part 2, p. 12.

13. Hinrich Elmenhorst, *Dramatologia Antiquo-Hodierna* (Hamburg, 1688), p. 100.

14. Text from Angelus Silesius, *Heilige Seelenlust* (Breslau, 1657), p. 101.

15. Text from Ahasverus Fritzsch, *Himmels-Lust und Welt-Unlust* (Leipzig, 1679).

16. Archiv der Hansestadt Lübeck, *Lübeckische Verordnungen*, xiii.

17. For a list of Buxtehude's poems, see Snyder, *Dieterich Buxtehude: Organist in Lübeck*, p. 438.

18. Maxton changed this word to "Sünden-haven" in his edition (*Das Jüngste Gericht*, p. 126).

19. These librettos are published in facsimile in Georg Karstädt, *Die "extraordinairen" Abendmusiken Dietrich Buxtehudes: Untersuchungen zur Aufführungspraxis in der Marienkirche zu Lübeck* (Lübeck: Max Schmidt-Römhild, 1962).

20. Johann Wolfgang Franck, *Arien aus dem Sing-Spiel Vespasian Mit ihren Ritornellen* (Hamburg: author, 1681).

21. Krummacher, *Die Choralbearbeitung in der protestantischen Figuralmusik zwischen Praetorius und Bach*, pp. 166–73.

22. See Snyder, *Dieterich Buxtehude: Organist in Lübeck*, pp. 204–6.

23. Ibid., p. 474.

24. Letter from Dieterich Buxtehude dated 7 February 1683 (Lübeck, Archiv der Hansestadt, Nr. 15116; until recently in the custody of the German Democratic Republic, Staatliche Archivverwaltung); transcribed in Snyder, *Dieterich Buxtehude: Organist in Lübeck*, p. 477.

25. Lübeck, Archiv der Hansestadt, Nr. 5290 [St. Mary's Accounts, 1678–85], fol. 4r; until recently in the custody of the German Democratic Republic, Staatliche Archivverwaltung; transcribed in Snyder, *Dieterich Buxtehude: Organist in Lübeck*, p. 473.

26. Liselotte Krüger, *Die Hamburgische Musikorganisation im XVII. Jahrhundert* (Strasbourg: Heitz, 1933), pp. 237, 241.

27. *Natalitia Sacra, Oder Verzeichnüß aller Texte, Welche in bevorstehenden Heiligen Festen, als Weinachten, Neuen Jahr und Heil. drey Könige allhie zu St. Marien sowohl Vor- als Nachmittag, theils vor und nach den Predigten, theils auch unter der Communion mit genugsamer Vocal-Hülffe sollen musiciret werden* (Lübeck: Moritz Schmalhertz, 1682; reprinted in Martin Geck, *Die Vokalmusik Dietrich Buxtehudes und der frühe Pietismus*, Kieler Schriften zur Musikwissenschaft, no. 15 (Kassel: Bärenreiter, 1965), pp. 230–37.

28. On the repertory of the *Kantorei* see Snyder, *Dieterich Buxtehude: Organist in Lübeck*, pp. 93–97.

Part Three

Seventeenth-Century
German Theory and Notation

12

Vocal Polyphony in the Lüneburg Tablatures: A Double Repertory of Solo Organ Literature and Accompanimental *Absetzungen*

Curtis Lasell

Erstlich wißen meine geneigten Herren, daß ein guter Regalist sein muß, der den General Bass aufs Positiv richtig führet, alle Woche selbst durchstimmet und waß in absetzung von mir dargereichet wird, zu papir bringe und allemahl bereit sey.
Michael Jacobi, 1652

In 1956—a half-dozen years after Lüneburg shared with other *Bachstädte* a bicentennial of her most illustrious alumnus—the city focused its attention inward in celebrating its own millenary (an anniversary measured from the first mention of the town in a privilege from King Otto I, which addressed the newly established Benedictine monastery there). A festschrift was published to mark this milestone. Among other articles which examine the history of the city's growth in the Middle Ages, its schools, churches, mint, and spa, the volume also contains a report by Friedrich Blume and Martin Ruhnke on the then-current state of research in Lüneburg's music history.[1] Drawing on both the research of local historians (Wilhelm Reinecke, Wilhelm Friedrich Volger, Wilhelm Görges) and the specifically musical studies of Wilhelm Christian Junghans, Richard Buchmayer, Gustav Fock, Max Seiffert, and others, the two authors present the fullest account up to that time of the musical curricula and practices in Lüneburg's post-Reformation *Lateinschulen,* the careers of the city's cantors, organists, and *Ratsmusikanten,* the collection of music prints and manuscripts—especially the highly prized mid-seventeenth-century keyboard tablatures—housed in the Ratsbücherei, and issues related to Bach's sojourn at the Michaelisschule. Provocative questions, often pointing the way to further research, punctuate Blume's and Ruhnke's article. Their urgent call for a thorough investigation of the "ungeahnt Vieles" buried amid Lüneburg archivalia was answered a decade later in the form of Horst Walter's excellent dissertation, which for the most part superseded all previous writings—and still remains the authority—on the general subject of music in Lüneburg through the tenure of the *Johannisorganist* Georg Böhm.[2]

This article will take up a particular question which has been left dangling these thirty-odd years: the question of the over 120 intabulations of vocal polyphony which hold so high a profile in the Lüneburg organ tablatures. In her *MGG* article on these manuscripts, Margarete Reimann underscored this "most problematic" of the issues surrounding their repertories.[3] And Professors Blume and Ruhnke write:

> The purpose served by these intabulations is a question which hitherto has never been fully explained. As far as concerns intabulated motets (or song settings, etc.) in four or five voices, they doubtless were intended as solo organ pieces; a solo voice might have sung along, perhaps with another solo instrument. But the reason behind intabulations of very large vocal compositions—up to sixteen voices and of enormous length—cannot be as readily explained. Were they really intended to be played on the organ? Or in these cases are the tablatures to be understood as a type of score? Did the organist perhaps conduct the *Chorus musicus* from the console? Did he accompany it? Both these hypotheses are improbable. The direction of vocal works or of concerti involving vocal and instrumental forces (i.e., figural music) fell to the cantor's responsibilities; organ accompaniment, if needed, was performed on a positive organ, which could be placed right beside the choir, rather than on the large organ. For the time being, then, the problems posed by the presence of these intabulations remain open.[4]

Just under 85 percent of all the Lüneburg intabulations are contained in the two large tablatures KN 209 and KN 210.[5] The latter manuscript in fact is devoted almost exclusively to the genre; only two "fugae" and a six-measure praeambulum stand apart from its main repertory of seventy-five intabulations.[6] KN 209, essential through its many unica to our knowledge of the chorale preludes and free organ works of Franz Tunder, Matthias Weckmann, and Heinrich Scheidemann, is at the same time the single most important source for Scheidemann's and Delphin Strungk's virtuosic intabulations of Lassus, Hassler, and others. Beyond the repertories of these two manuscripts and the two fascicle-manuscripts KN 207[2] and KN 207[3] (which will occupy us at some length below), only a handful of intabulations remain, distributed throughout the first volume of KN 208 (which contains mainly chorales and free preludes), the bifolium KN 207[18] (Scheidemann's intabulation of Hassler's *Verbum caro factum est*), the second fascicle of Mus. ant. pract. 697 (a single motet— Hassler's *Alleluia laudem dicite*), and the extensive and largely secular tablature KN 146.

By far the majority of intabulations are based on sacred polyphony—motets, some harmonized chorales (from Praetorius's *Musae Sioniae*), and a few sacred concerti. KN 210 alone contains eleven Italian madrigals and canzonettas, by both "oltramontani" (Bargnani, Nanino, and Palestrina) and Germans (Jacob and Hans Leo Hassler) alike.[7] None of the intabulations are of works which prescribe obbligato instruments beyond a continuo force.

Appendix A indexes the models of the entire repertory of intabulated works in the Lüneburg tablatures. In sheer weight of representation, Jacob Handl and Hans Leo Hassler stand out amid a roster of mostly German composers, their lives spanning a century and a half—from Lassus and even Johann Walter (his *Joseph, lieber Joseph mein* is intabulated under the carol's Latin title) to Andreas Hammerschmidt and Caspar Movius. The motets by foreigners (Bassano, Leoni, Faignient, Trombetti) were readily available in published German anthologies; a number of others by cantors such as Grimm, Elsmann, Palladius, and Calvisius, can only have been acquired through an active manuscript exchange.

An examination of the intabulations reveals most of them to fall squarely within the centuries-old tradition of the keyboard arrangement.[8] The context for these pieces is the same as that for the *ars nova* motets in the Robertsbridge fragment, or Bach's and Johann Gottfried Walther's organ arrangements of Italian instrumental concerti, or even Liszt's and Busoni's transcriptions of operatic and symphonic literature, in the sense that solo performers have always been attracted to pieces outside their medium and audiences have always enjoyed hearing their favorites rendered in a new and often virtuoso setting.

In the case of arrangements of vocal polyphony, the intabulation had its heyday in the sixteenth century. The decades which followed Andrea Antico's first book of frottola intabulations (1517) produced keyboard collections—printed and manuscript—filled with as many motets, madrigals, and chansons as the dances, ricercars, fantasias, toccatas, and other genres which we are more accustomed to regarding as "keyboard music." (Even a cursory browse through Howard Mayer Brown's *Instrumental Music Printed before 1600* reveals the vastness of this repertory.) German organists were the last in Europe to abandon the practice. The latest printed keyboard anthologies which still include groups of motets or madrigals are German and Swiss, respectively Bernhard Schmidt's *Tabulatur Buch* of 1607 and Johann Woltz's *Tabulatura* of 1617. But, as the Lüneburg tablatures attest, the tradition continued in manuscript and in practice until well past the middle of the century. In fact, I know of no more recent source than these where the intabulated motet commands so weighty a position in the repertory, or, for that matter, appears at all. North Germany, then, can claim for itself the final flowering of an ancient practice—indeed, the oldest keyboard tradition (along with the dance) of which musical examples survive.

The fourteen intabulations by Scheidemann and Strungk in the Lüneburg tablatures, exceptional in their bravura technique and their bottomless wealth of imaginative figuration patterns, are unquestionably jewels—long neglected—of the solo organ literature.[9] All the rest of the arrangements in these manuscripts are anonymous, and their quality falls far short of that which distinguishes Scheidemann and Strungk. At their best (and I use this superlative with reservations), these intabulations demonstrate a modest skill in figuration, usually at the eighth-note level, with the occasional sixteenth-note flourish or trill. The intabulations of Grimm's *Lobet den Herren* and the anonymous *Quare fremuerunt gentes* are such pieces—the former even gleams here and there with a spark of Scheidemannesque technique.[10] At their worst, though, the anonymous arrangements exhibit a clumsy and primitive hand, dull in what little figuration it attempts, and incapable of reducing inner voices to smooth harmonic or contrapuntal filler.

Most of the arrangements clearly establish the horizontal texture of the model at the outset, with each voice occupying its own line in the tablature. But in the majority of cases, the clear definition of the voices of the model deteriorates further into the piece. In the intabulation of Jacob Handl's *Exurge gloria mea* in KN 210 this deterioration already begins in the third bar (ex 12.1). For this measure alone, the intabulator invents a sixth voice, squeezed among the inner lines, which is allotted the first two notes of the Altus part.[11] From measure 4, the written texture narrows to four voices (a point which corresponds in the source to a shift to the second page of the opening). This generally holds for the remainder of the intabulation, which seldom realizes the full five-voice texture when it occurs in the model. As more voices enter, the intabulation conflates inner voices, a process which first occurs at measure 7, where the tenor flows directly from the Tenor II line into the Tenor I (dropping the tied a in the process). More pitches are dropped from the keyboard reduction as the texture thickens: the b of the Tenor II in measure 8, the e' sounding in the two Tenors on beat three of measure 8, the a and e' of the Altus in measures 7 and 9. On the other hand, pitches may be added to enrich a particular sonority, such as the soprano f' on the second beat of measure 6 (here at the expense of the counterpoint, where a direct fifth occurs with the tenor). At points of voice-crossing, the vertical sonorities are reordered in the intabulation to keep higher sounding parts visually on top (cf. Cantus and Altus in mm. 3 and 5, and Tenor I and Altus in m. 8). Where two voices strike a unison, the intabulator often displaces one of them with a rest (e.g., the d' of the Cantus and the Tenor II in m. 3). The modest ornamentation in this example is typical of the anonymous arrangements: the turn in the alto before the cadence in measure 6, and the figuration outlining the Cantus part in measure 9, are both at the eighth-note level. A more subtle embellishment appears in the passing eighth-note d' in the

Example 12.1.   Jacob Handl, *Exurge gloria mea,́ mm. 1–10*

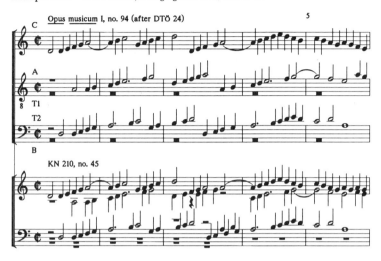

alto at measure 9. At no point in the piece is figuration applied where the imitative texture is dense (mm. 1–5, 7–8, etc.).

The arrangement of Handl's polychoral Easter motet, *Maria Magdalena et altera Maria* (ex. 12.2 and fig. 12.5), shows how, even when such surface features as ornamentation play a minimal role (cf. mm. 19, 21, 23), the hand of the intabulator can still be very much present. The texture of the eight-voice piece is antiphonal and largely homophonic and declamatory. In the eighty-six measures of the prima pars, tuttis occur at only three points, the longest being the five-bar closing passage. Thus, the intabulator needs to realize for the most part only four voices at a time, which he does note for note in most of the piece. The only places showing significant changes occur at junctures of choral entrances or exits, where overlapping joints are homogenized to uniform minim chords in each choir. A single minim rest in each line of the intabulation marks these points (cf. especially the truncated entry of Choir II in m. 12, and the truncated exit of Choir I in m. 27), and individual pitches may undergo adjust-

Example 12.2.   Handl, *Maria Magdalena et altera Maria,* mm. 9–27
                 See also figure 12.5.

Example 12.2, cont.

Example 12.2, cont.

Example 12.2, cont.

ment (m. 10, Tenor I; m. 12, Tenor II). As we have seen before, unisons may be renotated with a rest in one voice (Cantus II and Altus II at the end of m. 12, Altus II and Tenor II in m. 15). The tutti section beginning in measure 22 demonstrates how the intabulation deals with reducing the full complement of eight voices. Usually it retains the uppermost sounding voice of the two Cantus parts and the lowest of the two basses; the inner voices are reduced to static filler harmonies. The omission of one and one-half bars of music between measures 25 and 27 was probably the conscious decision of the intabulator, whose imagination was evidently incapable of dealing skillfully with the long static G-major harmony of measures 22–26. This particular intabulation drops more musical text further into the piece: measures 71–80 (an internal repeat of the alleluia section), one and one-half bars from the closing tutti, and half of measure 32 in the secunda pars.[12]

Liturgical ordinances for both Hamburg and Lüneburg mention the practice of solo motet intabulation. In Hamburg it was a matter of practical expediency:

for figural music, the four main churches in town shared one cantor and one choir, which rotated among them. At one or more points in any service, then, the organists of three churches had to supply an intabulation while the choir was performing at the fourth.[13] Even as late as 1655, the audition for the organist's position at St. Jacobi required improvised motet intabulation.[14] In Lüneburg, the Vespers and Matins ordinance of 1656 for the Michaeliskirche states specifically that the organist must hold the service together with intonations and with preludes, interludes, and postludes on liturgical items, and that he must play "fine pieces and motets" regularly.[15]

The Protestant liturgy was not the only place for motet intabulations. That so many German keyboard anthologies include motets along with chansons, madrigals, dances, and free pieces shows that all genres together formed a repertory for private and public entertainment. (The even longer list of sources for sixteenth- and early seventeenth-century lute music, which preserve an identical repertory, points to the same conclusion.) In the third volume of his *Syntagma musicum* (1619), Michael Praetorius advises the organist or lutenist who entertains "in Conviviis" to seek diversity and expression in his program by opening with a motet or a madrigal played very slowly and gravely, then continuing with perhaps an allemande, intrada, branle, or galliard, followed in turn by another motet, madrigal, pavane, or fugue.[16]

Thus it is not difficult to establish a context for the presence of most of the motet intabulations in the Lüneburg tablatures, and examples 12.1 and 12.2 demonstrate the danger of a casual look at the repertory. With all parts allotted a line at the beginning, an intabulation could give the false impression of a full-voiced transcription, when in fact the piece has been arranged through a variety of techniques for solo performance, thoroughly purged of any technical problems of execution. Clearly "corrupted" intabulations such as these could hardly serve any purpose as conducting or accompanying scores, and belong instead to the literature for solo organ.

But over one-quarter of the intabulated motets in the Lüneburg tablatures are not keyboard arrangements. Rather, they are full scores in tablature notation, and cannot be played on the organ as written if the composition, at best, is in more than five or six voices. A consideration of the intabulation must distinguish, then, between solo arrangements and literal transcriptions. KN 209 and KN 210 include both kinds, but other Lüneburg manuscripts contain exclusively the second type—what I prefer to call tablature scores. It is to this body of intabulations that we must redirect Blume's and Ruhnke's questions: Were they copied with the intention of organ performance (as the basis for either an improvised solo or an accompanimental part), or are they actually conductors' scores? Recalling the vast manuscript collection at Uppsala amassed by Gustav Düben toward the end of the seventeenth century, which preserves in tablature score hundreds of vocal works (primarily cantatas and sacred concerti), one could also ask whether the Lüneburg motets were compiled in order to preserve a repertory for reference purposes.[17]

Inasmuch as most of the motets in KN 210 are arrangements for solo organ, we would first surmise that an organist prepared the volume for his own use. The identification of one of its two copyists supports this hypothesis. Margarete Reimann long ago recognized the manuscript's primary hand in four other keyboard or organ manuscripts: KN 207[18], the two volumes of KN 208, and most of KN 146 (which shows three hands). Years later, Renate Brunner identified the hand as that of Franciscus Schaumkell (ca. 1589–1676), the long-lived organist of Lüneburg's Johanniskirche.[18] The other hand in KN 210 belongs to an anonymous organist who worked closely with Schaumkell—their hands alternate nine times in the manuscript, and the unknown scribe copies the same set of motets (nos. 15–17) which Schaumkell enters farther into the manuscript (nos. 43, 44, 41).

Similarly, KN 209 is predominantly an anthology of solo organ music, and contains, in addition to chorale preludes, toccatas, etc., twenty-three motet arrangements (clustered at the beginning of the manuscript) and six tablature scores of motets (clustered in the middle). This source shows close ties to KN 210 through a number of concordances, including the same group of three intabulations mentioned above.[19] The presence of tablature scores alongside "real" organ music in these two collections, then, most likely refutes an explanation which claims their use as conducting scores.

The pan-European practice of scoring all parts of a vocal composition into keyboard tablature (and I use the word tablature here in its broadest sense) goes back at least to the beginning of the sixteenth century. Sebastian Virdung in 1511 centers his entire discussion of instrumental literature, including that for keyboard, on vocal music and how the instrumentalist transfers "eynen Gesang" into tablature.[20] His example is a four-voice setting of some German Marian paraphrases, which he transcribes note-to-letter from the staff notation into Old German organ tablature and into tablatures for lute and flute. (In German, the process is called *absetzen*.) In the same vein, Juan Bermudo in chapter 41 of his *Declaración* (1555) comments how a keyboardist must draw on the masterworks of foreign composers to build his repertory ("since so little of value is available in Spain") and lists three ways to do this: one must learn to read directly from a choir-book, which he admits is very difficult; one must prepare a barred vocal score; or one must intabulate the piece, whereupon he describes his own numerical system of tablature.[21]

Additional documents from Italy and Germany suggest that European organists spent a good deal of time transcribing music from part-books into score. The publication of keyboard music in part-books is rare,[22] but examples do occur throughout the sixteenth century—such as *Musica nova,* a set of part-books printed in Venice in 1540 containing pieces "accommodata per cantar et sonar sopra organi, et altri strumenti"—and even at the beginning of the seventeenth century, when Michael Praetorius published eight organ chorales in the seventh part of his *Musae Sioniae* and in his *Hymnodia sacra*. Taking a broader perspective, though, I think the many sixteenth-century vocal prints whose title-pages describe their selections of motets, chansons, and Lieder as "omnis generis instrumentis accomodatae," or "convenables tant aux instrumentz comme à la voix," or "lustig zu singen, und auff allerley Instrument dienstlich," do not exclude the organ, harpsichord, and clavichord from their options of performance medium.[23]

This still does not solve the problem of the eight-voice motet scores in the Lüneburg tablatures, none of which are particularly "accomodatae" to keyboard performance.[24] Here again, Italian and German musical sources provide a clue. It is clear from prefatory comments and instructions in the organ parts to numerous Venetian and Milanese motet collections from the 1590s, that organists did at times accompany choirs from a full score.[25] For example, Aurelius Ribrochus, who edited Giuseppe Galli's *Sacri operis musici* in Milan in 1598, says he has saved the organist a lot of work by preparing the four-voice *partitura* for him in this edition; he also comments on the unpleasant dissonances which arise when organists do not play from a *partitura*, but just from the bass line.[26]

In much of his discussion on the new concepts of *General Bass*, Michael Praetorius defers to Italian authors. Quoting from Bernardo Strozzi's now-lost third volume of sacred concerti, *Affettuosi concerti ecclesiastici*, he addresses the origin of basso continuo:

> The tablature of all parts was in fact invented before this time, so that the part would be correctly played, as it stood in the score; this was a good idea, and he who understands it well, and can improvise well from the part, will play from it as best he can. But inasmuch as it is very difficult—and tiresome, too—to play such a part well, . . . the need then arises . . . to relieve oneself of this burden. So in order that one could play along in a *Concert* and at the same time avoid the difficulties of reading a part with its voices spread all over the page, the Bassus Continuus . . . was invented.[27]

Nevertheless, in speaking for himself Praetorius denies that basso continuo was "invented as a convenience for lazy organists who disliked the trouble of preparing a tablature, but rather in order that it might form the foundation of a score or tablature from which the Organist might construct his part."[28] And in the same year that Praetorius published this admonition, Heinrich Schütz similarly advised the organist who would accompany his *Psalmen Davids:* while confident in his ability to be able to play the continuo part for the psalms (which are in "stylo recitativo"), Schütz recommends he score up the more complicated "Moteten vnd Concerten" (beginning with no. 19, *Ist nicht Ephraim mein teurer Sohn*).[29] Even years later, at the middle of the century, Schütz still advocates a score—whether in staff notation or tablature—for the accompaniment of *prima prattica* motets.[30]

In turning to two smaller manuscripts in the Lüneburg collection, we can begin to document the relationship between the tablature scores they contain and the *absetzen* tradition in Germany in the seventeenth century. KN 207[2] and KN 207[3] are both single-fascicle manuscripts, the former of eight leaves and the latter of eighteen. The music in the two manuscripts begins on the verso of their first folios, and is written across both pages of each opening. KN 207[3] is ruled into four horizontal systems, KN 207[2] into five. A vertical ruling in KN 207[3] produces fourteen equally spaced, upright rectangular "measures" per system (over the entire opening), each of which may contain anywhere from a single semibreve's to two semibreves' worth of music, depending on the local rhythmic activity; usually each measure corresponds to a breve. In all but the last number in KN 207[3], the bottom line of each system carries the motet text, aligned with the bass part. KN 207[2] has no vertical rulings, nor are any of its pieces texted.[31] (See figs. 12.1, 12.2, and 12.4.)

Tables 12.1 and 12.2 inventory the contents of these two tablatures, each a small compilation of eight-voice motets. The first six numbers in KN 207[3] are solidly represented in German prints, especially the major, multipart collections—the *Opera musici*—of Jacob Handl (1586–90) and Hieronymus Praetorius (1618–25), and Erhard Bodenschatz's widely disseminated, two-volume *Florilegium Portense* (1618–21). Except for the missing part-books in the single Dresden concordance for Grimm's *Alleluia Lobet den Herren*, the only real problem in the two remaining, unpublished motets concerns the identity of the composer of no. 7, Andreas Marquardt. Of the seven sources at Dresden for *Ich hab einen guten Kampf gekämpfet*, only Pirna 57 supplies an attribution ("Andr Marquardius"), and no other works appear by him in Dresden manuscripts, or, for that matter, in any other inventories I have consulted.[32] None of the standard biographical reference works list him (*New Grove, MGG*, Eitner, Fétis, Gerber, Walther), nor do the RISM volumes of printed anthologies or *Einzeldrucke*, or, for instance, Reinhard Vollhardt's *Geschichte der Cantoren und Organisten von den Städten im Königreich Sachsen* (Berlin, 1899; rev. ed., 1978). Andreas Marquardt is a disembodied name, and, for the time being, is little better than anonymous.

The repertory of KN 207[2] is more problematic. The two motets by Hartmann are the only ones to have concordances in print, yet the Lüneburg tablature curiously misattributes one of them to Luca Marenzio. Two of the remaining three compositions are unica, and *Ich habe den Herrn alle Zeit für Augen* suffers an unresolvable attribution conflict.[33] Furthermore, the identity of "Eysenkrautt," the composer of *Cor mundum*, is only slightly less enigmatic than that of Marquardt; in the absence of any other likely candidate, the ascription could well refer to the Halle organist Wolfgang (Wolff) Eisentraut (1560–1629).

Table 12.1   Inventory of KN 207^2 [34]

Opening	No.	Composer	MS Entry	Concordances
2–3	1	[?Wolff Eisentraut]	Cor mundum | crea in me | Deus et | Spiritum | Eysenkrautt.	–
4–5			[concl. of no. 1]	
6–7	2	?Heinrich Grimm [?Samuel Rühling]	Ich Habe den | Herren alle Zeit | für Augen, den | er ist mir zur | rechten. | H. Grimmius.	Bs 40040:19 Bs 40158:61 Dl 8/70:114 Dl 10:27 Dl 59:48
8–9			[concl. of no. 2]	Dl 69:51 Ds 41:17
10–11	3	[Heinrich Hartmann]	Lobe den Herren | meine Seele | a: 8. voc.	HH 1618:21 1621^2:39 (CW 98:4)
12–13	4	Sethus Calvisius	Zion spricht | der Herr | hat mich ver-| laßen. | Sheti Calvisij.	–
14–15			[concl. of no. 4]	
	5	[Heinrich Hartmann]	Ist nicht Ephraim | mein Trewer Sohn | vnd mein trawteß | kint. | a 8 Voc. | [misattr. to] Luc: Marentjo.	1618^1:107 HH 1618:18 (var.) (CMM 72^3:12)
16			[concl. of no. 5]	

We are fortunate to be able to identify the scribes of both KN 207^2 and KN 207^3, and this identification fixes a local origin for both manuscripts. The scribal hand in KN 207^3 compares favorably with the handwriting of Joachim Dralle, whose career included a decade of service as organist of Lüneburg's Nicolaikirche. From his abundant thirty-year correspondence with the city council, it is not difficult to establish him through handwriting comparison as the copyist of KN 207^3 (cf. figs. 12.1, 12.2, and 12.3).[35]

Dralle was born in March, 1642.[36] Both his grandfather, Paulus Blocius, and his father, Hilmar Dralle, devoted most of their careers to teaching at Lüneburg's Latin school, the Johannisschule. Blocius was its rector for over thirty-five years, and the senior Dralle, evidently a native of nearby Gellersen,[37] entered the faculty as *collega quinta* (teacher of the fifth class) in July, 1634; years later he was promoted to *collega quarta*. Joachim's basic musical training formed part of the curriculum at the Johannisschule, where he acquired his

Table 12.2   Inventory of KN 207³

Opening	No.	Composer	MS Entry	Concordances
2–3	1a	Hieronymus Praetorius	Tulerunt Dominum | meum | 8 Voc. | Hieron. Praetor.	HP I:24–25 1618¹:67
4–5			[concl. of no. 1a]	
	1b		Secunda Pars | Cum ergo fleret. | 8. Voc.	
6–7			[concl. of no. 1b]	
8–9	2a	Jacob Handl	Maria Magdalena | 8 Voc. | Jacob Händl.	JH II:31 (DTÖ 30:31)
10–11	2b		Secunda Pars | Cito euntes. | 8 Voc.	
12–13	3a	Jacob Handl	O quam metuendus | est locus iste | Jac. Gallus | 8 Voc.	JH III:27 1607⁶:36–37 1618¹:29 (DTÖ 40:27)
14–15	3b		Secunda Pars | Orantibus in loco | isto. | 8 Voc.	
16–17	4	Caspar Movius	Schaff in mir Gott | ein reines Hertz | 8 Voc. | Casp. Movius	CM 1640:4
18–19			[concl. of no. 4]	
20–21	5	Hieronymus Praetorius	Venite exultemus | Domino | à 8. | Hieron. Praetorii	HP II:3 1618¹:97
22–23			[concl. of no 5]	
24–25	6	Hieronymus Praetorius	Cantate Domino | canticum novum | ab 8 | Hieron. Praetor.	HP II:4 1618¹:96 (RRMR 18:3)
26–27			[concl. of no. 6]	
28–29	7	[Andreas Marquardt]	Ich hab einen guten | Kampf gekämpfet | ab 8 Voc.	Dg 24:2 Dl 33:7 Dl 54:7 Dl 59:76
30–31			[concl. of no 7]	Dl 66:31 Dl 67:86 Dp 57:1

Table 12.2, cont.

Opening	No.	Composer	MS Entry	Concordances
32–33	8	Heinrich Grimm	Alleluja | Lobet den Herren in | seinem Heiligthumb | H. G. | ab 8	Dl 53:21
34–35			[concl. of no. 8]	
36	—	—	[blank]	—

primary education. (The schoolboys were responsible, under the cantor, for providing all the civic churches in town—St. Johannis, St. Lamberti, St. Nicolai, and St. Spiritus—with plainchant, chorale singing, and figural music.)[38] He completed his education with three years of study at the University of Leipzig, where he matriculated in the summer semester of 1663.[39]

We can first document Dralle's return to Lüneburg at the end of 1668, for it is his hand which copies his father's letter of 9 December (a testimonial for Joachim aimed at gaining him entry into the Johannisschule faculty). But over the next three years he made no progress in this direction. In the absence of any immediate promise of a career there, Dralle applied successfully in 1672 to succeed the late Martin Hudemann as organist of St. Nicolai.

Dralle was fully prepared to do this. In addition to his musical education at the Johannisschule, Joachim as a youth had enjoyed lessons on the side in "die Clavier-Kunst." And he had become proficient enough on the organ, according to his father, that he once deputized for the aging and ailing Franciscus Schaumkell on the large organ at St. Johannis for an entire year. (This could be evidence that Dralle had studied with Schaumkell, since the latter probably would have had one of his own students substitute for him.)[40] For the next ten years Dralle was forced to pursue what he viewed as an avocation, and his tenure at St. Nicolai was punctuated with repeated applications to the city council as positions opened up at the Johannisschule.[41] He finally met with success in the spring of 1682, and formally entered the faculty on 2 June. Ten years later he advanced to *subconrector,* his last position at the school. In 1697 Dralle fell ill, forcing his early retirement, and he remained on a disability pension until he died in September of 1702.

Joachim Dralle's musical development at the Johannisschule had ultimately been at the hands of the cantor Michael Jacobi. Jacobi was young and vigorous (at his death in 1663 he was only forty-five), and single-handedly revitalized and modernized musical practice in his adopted city at a time when it had declined through the economic repercussions of the Thirty Years' War and the coincident tenure of his poorly organized predecessor, Georg Cossius.[42] Much to his credit, Jacobi established a rotating schedule to supply all three civic churches, rather than just St. Johannis, with figural music; brought the neglected music library up to date; initiated annual Passion performances; battled with the administration of the Johannisschule to authorize the production of staged musical/theatrical works; and, in a word, did all he could to introduce the "itzigen Manier der Music."[43]

Soon after his appointment in 1651, Jacobi recognized the sore need for reforms in the administration of church music. In his "Musicalische Supplication" of 15 December 1652 to the board (*Juraten*) of the Johanniskirche, he particularly stresses budgetary needs: for salaried bellows pumpers (rather than schoolboys), for proper honoraria for instrumental musicians, and for his own reimbursement for growing expenditures towards instruments, music and music paper, honoraria, etc. But "first of all . . . there must be a good *Regalist*, who can properly handle the *General Bass* on the positive, tune it himself every week, and put down on paper whatever I set before him in *absetzung* and always be prepared."[44] The regalist was the accompanist of the *chorus symphoniacus* (the Johannisschule's most advanced choir, which was trained in polyphony). In the Johanniskirche, and presumably in the other churches, the choir performed "auf dem Chor," that is, in the chancel, where a regal and a positive organ were kept for its use.[45] In establishing the position of a salaried regalist, Jacobi directed his energy to all that related to it: in the fall of 1654 the church acquired a new positive organ; in 1651 and 1659 the school received gifts of a regal and a harpsichord (among other instruments); and a sudden flurry in the St. Johannis accounts of fairly regular expenses related to the positive and the regal (salaries, maintenance, etc.), which are entirely absent for decades prior to this, coincides with his arrival in Lüneburg (see appendix C).

Expenditures directed specifically to a regalist (five *Reichsthaler,* or ten marks, per semester) first appear in the St. Johannis accounts in 1655, but Jacobi was already employing accompanists much earlier than this.[46] An entry for 1652 records that "the cantor was reimbursed four marks which he paid [to someone] for playing the positive." (The "someone" was probably either one Theodor Jordan, or an unidentified student of Martin Hudemann's, as both these musicians served Jacobi in an apparently unofficial capacity in 1651 and 1652.)[47] For 1662 and a few years beyond, the accounts provide regalists' names, and at the head of the list stands Joachim Dralle, who was paid for a semester's work on 18 October. With this data, Horst Walter confidently reconstructs Dralle's line of succession for the rest of the decade: Emanuel Hemmerde (1662–65), Georg Krusemarck (1665–66), Caspar Arnold Grumbrecht (1667–69), and, once again, Dralle himself, who held the post until his election as Nicolaiorganist.[48]

By this roster, Walter seems to imply that the accounts of St. Johannis show regular entries for the biannual payments. According to Gustav Fock, however, the expenditures for the regalist are recorded only sporadically. Fock's

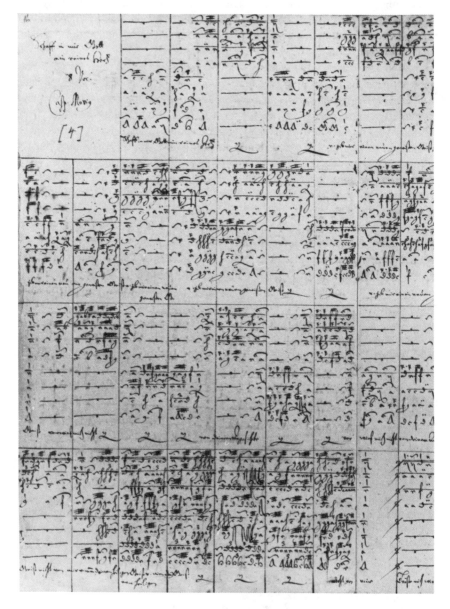

Figure 12.1. Caspar Movius, *Schaff in mir Gott ein reines Hertz*
(Luneburg, Ratsbücherei, Mus. ant. pract. KN 207³, p.16)

Figure 12.2. Heinrich Grimm, *Alleluja Lobet den Herren*
(Lüneburg, Ratsbücherei, Mus. ant. pract. KN 207³, pp. 32–33)

Figure 12.2, cont.

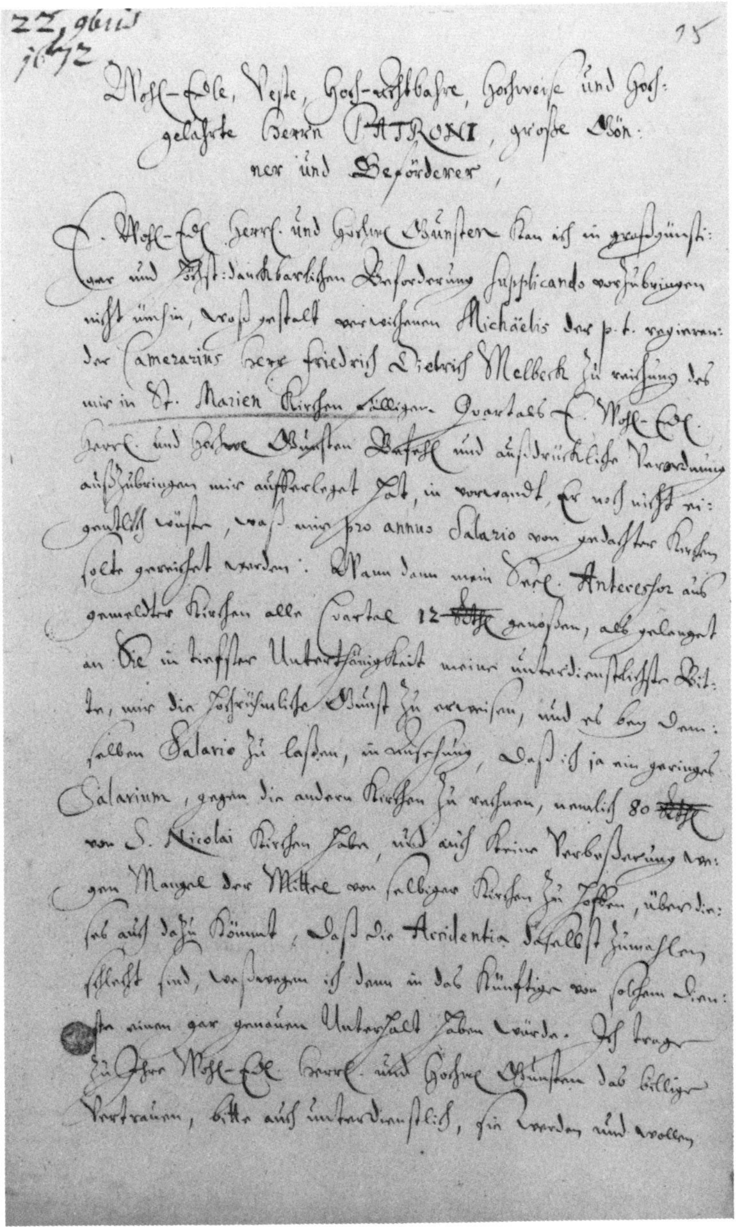
22, 96…
1672 15

Wohl-Edle, Veste, Hoch-achtbahre, Hochweise und Hoch-
gelahrte Herrn PATRONI, grosse Gön-
ner und Beförderer,

E. Wohl-Edl. Herrl. und Hochw. Gunsten kan ich in grosgünsti-
ger und höchst-dankbarlichen Beförderung supplicando vorzubringen
nicht umhin, wasgestalt verwichenen Michaëlis der p.t. regieren-
der Camerarius Herr Friedrich Dieterich Melbeck zu reichung des
mir in St. Marien Kirchen billigen Quartals E. Wohl-Edl.
Herrl. und Hochw. Gunsten Befehl und ausdrückliche Verordnung
auszubringen mir aufferleget hat, in verwandt, er noch nicht eigentlich wüste, was mir pro annuo Salario von gedachter Kirchen
solte gereichet werden. Wann dann mein Herr Antecessor aus
gemeldter Kirchen alle Quartal 12 Rthl genossen, als gelanget
an Sie in tiefster Unterthänigkeit meine unterdienstlichste Bitte, mir die hochrühmliche Gunst zu erweisen, und es bey demselben Salario zu lassen, in ansehung, dass ich ja ein geringes
Salarium, gegen die anderen Kirchen zu rechnen, nemlich 80 Rthl
von S. Nicolai Kirchen habe, und auch keine Verbesserung wegen Mangel der Mittel von selbiger Kirchen zu hoffen, überdie-
ses auch dazu kömmt, dass die Accidentia daselbst zumahlen
schlecht sind, wessentwegen ich dann in das künftige von solchem Dienste einen gar genauen Unterhalt haben würde. Ich trage
zu Ihrer Wohl-Edl. Herrl. und Hochw. Gunsten das billige
Vertrauen, bitte auch unterdienstlich, sie werden und wollen

Figure 12.3. Letter of Joachim Dralle, 20 Nov. 1672
(Lüneburg, Stadtarchiv, E le Nr. 15, ff. 15ʳ and 15ᵛ)

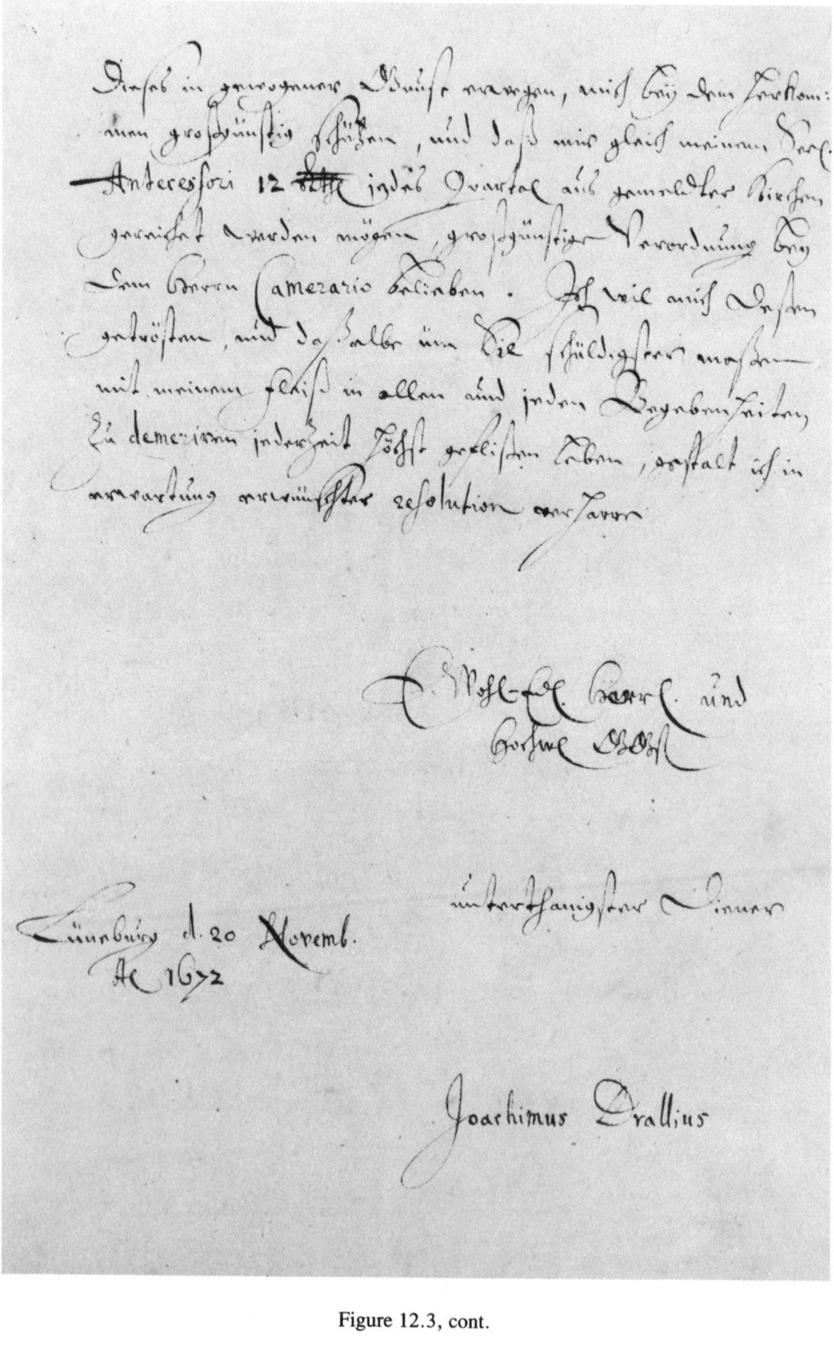

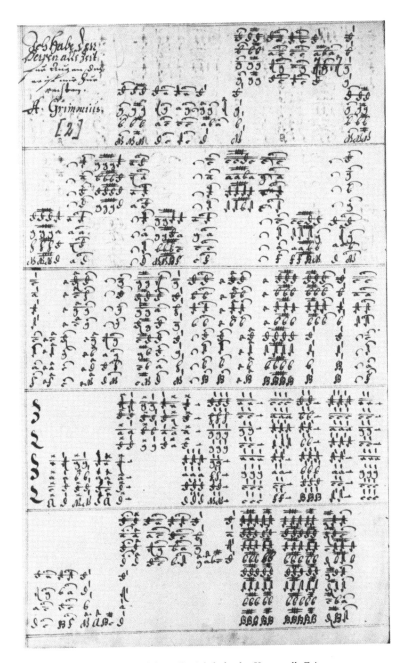

Figure 12.4. Heinrich Grimm (?), *Ich habe den Herren alle Zeit*
(Lüneburg, Ratsbücherei, Mus. ant. pract. KN 207², pp. 6–7)

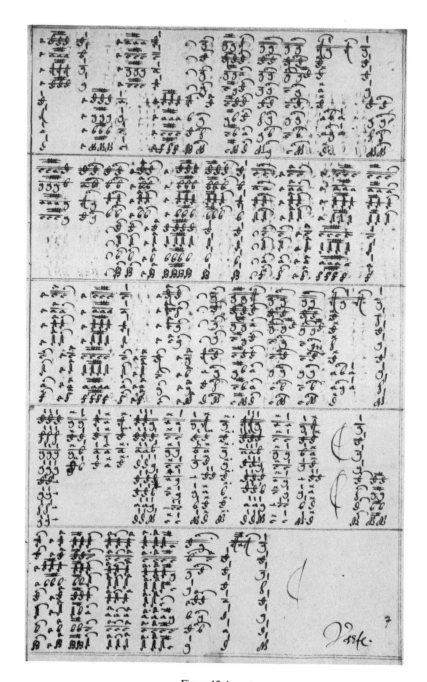

Figure 12.4, cont.

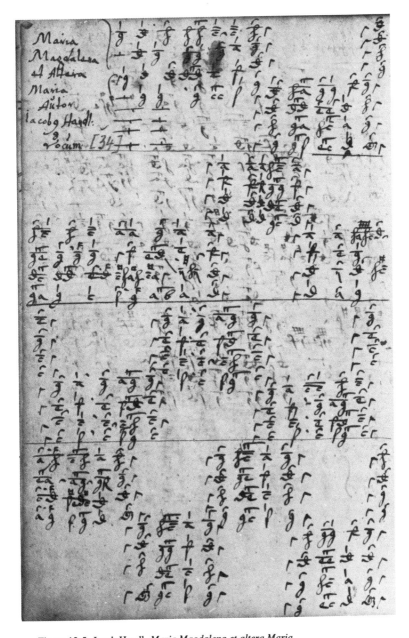

Figure 12.5. Jacob Handl, *Maria Magdalena et altera Maria*
See also example 12.2.
(Lüneburg, Ratsbücherei, Mus. ant. pract. KN 210, ff. 46ᵛ and 47ʳ)

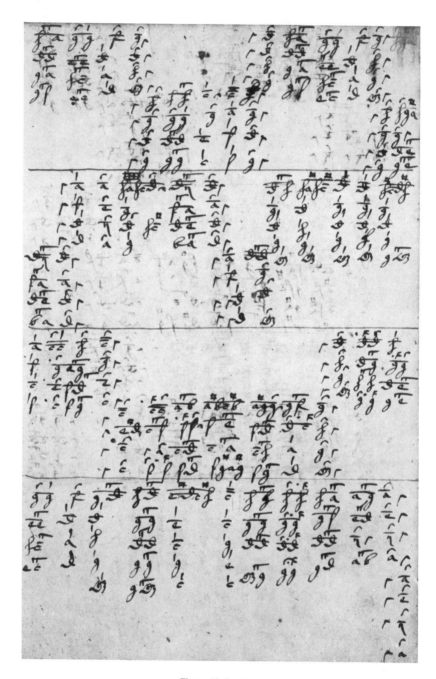

Figure 12.5, cont.

transcripts of items related to music in the St. Johannis accounts include no entries mentioning the regalist for the years 1657–61, 1664–65, 1668, or 1671–72, and only one semester's or one quarter's payment is recorded in all the other years under discussion except for 1669, which is fully accounted for.[49]

Table 12.3 summarizes Fock's transcripts from 1662 through 1672. If they are complete (I have not examined the St. Johannis accounts), I'm not sure Walter can presume that Emanuel Hemmerde, whose salary is entered only once on 25 April 1663, necessarily continued as regalist through the rest of that year and on through the two succeeding years, for which Fock lists no payments. Walter is more justified, perhaps, in assuming continuous service for Caspar Arnold Grumbrecht (to whom payments are recorded only on 1 July 1667 and 20 June 1669); furthermore, we can probably give Grumbrecht the benefit of the doubt for being the unnamed regalist who was paid only a quarter's salary in the fall of 1669 "because he moved away." The proposal that Joachim Dralle's second tenure was continuous into 1672 is reasonable, too, and finds support in remarks of his father's from March of that year, which relate that "at the current time, he is once more participating in harmonious service 'auff dem Chor' and skillfully playing the *General-Bass,* which is the foundation of the organist's entire art."

At this point, the evidence which links KN 207[3] to the regalist's duties in Lüneburg is circumstantial. We know that organists in Europe in the sixteenth and seventeenth centuries commonly scored motets and other vocal music into tablature. While they thereby expanded their solo repertory, we have shown above that they also accompanied choirs from such scores; evidence for this is

Table 12.3   Regalists at St. Johannis, 1662–1672

Year	Easter	Johannis	Michaelis	Christmas
1662	—	Dralle	Dralle	Hemmerde
1663	Hemmerde	—	—	—
1664	—	—	—	—
1665	—	—	—	—
1666	Krusemarck	Krusemarck	—	—
1667	Grumbrecht	Grumbrecht	[Grumbrecht]	[Grumbrecht]
1668	[Grumbrecht]	[Grumbrecht]	[Grumbrecht]	[Grumbrecht]
1669	Grumbrecht	Grumbrecht	[Grumbrecht]	Dralle
1670	Dralle	Dralle	[Dralle]	[Dralle]
1671	[Dralle]	[Dralle]	[Dralle]	[Dralle]
1672	Dralle	[Dralle?]	—	—

especially rich from Italy and Germany. Even well after the introduction of figured bass, we know from Praetorius's and Schütz's remarks that under certain circumstances organists in Germany still followed—and were encouraged to follow—the old practice. In Lüneburg, it was the regalist's job in the second half of the century to accompany the school choir in church polyphony, and the hand of one particular regalist, Joachim Dralle, prepared the tablature score KN 207³. It seems improbable that Dralle would have bothered to enter the motet texts into the manuscript if he were preparing an intabulation for himself as a guide to solo improvisation.

Certainly it is conceivable that Dralle's duties as organist at St. Nicolai might have extended to some choral accompanying. However, physical evidence in KN 207³ is more consistent with an origin prior to his appointment there. The watermark in the manuscript shows a lion standing before three trees, contained within a shield. Piccard localizes this watermark type to the region around Celle, ca. 1650.[50] My own gleanings in the Lüneburg Stadtarchiv uncovered eleven exemplars of this watermark type in documents written in Lüneburg between 1649 and 1674, a period which embraces Dralle's two terms as regalist.

One last consideration strengthens our case for an earlier dating: the presence in the manuscript of Andreas Marquardt's motet. The text of *Ich hab einen guten Kampf gekämpfet* is the well-known couplet from 2 Tim. 4, and was common stock for funeral motets: "I have fought the good fight, I have finished the race, I have kept the faith. Henceforth there is laid up for me the crown of righteousness, which the Lord, the righteous judge, will award to me on that Day, and not only to me but also to all who have loved his appearing." (The verse just preceding this concludes, "The time of my departure has come.") We can show numerous instances of this text's having been set specifically for the obsequies of particular individuals. Table 12.4 lists those composers who

Table 12.4   Occasional Settings of *Ich hab einen guten Kampf*[52]

1622 (Coburg)	Melchior Franck (RISM A/I, F 1715)
1631 (Leipzig)	Samuel Michael (Mueller, 261)
1638 (Kbg.)	Heinrich Albert (DDT, 12:xxi, 9f)
1651 (Nbg.)	Joh. Er. Kindermann (Samuel, 379 no. 21; EDM, 79:45f, 136)
1654 (Nbg.)	Kindermann (Samuel, 381 no. 25; MAM, 3:vii, 1)
1655 (Rostock)	Nicolas Hasse (RISM A/I, H 2314)
1657 (Nbg.)	Paul Hainlein (Samuel, 340 no. 5)
1659 (Nbg.)	David Schedlich (Samuel, 473 no. 14)
1665 (Nbg.)	Paul Hainlein (Samuel, 138–42, 345 no. 19)
1672 (Gotha)	Joh. Georg Reimann (RISM A/I, R 1010)

published settings of the verses as elegies for ranking citizens of the cities in which they worked. (Melchior Franck in fact eulogizes the late Duke Friedrich of Saxony, who fell in the battle of Fleurus in the service of the Palatine forces;[51] hence the verses take on a literal significance.) Heinrich Albert and the Nuremberg composers set not the biblical text, but poems whose strophes elaborate upon it, always quoting or paraphrasing the beginning of verse 8 in the first line. To these occasional publications we can add the funerary setting by Petrus Laurentius Wockenfuss, cantor in Kiel, which opens a manuscript collection in Berlin entitled "Musikalischer Todes-Gedancken" (Mus. Ms. 23220), and that by Christian Ritter.[53]

The obligations of the *chorus symphoniacus* at St. Johannis included attendance at funerals. At these, as at other times, they normally sang to the accompaniment of a regal or a positive. But on 2 March 1672, the *Johanniscantor* Friedrich Funcke (Jacobi's successor) was notified that a half-year's salary was to be withheld from him because he had allowed his choir to perform with instrumental accompaniment at a local funeral, a practice which had been forbidden. In his defense of three weeks later (see appendix B, part 3), Funcke responds that his presence before the choir at the funeral in question (that of his late brother-in-law, Jacob Hasse) had not been possible, and that his assistants were in charge; under these circumstances, the choir could fare well only with accompaniment. (Funcke speaks of his "Abwesenheit": we cannot tell if he means absence from his duty as choirmaster, and that he possibly had another function at his brother-in-law's funeral, or if he in fact wasn't at the event at all.) He continues, claiming that he had been using such a "Fundament" with the choir at funerals since 1665 (the year after he was hired), and that he realized he had previously been forbidden to use accompaniment at the funeral of the late Heinrich von Bücken, but that he had thought this an isolated instance, not a general ban. He had obeyed the order that time, and had received no reprimands for continuing to use the organ during the intervening period.

Despite the severity of the fine and the solemnity of Funcke's own promise never to repeat this violation ("In the future, and for the rest of my days, I will never permit any viol, let alone a single keyboard instrument, to make a sound at burial services"), the case did not close here. At the end of the same year, Funcke received further reproval for the identical offence, this time involving the funeral of the late *Bürgermeister* Augustus Busche. A report from a grand jury records Funcke's case:[54] he thought the council's ban concerned only ordinary citizens but not "Bürgermeister- und Rahtstandes Persohnen," and he insists that the family had requested the use of instruments at the funeral, from which he had tried to discourage them; furthermore, he had recently used the regal at the funerals for Johann von Cölln (19 May) and *Bürgermeister* Friesendorff (13 October) without complaint from anyone.

The report recommends Funcke's exculpation, and the civil acts contain no further charges against him for subsequent violations of this sort. Evidently, then, the city council's insistence that funeral music be unaccompanied held sway after this, at least for some time. It follows that the year 1672 must be the last year that Dralle would have accompanied the chorus at funerals, whereby we establish a *terminus ante quem* for the copying of Marquardt's funeral motet, and hence for KN 207[3]. Evidence thus favors a dating for the manuscript either between 1670 and 1672, or within a period—possibly several years long— ending in September 1662.[55]

We noted above that the small motet tablature KN 207[2] also had its origins in Lüneburg. The handwriting in the manuscript agrees with that in not only KN 209, the largest and arguably the most important manuscript of the collection, but also KN 207[15] and KN 207[16] (two volumes of preludes which, like KN 209, are sources for works by Weckmann, Scheidemann, and Tunder).[56] Furthermore, this same hand belongs to the secondary scribe in KN 146, where it several times shares the copying of a single piece with Franciscus Schaumkell.[57] The copyist of all these manuscripts is one whose name has been known since Wilhelm Christian Junghans first described Lüneburg's musicalia over a century ago.[58] KN 209 bears his collophon in its inside front cover: "Heinrich Baltzer Wedemann." For decades, the absence of any clue to the identity behind the name left musicologists with the tentative and generally tacit assumption that it belonged to a former owner of the manuscript.[59]

From 1678 until his death in 1718, Heinrich Baltzer Wedemann was organist at St. Nicolaihof, a small community outside Lüneburg's walls (closer, in fact, to Bardowick) whose chapel was under Lüneburg's administration.[60] Ironically, Wedemann's position was more that of a civil servant than a musician. Like so many organists' posts elsewhere in northern Germany—posts held by the eminent likes of Buxtehude, Tunder, Scheidemann, and Weckmann—the job at St. Nicolaihof demanded bookkeeping and other clerical skills in addition to musical experience. In Wedemann's case, the offices of *monitor* (the accountant for St. Nicolaihof's extensive agricultural interests) and sexton which he embodied vastly overshadowed his role as organist for the rural chapel, and existing documents are all but silent on details relating to his musical background and responsibilities.

The registers of Lüneburg's Nicolaikirche record Wedemann's baptism in 1646 and marriage in 1681, both in the month of November. That his father, Peter Wedemann (whom I have been unable to trace), was an organist, and that Baltzer himself, before his appointment at St. Nicolaihof, had been *praeceptor* to the von Dassel family (one of Lüneburg's prominent *Patriziergeschlechte*), are the only bits left to fill out his scanty biography. We cannot even show that Wedemann attended the Johannisschule, though he could hardly have held tutorial and accounting jobs without such an education.

The little we do know about Wedemann, though, begins to outline a surprising parallel to Joachim Dralle's biography. Before landing a job with the city, Dralle, too, made ends meet as a private tutor; Dralle probably apprenticed under the organist Schaumkell, which seems also to have been the case for Wedemann (the presence of both Wedemann's and Schaumkell's hands in KN 146 attests to this); and both Dralle and Wedemann copy out in tablature score a little fascicle-manuscript of eight-voice motets. The bonds which draw Schaumkell, Dralle, and Wedemann together grow tighter still through the presence of Dralle's colophon, dated 1650, in KN 146. In that year Dralle was eight and Wedemann was four, yet Wedemann's hand appears first in the tablature and Dralle's never appears at all.[61]

The hypothesis we have proposed above for KN 207³ thus significantly affects our interpretation of both the provenance of KN 207² and further details about Wedemann's background. Do we have in him another of Jacobi's or Funcke's regalists? If so, we could consider dating KN 207² either between 1672 (when Dralle leaves the post) and 1678 (the year of Wedemann's appointment at St. Nicolaihof), or else between 1663 and 1666 (the vacant slot in our roster of regalists). To resolve this requires incorporating evidence from all five of Wedemann's manuscripts and analyzing their relation to one another, a task which is beyond the scope of this article. (KN 209, for instance, whose scribal link with KN 207² is strengthened by its six tablature scores [nos. 49–54], bears the date of 1663 at the end of its penultimate piece, a chorale by Peter Morhardt. This could be a date of composition or a date of copying.)

Identical questions loom up when we approach KN 210. Most of the motets in the manuscript are organ arrangements, copied either by Schaumkell or by his anonymous associate. But ten successive motets in tablature score, several with texts, open the manuscript in the hand of the unknown scribe.[62] Does this lead us to conclude that KN 210, too, was assembled—at least in part—by one of Lüneburg's regalists as a repertory of *Absetzungen?* I think it likely. We might even have already met him, recalling that Emanuel Hemmerde's tenure included at least the semester ending with Easter 1663: the only date in KN 210 is (coincidentally?) the year 1663, entered after no. 31, an intabulation of Melchior Franck's Easter motet *Quia vidisti me Thoma.* At points like this, otherwise utterly insignificant names such as Hemmerde's rise to prominence and call out for scrutiny.

The intabulations we have examined are a Janus-faced repertory. On the one hand, the solo motet intabulation, looking back over a tradition four centuries old, draws its last breath in the Lüneburg tablatures. On the other, the presence of tablature scores in Lüneburg at this specific point in time demonstrates that more removed parts of Europe were still anticipating the complete adoption of modern continuo practice. As late as the 1660s or even the 1670s, provincial organists like Dralle and Wedemann—and, more than likely, Hemmerde, Grumbrecht, and their compatriots—were still laboriously drawing up their *Absetzungen*. Two generations after its invention, literacy in figured bass had not yet completed its migration across Europe, and even the progressives Schütz and Jacobi would still qualify its value in practice: "Copy this into score and be ready with it."

The insight which characterizes Blume's and Ruhnke's vision is nowhere more evident than in their appeal for a consideration of the intabulated repertory equal in scope to that already accorded "real" organ compositions. The passage from their study quoted above is soon followed by their prophetic analysis of the import of the Lüneburg intabulations:

> The opposite side of this interest [shown in the Lüneburg tablatures by Seiffert, Reimann, and Straube for their research and editions] in originally conceived [organ] compositions and their application in practice, is that in the meantime an investigation into the intabulations has been entirely neglected, despite the far-reaching disclosures which they promise regarding performance practice, the use to which they were put—indeed, even the very origin and compiler (or copyist) of the tablatures themselves.[63]

For now the question of how our theory might apply to other repertories remains open. The famous volumes at Pelplin date from the 1620s, and the less well-known tablatures at Schmölln (near Leipzig) from the same time; the Braunschweig tablatures were copied forty years before that.[64] These three huge collections of tablature scores, and many others besides, could well be additional witnesses to the practice of using motet scores as protocontinuo parts.[65] It matters little that the eight- or twelve- or sixteen-voice compositions cannot be played as written; as Bernardo Strozzi said above, the organist will play from the part as well as he can. Further ramifications of this hypothesis crop up outside German-speaking lands: for example, what implications (if any) does it carry with regard to Edward Lowinsky's theories on the development and use of score notation in Italy? (Professor Lowinsky dismisses late sixteenth-century Italian organ scores from practical keyboard use because their texts are unplayable as written.)[66] To be sure, Blume's and Ruhnke's prophecy encompasses an area which extends far beyond Lüneburg's thousand-year-old walls.

Appendix A: Index to Intabulated Vocal Polyphony in the Lüneburg Tablatures[67]

Ottavio Bargnani	*Clori mia bella* a 5	210:67
	Quel sospir che dal core a 5	210:68
Giovanni Bassano	*Dic nobis Maria* a 6	209:15 HS
Joachim a Burck	*Wie lieblich und wie schöne* a 4	210:29
Sethus Calvisius	*Zion spricht, der Herr hat mich verlassen* a 8	207²:4*
?Wolff Eisentraut	*Cor mundum crea in me* a 8	207²:1*
Heinrich Elsmann	*Ein freundlich Weib ist ihrem Manne* a 5	209:52*
Noë Faignient	*Laudate Dominum omnes gentes* a 8	209:11; 210:57
?Arnoldus de Fine[68]	*Das alte Jahr vergangen ist* a 4	210:27
Melchior Franck	*Cantabo Domino in vita mea* a 7	209:12 = 210:47
	Fürchte dich nicht a 6	210:59
	Quia vidisti me Thoma a 6	210:31
	Was mein Gott will a 8	210:69
Heinrich Grimm[69]	*Alleluia. Lobet den Herren in seinen Heiligtum* a 8	207³:8*
	Ein freundlich Weib erfreuet ihren Mann a 8	209:51*
	Freue dich du Tochter Zion a 8	209:53*
	Ich habe den Herrn alle Zeit a 8	207²:2*
	(Sam. Rühling?)	
	Lobet den Herren alle Heiden a 6 (a 8?)	209:22
	Wie schön leuchtet der Morgenstern a 6	209:1 = 210:46
Andreas Hakenberger	*Exultate iusti in Domino* a 6	209:50*
Andreas Hammerschmidt	*Alleluia. Ach mein herzliebes Jesulein* a 6	209:54*
Jacob Handl	*Audi tellus audi omne* a 8	210:10**
	Exultate Deo adiutori nostro a 5	210:42
	Exultate iusti in Domino a 8	210:51
	Exurge gloria mea a 5	210:45
	(= secunda pars to *Repleatur os meum*)	
	Factus est repente de caelo a 4	210:37
	Gloria et honore coronastieum a 8	210:58
	Hierusalem gaude gaudio magno a 6	209:8; 210:21
	Hodie nobis caelorum rex a 8	210:25
	Laus et perennis gloria a 8	210:52
	Maria Magdalena et altera Maria a 8	210:34; 207³:2**
	O beata trinitas coaequalis a 4	210:39
	O quam metuendus est a 8	207³:3**
	Omnes gentes plaudite manibus a 8	210:35
	Veni sancte spiritus a 4	210:36
Heinrich Hartmann	*Ist nicht Ephraim mein teurer Sohn* a 8	207²:5*
	Lobe den Herren meine Seele a 8	207²:3*
Hans Leo Hassler[70]	*A Domino factum est istud* a 8	210:5**
	Alleluia. Laudem dicite Deo nostro a 5	208¹:40 HS; 209:10; 210:3*; 1r 697*
	Canite tuba in Sion a 5	210:20
	Dixit Maria ad angelum a 4	209:4 = 210:16 = 210:44; 209:20 HS
	Domine Dominus noster a 5	209:6 = 210:18
	Dum complerentur dies Pentecostes a 8	210:38

	Ecce quam bonum a 5	209:3 = 210:15 = 210:43
	Expurgate vetus fermentum a 5	209:5 = 210:17 = 210:41
	Hodie Christus natus est a 10	210:24
	Laudate Dominum omnes gentes a 8	209:49*
	Laudate Dominum in sanctis eius a 8	210:48
	Pater noster a 8	209:13 = 210:50
	Verbum caro factum est a 6	207[18] HS; 209:9; 209:23 DS; 210:1*
	Chi mi dimandar a 4	210:55c
	Donna se lo mio core a 4	210:55b
	Ridon di maggio a 4	210:55d
	Sospira core a 4	210:55c
Jacob Hassler[71]	*Amate mi ben mio* a 6	210:55
	Quest' arder mio a 6	210:55a
Orlando de Lassus	*Benedictum Dominum in omni tempore* a 5	4209:7 = 210:19 HS
	De ore prudentis a 5	209:18 HS
	Domine Dominus noster a 6	210:53
	Ecce Maria genuit nobis a 5	210:26
	Ego sum panis vivus a 5	210:40 HS
	O decus celsi genus a 6	210:54
	Surrexit pastor bonus a 5	209:16 DS; 209:17HS; 210:32
	Tibi laus tibi gloria a 5	209:19 DS
Volckmar Leisring	*Wer mich liebet* a 5	210:12*
Leone Leoni	*Tribularer si nescirem* a 8	210:65
Andreas Marquardt	*Ich hab einen guten Kampf gekämpfet* a 8	207[3]:7**
Jacob Meiland	*Non auferetur sceptrum* a 6	210:22
Caspar Movius	*Schaff in mir Gott* a 8	207[3]:4**
Giovanni Maria Nanino	*Erano i capei* a 5	210:64
G. P. da Palestrina	*Vestiva i colli* a 5	210:13
David Palladius	*Vespera iam venit nobis* a 6	210:63
Hieronymus Praetorius	*Benedicam Dominum in omni tempore* a 6	209:21 HS
	Cantate Domino canticum novum a 8	207[3]:6**
	Domine Dominus noster a 8	210:7–8*
	Tulerunt Dominum meum a 8	207[3]:1**
	Venite exultemus Dominum a 8	207[3]:5**; 210:4**
Michael Praetorius	*Ein schönes Liedlein singen wir* a 4	210:28
	Das alte Jahr ist nun vergahn a 4	210:27b
	Das alte Jahr vergangen ist a 4	210:27a
	Mein Hüter und mein Hirt a 8	209:14
	Nunc angelorum gloria a 4	210:30
?Samuel Rühling	*Ich habe den Herrn alle Zeit* a 8 (?Heinrich Grimm)	207[2]:2*
Michael Tonsor	*Dum transisset sabbatum* a 5	210:33
Ascanio Trombetti	*Paratum cor meum* a 5	210:11*
Melchior Vulpius	*Zion spricht, der Herr hat mich verlassen* a 5	210:62
Christoph Thomas Walliser	*Nun lob mein Seel den Herren* a 5	210:66
	Wohl dem der in Gottes Fürchten steht a 5	209:2 = 210:14; 210:49*

Johann Walter	*Resonet in laudibus* a 5	208¹:7
	(*Joseph, lieber Joseph mein*)	
Erasmus Widmann	*Ich bin die Auferstehung* a 6	210:6*
Nicolaus Zangius	*Hierusalem gaude gaudio magno* a 8	209:8; 210:23
Anonymous⁷²	*Cantate Domino canticum novum* a ?	210:60
	Hosianna dem Sohne David a 5	146:41 = 210:56;
		208¹:19
	O Jesu mi dulcissime a 3	210:9**
	Quare fremuerunt gentes [a 8 ?]	210:61
	[untitled madrigal] [a 4 ?]	210:2

Appendix B: Documents

1. Hilmar Dralle to Friedrich Theodor Melbeck and Georg von Dassel, Jr., 9 December 1668 (Ls, S 3b Nr. 3).

Wohl-Edle . . . Beförderer,
Nach dem nunmehro am Tage ist, daß unser Sub-ConRector Michael Jordan*us* mutieren und seinen so lange bedienten Dienst verlaßen wird, wodurch denn eintzige Vacantz sich an unseren Schuldiensten ereignet, welche wiederum zu bekleiden Ihre WohlEdle und Hochweise Gunsten, als ihrer Schulen Höchstgetreue Versorger, sich ehisten werden angelegen sein laßen, um welche Bekleidung denn sich vermuhtlich meine beyde Herren Col legen werden bemühen, auf welcher Beforderung auch die unterste Stelle in unserm Collegio Scholastico erlediget würde. Nun wil ich nicht verhoffen, Daß meine Großgünstige Herren Patroni, soferne sich solche Stelle ambirete, mich praeteriren würden, weil ich nunmehro an ihrer Schulen mügligstem und menschlichem Fleiße nach in die 35. Jahre gearbeitet habe. Dieweil ich aber meine Jahre erreichet, und ein Mann bin, der fast auff der Gruben gehet, so wil ich mich solcher Anwartung begeben, und einem meiner Collegen solchen Dienst hertzlich gönnen, mehr vor meine Kinder als für mich sorgende. Weswegen denn hiemit an Eure WohlEdle und Hochweise Herrligkeiten und Gunsten meine unterthänigste Bitte gelanget, Mir doch die große Willfahrung zu erweisen, und meinen Sohn Joachimum, welchen ich mit schweren Unkosten 3. Jahr auff der Universität Leipzig zum Studieren gehalten habe, vor andern zu der untersten Stelle in unserm Collegio zu befördern, er soll nechst Göttlicher Verleihung seinem Dienste vorstehen, daß die Herren Patroni sollen satsahme Genüge daran haben. Denn es ist ihm fast die SchulArbeit angeerbet, theils von mir, als der ich meine graue Haar bey Information der Jugend erlanget, theils auch von seinem seel*igen* GroßVater Paulo Blocio, welcher an Ihrer Schulen auch 45. Jahr gearbeitet hat. Zwar hätte mein Sohn schon längst einen guten Cantor-dienst bekleiden können in Holstein, wenn ich nicht auf zurathen Ihro Wohlweißheiten Herrn Tzarstedten, Damahligen Gerichts Praesidenten und Scholarchen ihn der Music zum Besten, und dem seeligen Jacobi zu Hülffe noch ein Jahr hätte auffgehalten. In Erinnerung, aber nicht Erwiederung dieses, bitte ich nochmahlen unterdienstlich, meine unterthänigste Bitte doch anzunehmen, und mir auf solche eine großgünstige Resolution zu ertheilen. . . .

2. Hilmar Dralle to the City Council, 11 March 1672 (Ls, E 1d Nr. 56).

Wohl-Edle . . . Herren Patroni . . . ,
Daß ich mit gegenwärtiger Bitt-schrift anjetzo vor Ihre Hoch- und Wohl-weise Gunsten unterthänigst trete, werde ich auß väterlicher Liebe und angebohrner Vorsorge erkühnet, in Ansehung und Betrachtung des anjetzo zu St. Nicolai entledigten Organisten dienstes, zu welches wiederersetzung und Bestellung ohne Zweiffel auf das ehiste ein Subjectum, welches auff hochverständiges Gutachten darzu geschickt, wird gewürdiget werden. Gelanget derowegen an Sie, als meine hochgeehrte Herrn Patronen, mein unterdienstliches Suchen und Bitten, Sie wollen doch großgünstig geruhen, und

meinen Sohn Joachimum, auff welchen ich in dieser Kunst etliche Jahr ein ehrliches gewendet, durch einstimmige Wahl mit solchen Dienst vor andern begünstigen, welche höchstrühmliche Gewehrung ich alß eine angenehme Erwiederung und Belohnung meiner und seines Seel*igen* Großvaters Blocii vielerjährigen blutsauern Schul- und zu St. Nicolai Kirchen Arbeit danckbarlich empfinden werde, bey versicherten Versprechen, daß mein Sohn solchem Dienste vorstehen soll, durch mügligsten Fleiß und Vermeidung alles ermangelnden begehren; Es möchte sich zwar bey seiner Geschickligkeit ein Mißtrauen ereignen, in Einwurff: Er hätte ja die Clavier-Kunst nicht als ein Selbst-Werck, sondern nur als ein Neben-Werck bey seinen Studiis getrieben, da es doch einen gantzen Menschen erforderte, welcher nicht alleine der Kunst fähig, sondern auch des Orgelwerckes, wegen Reinstimmung und Fertighaltung, wohl kündig seyn müste! Diesem zu begegnen, so ist nicht alleine bekandt, daß er das große Werck zu St. Johannis ein gantzes Jahr, wegen zugefallner und anhaltender Kranckheit des Organisten Schaumkellens, unter seinen Händen gehabt, welches er nicht allein gebührend, wie man dazumahl gehöret, bespielet, sondern auch durch kündige Aufsicht allezeit wohlgestimmet und fertig gehalten hat, daß keine Klage darüber jemahls ergangen, viel weniger dem Wercke Schaden zuge wachsen ist; Wegen seiner Kunstfähigkeit aber geben ihm nicht alleine Zeugnüß seine SchülerJahre, in welchen er das Positiv- und Regal unter dem Directorio musico des Seel*igen* Jacobi schon verwaltet, sondern auch gegenwertige Zeit, da er ebenmäßig wiederüm auff dem Chor mit auffwartet, und den General-Bass, als der gantzen Organisten-Kunst Grund, kunstgemäß spielet, daß also verhoffentlich sich man keine fernere Gedancken deßwegen wird machen können. In Ansehung deßen nun bitte ich nochmahl demühtigst, Ihre Hoch- und Wohlweise Gunsten geben doch meinem väterlichen Suchen ein gewehrendes Ohr und beseeligen mich, als ihren alten und auf der Grube gehenden Schulbedienten, doch in meinen grauen Jahren noch mit einer freudigen Ergetzung durch verleihung des entledigten Dienstes vor meinen Sohn, Ich werde nicht unterlaßen schüldigster maßen solche hohe Gunst-gewogenheit üm Sie allerseits gegen Gott mit einem inbrünstigen Gebet, samt allen denen lieben Meinigen wiederüm zu verschulden. . . .

3. Friedrich Funcke to the City Council, 27 March 1672 (Ls, S 3b Nr. 8, fasc. 1, ff. 89–91).

Wohl-Edle . . . Herrn Patroni . . . ,
Wiewohl ich jederzeit vermeinet und mir eingebildet habe, daß ich aller Gunst eines Hochweisen Rahts versichert wäre, weßwegen ich mich denn nach mügligsten Fleiß auch allezeit dahinn befliessen, daß nichts möge ermangeln, so viel an mir gewesen, was mir in meinen Amts-Verrichtungen oblieget, so habe ich doch den 2 Martij, leider! ein wiedriges erfahren, in dem mir von den Hn. Scholarchen Hn. Georg Büschen durch den Marckt-Voigt wegen der aus höchster Nohtwendigkeit eintzig angezogenen gedockten Stimme bey meines seel*igen* Schwagers Jacob Hassens Beerdigungs-Music der ungünstige Straff-Schluß, nemlich eine halb-jährige Besoldungs-Zurück-Behaltung ist angekündiget worden. Nun hätte ich zwar nicht gemeint, daß mann auf mich deßwegen eine solche unerträgliche Ungunst hätte werffen sollen, alldieweil solches warhaftig weder auß Ungehorsam kegen meine Hochweise Obrigkeit, wofür mich mein Gott behütten wolle, weder auß sonderlicher Pracht, sondern auß erheischender Nohtwendigkeit, wegen Abwesenheit meiner Person, auß Furcht, daß meine Adjuvanten ohne Fundament nicht möchten zurechte kommen, wie meinem Regalisten bewust, welchen Schimpf ich auch nicht gerne hätte haben wollen: denn ich bemühe mich ja auf das höchste, daß ja bey Beerdigung derer mit nicht Verwandten nichts möge unterlaßen werden, was denen seelig-Verstorbenen zur letzten Ehre und denen hinterbliebenen zu angenehmen Gefallen gereichen möge, wie ich denn von Anno 1665 an biß auf meinen seel*igen* Schwager bey vieler Beerdigung, ohne Entgeldt, wie auß beygelegten Verzeichnüß zu ersehen, habe theils das Positiv, theils das Regal in unterschiedenen Kirchen spielen lassen. Zwar muß ich gestehen, daß kurtz vor Heinrichs von Bücken Ihro Wohlweißheiten oberwehnter Herr Scholarche durch den auch gedachten Marckt-Voigt mir einen Zettul zugesendet, in welchen, so warhaftig alß der höchste Gott lebet, Er mir nur alleine hat lassen verbiethen im Nahmen eines Hochweisen Rahts, daß doch bey Beerdigung

see*liges* Heinrichs von Bücken kein Regal oder Positiv möge gerühret werden, welchen Verboht ich auch unterthänigst gehorsamet, aber nicht gewust und gemeinet, daß solches ein allgemeines Verboht sey, weil solches in gemeldten Zettul nicht enthalten, sondern nur alleine Heinrichs von Bücken darinn gedacht worden; wäre mir solches über-all verbothen worden, ey so soll mich mein getreüer Gott dafür behüttet haben, daß ich nur ein eintzigs Clavier hätte sollen regen lassen, wenn mir auch der Verstorbene noch näher wäre Verwandt gewesen. Weil es aber von Anno 1665 her so manchmahl geschehen ist so wohl Standts- alß Bürgers Persohnen zu Ehren, und mir niemahls nicht ein wordt ist davon gesaget worden, sondern ist von denen hinterbliebenen vielmehr danckbarlich gelobet worden, habe ich mich auch bey meines see*ligen* Schwagers Beerdigung von einen Hochweisen Raht keiner Ungunst und Leids wegen Rührung deß blossen Positivs, weil ich selbsten nicht zukegen war, befahret habe ich mich aber irgends mit der Beerdigungs-Music des see*ligen* Hn. Superintenden-ten verstossen, bitte ich um Verzeihung, mit unterthänigsten Angeloben, daß ich in das Künftige nicht alleine keine Viole sondern auch nicht ein eintzigs Clavier meine Lebens-Tage will rühren lassen bey der Verstorbenen Beerdigung, sondern allezeit meiner hochzuehrenden Hn. Patronen Ver- und Ge-Boht hirinnen schuldigst und willigst Folge leisten. Ist denn nun alßo, daß solche Beerdigungs-Music des see*ligen* Herrn Superintendenten der unerträglichen Ungunst Grund ist, wie ich mir denn fest einbilde, weil das Verboht des Grund-Spiels alsobaldt nach solcher gefolget, so kann ich gleichwohl meinen hochzuehrenden Hnn. Patronen nicht enthalten, daß ich eine solche Instrumental-Traur-Music schon *Anno* 1668 vorgehabet bey Beerdigung der see*ligen* Jungefrauen Irer Magnificentz Hn. BürgerMeister Hieronymi von Lafferdts, wie auß Beylage zuersehen, welches Traur-Stück ich der see*ligen* Jungefrau zu Ehren gesetzet, wenn es mir nicht der see*lige* H. Superin-tendens und der see*lige* H. Licentiat Schwencke, welche es den Tag vorher erfahren, fast verbohts-weise wiederrathen hätten, wegen etlicher von Ihnen angeführten Ursachen, daß alßo meine hochzuehrenden Hn. Patroni sehen, daß ich mich ja nur eintzig und alleine bemühet habe, wie ich meiner Herrn Obern Gunst durch mein mügligstes Bemühen allezeit in etwas erwiedern möchte. . . .

Appendix C: Extracts from the St. Johannis Accounts Which Cite the Regal and Positive, 1650–1675[73]

1652	Dem Hr. Cantori laut Quittung gezahlet, so er wegen des Positivs zu schlagen gegeben Nr. 19	4 M
1654	16. September Marcus Röder für das Positiv in Hamburg an das Schiff zu bringen gegeben	1 M
	Auch die Fracht ihm zugestellt	3 M
	Vier Schipsknechten, welche das Positiv vom Kaufhause nacher Kirchen getragen	12 B
	Dem Orgelmacher, welcher bei dem Positiv gearbeitet einen Hangk Leuchter holen lassen, so er zu der Arbeidt gebrauchet	[?]
	4. October dem Orgelmacher für das Positiv zu verfertigen gegeben, weilen er 26 Rthl. gefordert, ihm aber 21 Rthl. gegeben, Laut Quitung Sub Litt.V	42 M
	7. October dem Orgelmacher auf Vorbitten des Hr. Cantoris weilen sich ein Schaden auf der grossen Orgel befunden, selbigen Schaden verfertigen müssen, auch das Positiv 2 mahlen hat stimmen müssen	4 M
1655	Osterquartal: Dem Regalisten für 1/4 Jahr das Regal zu spielen	5 M

1656	Dem Regalisten für 1/2 Jahr Besoldung	10 M
	Den Knaben, das Regal und Positiv zu heben	1 M
	20. December wegen des kleinen Regals, so auf dem Chor stehet, dem Hr. Cantori Michaeli Jacobi bezahlet mit Consentirung der Conjuraten; so von dem Orgelmacher in Andreas Rimbacken Hause logieret 30 Rthl. tuet	60 M
1657	23. November Hinrich Trahn dem Mahler für das Positiv anzustreichen gegeben laut Quitung Nr. 3	5 M
	25. November Magnus Grimm dem Orgelbauer zu renoviren das Kirchen-positiv laut Quitung Nr. 5	4 M
1658	11. November Magnus Grimm dem Orgelmacher bezahlt, so er an der Orgel gemachet laut Quitung Nr. 8	6 M

Die Quittung Nr. 8 lautet:

Ao. 1657 gegen Weihnachtfest das dobbeldt Regall zurecht gemacht vnd die Windtrohr angeleimbt. Jtem das Positive rein gestimmett vndt etzlich Mangel benommen.

Ao. 1658 gegen Ostern abermahl ein grosse Mangell benommen vndt folgendt noch 2 mahl rein gestimmet.
Magnus Grim; Orgelist.

1659	16. Martii 1660 Jonas Weigel, dem Orgelmacher aus Braunschweig bürtig, für Reparirung des Regals und Positivs auf dem Chor laut Quitung Nr. 20	14 M
1660	2 Knaben für das Positiv zu heben	1 M
	30. Mai Dem Orgelbauer das Positiv und Regal aus der Kirchen in sein Quartir, als Ditmers Haus auf dem Sande und aus diesem in die Kirche wieder getragen, in allem gegeben	14 M
1662	18. October Dem Regalisten Joachimus Drallius sein halbjähriges Salarium	5 Rthlr.
	20. December Dem Orgelbauer Michael Berigel für unterschiedliche Arbeit an Positiv und Regal laut Scheins Nr. 21	4 M
1663	Den 2 Knaben, das Positiv zu heben	1 M
	25. April Dem Regalisten Emanuel Hemmerde für das Positiv zu schlagen sein halbjähriges Salarium	10 M
1665	10. October Dem Orgelmacher Michael Berigel für reparirung des Regals auf dem Chor laut Scheins gegeben Nr. 24	12 M
	21. November Dem Orgelmacher Michael Beriegel für reparirung des Positivs auf dem Chor gegeben laut Scheins Nr. 26	20 M
1666	31. Juni Dem Regalisten Georg Crusemarc, Perlemontanus Marchicus, für Aufwartung des Positivs sein 1/2 jähriges Salarium	10 M

1667	1. Juli Dem Regalisten Casparus Arnold Grumbrecht sein Salarium für 1/2 Jahr	10 M
1669	20. Juni Dem Regalisten Casp. Arnold Grumbrecht sein Salarium	10 M
	Michaelis Quartal: Dem Regalisten wegen 1/4 Jahrs Bedienunge, weiln er weggezogen, laut Quitung Nr. 22	5 M
	4. Januar 1670 Dem Regalisten Joachim Dralle sein Salarium von 1/4 jahr	5 M
1670	Johannis Quartal: Dem Regalisten Dralle laut des Hr. Cantoris Quitung sein [halb]jähriges Salarium Nr. 11	10 M
	2. Januar 1671 Für 1 Schlüssel zum Positiv so zerbrochen	[?]
1675	2. März Zu nageln, die kleine Orgel aufm Chor damit zuzunageln	1 ß
	7. May Dem Orgelmacher Michel Beriegel wegen Reparirung des Positivs und Regals auf dem Chor	8 M

Notes

1. Friedrich Blume and Martin Ruhnke, "Aus der Musikgeschichte der Stadt Lüneburg," in *Aus Lüneburg's tausendjähriger Vergangenheit,* ed. Ulrich Wendland (Lüneburg: Heliand, 1956), pp. 109–38.

2. *Musikgeschichte der Stadt Lüneburg vom Ende des 16. bis zum Anfang des 18. Jahrhunderts* (Tutzing: Hans Schneider, 1967).

3. "Lüneburger Orgel- und Klavier-Tabulaturen," *Die Musik in Geschichte und Gegenwart* (Kassel: Bärenreiter, 1960), vol. 8, col. 1283.

4. Blume and Ruhnke, "Aus der Musikgeschichte," p. 129: "Denn zu welchem Zweck eigentlich die 'Intavolierungen' dienen, ist eine bisher nicht ganz geklärte Frage. Soweit 4- oder 5-stimmige Motetten, Liedsätze u. dergl., die sich einigermaßen auf zwei Manualen und einem Pedal wiedergeben ließen, intavoliert wurden, dienten sie zweifellos dem solistischen Orgelspiel, bei dem evtl. eine Singstimme oder auch ein Melodieinstrument mitgehen konnte. Doch zu welchem Zweck eigentlich riesige Vokalwerke (bis zu 16 Stimmen) und von großer Länge 'intavoliert' worden sind, ist nicht ohne weiteres ersichtlich: haben sie wirklich zur Wiedergabe auf der Orgel gedient? oder ist die Tabulatur in diesen Fällen als eine Art Partiturersatz zu verstehen? hat etwa der Organist den Chorus musicus von der Orgelbank aus geleitet? hat er ihn begleitet? Beides ist unwahrscheinlich. Die Leitung von Vokalstücken oder von 'Konzerten' gemischt vokal-instrumentaler Besetzung (also der 'Figuralmusiken') war Sache des Kantors, und die dazu etwa benötigte Orgelbegleitung führte man statt auf der großen Kirchenorgel lieber auf einem Positiv aus, das dicht bei dem Chor stehen konnte. So bleibt für diese 'Intavolierungen' also vorerst noch manches Problem offen."

5. The discussion of intabulations in this article does not extend to the songs drawn from collections by Johann Rist, Gabriel Voigtländer, Heinrich Albert, and the like, nor to the intabulations of ensemble dance music by Michael Praetorius, Isaac Posch, William Brade, Thomas Simpson, and others. (This music is contained in KN 146 and KN 148.)

6. Lydia Schierning probably based her misleading reference to four anonymous "Choralbearbei-
    tungen" in KN 210 (*Die Überlieferung der deutschen Orgel- und Klaviermusik aus der ersten
    Hälfte des 17. Jahrhunderts: Eine quellenkundliche Studie*, Schriften des Landesinstituts für
    Musikforschung Kiel, vol. 12 [Kassel: Bärenreiter, 1961], p. 106) on the modern summary of
    the manuscript's contents, written on its first recto, which includes "Orgelchoräle." Neither of
    these descriptions should be read to suggest the presence of chorale preludes in KN 210. On
    the contrary, two of the "Choralbearbeitungen" Schierning names are intabulations of motets:
    Grimm's six-voice *Wie schön leuchtet der Morgenstern* (no. 46; for its several Dresden concor-
    dances, see Wolfram Steude, *Die Musiksammelhandschriften des 16. und 17. Jahrhunderts in
    der Sächsischen Landesbibliothek zu Dresden*, Quellenkataloge zur Musikgeschichte, vol. 6
    [Wilhelmshaven: Heinrichshofen, 1974], p. 14, no. 24) and Arnold de Fine's (Joseph Schle-
    gel's?—see n. 68 below) imitative, four-voice *Das alte Jahr vergangen ist* (no. 27), which
    apparently has no basis in a chorale melody at all. (The gracious assistance of Prof. Dr.
    Burgemeister and of Dr. Ortrun Landmann, both of the Sächsische Landesbibliothek, was
    invaluable in establishing the nature of the intabulation of Grimm's composition, and I grate-
    fully acknowledge it. I thank the library and its Music Division also for the microfilms of
    manuscripts in the Grimma, Löbau, Pirna, and Schwarzenberg collections, with which their
    staffs generously supplied me.) The other two pieces in Schierning's list, *Das alte Jahr
    vergangen ist* (no. 27a) and *Das alte Jahr ist nun vergahn* (no. 27b), appear at the head of a
    cluster of Christmas and New Year's songs, in four-voice homophonic harmonizations and a
    dance-like triple meter, taken from Michael Praetorius's *Musae Sioniae* (1607[12], 1609[9]); the
    set continues in KN 210 with *Ein schönes Liedlein singen wir, Nunc angelorum gloria*, and
    Joachim a Burck's *Wie lieblich und wie schöne* (nos. 28–30). These intabulations incorporate
    only minimal changes in the polyphonic lines, on the order of slight rhythmic adjustments
    minor modifications of pitch (some of which could be copying errors), or a vertical realignment
    where voices cross. (*Nunc angelorum gloria* is a literal transcription, though its note values are
    reduced by one-quarter. The homophonic setting of *Das alte Jahr vergangen ist* retains Praeto-
    rius's outer parts, but at many places the inner voices depart considerably from the model.)

7. It is not surprising to find among these Palestrina's *Vestiva i colli* (copied only through m. 51,
    and left incomplete) and Nanino's *Erano i capei*, which both enjoyed widespread reprinting
    as well as quotation in intabulations, contrafacta, and parodies.

8. Literature on intabulation per se is slim; most studies in the genre treat limited repertories or
    draw on intabulations for data pertaining to other issues, such as musica ficta or ornamentation
    technique. A comprehensive survey of the practice in Germany can be found in Cleveland
    Johnson's recent dissertation, *Keyboard Intabulations Preserved in Sixteenth- and Seventeenth-
    Century German Organ Tablatures: A Catalogue and Commentary*, Ph.D. diss., Oxford Uni-
    versity, 1984. See also Malcolm Boyd, "Arrangement," *The New Grove Dictionary of Music
    and Musicians*, ed. Stanley Sadie (London: Macmillan, 1980), vol. 1, pp. 627–32; Howard
    Mayer Brown, "Intabulation," *New Grove*, vol. 9, pp. 255ff; Willi Apel, *The History of
    Keyboard Music to 1700*, rev. ed. by Hans Tischler (Bloomington: Indiana University Press,
    1972), pp. 288–90; Schierning, *Überlieferung*, pp. 101–9; and Howard Mayer Brown, "Embel-
    lishment in Early Sixteenth-Century Italian Tabulations," *Proceedings of the Royal Music
    Association* 100 (1973–74), pp. 49–83 (which has a good introduction to the genre).

9. Werner Breig provides an introduction to Scheidemann's intabulations in his study, *Die Orgel-
    werke von Heinrich Scheidemann*, Beiträge zum Archiv für Musikwissenschaft, vol. 3 (Wies-
    baden: Franz Steiner, 1967), pp. 95–100. To my knowledge, the only commentary of any
    length on Strungk's intabulations is to be found in Ardyth June Lohuis's D.M.A. thesis,
    Delphin Strungk: The Organ Compositions Found in Lüneburg Tablature KN 209, University
    of Cincinnati, 1970.

10. Transcriptions of these two pieces, as well as Scheidemann's and Strungk's intabulations in Lüneburg sources, can be found in volume 3 of my forthcoming dissertation, *Origins of the Lüneburg Keyboard Manuscripts* (Princeton University).

11. In discussing the following examples, I refer to the voices of the vocal models by the names assigned them in their source (in uppercase), and to the lines in the intabulation by modern equivalents (in lowercase). In examples 12.1 and 12.2 I have tried to adhere to the original notation as closely as possible. This is especially noticeable in example 12.2, where I use three staves to retain a sense of the spatial distribution of the "eight" voices in the tablature; obviously two staves would be sufficient for a less diplomatic transcription. In both examples, all pairs of notes tied across a barline appear as semibreves, dotted semibreves, or dotted minims (as appropriate) in KN 210, except for the tied *a'* at the end of measure 3 in example 12.1, which is so written in the source. The line of conjunction (which clarifies voice-leading) is reproduced as it is used in the tablature (ex. 12.1, mm. 6–7; ex. 12.2, m. 15). The superfluous minim rests in measure 22 of ex. 12.2 appear in the source.

12. *Maria Magdalena* is not the only motet which loses text in the intabulation process: cf. KN 210, nos. 22, 24, 38, and 42.

13. Liselotte Krüger, *Die Hamburgische Musikorganisation im XVII. Jahrhundert*, Sammlung Musikwissenschaftlicher Abhandlungen, vol. 12 (Strasbourg: Heitz, 1933), pp. 109–12.

14. In this instance it was the audition of Matthias Weckmann, who, as his student Johann Kortkamp reports, improvised an intabulation from the bass partbook of a motet by Hieronymus Praetorius. See Krüger, *Hamburgische Musikorganisation*, p. 110, and *idem* "Johann Kortkamps Organistenchronik, eine Quelle zur Hamburgischen Musikgeschichte des 17. Jahrhunderts," *Zeitschrift des Vereins für Hamburgische Geschichte* 33 (1933), p. 206.

15. The ordinance is reproduced in Gustav Fock, *Der junge Bach in Lüneburg, 1700 bis 1702* (Hamburg: Merseburger, 1950), pp. 105–10; cf. §1: "Deß Sonnabendts wie auch in vigiliis der hohen Feste soll die gantze Schule zur gewöhnlichen Vesperzeit . . . in die Kirche aufs Chor gehen und nebst dem üblichen Teutschen Magnificat noch drey Geistliche Lieder gesungen vnd dan zwischen, wie auch zum Anfang, vnd wan daß Benedicamus gesungen, zum Beschluß die Orgel gerühret werden. Da sich dan der Organist zu befleißigen, daß er zum öfteren, wo nicht allemahl, nach beendigtem Gesang ein oder Paar feiner Stücke oder Moteten schlage. . . ."

16. P. 110 (misprinted as 130): "Welches dann auch ein Organist oder Lautenist vor sich alleine in acht nemen kan, daß wenn er in Conviviis, eine Mutet oder Madrigal fein langsam vnd Gravitätisch gespielet, also bald darauff ein frölich Alemande, Intrada, Bransle oder Galliard anfange; hernacher wiederumb etwa eine andere Mutet, Madrigal, Pavan oder kunstreiche Fugam vor sich neme."

17. Cf. Kerala J. Snyder, *Dieterich Buxtehude, Organist in Lübeck* (New York: Schirmer, 1987), pp. 309, 314f.

18. Reimann, "Lüneburger Tabulaturen," col. 1282; Renate Brunner, "Franz Schaumkell und die Lüneburger Tabulaturen," *Die Musikforschung* 26 (1973), pp. 208–10. I fully agree with Fr. Brunner's identification, having arrived at the same conclusion independently before learning of her article. (A number of Schaumkell's autograph letters survive in the Lüneburg Stadtarchiv.) The interested reader may compare Schaumkell's signature, reproduced in Walter, *Musikgeschichte Lüneburg*, in the plate opposite p. 144, with the facsimiles in Reimann, *Die Lüneburger Orgeltabulatur KN 208¹*, Das Erbe deutscher Musik, vol. 36 (Frankfurt/Main: Henry Litolff, 1957), pp. xi–xv, and with figure 12.5 in the present article.

19. In this short space we can only scratch the surface of the complex cross-relationships of scribal and repertorial concordances which link together a core group of some ten tablatures. As will be seen further below, a second, hitherto unrecognized set of scribal concordances in the hand of a Lüneburg organist, involving KN 209 and drawing on the Schaumkell tablatures, contributes to the intricacy of the network. A detailed analysis of this source complex is the major task of my dissertation, to which I refer the reader.

20. *Musica getutscht*, sig. H3r-04v.

21. Robert M. Stevenson, *Juan Bermudo* (The Hague: Martinus Nijhoff, 1960), p. 54.

22. See Friedrich W. Riedel, "Strenger und freier Stil in der nord- und süddeutschen Musik für Tasteninstruments des 17. Jahrhunderts," in *Norddeutsche und nordeuropäische Musik: Referate der Kieler Tagung, 1963*, ed. Carl Dahlhaus and Walter Wiora, Kieler Schriften zur Musikwissenschaft, no. 16 (Kassel: Bärenreiter, 1965), p. 64; H. Colin Slim, "Keyboard Music at Castell'Arquato by an Early Madrigalist," *Journal of the American Musicological Society* 15 (1962), p. 41f; and Egon F. Kenton, "A Note on the Classification of 16th-Century Music," *Musical Quarterly* 38 (1952), pp. 203–5, 208.

23. See, for example, RISM 1534[17], 1552[12], 1569[7], etc.

24. Contrary to Blume and Ruhnke's claim above, the keyboard tablatures do not contain any intabulations of pieces in sixteen voices. I presume they got this idea by including KN 206 in their discussion, an error which has plagued and complicated the nature of the intabulation problem for decades. (Even *New Grove* enters this manuscript under its rubric for keyboard sources [vol. 17, p. 727].) KN 206 is not a keyboard manuscript, but an anthology of scores—in staff notation—of Italian and German vocal concerti copied by Matthias Weckmann in the early 1640s, presumably for his own study. I am grateful to Prof. Alexander Silbiger, who kindly shared his views on this manuscript with me. His paper, "The Autographs of Matthias Weckmann: A Reevaluation," which he presented at the International Symposium on *Heinrich Schütz and Musical Life in Denmark during the Reign of Christian IV* (Copenhagen, November 1985), is due to be published in the *Proceedings* of that symposium.

25. Much of this material is covered in Max Schneider, *Die Anfänge des Basso continuo und seiner Bezifferung* (Leipzig: Breitkopf & Härtel, 1918), pp. 9–19, 52–82; Otto Kinkeldey, *Orgel und Klavier in der Musik des 16. Jahrhunderts* (Leipzig: Breitkopf & Härtel, 1910), pp. 187–226; and in the first hundred pages of Frank T. Arnold, *The Art of Accompaniment from a Thorough-Bass as Practised in the XVIIth & XVIIIth Centuries* (London: Oxford University Press, 1931). See also Howard Mayer Brown, *Sixteenth-Century Instrumentation: The Music for the Florentine Intermedii*, Musicological Studies and Documents, vol. 30 (N.p.: American Institute of Musicology, 1973): 21–26, where the author fully develops the role of keyboard accompaniment within the context of secular Italian ensemble music.

26. Kinkeldey, *Orgel und Klavier*, pp. 198–200.

27. *Syntagma musicum* III, p. 129: "Die Tabulatur aller Parteyen ist zwar vor dieser zeit erfunden worden, daß man sie solte recht schlagen, wie sie abgesetzt stünde, vnd war gar wol gethan, vnd wer sie recht verstehet, vnd extempore daraus wol schlagen kan, der folge jhr auffs beste er jmmer kan. Aber dieweil es gar ein schwehr ding ist, vnd auch langweilig, dieselbe recht secur zuschlagen, . . . so wer es von nöthen, . . . sich der mühe auch zu vberheben. Darmit man aber in einem Concert ohne solche weitläufftigkeit vnd difficultet alsobald zugleich mit einschlagen könte, so ward der Bassus Continuus . . . erfunden."

28. Arnold, *Art of Accompaniment*, p. 93. See *Syntagma musicum* III, p. 124 (misprinted as 144): "Nun ist der General Bass nicht vmb etlicher nachlessigen oder verdrossenen Organisten willen, die ohne das vngern absetzen, sondern fürnemblich darumb erfunden worden; Daß ein Organist, ob er gleich aus demselben im anfang nicht alsobald mit einschlahen könne, doch daraus in seine partitur, oder Tabulatur desto leichter bringen, vnd alsdenn die eine, zween, oder drey Stimmen darüber setzen, vnd wie es gegen einander stehet, mit besonderm fleiß acht haben, vnd auffmercken sol. Dahero er dann darnechst, aus dergleichen Basso generali seine Partey zu machen, sich vmb so viel leichter vnd füglicher darzu gewehnen kan."

29. Cf. the note to the reader, §7: "Der Basso continovo ist eigentlich nur für die Psalmen gemeinet, von der Motet an: Ist nicht Ephraim, biß zum Beschluß deß operis werden sich fleissige Organisten mit absetzen in die Partitur zu bemühen. . . ."

30. *Geistliche Chormusik* (1648), note to the reader: "Da auch iemand von den Organisten etwa in dieses mein ohne Bassum Continuum eigentlich auffgesetztes Wercklein, wohl und genaw mit einzuschlagen Beliebung haben, und solches in die Tabulatur oder Partitur abzusetzen sich nicht verdriessen lassen wird: lebe ich .der Hoffnung, daß der hierauff gewandte Fleiß und Bemühung ihn nicht allein nicht gereuen, sondern auch diese Art der Music desto mehr ihren gewüntschten Effect erreichen werde." For more detailed analyses of Schütz's remarks, see Gerhard Kirchner, *Der Generalbass bei Heinrich Schütz* (Kassel: Bärenreiter, 1960), and Hans Heinrich Eggebrecht, "Arten des Generalbasses in frühen und mittleren 17. Jahrhundert," *Archiv für Musikwissenschaft* 14 (1957), pp. 66–69. For a discussion of the various notational systems used in seventeenth-century German accompanimental practice, see Cleveland Johnson, "New German Organ Tablature: Its Rise and Demise," in *Charles Brenton Fisk, Organ Builder,* ed. Fenner Douglass, Owen Jander, and Barbara Owen (Easthampton, Mass.: Westfield Center for Early Keyboard Studies, 1986), vol. 1, pp. 98–101. (I would correct Professor Johnson's note 13 on page 98: none of the intabulations in KN 209 or KN 210 are of the skeletal soprano/bass type, which omits inner voices.)

31. See my dissertation for a more complete description of these two manuscripts.

32. Cf. Steude, *Musiksammelhandschriften,* p. 194, etc.

33. The composition by Calvisius is an entirely different piece from his eight-voice *Zion spricht* in Bodenschatz's second volume; the latter, in fact, is a parody of Alessandro Merlo's napolitana *a 5, Madonna più che mai.* Two of the Löbau sources for *Ich habe den Herrn alle Zeit* share the attribution in the Lüneburg tablature to Heinrich Grimm, who was cantor in Magdeburg and Braunschweig, whereas the two Berlin manuscripts bear ascriptions to the Dresden cantor Samuel Rühling. The attribution problems in this manuscript receive more thorough coverage in my dissertation.

34. The following abbreviations are used in tables 12.1 and 12.2. All sources refer after the colon to the number of the piece within the collection. Items in parentheses are modern editions of the works in question. Abbreviations which appear in the original text (e.g., Latin suffixes) are realized in Italic type. (This practice is followed also in appendix B.) Bs—Berlin, Staatsbibliothek Preussischer Kulturbesitz, Mus. Mss. 40040, 40158; CM 1640—Caspar Movius, *Triumphus Musicus Spiritualis: Das ist: Newe Geistliche Triumph Lieder . . . Mit 6. vnd 8. Stimmen sampt dem Basso Continuo. . . .* Rostock, 1640; CMM 72³—*Corpus mensurabilis musicae,* vol. 72, *Luca Marenzio. Collected Works,* vol. 3, edited by Roland Jackson (Neuhausen-Stuttgart: American Institute of Musicology/Hänssler, 1979); CW 98—*Das Chorwerk,* vol. 98, *Heinrich Hartmann. Vier deutsche Motetten, . . .* edited by Adam Adrio (Wolfenbüttel: Möseler, 1965); Dg—Dresden, Sächsische Landesbibliothek, Grimma collection, Mus. Ms. 24; Dl—ibid., Löbau coll., Mus. Mss. 8 and 70, 10, 33, 53, 54, 59, 66, 67,

69; Dp—ibid., Pirna coll., Mus. Ms. 57; Ds—ibid., Schwarzenberg coll., Mus. Ms. 41; DTÖ 30, 40—*Denkmäler der Tonkunst in Österreich*, vols. 30 and 40, *Jacob Handl (Gallus). Opus musicum: Motettenwerk für das ganze Kirchenjahr*, pts. 3 and 4, ed. Emil Bezecny and Josef Mantuani (Vienna: Artaria, 1908–13); HH 1618—Heinrich Hartmann, *Erster Theil, Confortativae Sacrae Symphoniacae, Das ist: Geistlicher Labsal, vnd Hertzstärckung . . . mit fünff, sechs, acht, vnd mehren Stimmen . . .*, 2nd ed. (Erfurt, 1618); HP I, II—Hieronymus Praetorius, *Opera Musici*, vol. 1, *Cantiones Sacrae De Festis Praecipuis Totius Anni. . . .* (Hamburg, 1622; 1st edition, 1599), and vol. 2, *Canticum B. Mariae Virginis. Seu Magnificat Octo Vocum . . . Motectis aliquot 8. 10. & 12. Vocum auctus. . . .* (Hamburg, 1622); JH II, III—*Jacob Handl, Secundus (Tertius) Tomus Musici Operis, Harmoniarum Quatuor, Quinque, Sex Octo Et Plurium Vocum. . . .* (Prague, 1587); RRMR 18—*Recent Researches in Music of the Renaissance*, vol. 18, *Hieronymus Praetorius. Polychoral Motets*, ed. Frederick K. Gable, pt. 1 (Madison: A-R Editions, 1974); 1607[6]—Michael Praetorius, *Musarum Sionar: Motectae Et Psalmi Latini . . . I. Pars* (Wolfenbüttel, 1607); 1618[1]—Erhard Bodenschatz, ed., *Florilegium Portense, continens CXV. Selectissimas Cantiones. . . .* 2nd ed. (Leipzig, 1618); 1621[2]— idem, *Florilegii Musici Portensis, Sacras Harmonias sive Motetas . . . Pars Altera. . . .* (Leipzig, 1621).

35. Points of correspondence are especially clear in the uppercase letters *C, E, F,* and *L,* the Latin *M,* and the German *S, H* (two forms), and the especially unique *G.* The sometimes exaggerated swoop to the left in the descender of the lowercase *G* contributes considerably to the general duct of the handwriting. Compare also the shape of the squiggle over the lowercase *U,* and the loop to the left on the ascender in the terminal German *S.*

36. Joachim's baptism on 22 March is entered into the baptismal registry of the Johanniskirche. Documents in the Lüneburg Stadtarchiv (hereafter Ls) supply most of the data used to construct Dralle's biography, the letters written by Joachim and his father in the collections S 3b Nr. 3 and E 1d Nr. 56 being of particular importance in this regard. The so-called Büttner-Album (Ls, NBü 23) is also a major source of data. Appendix B reproduces two of Hilmar Dralle's letters from the years 1668 and 1672, from which comes all information attributed to him below.

37. In the revised *Schulordnung* of 1670–71 (Ls, AB 829i, ff. 82r-83r), Hilmar Dralle signs himself "Hilmarus Drallius Gelleresâ Luneburgius."

38. Joachim's father could have participated in his son's earliest music instruction. As a teacher of one of the three lower classes, he needed a minimum of musical competency to lead his pupils and the congregation in monophonic song at St. Nicolai and St. Lamberti. (Normally the cantor would direct the services at the *Hauptkirche*, St. Johannis, using the older boys, and his subordinate colleagues would take the younger classes to the secondary churches). See Walter, *Musikgeschichte Lüneburg*, p. 137; for Walter's full account of the musical organization under the *Johanniscantor*, see pp. 136–227.

39. Georg Erler, *Die Iüngere Matrikel der Universität Leipzig 1559–1809. . . .* (Leipzig: Giesecke & Devrient, 1909), vol. 2, p. 81. I do not know how Horst Walter concludes that Joachim Dralle studied at Leipzig from 1666 to 1668, nor what the source is for his reference to "Lüneburger Stipendium" for Dralle (*Musikgeschichte Lüneburg*, p. 134). (Hilmar Dralle reminds the city council of the "schweren Unkosten" he himself paid for his son's higher education). Nonetheless, I do think it possible that Joachim remained in Leipzig for a time after 1666. In his letter of 10 August 1691 (Ls, S 3b Nr. 3; see also his letter of 25 September 1675 in the same collection), he says that he privately tutored students in the classical curriculum of the Johannisschule during the years 1669–71. Dralle also first returns to his old job as regalist

late in 1669 (see below). One might think that if he were back home much before that time, and without a steady job (which was apparently the case), he would not have delayed in taking on jobs such as these during the interim.

40. The process of elimination relegates Dralle's year as substitute to the time before his departure for Leipzig in 1663. Schaumkell had gone on permanent disability by May of 1668, and the *Lambertiorganist* Christian Flor was formally appointed deputy and expectant to the post. (The accounts of St. Johannis already show a payment to Flor on 19 October 1667 "für etzliche Wochen auf der Orgel aufgewartet;" see Gustav Fock, "Musiknachrichten aus den Rechnungen der Lüneburger Johanniskirche von 1559–1884" [typescript housed in the Lüneburg Stadtarchiv], 45.) Thus Flor controlled both benches from this time on, and when he needed to be in two places at once, he most likely had one of his more advanced students fill in for the less important service. Joachim Dralle probably wasn't one of these. In a contest with the city council which lasted over two years, Dralle bitterly denounced Flor for infringing upon a portion of his salary due him from his auxiliary position as organist of the small chapel of St. Marien. This building had just been condemned in 1675, and, while some of the services were transferred to St. Nicolai, most were being held in St. Lamberti, thus causing friction between Flor's position there and Dralle's perquisites as *Marienorganist*. In the letters in which Dralle addresses this issue (Ls, E le Nr. 15, ff. 16–31), he never calls Flor his teacher. On the contrary, he says that Flor allows no one but his own students near the organ loft at St. Lamberti, an exclusion which would not be due Dralle if he had studied with Flor. Dralle angrily rebukes Flor's students and speaks in terms which no apprentice would apply to his master. For these reasons and others (which will become clear below), I am more inclined to place the young Dralle in Schaumkell's circle of apprentices rather than, as Walter has suggested, Flor's (*Musikgeschichte Lüneburg*, p. 134).

41. In September, 1675 (on the death of the *collega quinta*, Rogerus Mirovius); at sometime before this for *collega sexta*, the bottom rung; and again in 1679 (on the death of his own father). See Dralle's letter of 25 September 1675 and his undated letter (from the end of February or the beginning of March 1679, his only one in Latin) in Ls, S 3b Nr. 3.

42. More than once, Walter refers to Cossius in this way (*Musikgeschichte Lüneburg*, pp. 171, 172).

43. Ibid., p. 179.

44. Ibid., p. 173; the original German is quoted at the head of this article.

45. Ibid., pp. 136f, 163.

46. Fock, "Musiknachrichten." See appendix C.

47. Walter, *Musikgeschichte Lüneburg*, p. 163.

48. Ibid., pp. 134, 163.

49. Fock, "Musiknachrichten," pp. 33–47. See appendix C.

50. Gerhard Piccard, *Die Wasserzeichenkartei Piccard im Hauptstaatsarchiv Stuttgart*, Veröffentlichungen der Staatlichen Archivverwaltung Baden-Württemberg, vol. 15², *Wasserzeichen Raubtiere* (Stuttgart: W. Kohlhammer, 1987), no. 1955.

51. Wilderich Weick, *Histoire de la maison de Saxe-Cobourg-Gotha*, trans. Auguste Scheler (Brussels: D. Raes, 1846), p. 187.

52. Abbreviations: DDT 12—*Denkmäler deutscher Tonkunst*, vol. 12: *Arien von Heinrich Albert*, ed. Eduard Bernoulli (Leipzig: Breitkopf & Härtel, 1903); EDM 79—*Das Erbe deutscher*

Music, vol. 79: *Threnodiae sacrae: Beerdigungskompositionen aus gedruckten Leichenpredigten des 16. und 17. Jahrhunderts*, ed. Wolfgang Reich (Wiesbaden: Breitkopf & Härtel, 1975); Kbg.—Königsberg; Krummacher—Friedhelm Krummacher, *Die Überlieferung der Choralbearbeitungen in der frühen evangelischen Kantate: Untersuchungen zum Handschriftenrepertoire evangelischer Figuralmusik im späten 17. und beginnenden 18. Jahrhundert*, Berliner Studien zur Musikwissenschaft, vol. 10 (Berlin: Merseburger, 1965); Kümmerling—Kümmerling, *Katalog;* MAM 3—*Musik alter Meister*, vol. 3, *Begräbnisgesänge Nürnberger Meister für Exulanten aus der Steiermark*, ed. Hellmut Federhofer (Graz: Akademische Druck- und Verlagsanstalt, 1955); Mueller—Joseph Mueller, *Die musikalischen Schaetze der Koeniglichen- und Universitaets-Bibliothek zu Koenigsberg in Preussen . . . Ein Bei-trag zur Geschichte und Theorie der Tonkunst* (Bonn: Adolph Marcus, 1870); Nbg.— Nuremberg; RISM A/I—*Répertoire international des sources musicales*, vol. A/I: *Einzeldrucke vor 1800*, ed. Karlheinz Schlager et al., 9 vols. (Kassel: Bärenreiter, 1971–81; numbers refer to the alphabetical serial number which appears after each entry in the catalogue); Samuel—Harold E. Samuel, *The Cantata in Nuremberg during the Seventeenth Century*, Studies in Musicology, no. 56 (Ann Arbor: UMI Research Press, 1982).

For numerous instances of the incorporation of Albert's song—to his own melody and to others—into Protestant *Gesangbücher* (where it appears under rubrics for funerals or burials), see Johannes Zahn, *Die Melodien der deutschen evangelischen Kirchenlieder* (Gütersloh, 1889–92; reprint, Hildesheim: Georg Olms, 1963), vol. 6, nos. 6288b and 6290–6308. Several more composers have set the two lines from 2 Tim., and it is possible that their manuscript sources (which I have not examined) may contain rubrics identifying them specifically as *Grabgesänge:* Reinhard Keiser (Kümmerling, no. 496), Christian Liebe (Krummacher, 534; Kümmerling, no. 600), Georg Österreich (Kümmerling, no. 653), Michael Österreich (Kümmerling, no. 704), and Johann Melchior Gletle (a lost setting of the Latin reading, *Bonum certamen certavi*—see Max Seiffert, "Die Chorbibliothek der St. Michaelisschule in Lüneburg zu Seb. Bach's Zeit," *Sammelbände der Internationalen Musikgesellschaft* 9 [1907–8], p. 606). Two further printed compositions by Stephen Otto (*Kronen Krönlein* [Freiberg, 1648], no. 15) and Salomon Hossmann (*Opusculum musicum* [Polnisch Lissa, 1653], no. 18) make no specific references to funeral usage.

53. Harald Kümmerling, *Katalog der Sammlung Bokemeyer*, Kieler Schriften zur Musikwissenschaft, vol. 18 (Kassel: Bärenreiter, 1970), no. 1060; Richard Buchmayer, "Christian Ritter, ein vergessener deutscher Meister des 17. Jahrhunderts," in *Riemann Festschrift, Gesammelte Studien: Hugo Riemann zum sechzigsten Geburtstage* (Leipzig: M. Hesse, 1909), pp. 365, 379 (see also Krummacher, p. 545). Another setting of 2 Tim. 4 is one of four compositions that conclude the fourth part of Johann Staden's *Hauss-Music* (Nuremberg, 1628), constituting a group ostensibly related to an obsequial theme. While such an association is not explicitly attached to *Ich hab einen guten Kampf* (no. 29, published in *Denkmähler der Tonkunst in Bayern*, Jg. 7[1] [1906], p. 95f), the two pieces directly preceding it are dedicated to Staden's late daughter, Maria Magdalena (d. 2 September 1627) and were sung at her burial, and the text of no. 30, from Isaiah 57, also falls within the catagory of *Sterbgesänglein* ("The righteous are taken away from calamity, and enter into peace; they who walk in uprightness rest in their beds").

54. The "Gerichtliche Relatio" of 30 December 1672, in Ls, S 3b Nr. 8, fasc. 1, ff. 92–94.

55. The accounts at St. Johannis record no regalists' salaries for the five years before Michaelis, 1662 (when Dralle is first paid), yet Hilmar Dralle says his son was regalist under the cantor Jacobi "during his years as a schoolboy." Since Joachim was twenty in 1662—a bit overaged to be attending the Johannisschule—his first appointment as regalist could conceivably date back to the late 1650s. And we can dismiss the year 1669 (when Dralle returns to the job) in

considering a date for KN 207³, since the manuscript opens with the two Easter motets by Praetorius and Handl: at Easter in 1669 Caspar Grumbrecht was still regalist, not Dralle.

56. Again, the interested reader might care to compare the handwriting in KN 207² (see fig. 12.4) with that in the other manuscripts. Facsimiles of pages in KN 209 are especially abundant, appearing in Franz Tunder, *Sämtliche Orgelwerke,* ed. Klaus Beckmann (Wiesbaden: Breitkopf & Härtel, 1974), pp. 53, 57; Matthias Weckmann, *Choralbearbeitungen,* ed. Werner Breig (Kassel: Bärenreiter, 1979), p. xii; Gisela Gerdes, *46 Choräle für Orgel von J. P. Sweelinck und seinen deutschen Schülern,* Musikalische Denkmäler, vol. 3 (Mainz: B. Schott, 1957), pl. 1; Josef Hedar, *Dietrich Buxtehudes Orgelwerke: Zur Geschichte des norddeutschen Orgelstils* (Stockholm: Nordiska, 1951), p. 21; Friedrich Welter, *Katalog der Musikalien der Ratsbücherei Lüneburg,* (Lippstadt: Kistner & Siegel, 1950), p. ii; *Die Musik in Geschichte und Gegenwart,* vol. 8, pl. 64 (opp. col. 1280). A facsimile from KN 207¹⁵ (ff. 5v-6r) appears on the covers of both volumes of John R. Shannon, ed., *The Free Organ Compositions from the Lueneburg Tablatures* (St. Louis: Concordia, 1958).

57. It copied twelve entire pieces in KN 146, and shared with Schaumkell the copying of six more (both their hands appear in nos. 5, 18, 29, 51, 64, and 152).

58. *Johann Sebastian Bach als Schüler der Partikularschule zu St. Michaelis in Lüneburg; oder Lüneburg, eine Pflegstätte kirchlicher Musik. Aus dem Ostern 1870 herausgegebenen Programm des Johanneums zu Lüneburg abgedruckt* (Lüneburg: Stern, 1870), pp. 25–36.

59. Besides Wedemann's colophon in KN 209, the evidence which establishes him as copyist of these five manuscripts includes comparison of existing records and receipts in his hand (in Ls, S 10h 3a Nr. 3, dating from 1708 and 1709), and the hitherto unobserved presence of his monograms, *HBW* and *HBWM,* written three times on the inside back cover of KN 207¹⁵. Wedemann's identification, biography, and role as copyist are discussed fully in chapter 2 of my dissertation.

60. The documents in Ls, S 10h 3g Nr. 10, are the primary source for this summary of Wedemann's biography and his position at St. Nicolaihof.

61. Clearly the current theory that KN 146 served as Dralle's beginning music book (Brunner, "Franz Schaumkell," pp. 209–10) must be reconsidered in view of the new evidence on Wedemann. See my dissertation.

62. This count excludes the secular intabulation (no. 2) which Schaumkell added later in the space left at the bottom of the opening, ff. 2v-3r.

63. Blume/Ruhnke, "Aus der Musikgeschichte," p. 130: "Die Kehrseite dieses Interesses an den originalen Kompositionen und deren Ausnutzung ist, daß bisher die 'Intavolierungen' üdberhaupt noch nicht untersucht worden sind, obwohl sie weitgehende Aufschlüsse für die Aufführungspraxis, den Verwendungszweck, ja auch über Herkunft und Verfasser (Schreiber) der Tabulaturen versprechen."

64. The lavishly produced edition of the Pelplin tablatures fills vols. 1–10 of *Antiquitates musicae in Polonia* (Graz: Warsaw University Press, Akademische Druck- und Verlagsanstalt, 1963–70). References to the Schmölln tablatures appear in Werner Breig, "Samuel Scheidts Bearbeitungen alter Motetten," *Archiv für Musikwissenschaft* 19–20 (1962–63): 58, 60, and Heinrich Sievers's short description of "Die Braunschweiger Tabulaturen" is in the *Kongress-Bericht; Gesellschaft für Musikforschung Lüneburg, 1950* (Kassel: Bärenreiter, n.d.), pp. 97–99.

65. See, for instance, Otto Kinkeldey's conclusions about the volumes of intabulations at Breslau (*Orgel und Klavier,* p. 191).

66. Edward E. Lowinsky, "Early Scores in Manuscript," *Journal of the American Musicological Society* 13 (1960), pp. 126–71; cf. esp. p. 143f.

67. This index treats the contents of KN 146, KN 207², KN 207³, KN 207¹⁸, KN 208¹, KN 209, KN 210, and Mus. ant. pract. 697. A semicolon separates different intabulations of the same piece; if two or more keyboard arrangements are identical, an equals sign (=) stands between them. Starred numbers mark motets or sacred concerti copied in tablature score; double-starred numbers are tablature scores with text underlay. The initials HS and DS designate intabulations by Heinrich Scheidemann and Delphin Strungk. All items are referred to by their modern number in the source. (The inconsistencies in this numbering system show up in KN 210 in Hassler's Italian canzonettas, two of which are assigned the number 55c, and in Hieronymus Praetorius's *Domine Dominus noster,* whose first and second parts are given separate numbers. The scribe of KN 209 erroneously labels Nicolaus Zangius's *Hierusalem gaude* as the secunda pars to Handl's setting of the same text, producing further numbering problems.)

68. Regarding the double attribution of this motet—which is so often transmitted anonymously—to Arnoldus de Fine and Joseph Schlegel, see Breig, "Scheidts Bearbeitung," p. 58f.

69. Grimm's original setting of *Lobet den Herren* does not survive. The title entry in KN 209 refers to a six-voice model, but other evidence suggests the model could be Grimm's lost setting for eight voices and continuo, which he published as a wedding motet in 1623. See the commentary on this intabulation in my dissertation.

70. KN 210 misattributes Hassler's *Laudate Dominum in sanctus eius* to Noë Faignient.

71. No. 55a in KN 210 is apparently a pasticcio, its first ten bars quoting the opening of Jacob Hassler's madrigal *Quest' arder mio.* The piece continues with as yet unidentified music.

72. Two of the anonymous pieces have appeared more than once in print: the popular *Hosianna dem Sohne David* in the numerous editions of Bartholomäus Gesius's *Geistliche Lieder* (1601ff), in the fifth part of Praetorius's *Musae Sioniae* (1607¹²), and in Gottfried Vopelius's *Neu Leipziger Gesangbuch* (1682); and *O Jesu mi dulcissime,* doubly texted in German and Latin, in 1637³ and 1643⁴.

73. Drawn from Fock, "Musiknachrichten," pp. 33–47.

13

A Keyboard Diminution Manual in Bártfa Manuscript 27: Keyboard Figuration in the Time of Scheidt

Cleveland Johnson

Unlike the many sixteenth-century performance manuals for wind, string, and vocal performers, keyboard treatises seem to avoid exhaustive discussions of diminution. Keyboard manuals, such as those by Bermudo, Buchner, Sancta Maria, and Diruta,[1] cover a broad range of issues including counterpoint, modal theory, improvisation, as well as many practical matters such as hand position and fingering; but the importance of diminutions, which is revealed and emphasized even in the titles of most nonkeyboard treatises,[2] is not stressed by the keyboard authors. These writers do not provide the quantities of raw information—lengthy tables of diminution formulae—that are common in many nonkeyboard manuals.

Despite this scarcity of didactic evidence, the keyboard music of the period is evidence enough that diminution was a vital part of keyboard style. Diminutionlike figuration is seen in most genres of sixteenth- and seventeenth-century keyboard composition, and, continuing in a much older tradition, one can also assume that such figuration was still part of the improvisatory style. This study seeks to confirm that assumption; diminutions were just as important to a keyboardist as to any other instrumentalist or vocalist of the time.

The evidence to be discussed is Manuscript 27 of the Bártfa Collection, housed in the National Szèchènyi Library of Budapest. Bártfa, the location of this collection until early in World War I, is located in the mountainous Zips region of eastern Slovakia. This area was inundated by German settlers in the twelfth century, and by the sixteenth and seventeenth centuries this transplanted, Germanic culture had blossomed into a flourishing artistic society.[3] In the seventeenth century, for example, many German churches in the area maintained impressive musical establishments and performed a sophisticated repertory, perhaps old-fashioned, but otherwise not unlike that performed in major German cities. The Bártfa Collection, containing the music once owned by Bártfa's St. Aegidi church, attests to this active musical life; among the fifty-one musical publications there, music by Christoph Demantius, Hans Leo Hassler, Orlandus di Lassus, and Hieronymus Praetorius can be found.[4]

In addition to the printed volumes from the St. Aegidi library, twenty-nine manuscripts also survive, including four organ tablatures (mss. 25–28). The tablatures numbered Manuscripts 25, 26, and 28 appear to have been copied and owned by Zacharias Zarewutius, organist at St. Aegidi from 1625–67. These volumes were probably compiled during the last decade of his service there, even though they contain intabulations based on published vocal works from sixty or seventy years earlier. They also contain several large vocal works by Zarewutius himself which show him to be a competent composer.

Manuscript 27, the tablature of importance to this discussion, is of a distinctively different paper from the other three tablatures and is also in a different hand. Otto Gombosi proposed that its author may have been Samuel Medvetzki who was the successor of Zarewutius in Bártfa,[5] but this attribution has more recently been called into doubt by Lydia Schierning.[6] Whoever this author may be, he definitely had different musical interests than did Zarewutius. Although some interest is shown in intabulating vocal works, the Manuscript 27 writer devotes the majority of his tablature to the copying of original keyboard works. Thus, Bártfa Manuscript 27 is already familiar to many keyboard scholars today as a tablature source of chorale and dance variations by Sweelinck and Scheidt.[7] Unfortunately, the mere presence of these important original compositions may have distracted attention from the tablature's most remarkable contents, a seemingly insignificant group of intabulations at the beginning of the volume[8] and nine pages of closely packed diminution formulae at the end. To remedy the situation, this article will largely ignore the compositions of this famous teacher/student duo and will focus instead on the lesser-known contents of Bártfa 27.

Figure 13.1 shows part of what may be regarded as a "homespun" keyboard diminution manual, a collection of 643 formulae compiled in a separate fascicle of five folia (ff. 55–59) at the end of the manuscript (and reproduced in its entirety in appendix A). The paper, although its watermark is too deteriorated to identify, is decidedly different from that in the main body of the manuscript. The writing, however, is in the same hand. Apparently, these formulae were collected in the latter half of the seventeenth century by the Bártfa scribe to serve as a personal diminution manual.

Despite the manuscript's late date, the spirit behind this endeavor immediately reminds one of printed sixteenth-century diminution manuals for wind and string instruments; each microscopic row of tablature in this handwritten manual represents a single embellished formula that can substitute for a basic melodic progression. Unlike these published manuals, however, the Bártfa manual is little more than a lengthy list of formulae. It is not a didactic manual with

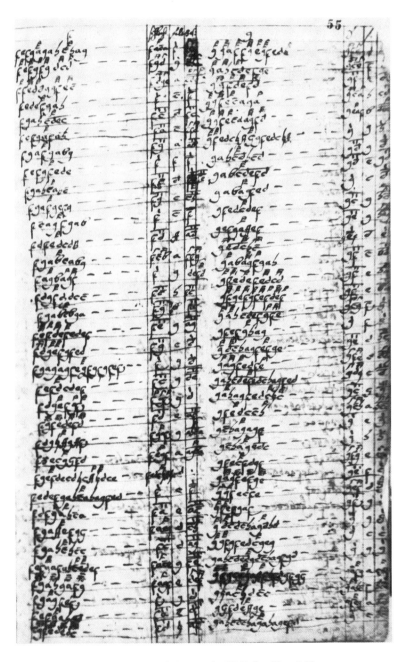

Figure 13.1. Bártfa Manuscript 27, Folios 55ʳ and 55ᵛ
(Budapest, National Szèchènyi Library)

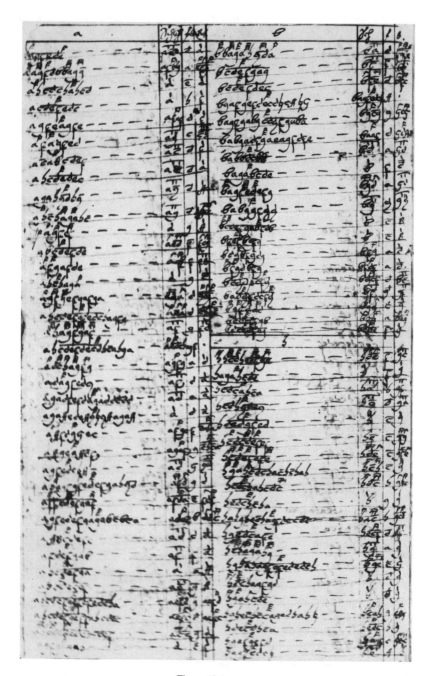

Figure 13.1. cont.

instructions for applying the formulae, nor does it suggest in any way what its practical intent may have been. The Bártfa manual follows its own unique plan and does not acknowledge any debt to published sources. Indeed, it is the only example from the sixteenth or seventeenth century to provide such thorough diminution tables for keyboard instruments.

On first appearance, each page looks well organized: the page is always divided into two columns, and each column is subdivided into four fields of information. Adjacent columns are basically unrelated; the top of the right column simply continues from the bottom of the left column. Within each column, however, the four vertical fields do correspond. Notice the headings above each field: *schlicht, felt,* and *Baß*. The first field, the one without a heading, contains the diminution pattern itself; this pattern always equals one whole note in total duration. The second field shows the bare melodic outline that the diminution elaborates: *schlicht*, meaning "simplified," is an appropriate tag. The third field, labeled *felt*, shows *was fehlt* ("what is missing"); it indicates the next note in the melodic progression. The fourth field, labeled *Baß*, shows the contrapuntal motion of a second voice against which the diminutions would sound. The label here is slightly misleading, because this voice does not necessarily act as a bassline. The *Baß* frequently represents a contrapuntal line *above* the embellished voice.

Within the neatly aligned columns and fields, the individual formulae show no apparent organization. Printed manuals often organized their formulae according to the interval to be embellished and by the complexity of the embellishment. For example, all diminutions that embellished a descending second would be printed together beginning with the simplest formula and ending with the most complex. In the Bártfa manual, although there are sixty-eight ways shown to embellish a descending second, these examples are scattered randomly throughout the manual. For this article, a computerized database was developed to organize the formulae by interval, but without such an index, the Bártfa manual could not possibly be used in the same way as the published manuals. The performer could not take a simple melodic interval from a composition and "look up" an embellished substitute for that interval. The manual was obviously not designed for that use.

Avoiding this traditional intervallic organization, the Bártfa author lacks an efficient system to keep track of his ideas. Apparently the manual was compiled chronologically—not a very good way to produce a useful diminution manual. His list is not *more* convoluted only because he chose to give examples for each diatonic pitch between F and A″. Thus, the manual begins with thirty-four patterns originating on tenor F, followed by thirty-four on G, thirty-five on A, nineteen on Bb, twenty on B♮, etc. until the list of 643 formulae has been subdivided into nineteen more manageable groups. This approach does avoid total chaos, but within each group the organization is still random.

It is interesting to follow the author's mind as he moves often haphazardly from one individual pattern to the next. Often there is no logical relationship between successive formulae, but in some cases a definite influence can be seen of one formula on the next. The stepwise descending thirds in #13, for example, may have been the inspiration for the stepwise ascending thirds in #14. Examine also the systematic string of eighth-note patterns from #4–16, the similar beginning of #251 and #252, or the transposition of #257 from #256. Other examples of such thought continuity can be found throughout the manual, but they are not systematic and do not make up for an overall lack of order.

The most puzzling problem remains this subdivision by pitch because, in general, most of the diminutions would work on several pitch levels. In fact, the same formula often shows up on several different pitches, perhaps without the author's conscious knowledge of the repetition; at least sixty-five formulae can be identified that are replicated elsewhere in the manual. Thus, the author seems to contradict his own organizational premises by recycling over 25 percent of his formulae. For example, the melodic pattern in example 13.1 is used fourteen times and appears on every scale degree except B♭.

This reuse of formula does not imply that there are not subtle differences between patterns at different pitch levels and in different ranges. For example, the patterns early in the manual are used as basslines, whereas those on tenor B♮ and above are treated more often as an upper voice. Certain constraints appear when the starting pitches move into the soprano octave; because the keyboard compass allows little room to go up, these formulae dwell in the octave below the starting pitch. These higher formulae also appear to be more virtuosic. The tonal context of the starting pitch also influences the formula, because this initial tone is not necessarily the tonic of a key or the root of a chord. Patterns on B♮, for example, alternate between those that elaborate the tonic of B Minor, those that elaborate the tonic of G Major (beginning on the third of the chord), and those that elaborate the leading tone of C Major. Such patterns are intrinsically different but are grouped by the Bártfa author into the same category.

With his lengthy list of formulae, the question that now arises is whether the author actually applies these diminutions to music elsewhere in the tablature. Such evidence would most likely be found at the beginning of this source, where a group of six vocal works are intabulated and embellished. On the surface, the idea of supplying embellished examples seems to follow that of the printed manuals where, along with the usual diminution tables, the diminutions are also applied to specific compositions. In this manuscript, however, very few of the formulae are actually used in the embellished works.[9]

These opening intabulations show a musician grappling with technique. They do not look like pieces that have been embellished by a man who just compiled a manual of 643 diminution patterns. They do, however, show a man

Example 13.1

who is concentrating on *the embellishment process* itself. First of all, he reduces the number of voices in each intabulation to a bare, outer-voice framework. This reduction allows him to concentrate on the diminution process. Second, he supplies both the embellished and the unembellished lines. This offers a point of comparison or reference. And third, although he is somewhat inept, he is seen trying a wide variety of techniques and alternative patterns on the same material.

The first piece in this manuscript, an intabulation of Palestrina's popular madrigal *Vestiva i colli,* is a good example of the author's embellishment process. The intabulator allows the opening point of imitation to pass through each voice before he commences with the embellishments. (Remember that the two voices here are composite voices, since this intabulation is reduced from an originally five-voice work.) The initial diminutions, predominantly sixteenth-note patterns, are applied to the lower voice, where the focus of attention remains through measure 40. At this point the structure of the vocal model becomes significant, because measures 41–81 are essentially a repeat of this opening section (see table 13.1). The Bártfa intabulator takes his cue from Palestrina's original repetition and decides to repeat this first section over and over again, each time with different diminutions. Thus, measures 41–80 in the intabulation treat the upper voice with consistent eighth-note patterns, measures 81–122 repeat this section a third time but now use sixteenth-note embellishments in the upper voice, and measures 123–60 repeat the material a fourth time

Table 13.1   Palestrina, "Vestiva i colli"
Parallel horizontal lines indicate repeated musical material.

Vocal model (à 5)

m. 1	m.40
m.41	m.81 m.93

Intabulation* (à 2):

m. 1 bass: ** ♬♬, ♪♪, ♬♪, ♬♪	m.40
m.41 sop.: ♪♪ bass: ♪♪, ♪♪♪, ♩. ♪	m.80
m.81 sop.: ♬♬, ♪♪, ♬♪ bass: ♪♪, ♬♪, ♬♬	m.120
m.121 sop.: ♬♪, ♬♬, ♪♪, ♪♪, ♬♪, ♬♬	m.158
m.159 sop.: ♬♬, ♬♪, ♪♪, ♪♪♪, ♪♪	m.199 ♬♬, ♪♪ m.208
bass: ♬♬, ♬♪, ♪♪, ♩. ♪	♬♬

*Budapest, National Library: Mus. ms. Bártfa, ff. 1–4
**Rhythmic patterns (occuring more than once) are shown here in order of frequency.

using a greater variety of melodic patterns and rhythms. At measure 161 the intabulator ceases his repetition of the opening section and hooks back into the model at measure 41 (which you will remember is still a repetition of the opening forty bars). Beginning at this point and continuing to the conclusion, diminution is applied to *both* voices, sometimes in alternation but often simultaneously.

Unfortunately, the quality of the diminutions is not very high. The melodic beauty of the original lines is not enhanced at all by these embellishments, the static eighth- or sixteenth-note patterns add little to the rhythmic interest, and the frequent occurrence of consecutive fifths and octaves is a significant contrapuntal embarrassment. The intabulator has obviously not mastered the requisite skills for embellished intabulation.

The Bártfa author may have recognized these many weaknesses and decided, as a result, to compile a diminution manual which addressed his musical deficiencies. For example, after the obvious rhythmic monotony of the embellished intabulations, he seems to be striving for greater rhythmic variety in his manual. His most severe problem, that of forbidden parallel motion, is also systematically worked on as he forces himself to supply a correct contrapuntal voice for each diminution formula. Since many contrapuntal mistakes occur when separate patterns *join,* he also decides to project the note to which each formula should lead (to show *was fehlt*).

The fact that the Bártfa author was not a skilled, sophisticated musician (a view which is also borne out by his corrupt copies of the Sweelinck and Scheidt pieces), also helps explain why he organized his manual in such an odd way. His organization by pitch, instead of by interval, shows a very pragmatic musician, not a relativistic one. In other words, it was easier for him to perceive a formula on a fixed pitch than to deal with a movable, abstract formula. It is exactly these features, directly related to the author's specific insecurities, that make the Bártfa manual unique.

Despite his problems, the Bártfa author should be praised for his independence. No evidence suggests that he drew upon (or even knew of) other diminution manuals, nor can significant correspondences be found between his formulae and the figuration patterns of other seventeenth-century composers. His manual has been compared with the published manuals of Bassano, dalla Casa, Ganassi, Ortiz, and others, and comparisons have also been made with selected compositions by Ammerbach, Buxtehude, Froberger, Poglietti, Scheidt, Sweelinck, and Samuel Marckfelnera (a seventeenth-century Slovakian keyboard composer). Special attention was paid to the Sweelinck and Scheidt works in Manuscript 27 itself (they could logically have been models from which the author drew his inspiration), but this search for significant correlations was unsuccessful.

What was revealed by comparing the Bártfa diminutions to other sources is just how diverse the possibilities of figuration really are. At first the sixty-eight Bártfa examples of embellishing a descending second seem adequate, but looking in other diminution manuals, dozens of alternatives for embellishing this same interval can be found. In the seventeenth-century keyboard repertory, although positive matches could be made in 5 to 10 percent of the searches, hundreds of patterns were found that were not listed in Bártfa.[10]

With such an immense failure rate, the tactics of this search were eventually reversed to identify typical figurations that are *not* overwhelmingly represented in the Bártfa manual. The examples below show several such patterns, each of them frequently found in the music of Scheidt and Sweelinck.[11] Example 13.2 shows sixteenth-note patterns that begin with a sixteenth rest. There are no examples of this rhythm in the Bártfa manual. Example 13.3 shows a pattern that leads to a radically different range. Of course, many such examples in the keyboard repertory will turn around in the following measure and descend back into the original range. The one-measure Bártfa examples, however, cannot allow for this possibility, and hence this type of pattern is seldom found. Examples 13.4a and 13.4b are the ubiquitous parallel thirds and sixths, broken here into consecutive motion. Although some examples of this type are present in Bártfa, their frequency cannot begin to match that in Scheidt's or Sweelinck's music. The remaining examples are self-evident: example 13.5 shows a pattern with an unusually large leap; example 13.6 stands out because of its repeated notes; example 13.7 is a type of "octave echo"; example 13.8 shows chord-outlining figuration; example 13.9 shows triplets (totally absent in the Bártfa manual); and example 13.10 shows a popular pattern characterized by its "lower neighbor" motion. None of these is common in the Bártfa manual.

Needless to say, this comparison project did not lead to the fascinating results that were first envisioned. No claim can be made that the Bártfa tablature accurately codifies the figuration practice of the time; the vast number of possible figuration patterns is simply too enormous for any manual of several hundred formulae to be representative.[12] These results also suggest that we are wrong to think of diminution manuals as stockpiles of figurations which can simply be plugged into the music. Instead, the manuals supply diminution models from which creative musicians might develop their own individual techniques. The Bártfa manual is, in many ways, an imperfect model, but it does give evidence that early keyboard performers concerned themselves with diminution.

The Bártfa author was simply not content to perform the elaborate, precomposed figuration of Sweelinck and Scheidt; he wanted to understand how to use such exciting embellishments himself. From this perspective, his manual takes on the character of an extended exercise as he deals methodically with diminutions on each individual pitch. By codifying his own personal practice and compiling his own *vade-mecum* of diminution, this unknown village organist in seventeenth-century Bártfa should inspire early keyboard performers to try diminutions for themselves. The precedent has been set.

Example 13.2. S. Scheidt, *Herzlich lieb hab ich dich, o Herr,* verse 2, mm. 34–35

Example 13.3. J. P. Sweelinck (?), *Herzlich lieb hab ich dich, o Herr,* m. 103

Example 13.4a. Scheidt, *Vater unser im Himmelreich,* var. 1, m. 1

Example 13.4b. Scheidt, *Passamezzo,* var. 11, mm. 16–17

Example 13.5. Sweelinck (?), *Herzlich lieb hab ich dich, o Herr,* m. 102

Example 13.6. Sweelinck (?), *Herzlich lieb hab ich dich, o Herr*, mm. 216–17

Example 13.7. Scheidt, *Passamezzo*, var. 11, mm. 24–26

Example 13.8. Scheidt, *Passamezzo*, var. 11, mm. 21–22

Example 13.9. Sweelinck (?), *Onse Vader in hemelrijck*, mm. 69–70

Example 13.10. Scheidt, *Soll es sein*, var. 5, mm. 9–10

Appendix A: Keyboard Diminution Manual from Bärtfa Manuscript 27

Appendix A, cont.

Appendix A, cont.

Appendix A, cont.

Appendix A, cont.

Appendix A, cont.

Appendix A, cont.

Appendix A, cont.

Schlicht   Felt   Baß

Appendix A, cont.

Appendix A, cont.

Appendix A, cont.

Appendix A, cont.

Appendix A, cont.

Schlicht   Felt   Baß

Appendix A, cont.

Appendix A, cont.

Appendix A, cont.

Appendix A, cont.

Appendix A, cont.

Appendix A, cont.

Appendix A, cont.

Appendix A, cont.

Appendix A, cont.

Appendix A, cont.

Appendix A, cont.

Schlicht   Felt   Baß

Appendix A, cont.

Appendix A, cont.

Appendix A, cont.

Appendix A, cont.

Appendix B: Bártfa Diminution Manual Statistics

Number of formulae on each pitch:

f	34	c′	36	c″	59
g	34	d′	37	d″	37
a	35	e′	35	e″	35
b	19	f′	35	f″	37
h	20	g′	37	g″	37
		a′	36	a″	24
		b′	18		
		h′	38		

Number of formulae on single intervals which occur within the space of one measure (additional intervals are created when the pattern continues to the next measure):

Example: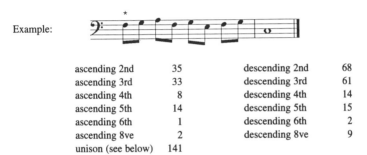

ascending 2nd	35	descending 2nd	68
ascending 3rd	33	descending 3rd	61
ascending 4th	8	descending 4th	14
ascending 5th	14	descending 5th	15
ascending 6th	1	descending 6th	2
ascending 8ve	2	descending 8ve	9
unison (see below)	141		

Number of formulae on the unison which, when completed by the first note of the following measure, embellish a single interval:

Example: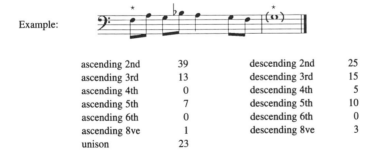

ascending 2nd	39	descending 2nd	25
ascending 3rd	13	descending 3rd	15
ascending 4th	0	descending 4th	5
ascending 5th	7	descending 5th	10
ascending 6th	0	descending 6th	0
ascending 8ve	1	descending 8ve	3
unison	23		

262	single intervals (one measure)
141	single intervals (created by motion to m. 2 from a unison pattern in m. 1)
231	multiple intervals
9	miscellaneous (illegible)

643	Total

Notes

1. Juan Bermudo, *El libro llamado declaracion de instrumentos musicales* (Ossuna, 1555); Girolamo Diruta, *Il Transilvano* (Venice, 1593); and Tomás de Sancta Maria, *Libro llamado arte de tañer fantasia* (Valladolid, 1565). Bermudo's treatise is published in facsimile, Macario Santiago Kastner, ed., *Documenta musicologica*, vol. 1/11 (Kassel: Bärenreiter, 1957). Sancta Maria is partially translated by Julia Aranguren and Orpha Ochse in *How to Play with Complete Perfection and Excellence by Thomas de Sancta Maria: Instructions for Keyboard Performance from "Libro llamado Arte de tañer Fantasia . . ." (1565)*, chapters 13–19 (Whittier, Calif.: Organ Press, 1979). Diruta is published in translation by Murray C. Bradshaw and Edward J. Soehnlein in *Il Transilvano*, Musicological Studies, vol. 38 (Henryville: Institute of Mediaeval Music, 1984) and in facsimile, Bradshaw and Soehnlein, ed., *Bibliotheca Organologica*, vol. 44 (Buren: Frits Knuf, 1983). Hans Buchner's manuscript *Fundamentum* (Basel, Öffentliche-Bibliothek der Universität: Ms. F. I. 8a) is published in German translation by Jost Harro Schmidt in *Hans Buchner. Sämtliche Orgelwerke*, Das Erbe deutscher Musik, vol. 54 (Frankfurt: Henry Litolff, 1974).

2. Silvestro di Ganassi, *Opera intitulata Fontegara* (Venice, 1535); Diego Ortiz, *Tratado de glosas sobre clausulas* (Rome, 1553); Girolamo dalla Casa, *Il vero modo di diminuir* (Venice, 1584); Giovanni Bassano, *Ricercare, Passaggi et Cadentie* (Venice, 1585) and *Motetti, madrigali et canzoni francese . . . diminuiti* (Venice, 1591); Richard Rogniono, *Passaggi per potersi essercitare nel diminuire* (Venice, 1592); Giovanni Luca Conforto, *Breve et facile maniera d'essercitarsi ad ogni scolaro . . . a far passaggi* (Rome, 1593); Giovanni Battista Bovicelli, *Regole, passaggi di musica, madrigali e motetti passeggiati* (Venice, 1594).

3. See J. Paul Tomásek, "Geschichte der evangelischen Gemine in Leutschau," *Andenken an die 300jährige Jubelfeier der evangelischen Gemine in der k. Freistadt Leutschau* (Leutschau: Johann Werthmüller, 1844).

4. More modern tastes seem to have reigned in nearby Levoča, where editions of music by Johann Hermann Schein and Heinrich Schütz are preserved. See Cleveland Johnson, *Keyboard Intabulations Preserved in Sixteenth- and Seventeenth-Century German Organ Tablatures: A Catalogue and Commentary*, (Ph.D. diss., Oxford University, 1984), vol. 1, pp. 79–81.

5. Otto Gombosi, "Die Musikalien der Pfarrkirche zu St. Ägidi in Bártfa: ein Beitrag zur Geschichte der Musik in Oberungarn" in *Musikwissenschaftliche Beiträge. Festschrift für Johannes Wolf zu seinem sechzigsten Geburtstag* (Berlin: M. Breslauer, 1929), p. 46.

6. Lydia Schierning, *Die Überlieferung der deutschen Orgel und Klaviermusik aus der 1. Hälfte des 17. Jahrhunderts*, Schriften des Landesinstituts für Musikforschung Kiel, vol. 12 (Kassel: Bärenreiter, 1961), p. 95.

7. See Alan Curtis, *Sweelinck's Keyboard Music: A Study of English Elements in Seventeenth-Century Dutch Compositions* (London: Oxford University Press, 1969), p. 105; Otto Gombosi, "Ein neuer Sweelinck-Fund" in *Tijdschrift der Vereeniging voor Nederlands Muziekgeschiedenis* XIV (1935), pp. 1–13; Gustav Leonhardt, ed., *Jan Pieterszoon Sweelinck Opera Omnia*, vol. 1/2 (Amsterdam: Vereniging voor Nederlandse Muziekgeschiedenis, 1974), p. xxi; Schierning, *Die Überlieferung*, pp. 94–95; and Max Seiffert, ed., *Jan Pieterszoon Sweelinck Werken voor Orgel en Clavecimbel, tweede, aanzienlijk vermeerderd druk* (Amsterdam: G. Alsbach, 1943), p. XLVIII.

8. "Vestiva i colli" (f. 1, G. Palestrina), "Matka Rozkossna" (f. 3v, anon.), "Canzon" (f. 5v, anon.), "Nasce la pena mia" (f. 7v, A. Striggio), "Intrada Herrn von Losenstein" (f. 9, anon), "Pater noster" (f. 12, M. Vulpius). The diminution formulae are found on ff. 55–59.

9. In fact, as the order of the manuscript suggests, these pieces were probably intabulated and embellished some time before the diminution manual itself was compiled.

10. These positive matches were made using only the diminution portion of the Bártfa information; if I had expanded my comparison to use the contrapuntal second voice given with each Bártfa diminution, my success rate would have been practically zero.

11. These specific examples are taken from their original compositions in Bártfa 27.

12. Any basic interval can be embellished in *billions* of ways. A diminution pattern consisting of sixteen sixteenth-notes, falling within one octave above or below the starting pitch, beginning on the first note of the interval, striking the second note of the interval directly on the third beat, and using every note in the two-octave range can be formulated in 87,178,291,312 possible combinations. Of course, many of these patterns would be musical nonsense, but if logical musical results were produced by a mere one-tenth of one percent, the total would still amount to almost nine million!

14

Tablature versus Staff Notation: Or, Why Did the Young J. S. Bach Compose in Tablature?

Robert Hill

It is commonly held that German letter tablature, sometimes called New German Organ Tablature, was an inconvenient form of musical notation, cumbersome to write down and difficult to decipher, at least by comparison with the five-line staff notation standard since the beginning of the eighteenth century. The survival of tablature in Germany and Scandanavia up through the early eighteenth century has been attributed mainly to two factors: conservative attitudes among the musicians of those countries, and tablature's usefulness as a form of musical shorthand for notating brief passages in spaces too cramped for conventional staff notation. J. S. Bach's occasional use of tablature in the margins of his manuscripts is well known and has been described often. Yet as we learn more about Bach's early activities as a composer, it becomes clear that his use of tablature, at least for a period of his youth, extended well beyond occasional use as a shorthand. Indeed, it now appears that Bach used tablature as his original notation for a number of early keyboard works, including such well-known pieces as the organ Passacaglia in C Minor (BWV 582).[1]

Bach's intensive early involvement with tablature as a vehicle for notation is surprising, if tablature was in fact commonly regarded in his own time as an awkward and outmoded form of notation. One might try to account for his use of tablature as a consequence of his keen interest in the music of his elder contemporaries, particularly Buxtehude. In order to have access to much of the German music that interested him, Bach would have needed to be fluent in deciphering tablature. We can take it for granted that he would have acquired this fluency very early. The legendary manuscript containing works by Froberger, Kerll, and Pachelbel (which Bach is said illicitly to have copied out by moonlight while living with his brother Johann Christoph) may well have been notated in tablature.[2] While it is one thing to learn to read and perhaps even to perform from an outmoded form of notation, it seems quite another thing to notate new, complex pieces in a notation clearly doomed to extinction. What might Bach's motivation have been for cultivating this obsolete notation to the extent of composing in it himself? Clearly, if Bach found it of value to write some of his own compositions in tablature, tablature must have some inherent strengths that offset its limitations.

To be sure, its drawbacks are many, as complaints by writers of the period attest. Apparently developed around 1550,[3] New German Organ Tablature, so designated by Johannes Wolf and Willi Apel[4] to distinguish it from the older form of German tablature combining letter notation for the left hand with staff notation for the right, indicates pitch by the letters A–B–H (for B♮)–C–D–E–F–G. All chromatic alterations are expressed by the addition of the suffix "-is" to a letter, raising it a half-step. Thus the pitch E♭ must be expressed in tablature as "dis," or D♯. Register is indicated much as it is today: capital letters for the octave starting with the C (sometimes the B) two octaves below middle C, small letters for the octave immediately below middle C, a single stroke, placed horizontally over the letter, for the octave beginning with middle C, and so on. To indicate rhythm, separate signs are used, appearing over the pitch letters. The rhythmic signs begin with a short vertical slash signifying a whole note. Diminution by half is indicated by the addition of a horizontal stroke to the right of the vertical slash. Thus the symbol ⊢ indicates a half note, ⊨ a quarter note, and so forth.

The inconveniences of this form of notation become immediately obvious. Lacking the ability to make enharmonic distinctions, tablature is ill-suited to music that explores harmonic regions outside the limited range of keys possible within meantone temperament.[5] Its notation of rhythm, relatively well-suited to the notation of music composed mainly in whole, half, and quarter notes, becomes very cumbersome when the rhythmic values to be expressed include thirty-second notes. If we count the additional strokes needed to indicate register, notating a single sixteenth note A″: ≣ for example, requires seven separate strokes, each of which involves lifting pen from paper, not including the circular stroke required for the letter itself. Entering the same note in staff notation requires only from two to four independent strokes, depending on whether the pen is lifted from the paper in making the stem and flags. Even with the consolidation of rhythmic characters for groups of equal note-values and of register lines for notes in the same octave, it is apparent that a passage in tablature takes much more time to write than the same passage in staff notation, if care is taken to avoid ambiguity caused by slurring strokes together.

Jacob Adlung, writing in 1758, recognized the inadequacy of tablature for music written in small note values: "With today's many-flagged notes, [tablature] is unuseable." He adds that "[Andreas] Werckmeister prefers [tablature] to staff notation, but wants to make it easier."[6] Werckmeister, to whose championing of tablature we will return later, was one of many who recommended changes to tablature notation practice in order to streamline it. Acknowledging that the writing of tablature was laborious, he states "it does appear as if in writing lines and notes one could finish sooner than with today's German tablature. For in the latter, one has just too many varied characters. . . ."[7]

Not only was tablature tedious to write, it also proved very difficult to learn to read. Michael Praetorius, while occasionally advocating tablature, admitted that "it is quite a difficult—and tedious—thing to perform securely from tablature." Writing in 1619, he evidently already regarded tablature as somewhat old-fashioned: "the people who invented and taught it are already dead, or at least very old."[8] In his autobiographical contribution to Johann Mattheson's *Grundlage einer Ehren-Pforte* (Hamburg, 1740), Georg Philipp Telemann relates that the prospect of learning tablature, as well as the stodgy style of delivery he evidently associated with tablatures, their contents, and their proponents from contact with his first and only keyboard teacher, so frightened him that he gave up study after fourteen days: "I began keyboard lessons; but had the misfortune to study with an organist who frightened me away with the German tablature, from which he played as stiffly as perhaps his grandfather had done, from whom he had inherited [the book of tablature]."[9]

Despite the difficulties of reading tablature, some professional musicians could read it fluently. Adlung testifies that "tablature is difficult; nonetheless, my father could read it, as well as staff notation, as easily as another can read the latter."[10] In general, however, it seems clear that contemporaries saw the difficulty of sightreading as one of the major drawbacks of tablature. It was one thing to have enough time to prepare a part from tablature in a thorough manner, and quite another to have to read something on the spot. Talking no doubt from experience, Praetorius describes tablature as a "difficult and miserable thing, in which one can easily go mad, especially when one has to perform *ex improviso.*"[11] The difficulty of performing from tablature became particularly acute when the realization of keyboard continuo accompaniments entered the picture. Indeed, most contemporary criticism focuses on the perceived inability of tablature to accommodate sightreading needs in ensemble situations.[12]

Compensating for these many deficiencies were a number of advantages that tablature notation held for its users. We have already mentioned its economy of space compared to staff notation. For German organists of the seventeenth century, this factor may indeed have been a significant one. They typically collected pieces of music by copying them in tablature into miscellany volumes, often more than a hundred folios thick and sometimes containing hundreds of compositions. Given the vicissitudes of the seventeenth-century German economy and the low economic status of musicians, many organists may have been forced to use paper as sparingly as possible.

Not only did tablature have the advantage of economy, but it afforded that advantage with absolute transparency of line for polyphonic music: tablature is in essence an open score. Voices are kept discrete from each other by careful layering, one above the other from bass to treble. Thus, the progression of voices within a potentially very dense contrapuntal texture is kept uncompromisingly clear. In staff-notation practices of the time, a corresponding clarity could be achieved only with an open or full score, similar to today's string-quartet or orchestral score. In keyboard staff notation of the seventeenth century there were no conventions according to which the direction of stems specified the voice to which a note belonged. Moreover, notation of music in larger values, including stemless whole notes, was much more prevalent, so that keeping track of the progression of individual voices sharing a staff or crossing from one staff to the other could be difficult or impossible.[13]

Since tablature is open score by nature, musicians used it to notate not only keyboard music but vocal and instrumental ensemble music as well. Where a full score in staff notation might occupy a half or even a whole page, the same music in tablature might take up only a single system out of five or six on a page. For the notation of keyboard music, tablature had yet another advantage over open score: it could very flexibly adapt to changes in the number of voices represented. It was also less rigorous than open score in allowing a melody to migrate from one voice part to another simply by angling the line of letters up or down to the space allocated to the neighboring part. Another advantage was the lack of clef changes. In contemporary staff notation, clef changes were frequently introduced to keep voices within the staff, in an effort to avoid ledger lines. German players, feeling insecure at best about realizing a thoroughbass part, might easily have felt intimidated by clef changes introduced in the bass line.

Tablature has another important characteristic, recognized by contemporaries as a strength over keyboard staff notations. Whereas keyboard staff notation is a crude graphic representation of the keyboard, turned sideways so that the horizontal lines and spaces correspond roughly to the keys, the letters of tablature notation furnish no such visual link for the performer. On a staff, the physical distance between keys can quickly be assessed, and chords suggest the hand position or even the fingering to be used. The eye and the hand coordinate instantly and automatically, so that the accomplished player can sightread even quite difficult music of the period while scarcely listening or concentrating. In tablature, the only graphic clue to intervallic relationships is the superimposition of voices with bass at the bottom of a system, soprano on top. The relationship of pitches to each other must be reconstructed in the aural imagination, in the mind's ear, so to speak.

Perhaps because it encouraged a strong mental image of the sound of lines as they combined polyphonically, tablature was recommended as a notational vehicle for composition. Praetorius praises tablature as "correct, good, easy and more comfortable [than staff notation], not only to perform from, but also to compose in."[14] For conducting, Werckmeister considered command of tablature an alternative to skill at keyboard playing: "I know various conductors who sing and direct out of scores in German tablature. . . . And even if a conductor or singer can't play keyboard, he can still learn the harmony and musical art."[15] Elsewhere he implies that command of tablature makes for a better musician: "And I therefore say expressly, that it is easier, and makes for a more accurate singer and musician, when they have the tones in their head and know how they sound, and that one can very easily learn to sing and play from letters."[16]

For the organ music of Scheidemann and his contemporaries, tablature had yet a further advantage over contemporary staff notations. In organ pieces to be played on two manuals, the discrete layers within a tablature system allowed a composer to indicate manual divisions very precisely.[17] But the very affinity of tablature with the style of music it was used to notate underscores its most serious limitation and a basic reason for its demise: as the style of keyboard music changed, tablature notation could not adapt. We saw earlier that tablature was inadequate for the accommodation of key changes or modulations. Nor could tablature accommodate the change to improvised harmony realized at the keyboard as the foundation of modern ensemble music. Moreover, as works notated in tablature became passé, performers lacked the incentive to maintain the skills necessary to decipher them.

We should not forget, however, that by the time tablature became extinct, so too had the other forms of keyboard notation, aside from five-line staff notation, vanished. Open score for keyboard music had become outmoded with the stylistic change from a mainly four-voiced *prima prattica* contrapuntal texture to a simplified *seconda prattica* counterpoint with its bass-treble axis. Both Italian notation, with its unequal numbers of lines for bass and treble staff, and the Northern European notation with six lines for each, were limited by their function of indicating precisely the distribution of notes assigned to the left and right hands. Only five-line staff notation had the neutrality of function that allowed it to accommodate changes of style, and even five-line notation saw a gradual reduction in the number of clefs used, although variations according to place and period persisted.

Given the advantages and disadvantages inherent in tablature, can we now account for why the young J. S. Bach composed in this notation? Even if we cannot answer the question definitively, there are clues to why he might have done so. The earliest sources for all the early keyboard works of Bach for which tablature apparently plays a role in transmission are two large, related anthologies, the so-called Möller Manuscript (W. Berlin, Staatsbibliothek Preussischer Kulturbesitz, Musikabteilung Mus. ms. 40644. Hereafter abbreviated as MM) and Andreas Bach Book (Leipzig, Stadtbibliothek der Stadt Leipzig, Sammlung Becker III.8.4. Hereafter abbreviated as ABB). The two books were compiled roughly between 1703 and 1713 by Johann Christoph Bach, organist in Ohrdruf, Johann Sebastian's eldest sibling and his first keyboard teacher. Most of the more than twenty-five works by J. S. Bach in the two books appear to have been copied by J. C. Bach directly from his brother's autographs. Of the Bach works in MM and ABB, nine point to Bach's cultivation of tablature (see table 14.1).

Table 14.1   Early J. S. Bach Compositions for Which Tablature
Notation Plays a Role in Transmission

BWV	Title	Earliest Source	Comment
535a	Prelude and Fugue in G Minor	MM	autograph fair copy
563	Fantasia and Imitatio in B Minor	ABB	
582	Passacaglia in C Minor	ABB	
588	Canzona in D Minor	MM	
724	Gott, durch deine Güte	ABB	unicum
832	Suite in A Major	MM	
912a	Toccata in D Major	MM	
917	Fantasia in G Minor	MM	
deest	Fantasia in C Minor	ABB	unicum, autograph fair copy

The chorale prelude *Gott, durch deine Güte* (BWV 724) and the C-Minor Fantasia (BWV deest) are the only two works to come down to us in tablature notation. For two of the remaining seven works, the Fantasia and Imitatio in B Minor (BWV 563) and the Suite in A Major (BWV 832), the texts of the earliest copies suggest derivation from tablature copies probably not prepared by Bach himself.[18] In two cases, those of the Prelude and Fugue in G Minor (BWV 535a) and the Fantasia in G Minor (BWV 917), tablature transmission is indicated only obliquely by a few minor errors or notational anomalies. For the D-Major Toccata (BWV 912a), transcription from a presumably autograph tablature copy is suggested by a passage of nine measures in which the barline is displaced by half a bar. Since tablature has no barlines (other than a short *Strich,* or vertical slash, used rather rarely), an error of this sort can continue uncorrected indefinitely, until caught by the transcriber. Octave transpositions in the ABB and MM texts of the C-Minor Passacaglia and the D-Minor Canzona (BWV 588), doubtless copied directly by J. C. Bach from J. S. Bach autographs, provide clear indications that these autographs were notated in tablature.

To summarize, of the nine Bach works in MM and ABB for which there are indications of tablature transmission, two are actually notated in tablature (one of these is an autograph), three more show unambiguous signs of tablature transmission, and four have notational features that more indirectly suggest tablature transmission. One of the latter, BWV 535a, is also an autograph. For two of the remaining, BWV 563 and 832, the implied tablature copies were doubtless not autographs. While these intermediate tablature copies may derive from tablature autographs, this cannot be proven.

It is appropriate to ask why the young Bach apparently notated these works originally in tablature rather than in staff notation, while notating other keyboard works composed during the same period in staff notation. One explanation may be the style of the pieces with tablature background. In five of the nine pieces listed above (BWV 563, 588, 724, 917, and BWV deest), slow note values predominate. All are polyphonic and written in at least four parts, although some are more rigorously polyphonic than others. The style of all five works is retrospective, recalling the solid, vocally influenced counterpoint of mid- to late-seventeenth-century Middle German composers such as Froberger Pachelbel, and Kuhnau. The remaining four works, BWV 535a, 582, 832, and 912a, are written in the more modern North German keyboard idiom of Böhm and Buxtehude. From a stylistic point of view, therefore, the Bach pieces for which tablature transmission is indicated lie squarely in the German compositional tradition. While the suite BWV 832 incorporates elements of French style, it does so under the influence of Böhm and Fischer. Thus it seems that Bach's use of tablature to notate his works coincides with the period during which he was most actively assimilating German compositional models for his keyboard music.

Many of those models would have been notated in tablature in the copies in which Bach encountered them. Of the German works other than Bach's in MM and ABB, a high proportion, particularly in MM, were either transcribed into staff notation directly from tablature, or are closely descended from tablature copies. Two preludes and fugues by Nicolaus Bruhns in MM were left in tablature, perhaps because their notation in staff notation was nearly as cumbersome as their tablature notation (as a look at a modern staff-notation edition will show). In several cases, including works by Bruhns, Dietrich Buxtehude, and Peter Heidorn, we have cause to believe that the tablature copies from which copies in MM were prepared may have been manuscripts from J. S. Bach's own library.[19]

The fact that many pieces in MM and ABB are transcribed directly from tablature suggests that Johann Christoph Bach, although fluent in writing tablature, may have felt uncomfortable enough performing from it to take the trouble to transcribe almost every work in tablature that lay before him. He may have decided to leave the chorale prelude *Gott, durch deine Güte* (BWV 724) in tablature because its part-writing, with its relatively dense texture and slow note values, was more transparent in that notation than in staff notation.

J. S. Bach may have been more fluent in playing from tablature than his brother. His avid curiosity about the music surrounding and preceding him caused him to "love and study" the music of Froberger, Kerll, Pachelbel, Fischer, Strungk, Buxtehude, Reinken, Bruhns, and Böhm,[20] many of whose works he would have encountered in tablature copies. In particular, the study of works by these composers in rigorous counterpoint notated in tablature would have constituted excellent training. It may have been this benefit that Werckmeister had in mind when he praised the study of music notated in tablature: "I do not object, when one can play a good piece from tablature, for this is very good, and I think much of good pieces written in tablature, for thereby one can see what other capable organists have composed, and can see in them good *Manieren* and *Inventiones,* and can make use of them oneself, and reflect further upon them and have ideas from them."[21]

To be sure, one could learn these things from copies in staff notation as well, but the study of pieces in a notation that forced the mind to translate directly into a sound image was possible only with tablature. In a way, staff notation was too easy. By providing visual cues about the intervallic distances within a melody and between voices, staff notation substituted an immediately comprehensible, external visual picture of the musical score for the purely mental image of the music that had to be reconstructed from tablature. The skill to read from open score staff notation came closest to the skills required to read tablature, and it seems no coincidence that the two flourished concurrently. During the zenith of these two notations, musicians would routinely have acquired the necessary reading skills. By the early eighteenth century, however, it must have been unusual for someone to take the trouble to learn tablature or the art of playing keyboard music from open score. Telemann's shying away from tablature was probably a common reflex.

J. S. Bach, on the other hand, being absorbed in the process of assimilating the music of his German predecessors, practiced composition in the notation appropriate to that musical tradition. At the same time, he sensed that the musical language around him was changing, under French and Italian influences. Having steeped himself in the language and traditional notation of his own heritage, the young Bach turned his attention both to older and newer French and Italian musical models. We cannot fix with precision the time of this change of orientation, which must have occurred gradually. Nonetheless, there came a point after which Bach ceased to notate new compositions in tablature. If we can judge by the relative musical maturity of the pieces for which tablature figures as Bach's original notation, the C-Minor Passacaglia (BWV 582) and the C-Minor Fantasia (BWV deest) probably count among the last works Bach wrote in tablature. That these two works are found within thirty or so openings of each other in ABB may be coincidental, but if not, then that portion of the manuscript may well reflect the end of Bach's active involvement with tablature. It is difficult and risky to attempt to date Bach's composition of these pieces more precisely, but it seems likely that by the age of about twenty-five Bach had ceased to compose in tablature, and thereafter used it only as a shorthand for marginal entries.

Notes

1. See Dietrich Kilian's discussion of BWV 582 in his critical commentary to volume 4/7 of the Neue Bach-Ausgabe, forthcoming. See also Robert Hill, *The Möller Manuscript and the Andreas Bach Book: Two Keyboard Anthologies from the Circle of the Young Johann Sebastian Bach*, (Ph.D. diss., Harvard University, 1987; microfilm available through University Microfilms International, # 88–00787), chapter 6.

2. R. Hill, "'Der Himmel weiss, wo diese Sachen hingekommen sind': Reconstructing the Lost Keyboard Notebooks of the Young Bach and Handel," in *Bach, Handel, Scarlatti: Tercentenary Essays*, ed. Peter Williams (Cambridge: Cambridge University Press, 1985), pp. 161–72.

3. For a discussion of early tablature sources, as well as the demise of tablature, see Cleveland Johnson, "New German Organ Tablature: Its Rise and Demise," in *Charles Brenton Fisk, Organ Builder I: Essays in His Honor*, ed. Fenner Douglass, Owen Jander, and Barbara Owen (Easthampton, Mass.: Westfield Center for Early Keyboard Studies, 1986), pp. 93–110.

4. Johannes Wolf, *Handbuch der Notationskunde* II (Leipzig: Breitkopf & Härtel, 1919; reprint, Hildescheim: Olms, 1963), pp. 3–35, and Willi Apel, *The Notation of Polyphonic Music 900–1600*, 5th ed. (Cambridge, Mass.: Medieval Academy of America, 1953, pp. 21–37.

5. In keyboards tuned in meantone temperament, which flourished from the late fifteenth through early eighteenth centuries (in other words roughly contemporary with the lifespan of tablature), the D♯/E♭ key has to be tuned to one or the other of the notes, in order to form a pure third with B (in the case of D♯) or G (in the case of E♭). For an overview of meantone and other unequal temperaments, see Mark Lindley, "Temperaments," in *The New Grove Dictionary of Music and Musicians*, ed. Stanley Sadie (London: Macmillan, 1980) vol. 18, pp. 660–74.

6. "Bei ietzigen vielgeschwänzten Noten ist sie nicht brauchbar. Werckmeister zieht sie dem Notensystem vor, aber . . . will er sie leichter machen." Jacob Adlung, *Anleitung zu der musikalischen Gelahrtheit* (Erfurt, 1758), p. 186, footnote (s). Facsimile reprint edited by Hans Joachim Moser, *Documenta Musicologica*, series 1, no. 4 (Kassel: Bärenreiter, 1953).

7. Andreas Werckmeister, *Musicalische Paradoxal-Discourse* (Quedlinburg, 1707), p. 70. Facsimile reprint in *A. Werckmeister: Hypomnemata Musica und andere Schriften* (Hildesheim: Olms, 1970). For a more extended transcription and translation of the above passage, see C. Johnson, "New German Organ Tablature," pp. 104–6. Johann Gottfried Walther, *Musicalisches Lexicon* (Leipzig, 1732), p. 592, commented that the common practice of abbreviating rhythm signs to arabic numbers (for example, the number *4* represented the four horizontal strokes of the sixteenth note) was done "for the sake of comfort" ("um mehrerer Bequemlichkeit willen").

8. "Aber dieweil es gar ein schwehr Ding ist, und auch langweilig, dieselbe recht *secur* zuschlagen und die Menschen so sie erfunden und gelehret waren, zuvor gestorben, oder auffs wenigste gar alt ist." Michael Praetorius, *Syntagma Musicum* III (Wolfenbüttel, 1619), p. 129. Facsimile reprint edited by Wilibald Gurlitt, *Documenta Musicologica*, series 1. no. 5 (Kassel: Bärenreiter, 1958).

9. "liess ich mich auf dem Clavier unterrichten; gerieth aber zum Unglück an einen Organisten, der mich mit der deutschen Tabulature erschreckte, die er eben so steiff spielte, wie vieleicht sein Grosvater gethan, von dem er sie geerbet hatte." See Georg Philipp Telemann, *Singen is das Fundament zur Music in allen Dingen: Eine Dokumentensammlung*, ed. W. Rackwitz (Leipzig: P. Reclam, 1981), p. 196.

10. "Sie ist schwer; doch konnte nebsten der italiänischen mein Vater sie so fertig, als ein andrer die Noten." J. Adlung, *Anleitung zu der musikalischen Gelahrtheit*, pp. 186–87, footnote (s).

11. Tablature is "ein beschwehr und Verdriesslich ding, . . . darinnen man leichlich irre wird insonderheit wen man *eximproviso Musiciren* soll." M. Praetorius, *Syntagma musicum III*, p. 150.

12. Perhaps the most well-known example is the satirical fable related in the foreword to Friedrich Erhard Niedt's *Musicalische Handleitung* (Hamburg, 1700), in which the organist Tacitus, whose training is in tablature, fails an examination as a candidate for an organist job opening because of his inability to sightread figured bass. For a fine survey of the sources documenting the resistance of German organists to learning thoroughbass, see C. Johnson, *New German Organ Tablature*, pp. 101–3. See also Walter Heimann, *Der Generalbass-Satz und seine Rolle in Bachs Choral-Satz*, Freiburger Schriften zur Musikwissenschaft 5, ed. Hans Heinrich Eggebrecht (Munich: E. Katzbichler, 1973), pp. 26ff.

13. Perhaps because, like tablature, open score staff notation could represent polyphony unambiguously, it became common in the late sixteenth century in Italy, where tablature was not in use, to publish contrapuntal keyboard music in that format. By the early seventeenth century, however, the skill of reading from open score had apparently gone into decline. Frescobaldi, publishing his *First Book of Capricci* (1626) states in the preface that "the performance of these pieces may give difficulty to certain players . . . because the practice of playing from score has apparently become neglected"; and in his preface to *Fiori musicali* of 1635, "I consider it of great importance for the player to practice playing from score, not only because I think it necessary for those who wish to intensively study the form of these compositions, but particularly also because it is a test which distinguishes the genuine artist from the ignorant." Translations by Pierre Pidoux, ed., *Girolamo Frescobaldi: Orgel- und Klavierwerke*, vol. 2: *Das erste Buch der Capricci, Ricercari und Canzoni 1626* (Kassel: Bärenreiter, 1950) and vol. 5: *Fiori musicali 1635* (Kassel: Bärenreiter, 1954).

14. M. Praetorius, *Syntagma Musicum III*, p. 126.

15. "wie ich dann unterschiedliche *Directores* gekennet die ihre *Partituren* in teutsche *Tabulatur* gesetzet und daraus gesungen und *dirigiret*. Ich kan auch noch mit des vornehmen *Grimmii* eigener Hand bezeugen das Er aus der deutschen *Tabulatur*, oder Buchstaben *dirigiret* hat Und ob schon ein solcher *Director* oder Sänger das Clavier nicht verstehet so kan er doch durch die Buchstaben die *Harmonie*, und Singe-Kunst in den Kopf bringen." A. Werckmeister, *Musical-ische Paradoxal-Discourse*, p. 72. Werckmeister apparently had in his possession tablature manuscripts containing church music in the hand of Heinrich Grimm (1592/3–1637).

16. "Und also sage und befinde ausdrücklich dass es leichter sey und *accuratere* Sänger und *Musicos* mache wann sie die *Claves* im Kopffe haben und wissen wie sie klingen so wohl in *regular* als *fictis modis*, und *Compositionibus:* Und dass einer gar leichte durch die Buchstaben allein singen und spielen lernen könne" (ibid., p. 61). Werckmeister spent a good deal of *Musicalische Paradoxal-Discourse* assailing staff notation for its limitations as a pedagogical tool for teaching students to read and think clearly in music. The conventions of letter notation seemed to him simpler than the multiple ways of notating a single pitch in staff notation.

17. See Werner Breig, ed., *Heinrich Scheidemann Orgelwerke III: Praeambeln, Fugen, Fantasien, Canzonen und Toccaten* (Kassel: Bärenreiter, 1971), p. 79.

18. R. Hill, "The Möller Manuscript and the Andreas Bach Book," pp. 305–9, 338–41.

19. Ibid., pp. 160–63, 190–93, 222–25, 229–30.

20. Hans-Joachim Schulze, ed. *Bach-Dokumente*. Supplement to *Johann Sebastian Bach: Neue Ausgabe Sämtlicher Werke*. Volume III: *Dokumente zum Nachwirken Johann Sebastian Bachs 1750–1800* (Kassel: Bärenreiter, 1972). p. 288.

21. "Ich verwerffe hiermit nicht wann einer ein gut Stück aus der *Tabulatur* spielen kan es ist sehr gut und halte viel auf gute *Tabulatur* Sachen denn man kan darauss sehen was andere rechtschaffene *Organisten* gesetzt haben und kan von denen gute *Mani*eren und Inventiones sehen und sich dieselben zu Nutze machen und weiter darauf nachdencken und Zufälle davon haben." A. Werckmeister, *Harmonologia Musica* (Frankfurt and Leipzig, 1702), p. 68. Facsimile reprint in *A. Werckmeister: Hypomnemata Musica und andere Schriften* (Hildesheim: Olms, 1970). Werckmeister introduces these remarks in a context in which he is defending the need for improvisatory skill.

15

Modality, Tonality, and Theories of Fugal Answer in the Late Renaissance and Baroque

Paul Walker

Perhaps no compositional technique survived the change from modality to tonality in a more prominent position than fugue. Theorists of the late Renaissance and Baroque frequently reserved discussion of fugue for the closing chapters of their treatises, and they invariably praised it as the ultimate test of a composer's skill. Beginning with F. W. Marpurg's *Abhandlung von der Fuge* of 1753, entire treatises have been devoted exclusively to fugue and composers from Haydn to Wagner to Stravinsky have learned, under the tutelage of some of the best-known teachers of the day, the "proper" way to write a fugue. Nevertheless, although many of the contrapuntal elements of "good fugal writing" have remained remarkably consistent through the centuries, one fundamental component of composition—harmonic language—has been completely transformed from a modal system rooted in the melodic motion of Gregorian Chant to a tonal system based on inversion and root transposition of harmonic triads. Aside from its implications for the overall structure of a fugal composition, this change from modality to tonality has exercised its most profound influence on the way theorists and composers think about the opening statement and answer of the fugue's subject.

Modern explanations of fugal answers rely on the relationship between tonic and dominant keys.[1] In the simplest terms, fugal theory requires that the subject be written in the key of the tonic, either entirely or with a modulation to the dominant (no other modulation is acceptable). The answer is then produced by transposing the subject to the key of the dominant. To keep the answering voice from placing excessive emphasis on the key of the supertonic, however, the composer is permitted to alter the subject in two ways: (1) if the subject modulates from tonic to dominant, it is answered by a modulation from dominant to tonic, not to supertonic, and (2) prominent placement of the dominant note near the beginning of the subject requires that this note be answered by the tonic note, not the supertonic note. If neither alteration appears in a particular answer, that answer is then an exact transposition of the subject and is said to be real; otherwise, it is said to be tonal. In the overwhelming majority of cases, theorists illustrate these rules with examples from the instrumental fugues of J. S. Bach, including real answers that are exact transpositions of their subjects (ex. 15.1); tonal answers that modulate from dominant back to tonic (ex. 15.2); tonal answers that alter the subject's dominant notes to tonic notes (ex. 15.3); and even real answers that are entirely in the subdominant (in violation of the rules, ex. 15.4). Because Bach's fugues are now considered to set the standard for all fugal writing before or since, musicians frequently consider them to be "above the rules," and the validity of any particular rule is often judged according to Bach's observance or breaking of it.

Late-Renaissance and Baroque theorists, working within the traditional

Example 15.1. J. S. Bach, *Fugue in C* (BWV 545)

Example 15.2. J. S. Bach, *Fugue in C* (BWV 547)

Example 15.3. J. S. Bach, *Fugue in G Minor* (BWV 542)

Subject

etc.

Answer

etc.

Example 15.4. J. S. Bach, *Fugue in D Minor* (BWV 565)

modal system, also recognized an important relationship between opening imitation and mode. However, with each mode firmly grounded on a specific "final" (e.g., Dorian on D, Phrygian on E, etc.), subjects and answers could not be explained using our modern concept of tonic and dominant keys. As German composers of the mature Baroque moved intuitively toward the tonic/dominant polarity at the heart of the tonal fugue, German theorists struggled to explain musical practice using traditional modality. In the process, they stretched and adapted the old modal system in ingenious ways until they finally took it beyond its breaking point and created a theory of fugal answers consistent with the new system of tonality. In order for us to appreciate their accomplishment, we must first turn to the very beginning of the association between the Latin word *fuga* and music.

Fuga began its musical life in the fourteenth and fifteenth centuries as a term for canon and canonic technique, the earliest important type of imitative counterpoint in Western polyphony. The first theorist to define it, Johannes Tinctoris in his musical dictionary of ca. 1473, inaugurated the known history of fugal theory by insisting that the various voices of a fugue should follow each other with identical solmization syllables.[2] Taken in the context of the late-medieval hexachord system, this requirement ensured that only voices a perfect interval apart could produce proper fugues, since with only three hexachords (on C, F, and G) any given sequence of syllables (say, re-mi-fa) could be produced only three ways (D-E-F, G-A-Bb [at the fourth], or A-B-C [at the fifth]). Thus, already in the fifteenth century, fugal entries were implicitly associated with the intervals of unison, fourth, fifth, and octave, even though this association reflected not a concern for projecting the mode, but a desire for exact replication of intervals by the imitating voices.

As the octave solmization system replaced the hexachord system in the early sixteenth century, theorists began to make explicit the relationship between fugal entries and the perfect intervals. Like Tinctoris, Zarlino restricted fugue to imitative counterpoint in which all voices replicated exactly the pattern of whole and half steps stated by the first voice, and he specified that this exactness was possible only when the voices followed each other at the unison, fourth, fifth, or octave.[3] Elsewhere in *Le istitutioni,* Zarlino also remarked that a composition should begin with the perfect consonances in order to make the mode clear to the listener, and he specified that the individual voices of a piece that began imitatively should obey this rule by entering on final and dominant of the mode.[4] Nevertheless, he offered no further advice on how to construct a fugal theme or its answer, and he remained silent about any relationship between their melodic motion and the mode of the composition.

Another Italian theorist of the late Renaissance, Pietro Pontio, took the first step in addressing this relationship when he noted that a theme intended for imitative treatment should emphasize the important notes of the mode.[5] Example 15.5 shows his illustration of this principle, with the leading voice, in trans-

Example 15.5. Pontio, Imitative Counterpoint with Important Modal Notes
    Properly Emphasized
    (*Dialogo,* p. 46)

posed Dorian on G, emphasizing the notes G, B♭, and D. Pontio failed to discuss how the answering voice should be treated, however, or whether it should likewise emphasize the important modal notes. At another point in the book, he noted in passing the phenomenon of tonal answers and offered an example, but, as the lower voice of example 15.5 makes clear, he did not consider such answers necessary.

German theorists of the late Renaissance took a similar approach. Gallus Dressler described, in his *Praecepta musicae poeticae* of 1563, how the important notes of the mode (including final, dominant, psalm tone tenor, and primary and secondary cadence notes) should form the basis both for cadences and for fugal themes.[6] As Dressler noted, this procedure facilitated smooth transitions between points of imitation, since the note upon which a particular cadence took place would most likely also figure prominently in the ensuing theme. Dressler further specified that the opening measures of a composition—for which he borrowed the term *exordium* from the discipline of rhetoric—should project the mode clearly. Nevertheless, the examples that he cited in his text, nearly all by Clemens non Papa, show great variety in their handling of opening imitation. Types include fifth answered by fourth (ex. 15.6), fifth by fifth (ex. 15.7), fourth by fourth (ex. 15.8), and other irregular patterns (ex. 15.9, in the Phrygian mode on E). Clearly, a composer of the mid-sixteenth century felt free to allow himself a great deal of liberty when he set about establishing the mode of an imitative composition.

By the beginning of the seventeenth century, Italian musicians had concluded that proper projection of the mode in the opening measures of an imitative composition was insufficiently ensured by the vague rules of the past. Girolamo Diruta, writing in part 2 (1609) of his famous organ instruction manual *Il Transilvano,* complained that a theorist frequently had to concoct some sort of "mixed mode" in order to explain the opening of an imitative composi-

Example 15.6. Clemens non Papa, *Mane nobiscum Domine*
(*Corpus mensurabilis musicae,* vol. 4/4, p. 14)

Example 15.7. Clemens non Papa, *Domus mea*
(*Corpus mensurabilis musicae,* vol. 4/18, p. 84)

Example 15.8. Clemens non Papa, *Adesto dolori meo*
(*Corpus mensurabilis musicae,* vol. 4/13, p. 33)

Example 15.9. Clemens non Papa, *Domine Jesu Christe*
(*Corpus mensurabilis musicae,* vol. 4/18, p. 84)

tion. His solution to this problem represents the first theoretical description of the tonal answer:

> mà vi voglio dare un'altro avertimento sopra le modulationi delli Tuoni non meno importante de gli altri, qual è questo. Havete da modulare li Tuoni sopra qual soggetto vi piacerà, pur che il soggetto sia fondato sopra le sue proprie specie, cioè ch'una faccia la Quinta, & l'altra la Quarta. Come volendo voi fare una fantasia overo comporre altre Cantilene sopra il primo Tuono; le sue specie sono re la & re sol, contenute tra D la sol re, A la mi re, & D la sol re. Se la parte del Tenore overo del Soprano farà il soggetto, & che dica re, la, il Basso, overo il Contralto re sol, dal A la mi re, & D la sol re, questa sarà la sua vera formatione.[7]

> but I wish to give you another caution concerning the melodic lines in the [various] modes, which is no less important than the others. It is this: you can proceed in the modes with whichever subject you like, on the condition that the subject is based on its proper species, i.e., that one [voice] makes a fifth and the other a fourth. If you want to make a fantasy or compose other pieces in the first mode, its species are [the fifth] re-la and [the fourth] re-sol contained between D la sol re, A la mi re, and D la sol re. If the tenor or soprano part states the subject with re la, the bass or alto [answers] re sol, which is the true formation of A la mi re and D la sol re.

Diruta's reasoning differed in no important respect from that of his sixteenth-century predecessors. He tacitly assumed that the voices would enter on final and dominant, as recommended by Zarlino, and he agreed with Pontio and Dressler that themes should emphasize the principal notes of the mode, but he carried their thinking one step further to argue that fugal answers should likewise emphasize important modal notes. Thus, a theme that began with the upward leap of a fifth from final to dominant (in Diruta's case, from D to A in D Dorian) required a tonal answer that leapt from A to D in order to avoid stressing the unimportant modal note E. He also noted that this rule was more important at the beginning and end of a composition, where unambiguous projection of the mode was necessary, than in the middle. Without realizing it, Diruta and the composers of his generation had inverted the traditional thinking of Tinctoris and Zarlino to make exactness of imitation less important than unambiguous projection of mode in a composition's opening measures.

Diruta's rule may have been more restrictive than sixteenth-century practice, as the above examples by Clemens non Papa suggest, but most Italian musicians of the early seventeenth century considered it a necessary element of *prima prattica* composition. Thirty-four years after Diruta's *Transilvano II*, Marco Scacchi, the Roman-born composer and theorist employed by the Polish court in Warsaw, criticized Paul Siefert, organist in Danzig and student of J. P. Sweelinck, for introducing the fugal imitation shown in example 15.10 at the beginning of a piece in *stile antico*.[8] Scacchi's reasoning followed Diruta's exactly: in the strict, Renaissance style of composition, establishing the mode was more important than maintaining exact imitation. Just as Diruta had pre-

Example 15.10. Paul Siefert, "Psalm 33," Opening Measures
From *Psalmen Davids* (1640). Text omitted.

scribed, Scacchi insisted that the alto and bass voices of example 15.10[9] should begin A-D, emphasizing dominant and final, rather than A-E.

Before the 1640s, German treatises had made no mention of tonal answers in their chapters on fugue. Once Scacchi introduced Diruta's ideas north of the Alps, however, the problem of real vs. tonal answers quickly came to dominate German theory. As the Viennese organist and theorist Johann Jacob Prinner remarked in 1677, "Therefore most accomplished musicians argue even at the present day which is better, whether one should observe the mode more than the solmization [of the theme]."[10] Although Siefert tried to defend his compositions against Scacchi's stinging criticism by arguing that northern rules of *stile antico* polyphony differed from those of Italy, Scacchi was able to reply by publishing a great many letters written by prominent German musicians who agreed with him rather than with Siefert.[11] Heinrich Schütz, despite some reluctance to take sides in the quarrel, lent Scacchi the endorsement of one of the most highly esteemed musicians in Germany when he wrote, "Nevertheless, I must acknowledge that as a youth I too was drilled and instructed by my teacher Giovanni Gabrieli of blessed memory in a way similar to that in which Mr. Marco Scacchi teaches Mr. Siefert."[12]

The first major German theorist of the second half of the century, Christoph Bernhard, made real and tonal answers the focal point of his writing about fugue.[13] The willingness with which Bernhard accepted Scacchi's reasoning is reflected in the organization of his treatise, for which he placed the information on fugal answers among the chapters on mode rather than among those on fugue (the latter deal exclusively with canonic technique). Nevertheless, whereas Scacchi had argued only for tonal answers and Siefert defended only real answers, Bernhard set out to demonstrate the validity and proper uses of both in more systematic fashion. To do so, he focused on the tradition of assigning a mode to each voice of a polyphonic composition. A century earlier, Zarlino had noted that the voice ranges of tenor and bass (and likewise soprano and alto) were approximately a fourth apart and that if one voice took the ambitus of a particular authentic mode, the other voice took that of the related plagal.[14] Bernhard used this theory to explain tonal answers. When the imitation began with a tonal answer, the answering voice in a sense "completed" the mode of the leading voice, and its mode was therefore the authentic or plagal counterpart to that of the leading voice. For instance, if tenor and soprano were in mode 1 (identified by Bernhard as authentic C Ionian), alto and bass were in mode 2 (plagal C Ionian). Bernhard called this procedure *consociatio modorum*, an "association of modes." When the imitation involved a real answer, on the other hand, the alto's mode in a sense "paralleled" the tenor's mode, and therefore the alto took another mode a fourth or fifth removed from that of the tenor. That is, if tenor was in mode 1, alto might be in mode 7 (authentic F Lydian) or 9 (authentic G Mixolydian). This procedure was called *aequatio modorum*, an "equivalence of modes." In both cases, of course, the overall mode of the polyphonic composition was mode 1.

Although Bernhard's position is frequently described today as a compromise between Scacchi and Siefert, he actually followed Scacchi's (and Diruta's) reasoning closely. Like them, he argued that real answers were best reserved for the body of the work and that mode took precedence over exactness of imitation in the first few measures of a piece. Bernhard added the caution that stepwise themes more often received real answers and leaping themes more often tonal answers. This rule basically follows common sense. The character of a stepwise theme must be drastically altered for a tonal answer, since one of its steps must be answered by either a leap or a repeated note, while a leaping theme requires only that one leap be answered by another of slightly different size.

Bernhard's system represents a significant refinement of the way in which earlier theorists related fugal imitation to the modes. While a composer had formerly been forced to content himself with the vague admonition that at the beginning of a piece subject and answer should avoid going "outside the mode" and that fifths should be answered by fourths and vice versa, he now had in Bernhard's work a theoretical basis for constructing a proper answer to almost any theme. Once he had determined which type of answer was appropriate, he proceeded in one of two ways. For example, a tenor in mode 1 would have an ambitus of C-C with its important notes on C and G. For a tonal answer (i.e., in *consociatio modorum*) the alto would then be in mode 2, with an ambitus of G-G and important notes on G and C. Thus, the tenor's C would correspond to the alto's G and tenor G to alto C. For a real answer (i.e., in *aequatio modorum*) the alto could take on one of two possible modes. If the tenor's theme remained in the lower fifth C-G, the "analogous mode a fourth or fifth away" would be mode 9 (authentic G Mixolydian), and the alto would have an ambitus of G-G with important notes on G and D. In this case, tenor C would still correspond to alto G, but tenor G would now correspond to alto D rather than alto C. Similarly, if the tenor theme remained within the fourth G-C, the analogous alto mode would be mode 7 (authentic F Lydian), alto would have the ambitus F-F, and the important tenor notes G and C would correspond to the alto notes C and F. Modes 8 and 10, whose finals are also a fourth or fifth away, would not be appropriate because in either case the ambitus (C-C for mode 8, D-D for mode 10) would incorrectly place the alto in essentially the same vocal range as the tenor.

When Bernhard spoke of two modes, separated by a fourth or fifth, that were equivalent in part, he was stretching the modal system about as far as it could go without breaking down. For any two modes a fourth or fifth apart, the respective scales will differ at only one point, where a particular "scale degree" will be placed with a half step below and whole step above in one mode while in the other whole and half steps will be reversed. Mode 3 (authentic D Dorian), for instance, is equivalent to mode 11 (authentic A Aeolian) except for the sixth scale degree (B♮ in mode 3, F♮, not F♯, in mode 11); its equivalence with mode 9 (authentic G Mixolydian) extends to every degree but the third (F♮ in mode 3, B♮, not B♭, in mode 9). The reason for this phenomenon is the presence of the tritone interval F-B, which cannot be reproduced at any other pitch level in the modal system. Thus, when any mode is compared with the mode a fifth above, its note B (wherever that note should fall) will be paired with the second mode's F, i.e., at the interval of a diminished, rather than perfect, fifth; when it is compared with the mode a fourth above, F will be paired with B, an augmented fourth.

Theoretically, either of two modes can be chosen for the alto voice in Bernhard's *aequatio modorum:* one whose "scale degrees" 1 through 5 (from final to dominant) match those of the tenor's mode, the other whose "scale degrees" 5 through 8 match the tenor's mode. One of these modes will be a fifth away from the original mode, the other a fourth away. The mode selected for a particular point of imitation will depend on the theme and the notes of the mode touched on by that theme. If the theme includes an F, the proper mode to select for writing a real answer must be the mode a fifth above, so that F is answered by C rather than B. If the theme includes a B, a real answer can be written only with the mode a fourth above, so that B is answered by E rather than F. Any theme that includes both F and B cannot be given a real answer, a possibility for which Bernhard failed to allow. An alternative method for producing real answers, namely the adding of accidentals to either F or B, destroys the integrity of the modal system.

The impossibility of producing a real answer for a theme that touches on both F and B makes particularly difficult the handling of modes 5 through 8, in which these two notes are enclosed within the fundamental fifth (E-B or F-C). Bernhard acknowledged this problem when he pointed out that modes 5 and 6 (E Phrygian) were most often treated like modes 11 and 12 (A Aeolian) and that modes 7 and 8 (F Lydian) were rarely used.[15] In other words, in the first case the B was usually avoided in favor of the A below it, while in the second it was usually flatted to produce transposed mode 1. Table 15.1 summarizes the various possibilities for *consociatio* and *aequatio modorum* in all twelve modes.

This system and Bernhard's guidelines for its use provide well for a theme that emphasizes final and dominant and that remains within the range of the mode's fundamental fourth or fifth. Given such a theme a student composer could decide which of the three possible modes he should choose for the alto voice and how to relate the most important notes of tenor and alto to each other based on the type of motion of the theme, the location of the point of imitation in the piece, and the particular mode. On the other hand, any theme that ventured beyond either the fourth or the fifth might or might not allow for a real answer, and one that included the tritone interval F-B could not be answered exactly without the introduction of ficta.

Bernhard's *consociato* and *aequatio modorum* preserve in microcosm the mid-seventeenth-century conflict between outdated modal theory and incipient tonal theory. In trying to "equate" portions of two modes a perfect interval apart Bernhard was reaching toward the innovation of a small number of scale patterns transposed to different pitch levels, yet at the same time he held on to the tradition whereby each scale pattern was associated with a specific final. The precariousness of his position is made all the clearer when compared with the theory of Johann Jacob Prinner, who found himself unable to maintain the balance between the two harmonic systems.

Writing approximately fifteen years after Bernhard, Prinner made plain in his discussion of real and tonal answers the extent to which practice, guided primarily by the ear, had outdistanced theory by the last quarter of the seventeenth century. Following the quote given above in which he described the continuing quarrel on the subject, Prinner expressed a preference for preserving solmization at the expense of mode. To support his case, he composed two brief points of imitation, one built upon the five-note stepwise theme with solmization re-mi-fa-sol-la, the other upon its inversion (see exx. 15.11 and 15.12). Both were given real answers as prescribed for such themes by Bernhard, and Prinner justified the second in this way:

Aus dem vorgesetzten Exempl mechte mir aber einer Vorwerffen, und sagen, wie das das [*sic*] erste subiectum Primi toni, das andere aber secundi toni seye, also das es sich nicht in dem ersten sondern in dem andern ton Ende, dass ist gewiss ein guete frag, und braucht einer

Table 15.1   Relationship between Tenor and Alto Voices in Bernhard's
Consociatio and *Aequatio modorum*

Mode 1

consociatio (tonal answer)		*aequatio* (real answer) Theme emphasizes fifth and avoids B.	
tenor	alto (mode 2)	tenor	alto (mode 9)
C	G	(C)	(G)
G	C	G	D
C	G	C	G

		Theme emphasizes fourth and avoids F.	
		tenor	alto (mode 7)
		C	F
		G	C
		(C)	(F)

Mode 2

consociatio (tonal answer)		*aequatio* (real answer) Theme emphasizes fifth and avoids B.	
tenor	alto (mode 1)	tenor	alto (mode 10)
G	C	G	D
C	G	C	G
G	C	(G)	(D)

		Theme emphasizes fourth and avoids F.	
		tenor	alto (mode 8)
		(G)	(C)
		C	F
		G	C

Mode 3

consociatio (tonal answer)		*aequatio* (real answer) Theme emphasizes fifth and avoids B.	
tenor	alto (mode 4)	tenor	alto (mode 11)
D	A	(D)	(A)
A	D	A	E
D	A	D	A

		Theme emphasizes fourth and avoids F.	
		tenor	alto (mode 9)
		D	G
		A	D
		(D)	(G)

Table 15.1, cont.

Mode 4

consociatio (tonal answer)		*aequatio* (real answer) Theme emphasizes fifth and avoids B.	
tenor	alto (mode 3)	tenor	alto (mode 12)
A	D	A	E
D	A	D	A
A	D	(A)	(E)

Theme emphasizes fourth and avoids F.

tenor	alto (mode 10)
(A)	(D)
D	G
A	D

Mode 5

consociatio (tonal answer)		*aequatio* (real answer) Theme emphasizes fifth.	
tenor	alto (mode 6)	tenor	alto
E	B	(E)	real answer
B	E	B	requires ficta
E	B	E	(for interval F-B)

Theme emphasizes fourth and avoids F.

tenor	alto (mode 11)
E	A
B	E
(E)	(A)

Mode 6

consociatio (tonal answer)		*aequatio* (real answer) Theme emphasizes fifth.	
tenor	alto (mode 5)	tenor	alto
B	E	B	real answer
E	B	E	requires ficta
B	E	(B)	(for interval F-B)

Theme emphasizes fourth and avoids F.

tenor	alto (mode 12)
(B)	(E)
E	A
B	E

Table 15.1, cont.

Mode 7

consociatio (tonal answer)			*aequatio* (real answer) Theme emphasizes fifth.	
tenor	alto (mode 8)		tenor	alto
F	C		(F)	real answer
C	F		C	requires ficta
F	C		F	(for interval F-B)

Theme emphasizes fourth and avoids B.

tenor	alto (mode 1)
F	C
C	G
(F)	(C)

Mode 8

consociatio (tonal answer)			*aequatio* (real answer) Theme emphasizes fifth.	
tenor	alto (mode 7)		tenor	alto
C	F		C	real answer
F	C		F	requires ficta
C	F		(C)	(for interval F-B)

Theme emphasizes fourth and avoids B.

tenor	alto (mode 2)
(C)	(G)
F	C
C	G

Mode 9

consociatio (tonal answer)			*aequatio* (real answer) Theme emphasizes fifth and avoids F.	
tenor	alto (mode 10)		tenor	alto (mode 1)
G	D		(G)	(C)
D	G		D	G
G	D		G	C

Theme emphasizes fourth and avoids B.

tenor	alto (mode 3)
G	D
D	A
(G)	(D)

Table 15.1, cont.

Mode 10

consociatio (tonal answer)			*aequatio* (real answer) Theme emphasizes fifth and avoids F.	
tenor	alto (mode 9)		tenor	alto (mode 2)
D	G		D	G
G	D		G	C
D	G		(D)	(G)

Theme emphasizes fourth and avoids B.

tenor	alto (mode 4)
(D)	(A)
G	D
D	A

Mode 11

consociatio (tonal answer)			*aequatio* (real answer) Theme emphasizes fifth and avoids F.	
tenor	alto (mode 12)		tenor	alto (mode 3)
A	E		(A)	(D)
E	A		E	A
A	E		A	D

Theme emphasizes fourth and avoids B.

tenor	alto (mode 5)
A	E
E	B
(A)	(E)

Mode 12

consociatio (tonal answer)			*aequatio* (real answer) Theme emphasizes fifth and avoids F.	
tenor	alto (mode 11)		tenor	alto (mode 4)
E	A		E	A
A	E		A	D
E	A		(E)	(A)

Theme emphasizes fourth and avoids B.

tenor	alto (mode 6)
(E)	(B)
A	E
E	B

Example 15.11.   Prinner, *Musicalischer Schlissl*, Section on *Fuga*, p. 3.

Example 15.12.   Prinner, *Musicalischer Schlissl*, Section on *Fuga*, p. 4.

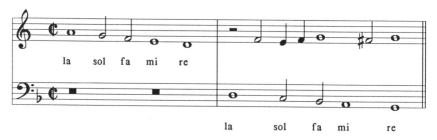

spitzfindigen ausslegung, Ich beandtworte aber solche auf dise weis, das, ich anfangs Ver-
meldet ehe ich das subiectum in anfang in das exempl gesetzt habe, das man, sovill miglich
bey der solmisation Verbleiben solle. Wan man dan darbey verbleibet, wie khan man dan
anders Verfahren als auf Vorgeschribene manir. Bleibt man aber nicht darbey, und will den
tonum observiren, so müste man der solmisation zu khurz thun.[16]

From the preceding example [15.12] one might wish to reproach me and ask how the first
subject can be of the first mode but the second of the second mode, i.e., so that it ends in the
second mode rather than in the first. That is certainly a good question and requires a subtle
explanation. I answer in this way: at the beginning [of the section] I announced, before I set
the subject in the beginning [of] this example, that one should remain as much as possible
with the solmization. If one then remains with it, how can one proceed if not in the manner
shown above? If one does not remain with it, however, and wishes to observe the mode, he
would have to make the solmization too short.

Prinner recognized that the themes of examples 15.11 and 15.12 could not
be given tonal answers without, as he put it, "shortening the solmization" (i.e.,
answering the theme's five steps with only four through the use of either a
repeated note or a chromatic progression). He disapproved of this solution, but
because he and the composers of his generation had become more interested in
writing monothematic fugues than in producing Renaissance-style motets, Prinner was unwilling to accept Bernhard's advice that stepwise themes and their

real answers be restricted to points of imitation in the body of the fugue. He argued, therefore, that since a composer should not be forbidden to write fugues with such themes and since the only "sensible" way to answer these themes was with real answers, the composer should be allowed to begin his fugue in this way, even if the mode was not perfectly outlined. In other words, Scacchi's demand that no piece begin with two fifths or two fourths was in Prinner's opinion too restrictive.

The question posed by Prinner's imaginary critic concerning the different modes of the two voices in example 15.12 is never directly answered in the text, but the implied answer is the same as Bernhard's justification for *aequatio modorum:* the two voices project two "equivalent" modes a fifth apart. To provide further theoretical foundation for real answers, Prinner drew up a chart, reproduced in example 15.13, in which he identified the "equivalent modes." The chart, comprising eight modes grouped in pairs and identified only by letter name, looks very different from the comparable chart derived from Bernhard's *aequatio modorum* (table 15.1). First of all, there is no trace of plagal vs. authentic, so that every note of the modal system (C, D, E, F, G, A, B♭, B♮) is given exactly one mode. The modes are then paired to produce (1) the "minor" modes on D and A, (2) the "major" modes on C and G, (3) the "major" mode C Ionian transposed to F with one flat and to B♭ with two, and (4) the Phrygian mode both at its original pitch and transposed to B with an F♯.[17] Like Bernhard, Prinner admitted that the two modes of each of the first two pairs were equivalent only in part, and he even identified the particular "scale degrees" that differed between a mode and its partner. He gave no indication, however, how this discrepancy between "equivalent" modes was to be handled or what effect it had on the preservation of solmization. Furthermore, the last two pairs comprise modes that are exact transpositions of each other rather than "equivalent," but this phenomenon is likewise passed over in silence. Prinner's chart demonstrates just how close musicians of the 1670s had come to the major/minor duality of the tonal system, but it leaves too many questions unanswered to be considered an improvement on Bernhard's *aequatio modorum*.[18]

Prinner mentioned tonal answers but offered no theoretical justification. He commented that they allowed fifths to be answered by fourths and fourths by fifths, but he did not repeat Bernhard's rule for matching different types of themes with different types of answers, nor did he suggest that tonal answers worked best at the beginning of a composition while real answers were best reserved for the body. In short, the predominance of arguments in favor of real answers and the lack of serious attention paid to tonal answers leave the reader of Prinner's text with the impression that, like Siefert, Prinner acknowledged the existence of tonal answers but preferred never to use them because they "destroyed" the solmization of the theme.

This impression is directly contradicted by ten pages of examples placed

Example 15.13. Prinner, Chart of Equivalent Modes for Use in Real
Answers
(*Musicalischer Schlissl*, Section on *Fuga*, pp. 6–7)

near the end of the material on fugue.[19] Prinner offered between ten and twenty examples of subjects and answers for each of the six modes with finals on D, E, F, G, A, and C. Each subject appears directly above its answer in order to indicate that either version may begin the composition, but beyond that not a single observation from Prinner's text is borne out by the almost 100 examples. Tonal answers outnumber real ones almost two to one (sixty tonal, thirty-five real); in fact, nineteen of the twenty examples in the D mode are tonal. As a result, the solmization for which Prinner professed such concern is preserved in only about one-third of the examples. Even more startling is example 15.14, in which the same theme used by Prinner in example 15.12 is given an answer that "cuts short" the solmization in the very way that Prinner had earlier condemned.[20]

The modes are frequently not paired according to the chart of example 15.13. In particular, the F mode seldom introduces a B♭ and is never paired with the B♭ mode, while the G mode is frequently paired with the D mode to which an F♯ has been added. In addition, musica ficta is often introduced in ways not explained in Prinner's text. For instance, a B♭ is frequently added to the D mode, making this mode a transposition of rather than an "equivalent" to the A mode. Finally, one example in the G mode even violates the rule about all voices beginning on final and dominant—its voices begin instead on final and subdominant.

Prinner's difficulty with abstract thinking and relating theory to practice reflects the no-man's-land between modality and tonality in which he was clearly trapped. Bernhard's *consociatio* and *aequatio modorum* had taken the old system as far as it could go, and Prinner's attempts to simplify Bernhard and bring his theories into line with current musical practice took the system beyond its breaking point. As it stands, the chart of example 15.13 is faithful neither to the modal system nor to the tonal system, but adding the kind of musica ficta that appears in Prinner's brief examples would bring it very close to eighteenth-century tonality.

A more successful refinement of Bernhard's system appears in a late seventeenth- or early eighteenth-century manuscript (East Berlin, Deutsche Staatsbib-

Example 15.14. Prinner, Section on *Fuga*, p. 9

liothek, Mus. ms. theor. 1595) made up entirely of excerpts quoted from various German treatises of the seventeenth century. One of the excerpts, a definition and discussion of *repercussio,* is well known today from Johann Gottfried Walther's manuscript treatise of 1708, but it also appears in a manuscript treatise ascribed to Johann Kuhnau, and its most likely author, indicated in the Berlin manuscript 1595, is Wolfgang Caspar Printz.[21] Using the idea of "repetition" inherent in the Latin word, Printz gave *repercussio* a musical definition that cleverly described the phenomenon of fugal answers. In part 1 of his *Satyrischer Componist,* Printz had already defined the word as "the most important notes of a mode," i.e., those "repeatedly" used in a particular mode: namely, final and dominant. The definition in manuscript 1595, on the other hand, adds a second sort of repetition, the "repetition of an interval." Thus, the explanation begins with the general statement that *repercussio* is nothing more than the "inverted repetition" of any two notes, e.g., E-F followed by F-E, or A-D followed by D-A.[22] In and of itself, *repercussio* was not terribly important, Printz noted, but in fugal writing this "inverted repetition" played a key role as an explanation for the traditional theory of tonal answers. In this context, Printz applied *repercussio* in both senses of the word. That is, he not only took for granted that the repercussions of each mode (i.e., the outer two notes of the fundamental triad) should figure prominently in a theme's melodic motion, but he also insisted that the answer of such a theme should include the "inverted repetition" of this interval (i.e., A-D answered by D-A) rather than an exact image (A-D answered by D-G).

Printz then proceeded to show in both theoretical and practical terms exactly how this was to be understood and effected. He began by drawing up two different octave scales side-by-side, one beginning on C (which he identified as "regular Ionian"), the other (unidentified) beginning on G (table 15.2a). The diagram represents, on the left, the scale of the original mode in which the theme is stated, and, on the right, the scale of the answering voice. Ordinarily, Printz pointed out, the composer would assume that each note on the left would be answered by the note directly beside it. The doctrine of *repercussio,* however, dictates that G on the left must be answered by C rather than D, and vice versa. Printz then drew lines of correspondence between notes on the left and notes on the right to create the diagram shown in table 15.2b. Thus, both F and G were properly answered by C, and B was answered by E rather than F (avoiding the tritone).

To demonstrate the diagram's usefulness, Printz offered a theme whose melodic motion spanned an entire octave from dominant to dominant (ex. 15.15). The theme opens with a stepwise descent from final to dominant. Its

Example 15.15.

Table 15.2   Prinz, Four Examples of Scalar Relationships for Leading and
Answering Voices

a. ordinary relationship	b. Ionian
C – G	G
B – F	C <
A – E	F
G – D	B – E
F – C	A – D
E – B	G
D – A	> C
C – G	F
	E – B
	D – A
	C – G

c. Dorian	d. Aeolian
D – A	A – E
G	D
C <	G <
F	F – C
B – E	B
A – D	E <
G	D – A
> C	G
F	C <
E – B	F
D – A	B
	> E
	A

initial motion covers precisely the portion of Printz's diagram where the doctrine of *repercussio* has caused a shift in the relationship between the two scales. That is, the notes G, A, and B on the left correspond to C, D, and E (rather than D, E, and F) on the right. As a result, the melodic progression C-C-B-A-G must be answered not with G-G-F-E-D, as in the original diagram above, but with G-G-E-D-C. Similarly, the second half of the theme rises triadically from final to dominant. In this portion of Printz's diagram, the two scales match up exactly as before, except for the note G on the left, which corresponds to C (rather than D) on the right. Therefore, the first two notes of this portion of the theme (C and E) are answered with G and B, but the last note G must be answered with C rather than D. The proper answer is shown in example 15.16.

Printz added two more octave-diagrams, one for D Dorian (table 15.2c),

Example 15.16.

the other for A Aeolian (table 15.2d). In the Ionian, the first shift in relationship
between the two scales takes place at the dominant of the mode, where both F
and G on the left correspond to C on the right. This shift leaves one extra note
in the scale on the right, which is accounted for at the top of the diagram, where
two notes on the right correspond to one on the left. In the Dorian, the similar
shift does not take place on the final and dominant notes of the mode, but again
on the notes C, F, and G. No explanation is offered, but this phenomenon does
provide the most satisfactory answer for the familiar troublesome theme that
ascends by step from final to dominant. In fact, when constructing a tonal
answer, a composer would most likely answer the theme D-E-F-G-A with A-B-
C-C-D, as provided for in the Dorian diagram, whereas the answer provided
by the Ionian diagram for the theme C-D-E-F-G, namely G-A-B-C-C, is a less
likely choice than G-A-B-B-C.

Printz's diagram for Aeolian reveals the impossibility of explaining all
details of the writing of tonal answers using the modal system. In this case, E
and A, the repercussions of the original mode, must always match up with A
and E of the octave to its right. However, if E is always paired with A, then the
F immediately above that E must be paired with B. But this is a tritone relationship and cannot be allowed. Consequently, the diagram contains additional
diagonal lines that allow a more flexible series of relationships between the two
scales in order to circumvent the problems caused by the prominent position of
the troublesome notes B and F in the scale of the answering voice. The possible
addition of accidentals, which is the solution offered by the tonal system, is not
considered.

From a purely practical standpoint, Printz's diagrams represent little more
than a fleshing-out of Bernhard's rule for *consociatio modorum*. Bernhard had
specified that if the tenor voice was in an authentic mode, the alto was in the
corresponding plagal, and vice versa. He did not explain, however, how the
tenor's five notes from C to G were to be answered by the alto's four notes from
G to C, or how the upper four tenor notes were to be answered by the corresponding five notes of the alto. Printz's diagram neatly supplies the missing
details.

The theories underlying the explanations of the two men differ considerably, however. In the first place, Printz made no mention of authentic and plagal
modes. Instead, he provided only the authentic scale for each of the three
primary modes, and he referred to each of their paired scales as simply the *scala*

or *octava* on G, A, or E, i.e., at the level of the primary mode's dominant. Thus, Printz's sample theme, which Bernhard would have assigned to plagal Ionian because of its ambitus from dominant to dominant, was labeled simply "regular Ionian," with its answer conceived not in the scale of authentic Ionian but in the scale based on the dominant note. Printz also made clear his preference for tonal answers in most, if not all, contexts. He thus eliminated altogether the two "closely related" modes—one a fourth above the original, the other a fifth above—that Bernhard had provided for *aequatio modorum*. As a result, whereas Bernhard offered a composer three modes from which to choose in answering a particular theme, Printz offered only a single "scale" beginning on the dominant of the given mode. Furthermore, Printz spelled out exactly how the original mode and its matching "scale" were to relate to each other, and the given relationship essentially guaranteed a tonal answer. Finally, Printz's selection of only three primary modes reveals the rapid approach of the major/minor system: the three are Ionian (i.e., major), Aeolian (minor), and Dorian (the most durable of the original eight modes). Only the absence of accidentals (most noticeably in the diagram for Aeolian mode) kept Printz within the modal system.

It was Johann Mattheson, in his *Vollkommene Capellmeister* of 1739, who finally translated Printz's theory into the tonal system. Mattheson began his discussion of fugal answers by identifying three general rules, listed in order of priority:

> Die allgemeine und in dreien Gliedern bestehende Fugen-Regel ist diese: Man soll die Gränzen der Ton-Art nicht überschreiten, weder unten noch oben; mit dem Gefährten nicht in einem dem Modo zuwiederlauffenden Klange anheben; übrigens aber die Intervalle bey der Versetzung so gleich und ähnlich machen, als nur mit guter Art geschehen kan. Das erste Glied ist das nothwendigste bey ordentlichen Fugen, nicht bey ausserordentlichen; und das dritte muss am meisten nachgeben. Es verdienet auch die Natur der Ton-Art allemahl mehr Achtung, als das übrige.[23]

> The general rule of fugue consists of three parts and is this: the boundaries of the key [Ton-Art] must not be overstepped either above or below; the answering voice must not begin on a note contradictory to the mode; moreover, the intervals must be made as equivalent and similar in the transposition [Versetzung] as can be done well. The first part is the most important, although it has its exception. The second is most important for ordinary but not for exceptional fugues. The third must yield the most. The nature of the key always deserves more attention than everything else.

This passage is followed by a number of examples, with clear preference given to tonal answers. Finally, Mattheson provided the novice with additional aid in the form of Printz's system of modal charts, which he expanded and updated according to the new system of tonality. He ignored Printz's charts for D Dorian and A Aeolian and created twelve diagrams, one for each note of the scale, according to the pattern of table 15.2b. He also fleshed out Printz's original scheme by inserting all chromatic notes within the octave, making the diagram applicable to any theme in any of the twelve major or twelve minor keys. Table 15.3 demonstrates Mattheson's pattern beginning on the note G.[24]

By incorporating chromatic notes and transposing Printz's original diagram to all twelve steps, Mattheson was able both to translate Printz's theory from the old modal system into the new tonal system and to correct a logical flaw. As Bernhard had noted, no two modes a fourth or fifth apart were entirely identical. Printz restricted his diagrams to pairings that worked relatively well, i.e., C & G and D & A. In these cases, the lower fifths of the two modes are identical, and the difference in configuration of whole and half steps is placed inconspicuously in the upper fourth, where it is less likely to pose difficulties for the composer. Printz failed to consider G Mixolydian, however. In this case, the mode a fifth above, D Dorian, has a minor rather than a major third, so that a theme emphasizing the fundamental triad G-B-D would presumably be answered D-F-A. The theory of fugal answers made no allowance for such blatant alteration of solmization, yet neither does the modal system provide for the use of the accidental F♯. Mattheson's chromatic scales remove this dilemma. The "closely related mode" is replaced by the "transposed mode" (Mattheson used the expression *versetzter Modus*), i.e., the key of the dominant, providing the composer with all accidentals necessary to write fugal answers at the dominant in any mode or key whatsoever. Furthermore, the doctrine of tonal answers prevented the answer from straying too far into the key of the dominant.

The dashed lines of table 15.3, like the extra lines of Printz's diagrams in tables 15.2b and 15.2c, represent an attempt to illustrate the system's flexibility. Mattheson explained them as follows:

> Denn Z.E. vom g ins dis als in die Sext hinauffgesprungen oder gegangen wird, so antwortet dem dis nicht das gegenüberstehende gis, sondern das b. Gehets aber abwärts vom g ins b so antwortet dem b das gegenüberstehende f richtig. Welches hier nur zur Probe angeführet wird um andere dergleichen Vorfalle darnach zu beurtheilen.[25]

> Thus, for example, if one proceeds upward from G to E♭ either by leap or step, the E♭ is answered not by the A♭ across from it, but by the B♭. If, however, it descends from G to B♭, the B♭ is properly answered by the F standing across from it. This is mentioned here only as an example by which other similar occurrences are to be judged.

He offered no systematic instruction for the interpretation of these extra lines, but left it to the composer to use them according to the rules for tonal answers as previously described. Despite the translation of Printz's diagram into the tonal system, however, Mattheson retained the traditional modes and modal terminology alongside the major and minor keys in order to discuss the proper way to construct fugal answers for chorale tunes.

Table 15.3   Mattheson, Diagram for G Major or Minor
(*Capellmeister*, p. 374; transl., p. 707.)

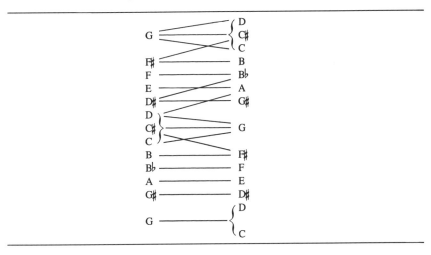

To summarize: the progression and refinement of theoretical argument concerning fugal answers might best be divided into three phases, roughly corresponding to the late Renaissance and *stile antico* in the early Baroque, the middle or mature Baroque, and the late Baroque. In the first, the relationship between imitative counterpoint and mode was viewed in terms of the individual notes constituting the mode's "scale." That is, the voices that began an imitative composition should enter on final and dominant (Zarlino), the theme to be imitated should have as its most prominent notes the principal notes of the mode (Pontio and Dressler), and the answer should likewise emphasize these important modal notes (Diruta and Scacchi). In the second phase, German theorists began to interpret fugal answers as transpositions of subjects, first to "analogous modes" a fourth or fifth away (Bernhard), then to a scalar pattern a fifth above the original mode (Prinner and Printz). Only Bernhard maintained the integrity of the modal system, however; both Prinner and Printz succeeded only in pairing modes that worked well together, namely Ionian on C (paired with Mixolydian on G) and Dorian on D (paired with Aeolian on A) while ultimately producing systems that were true neither to modality nor to tonality. In the final phase, Mattheson paired each of the twenty-four major and minor keys with its dominant key.

Meanwhile, musicians throughout this period continued to disagree about the relative merits of real and tonal answers. The Viennese theorists Prinner and Johann Joseph Fux agreed with Siefert that tonal answers destroyed the integrity of the theme and should be rarely used. Theorists in central and northern Germany, including Johann Beer, Johann Philipp Förtsch, Johann Mattheson, and many others, followed Scacchi in insisting that mode was more important and tonal answers therefore preferable in most instances. One Central-German writer, Andreas Werckmeister, wrote that chorale fugues should be excepted from this rule, probably because church organists who improvised fugues as introductions to congregational singing had as their most important task the projecting of the melody. Others disagreed.[26] In this respect, it is interesting to consider the subject and answer of Bach's so-called Little G-Minor Fugue (BWV 578; ex. 15.17). Bach's real answer, touching as it does on the supertonic, would seem to violate the rules of nearly all of his Central and North German predecessors and contemporaries: not only does it fail to conform to Printz's doctrine of *repercussio,* but it also violates Bernhard's warning against beginning a piece with such a real answer. A study of Bach's fugal answers could reveal much about his knowledge of theoretical sources and his attitude toward them.

Example 15.17. J. S. Bach, *Fugue in G Minor ("Little"; BWV 578)*

Notes

1. A great many authors could be cited in this context. Perhaps the most extensive modern treatise in English is Ebenezer Prout's *Fugue,* originally published in London in 1891 and now available in reprint (New York: Greenwood Press, 1969). André Gedalge's *Traité de la fugue* (Paris, 1901), used for many years at the Paris Conservatory, is also available in English translation (Norman: University of Oklahoma Press, 1965). The following summary is derived from a very brief article entitled "AGO Examinations: The Fugal Answer" by Harold Heeremans in *Music: The AGO & RCCO Magazine,* vol. 12/3 (March 1978), p. 36, and a follow-up article entitled "Still More on Fugal Answers" by Walter Hilse in *The American Organist,* vol. 22/3 (March 1988), pp. 78–79.

2. "Fuga est idemtitas [*sic*] partium cantus quo ad valorem nomen formam et interdum quo ad locum notarum et pausarum suarum." Johannes Tinctoris, *Terminorum musicae diffinitorium*, ed. and trans. Carl Parrish (London: The Free Press of Glencoe, division of Collier-Macmillan Ltd., 1963), pp. 32–33. On the dating of Tinctoris's *Diffinitorium*, which was published in 1495, see Heinrich Hüschen, "Johannes Tinctoris," *The New Grove Dictionary of Music and Musicians*, ed. Stanley Sadie (London: Macmillan, 1980), vol. 18, p. 839.

3. Not every example of imitative counterpoint at a perfect interval could be called fugue, however, but only those that involved the exact replication of the melodic intervals by the answering voice. See further James Haar, "Zarlino's Definition of Fugue and Imitation," *Journal of the American Musicological Society* 24 (1971), pp. 226–54, and Paul Walker, *Fugue in German Theory from Dressler to Mattheson* (Ph.D. diss., State University of New York at Buffalo, 1987), pp. 15–22.

4. *Le istitutioni harmoniche* (Venice: n.p., 1558; reprint, New York: Broude Brothers, 1965), pp. 173–74. Translated in Zarlino, *The Art of Counterpoint. Part Three of "Le istitutioni harmoniche," 1558*, trans. by Guy A. Marco and Claude Palisca (New Haven: Yale University Press, 1968), p. 55.

5. See Pietro Pontio, *Dialogo* (Parma: E. Viothi, 1595), p. 46.

6. A modern edition of Dressler's manuscript treatise, edited by Bernhard Engelke, is available in the *Geschichtsblätter für Stadt und Land Magdeburg* 49–50 (1914–15), pp. 213–50. On fugue, see esp. pp. 242–43.

7. Diruta, *Seconda parte*, Book III, p. 12; for another translation, see idem, *The Transylvanian*, vol. 2, p. 117.

8. *Cribrum musicum ad triticum Siferticum* (Venice: Alessandro Vincenti, 1643), p. 11.

9. This edition is taken from Hermann Rauschning, *Geschichte der Musik und Musikpflege in Danzig* (Danzig [now Gdansk, Poland]: Kommissionsverlag der Danziger Verlags-Gesellschaft, 1931), p. 162.

10. "Dahero Disputiren die meiste perfecten musici noch auf den heutigen tag, welches besser sey ob man nemblich mehr den tonum alss die solmisation beobachten solle." Johann Jacob Prinner, *Musicalischer Schlissl* [*sic*] (Manuscript, Washington, D.C., Library of Congress, Music Division, ML 95.P79). The manuscript is unpaginated; the quote can be found on the fifth page of the section on fugue.

11. This collection, entitled *Judicium cribri musici* and published ca. 1649, is now lost, but a manuscript copy survives in Bologna, Civico Museo Bibliografico Musicale.

12. "Attamen unicum hoc confiteor, et protector, quod hoc simili modo (quo Dominus Marcus Scacchius in Cribo suo Dominum Syfertum) ego in juventute mea a bone memoriae Johanne Gabriele Preceptore meo quoque fuerim instructus ac institutus." Heinrich Schütz, *Gesammelte Briefe und Schriften*, ed. Erich Hermann Müller (Regensburg: Gustav Bosse, 1931; reprint, Hildesheim: Georg Olms, 1976), p. 189.

13. Bernhard's primary treatise, the *Tractatus compositionis augmentatus* of ca. 1660, was never published but has been edited in modern times by Joseph Müller-Blattau in *Die Kompositionslehre Heinrich Schützens in der Fassung seines Schülers Christoph Bernhard*, 2nd ed. (Kassel: Bärenreiter, 1963), pp. 40–131. A translation by Walter Hilse appears in "The Treatises of Christoph Bernhard," *Music Forum* 3 (1973), pp. 31–196. The information on fugal answers can be found in the edition on pp. 98–106 and in the translation on pp. 133–44.

14. Zarlino, *Istitutioni*, 1558 ed., pp. 337–38. For a translation, see Zarlino, *On the Modes. Part IV of Le istitutioni harmoniche, 1558*, trans. by Vered Cohen (New Haven: Yale University Press, 1983), p. 92.

15. Bernhard, *Tractatus*, ed. Müller-Blattau, p. 101; trans. Hilse, pp. 136–37.

16. Ibid.

17. The grouping together of all modes with "major" fundamental triads (i.e., Ionian, Lydian, and Mixolydian) as distinct from those with "minor" fundamental triads (Dorian, Aeolian, and Phrygian) can be traced at least as far back as Zarlino's *Istitutioni*. For a detailed history of this phenomenon in Italy and Germany, see Joel Lester, "Major-minor Concepts and Modal Theory in Germany: 1592–1680," *Journal of the American Musicological Society* 30 (1977), pp. 208–53.

18. Prinner used black noteheads to indicate the location of half steps. Every half step is surrounded by two black notes. Whole steps are surrounded by either two white notes or one white and one black note.

19. Prinner, section on *fuga*, pp. 8–17.

20. Ibid., section on *fuga*, p. 9.

21. On all three of these manuscripts, and the likelihood of Printz's authorship of the material on *repercussio*, see Walker, *Fugue in German Theory*, pp. 432ff, and esp. note 135 on p. 436. According to Berlin ms. 1595, the passage is taken from Printz's *Satyrischer Componist*, probably the now-lost fourth part, which was never published. Walther's version of the passage, taken almost verbatim from Printz, can be found in his *Praecepta der musicalischen Composition*, ed. Peter Benary, Jenaer Beiträge zur Musikforschung, no. 2 (Leipzig: Breitkopf & Härtel, 1955), pp. 180–83.

22. "*Repercussio* ist eigendlich [*sic*] nichts anders, alss eine umgekehrte Wiederhohlung der Vorhergehenden *Clavium.*" D-Bds ms. 1595, fol. 31r.

23. Johann Mattheson, *Der Vollkommene Capellmeister* (Hamburg, 1739; reprint, Kassel: Bärenreiter, 1954), p. 387. A complete translation is available as *Johann Mattheson's "Der vollkommene Capellmeister,"* translated by Ernest C. Harriss (Ann Arbor: UMI Research Press, 1981). The translation given here is my own; Harriss's translation appears on p. 727.

24. Mattheson used the system of tablature notation, according to which all chromatic notes except B♭ are always indicated, regardless of context, as sharps. In the following discussion, I have translated sharps into flats when appropriate.

25. Mattheson, *Der vollkommene Capellmeister*, p. 374; see also Harriss, p. 707.

26. The various theorists' opinions on real vs. tonal answers are discussed at length at various places in Walker, *Fugue in German Theory*.

Index

Leipzig, 6, 7; opera theater, 128, 129; Stadtbibliothek der Stadt Leipzig, Sammlung Becker III.8.4 (Andreas Bach Buch), 353–56; Thomaskantors, 196; vespers practice in, 154
Leoni, Leone, 233
Leopold I, Emperor, 9; *sepolcri*, 181
Leyding, Georg: *Von Gott will ich nicht lassen*, 96–100
Lieder, 130, 131, 134
Lieferung und Beschlagung oder Probirung einer Orgel, 81
Linfield, Eva, 163–92
Lithuania, 198
Liturgical calendar, 56–57
Liturgy: and music, 31, 56, 240; reforms, 143–57
Longinus, 195
Lossius, Lucas, 152
Lowinsky, Edward, 262
Lübeck, Vincent, 90
Lübeck: 23, 24, 31, 182, 195, 198, 201; *Abendmusiken*, 9, 201, 205–24; Bach's visit to, 6–7, 9; Marienkirche, 4, 7, 12, 102, 155, 205; *Natalitia sacra*, 224; vespers practice in, 154; visits to, by musicians, 6–7, 9, 127–28
Lully, Jean-Baptiste, 8; *Achilles et Polixène*, 129; *Acis et Galatée*, 129
Lüneburg, 6, 231–62 *passim;* Johanneskirche, 241, 246–47; Johannesschule, 245–47, 260; liturgical ordinances, 239–40; Michaelisschule, 321–32, 240; motet scores, 231–32; Nicolaikirche, 244–62 *passim;* Ratsbücherei, 182, 232; tablatures, 232, 241, 243–61; Stadtarchiv, 258
Lustig, Jacob Wilhelm, 189
Luther, Martin, 24, 144–57 *passim*, 193–94, 200; *Deudsche Messe und ordnung Gottisdiensts* (1526), 146–48
Lutheran church, 24, 28, 34; organ playing, 25, 27, 31; vespers, 143–57
Lütkens, Peter, 128

Magdeburg: cathedral, 65n.11
Magnificat: in Lutheran vespers service, 152, 154; organ music, 31
Mahrenholz, Christhard, 43, 56–57
Marckfelnera, Samuel, 287
Marenzio, Luca, 243
Marpurg, Friedrich Wilhelm: *Abhandlung von der Fuge* (1753), 361
Marquardt, Andreas: *Ich hab einen guten Kampf gekämpfet*, 243, 258, 260
Mass: reconstruction of, 55–57; Schütz's *Musikalische Exequien* as, 119–22
Mattheson, Johann, 129, 130, 131, 351, 386; *Grundlage einer Ehren-Pforte* (1740), 351;

on the Phrygian mode, 169; on Preus, 80; on repertory of Hamburg opera, 129, 138–40; on the viola da gamba, 164; visit to Buxtehude, 7; *Vollkommene Capellmeister* (1739), 383–84
Maxton, Willy, 206, 224
Mecklenburg, 24
Medvetzki, Samuel, 280
Melanchton, Philipp, 152
Mendicanti: instrumental resources, 179
Merlo, Alessandro, *Madonna più che mai*, 273n.33
Merulo, Claudio, 27
Milton, John, 196
Mithobius, Hector: *Psalmodia Christiana* (1665), 28–29
Modality: and theories of fugal answer, 361–86
Modes: Schütz's treatment of, 117–18
Möller Manuscript, 19n.14, 353–56
Monatshefte für Musikgeschichte, 81
Monteverdi, Claudio, 8; early operas, 178
Works:
Lamento d'Arianna, 178
Orfeo, 177
Pianto della Madonna (1641), 182
Selva morale e spirituale (1641), 182
Morhardt, Peter, 261
Morley, Thomas: *Plaine and Easie Introduction to Practicall Musicke* (1597), 34
Moser, Hans Joachim, 111
Motet scores, 231–62
Movius, Caspar, 233
Musculus, Wolfgang, 147–48, 149
Musica nova (1540), 241

Nanino, Giovanni Maria, 233
Natalitia sacra (1682), 224
Netherlands, organists in, 27
New German Organ Tablature, 350
Nicolai, Philipp, 199–200
North, Roger, 163–64

Opera: in Hamburg, 8, 12, 30, 127–37; Italian, 189; in Rome, 179–80; social context, 30; theaters, 128; Venetian, 180
Opitz, Martin, 196
Oratorio, 8, 30–31
Organ builders, 198; malpractice, 71
Organ chorale, 9
Organ design and construction: standards, 67–82
Organ inspection: treatises on, 67–82
Organ motets, 31
Organ music, 5–6; of Buxtehude, 87–104; in northern Germany, 23–40; of Samuel Scheidt, 43–57
Organ recitals, 27
Organ ricercar, 31